M000300130

INSIDE HONORS:

Ratings and Reviews of Sixty Public University Honors Programs

©Copyright 2016 John Willingham

CONTENTS

CONTENTS

Cover photo © frannyanne photos

This book was not written to be entertaining. More than in the previous two attempts to rate public university honors colleges and programs, the present book is loaded with quantitative assessments—far too many, some will think; too complicated, others might say.

Here is the reason for all the data: Honors programs are in fact complicated and vary greatly. Often the variations seem impossible to quantify, much less to describe. Thank goodness this book is done!

Seriously, I have concluded that in the case of honors programs it is not the devil who resides in the details but, rather, the most significant indicators of excellence. For excellence is what honors programs augment in our public universities. Yet excellence can be elusive to define. You might think you know it when you see it, or when you feel it, but such is not always the case.

Some critics of honors programs say that they are elitist with their sometimes fancy dorms and other perks, and with the generous scholarships that they often provide. Others say that they exist mainly to raise the selectivity rankings of the universities to which they belong, meanwhile providing little of real value to the talented students they are supposed to serve. They talk a good game, but when all is done, they do not deliver. And it is sometimes the case that the universities in which honors programs are but a part do not support honors education as they should. Only a very few public universities have endowments that match those of the elite private institutions, and even if the public endowments are at a high level, the funds must still be spread among far more students than at an elite private university.

On the whole, however, many public universities *are* increasingly committed to honors education. In just the five years I have spent gathering and analyzing data about public university honors programs, I have observed dramatic growth in honors enrollment and in the private and institutional support for their mission. That mission, by the way, gains the most traction because of necessity, and not only financial necessity. Yes, highly talented students might find a place in a relatively small number of very selective institutions. The fact is, however, that many of the most selective schools reject 85% to 95% of applicants for reasons that no one fully understands.

If you have a son or daughter with an ACT of 29 or higher and a (new) SAT of 1360 or higher, the number of colleges and universities with student bodies that, on average, meet that profile is fewer than 100. The number of first-year places in all these schools is also less than the number of students with the credentials listed above. Only when public and private honors programs and colleges with similar admissions requirements are included does the number of places approximate the number of highly qualified students. Public honors programs provide the great majority of these additional places. (These views appear in detailed form on our website, in a post titled "Is It True that 80% of Elite Students Are Accepted by Elite Colleges?")

Granting this need for honors colleges and programs, how does one have any idea about the true quality of an honors program, assuming that the students enrolled have met high admission standards? Well-known college rankings generally focus on university-wide "inputs" and "outcomes" while often conflating the two. This book covers some of the same ground: class sizes and graduation rates, for example. These do not tell the full story, however.

Understanding what makes a program substantive must begin with an analysis of the "ground game," the time spent in honors classes, the thesis and research requirements, the specific mix of classes by discipline, the total number of honors sections—and, yes, the availability of special housing and perks.

PREFACE

It is not enough, for example, to know that University A has an excellent physics or political science department, and that one's son or daughter wants to major in one of those disciplines. If a family is trying to decide between one or more elite private universities and one or more public honors programs, it may be decisive to know that the public honors program has *honors level* courses in those subjects.

Or if a family is drawn to an excellent private liberal arts college that will require the student to open up, make and defend arguments, and learn to accept criticism, the option of a public honors program might depend on how many small honors classes are available in both discussion-based seminars and courses in the disciplines. Is the honors program really a combination of a "liberal arts college in the midst of a prominent research university, with all the advantages of both"? This typical description of public honors programs is sometimes true, sometimes misleading, and fairly often offset by equivalent values that are not mentioned in the hype.

And of course the choice almost always involves money. Is that private college that your National Merit Scholar has always dreamed of attending really worth an extra $30,000 a year, since all merit aid at the private college is need-based, and your income, even with a family of four, leaves such a big balance. In short, who can say exactly what fact or feature will help a family to decide?

It might be those eight honors math sections, or those interdisciplinary seminars at every class level, or that study-abroad stipend to attend Oxford in the summer, or that (mostly) quiet honors dorm with on-site dining, mentors, and study lounges on every floor, or the combination of writing, rhetoric, and honors business classes that will make your student a well-rounded success in life. And, often, it might be that merit award worth $10,000 a year, to go with a waiver of out-of-state tuition.

Yes, honors programs are complicated, but so are your college choice decisions. To understand *exactly* what those programs offer in order to make your decision, a parent, a prospective student, needs to look inside honors.

That is what this book tries to do, however many statistics it takes to do the job.

John Willingham, Editor

Ever since the *U.S. News Best Colleges* rankings commenced about three decades ago, the American public has been, if not obsessed with, then keenly interested in the numerical rankings of hundreds of colleges and universities.

Rankings are more interesting than ratings, and ratings are more interesting, to the general public at least, than "evaluations" or "assessments."

All have their uses, and their shortcomings.

Rankings presume a perfection that they cannot meet. If one claims that Princeton is better than Harvard based on a difference of one point out of a possible 100, then one is mighty certain that the methodology being used must inexorably lead to a real distinction arising from such a piddling difference. In the real world, inexorable truths are elusive, but the September ranking operettas featuring Harvard and Princeton—Stanford, Yale?—have taken on the aura of natural recurrences, like the stages of the moon or the orbital course of the planet.

Now, if the colleges were *rated* instead of *ranked*, who could have much doubt that both Harvard and Princeton—and Yale, Stanford, Chicago, Columbia, MIT, Penn, Duke—would all be in the highest group. For ratings are relatively humble, as against the hubris of rankings. It might seem un-American not to be Number One, or anyway not to assume that there *is* a Number One, but ratings are satisfied with a Number One *Group*. In the sciences, mathematics, computer science, and engineering, a methodology well applied to observable phenomena or established patterns can lead to precision, and sometimes to what abides as certainty. Yes, a university's football team might win the national title, but the whole university is a sprawling complex of traditions, cultural conflict, cutthroat politics, inspired or ill-fated leaders, competing ideologies, and students and professors of all stripes. No methodology can be precise enough to place a college on the sharp and narrow point of Number One. But, as Hemingway wrote, it is pretty to think so. And, by the way, a lot of fun. So hats off to *U.S. News* for being entertaining and for providing excellent data about class sizes, grad rates, test scores and so on.

We opted for rankings in the first edition, and it was a big mistake. If anything, honors colleges and programs are more heterogeneous than universities, being in some ways schools within schools. And speaking of heterogeneous, Malcolm Gladwell, writing in *The New Yorker* a few years back, argued that one can compare many things using a few criteria, but not many things using many criteria. Our own hubris, offset to some extent by the use of ratings instead of rankings, is that we are comparing 50 "things"—honors programs—using 13 criteria (and defying superstition). Whether or not that is too many criteria for Mr. Gladwell, one consolation is that *U.S. News* compares hundreds of colleges using even more criteria. What is significant is that we do recognize fully the variety and complexity of honors programs. People sometimes ask, Why don't you include a hundred programs—500 programs? Well, it has taken almost a thousand spreadsheets and documents to rate just 50 programs, each with 6-7 pages of narrative, so that is the best answer we have.

Finally, a word about evaluations and assessments. In the academic world, these terms are used to describe internal and external studies of academic components—individual departments, schools and colleges within the university, special programs, teaching effectiveness, faculty productivity, student learning, and so on. We actually considered producing a "study" that presented all of our data and resulting calculations in a more or less anonymous fashion, that is, without attaching any results to individual programs. It is possible that much of our data might have been more or less suitable for an academic paper or for assessment purposes, but that approach would not have given parents and prospective students any of the comparative information that they need in order to make the best decision possible about which college is best for them.

In the end this book is a hybrid: one part "study" replete with statistics, and the other part perhaps a distant relative of the *Fiske Guide to Colleges,* which has also used ratings instead of rankings. There is no number one, but we do identify (below) the top two groups, which include the honors colleges and programs in the top 44% of the overall ratings. But even these groups are only representative of the rated programs *in this edition.* It is all but certain that hiding out there in the growing universe of honors programs are several that could receive the highest rating.

We assign "mortarboards" instead of stars, asterisks, or other symbols that may represent a range of estimated quality. The highest rating overall or in a particular category is 5.

In this edition, the honors colleges and programs with an overall rating of 5 mortarboards would rank in the top 10, including ties. Here they are, in ***alphabetical*** order:

Arizona State, Barrett Honors College
Clemson, Calhoun Honors College
CUNY, Macaulay Honors College
Georgia Honors Program
Houston Honors College
Kansas Honors Program
New Jersey Inst of Technology (NJIT), Albert Dorman Honors College
Oregon, Clark Honors College
Penn State, Schreyer Honors College
South Carolina Honors College
UT Austin Plan II Honors Program

CUNY Macaulay, Houston, and NJIT were not rated previously. Oregon's Clark Honors College and Clemson's Calhoun Honors College have moved up to a 5 mortarboard rating. In the 2014 edition, the Michigan LSA Honors Program and the Echols Scholars Program at the University of Virginia were rated, and both received an overall rating of 5 mortarboards.

Honors colleges and programs in this edition with an overall rating of 4.5 mortarboards would rank in the 12-22 range, including ties. Here they are, again in ***alphabetical order:***

Arkansas Honors College; Delaware Honors Program; Illinois CHP Program; Maryland Honors College; Mississippi, Sally McDonnell Barksdale Honors College; New Mexico Honors College; UNC Chapel Hill Honors Carolina; Oklahoma State Honors College; Temple Honors Program; Texas Tech Honors College; UC Irvine Campuswide Honors Program; University of Central Florida (UCF), Burnett Honors College; and the University of Washington Honors Program.

Curriculum Requirements (20 pts): For each program, we (1) determine the highest level of honors completion, or an average level if there are multiple completion options; (2) determine the minimum number of credits required to fulfill the requirements; (3) calculate a small percentage credit for the number of engineering graduates from the university;* (4) take the total raw number derived from the previous steps; and (5) standardize and weight the raw data (the final step for all categories before they are summed to a total rating score).

*Developing an extensive honors curriculum in a university with a high percentage of engineering students puts a strain on honors programs (absent generous endowments) because those universities must allocate so many of their resources to engineering equipment, labs, and instruction. The greater demand on resources can limit the honors courses and requirements in several of these universities. The small proportional adjustment that we make for all programs is an attempt to even the playing field just a bit for those that operate in the context of an engineering-heavy university.

Number of Honors Classes (10 pts): Using the detailed data we received from respondents about the number and type of honors class sections, we (1) determine the total number of honors individuals (please see Glossary) enrolled for the term reported, (2) assign a prorated value to each honors credit section, depending on the number of credit hours and the percentage of honors student enrollment in each section, and (3) divide the number of individuals by the number of adjusted honors class sections.

Number of Honors Classes in Key Disciplines (10 pts): Using the same data as above, we (1) determine the total number of honors individuals enrolled for the term reported, (2) identify the class sections with a threshold percentage of honors enrollment in each key discipline, (3) prorate the value of each section as above, and (4) divide the number of individuals by the number of adjusted honors class sections in key disciplines. The key disciplines are biological sciences; business (all); chemistry; communications (especially public speaking); computer science; economics; engineering (all); English; history; math (all); philosophy; physics; political science; psychology; and sociology/anthropology/gender studies combined. *Each section has equal value, and there is no penalty for not having sections in one or more key disciplines.*

Extent of Honors Enrollment (10 pts): Each program provides the total number of honors students in good standing for the term reported. Not all of these students take an honors course in every term. For this measure, we divide the number of students in good standing by the total number of honors classroom "seats" occupied in the term reported. A desirable result is a number greater than 1.0, thus showing a reasonably high degree of honors enrollment and participation. In part, this can indicate whether honors students have honors course opportunities in the last two years of college. Most honors courses are offered in the first two years. (Please see Glossary for a definition of honors "seats.")

Average Class Size, Honors-only Sections (6.25 pts): For this measure, we add the total number of honors classroom seats in sections that have only honors students enrolled. We then divide this total by the number of honors-only sections.

Average Class Size, Overall (6.25 pts): On average, honors programs have six basic types of classes or activities that carry honors credit: (1) honors-only sections; (2) mixed sections, in which a sizable number of honors students shared the main section with non-honors students and, often, have additional honors-only labs or discussion sections; (3) contract (option, conversion, enhancement) sections, in which one or a few honors students in a regular non-honors section enter into a formal agreement with the instructor to do extra work for honors credit; (4) experiential courses or activities for honors credit, including internships, special research projects, leadership education, teaching assistantships, public service, and mentoring; (5) thesis preparation and completion; and (6) study abroad. For this measure, we count the *total* enrollment of students, honors and non-honors, in the *main* sections of classes in the first four categories. Many honors professionals believe that the relevant enrollment figures should only be for honors-only main sections or honors-only labs and discussion (breakout) sections, the latter offered primarily in introductory science courses and some business, economics, and political science courses. Our view is that when most parents think about class sizes, they have main course sections in mind. The overall average class size is *not a raw average of class sizes, however.* We do calculate the raw average class sizes for honors-only main sections, mixed sections, and contract sections—but then we use a proportional formula to arrive at the overall average class size. In other words, we take the percentage of enrollment in each section type (honors-only, mixed, contract) and then multiply the raw average class size for each type by the percentage of enrollment for each type. The products are then summed for the overall class size average.

Honors Graduation Rate (7.5 pts)--Using the six-year graduation rate for honors entrants, whether or not they completed the honors program, would essentially tie this metric to selection criteria—if you set the bar really high, a lot of the students you admit will graduate regardless. So we took the six-year honors entrant graduation data and then compared it to the honors graduation rates for other honors programs with the same test score range for admission. The result is an adjusted honors graduation rate.

Value-added Graduation Rate (2.5 pts): This rating simply compares the six-year graduation rate for honors entrants with the six-year graduation rate for the university as a whole.

Honors Staff (7.5 pts): Another simple rating, this one derives from dividing the total number of honors students in good standing by the number of full-time equivalent honors staff.

Priority Registration (2.5 pts): The maximum rating is assigned to programs that allow honors students to register for all courses, honors and non-honors, in the first group of students regardless of class year. Lesser points are assigned if honors students register first within their class year, or register with the class ahead.

Honors Residence Halls, Amenities (7.5 pts): We evaluated the room configurations, locations, amenities, and dining options of honors residence halls and then assigned values according to room type (suite-style and apartments receive the highest value), location, dining options, air-conditioning, proximity to honors administration and programming, in-house laundry, and options for housing upperclassmen as well as first-year students.

Honors Residence Halls, Availability (2.5 pts): For this measure, we (1) take the total number of honors dorm places, (2) count the total number of honors students in good standing, divide that total by two (= an approximation of first- and second-year students in good standing), and then divide the number of honors dorm places by the number of first- and second-year students.

Prestigious Awards (7.5 pts)--(1) We used raw totals for the entire history of the following: Rhodes, Marshall, Gates Cambridge, Churchill, Truman, Udall, and Goldwater; (2) we used raw totals for three most recent years of Fulbright Student and Boren, two most recent years of NSF GRG awards, and (3) a percentage of Gilman awards during the same period.

Much of the information in this edition is based on course and section data. Very few people know about or understand the different types of honors classes. To make an informed decision about choosing an honors college or program over a liberal arts college or an elite private university, parents and prospective students really need to consider the types of classes and how those offered by a given honors program will match the preferences and needs of the student.

First, the three major types of honors classes are honors-only classes, mixed sections, and contract (option, conversion) sections.

In most selective private colleges and universities, a class is a class. By this we mean that within each class section, there is not a mix of especially talented students with "regular" students. At the most elite level, this means that all classes at the college are presumably equal in their elite-*ness*.

Yes, there are some large classes, especially in the sciences and in extremely popular lecture sections. But most classes are relatively small, with the amount of discussion being limited more by the subject matter than by the number of students involved. Debate in a linear algebra section of 15 students is unlikely to be extensive; but in a seminar in history, philosophy, literature, or political science the same number of students might bring the roof down.

In public university honors programs, about 25%-30% of an honors student's coursework will be in honors classes, although in a few programs that can be as much as 40%. Some of these honors classes will be large, typically in the introductory science courses, but also perhaps in marketing, management, economics, and political science courses. The honors-only classes, especially in the first two years, are likely to be small—averaging 19 students across the 50 rated programs in this edition. So, in these classes, the comparability to liberal arts and private elite classes is greatest, especially in honors seminars and interdisciplinary sections in which class discussion is a prominent feature. These classes, along with an honors thesis requirement if there is one, are, in the public university setting, most likely to differentiate the honors and non-honors experience.

Unlike liberal arts colleges and elite private universities, some honors classes in the academic disciplines (e.g., biology, chemistry, computer science) are mixed honors sections or, especially in the last two years, honors contract sections, in any discipline. The offerings of some mixed and contract sections are still the norm, even though 44% of the rated honors programs in this edition (22 programs) offer honors-only courses almost exclusively.

The percentage of honors enrollment, by section type, for all fifty programs rated in this edition is 81.3% in honors-only sections; 13.6 % in mixed honors sections; and 5.1% in contract sections.

So…**what is a mixed section?** In honors programs, a mixed section for honors credit usually takes one of two forms. The majority of mixed sections are larger than honors-only sections, averaging 51.1 students, including honors *and* non-honors students (this is what makes them "mixed"). Some have no honors-only labs or discussion (breakout) sections in addition to the main mixed section. For these classes, the honors students may do extra work for honors credit, but often the sections are advanced and include students majoring in the discipline or pursuing departmental honors, as well as students in the honors program. Other mixed sections include "regular" students along with honors students, but the honors students meet in their own labs or in 1-2 credit discussion sections outside of the main section. In either of these instances, the mixed section is very likely an improvement over a regular class in the subject.

A contract section (also called an honors option, honors conversion, honors enhancement) is a regular section in which one or a few honors students enter into a written agreement with the instructor to do extra work for honors credit and, preferably, also to meet with the instructor one on one at regular intervals. Generally, honors staff must approve these agreements, but the amount of administrative oversight and quality of the extra work can vary considerably. In the best case, there is consistent oversight and evaluation of the contracts; in the worst case, which does exist, honors staff have little or no involvement in the process and might not even have a record of what the extra work was supposed to be.

This is not to say that honors contracts are necessarily inferior to honors-only courses or mixed honors sections. Even though the quality can be uneven, the contract courses can lead to extremely valuable mentoring relationships between instructors and students. Another positive factor is that students often take upper-division honors contract courses, sometimes including courses needed for majors, minors, or for graduating on schedule. The contract courses are also a way for motivated students to continue to be challenged while working on an honors thesis outside of class. Contract courses do tend to be larger, averaging 60.1 students per section. Proponents of honors contracts contend that the larger class sizes are more than offset by the one-on-one contact that should occur between the student and instructor outside of class. Out of 50 rated programs, 32 allow credit for contract courses, and 18 do not.

Much less typical than any of the three class types discussed above is the honors tutorial. In a tutorial, made famous by the British universities of Oxford and Cambridge, the whole course is a series of one-on-one meetings between the student and instructor. The only honors program to make extensive use of this method is the Honors Tutorial College at Ohio University in Athens, Ohio, but most honors students have at least one tutorial experience, especially if they are doing an honors thesis. Tutorials can be the most demanding, rewarding, and anxiety-producing experiences in undergraduate education (and graduate school, for that matter), depending on the personalities and expectations of the participants.

So what is the main takeaway for prospective students? Try to understand who you are, who you want to be, what you need in the way of change and development, which fears you want to overcome, and which subjects you want to study. Then decide if an honors program offers the right combination of honors classes and course types for *your* purposes. If you are comfortable with being assertive and participating in small classes, then look for those small classes and a sizable number of honors seminars. If you are uneasy about asserting yourself in class, then you can choose to confront that issue or select a program that emphasizes honors classes in the academic disciplines, especially courses in your proposed major. And if you want as much individual attention as possible, then look for a program with a good mix of class types and activities, including small seminars, undergraduate research opportunities, an honors thesis requirement—and maybe a couple of those contract courses too.

Undoubtedly, the current trend in higher education is to develop new honors colleges or to integrate existing honors programs into a separate honors college. This can lead to the perception that honors colleges are inherently better, more advanced, or more in tune with the need to create centers of greater excellence in public universities.

In the case of most of the public universities with an average *U.S. News* ranking of about 60 or higher, however, the preference is to offer an honors program--or programs--rather than establish a separate honors college within those universities. It is no coincidence that these schools, most notably Michigan, UCLA, UNC-Chapel Hill, Virginia, Illinois, UC Irvine, UW-Madison, Washington, and UT Austin have very strong overall academic reputations *and* high faculty rankings across all major disciplines. (UC Berkeley and William and Mary do not have any university-wide honors programs at all.)

When greater selectivity is combined with outstanding academic reputation and stellar faculty, students with Ivy-ish ambitions can say, with considerable confidence, that the smaller communities and classes created by the honors programs at these schools are the final steps that make them equivalent to (if different from) elite private universities. The university-wide academic reputation is present, and the faculty and most of the students are of a high caliber even in non-honors courses. For many extremely qualified students who care little about the prestige of an elite private college, these universities are sufficiently appealing as they are, with or without honors. There is no urgent competitive need, then, for these universities to establish a separate, often larger and more expensive honors college (please see "Size" comparisons at the end of this section).

There are exceptions, of course. When highly-ranked public universities receive generous private endowments or donations to establish honors colleges, they have done so. The Schreyer Honors College at Penn State is an outstanding example.

The University of Maryland Honors College is another exception. Though not named for wealthy benefactors, the college was created almost half a century ago, in 1966, making it one of the oldest and most respected honors colleges in the nation. The highly regarded Calhoun Honors College at Clemson is now in its sixth decade of operation.

Private endowments and remarkable institutional support can also fund honors colleges within flagships that are not rated among the top 60 national universities, making those honors colleges so notable that they often compete with public and private elites. Examples include the University of South Carolina Honors College, Clark Honors College at the University of Oregon, ASU's Barrett Honors College, and the Sally McDonnell Barksdale Honors College at Ole Miss. A new, generously endowed honors college is now opening at the University of Kentucky. The presence of these excellent honors colleges no doubt enhances the student profiles of the universities of which they are a part and makes the universities more competitive in keeping the brightest students in state. Often, the best honors colleges attract out-of-state students as well, especially if their resources permit generous merit scholarships.

As for **basic types of honors colleges and programs,** the type is not dependent on whether the university has an honors program or an honors college. Programs and colleges can all be roughly characterized as being **core programs, blended programs, or discipline (department)-based programs.**

Core Programs are almost always smaller in size, anywhere from a few hundred to about 800 students, although a few are larger than that. They emphasize interdisciplinary classes and lots of seminars in the first two years, especially, and these courses are offered directly by the honors college or program. Some have relatively few sections in the academic disciplines based in the various departments. The UT Austin Plan II Honors Program and Oregon's Clark Honors College, while they are essentially core programs, also offer their own courses in English, math, and physics.

Blended Programs offer a combination of seminars, interdisciplinary classes, and more courses across a broader range of subjects than core programs do. There are many examples, but the South Carolina Honors College is one of the best.

Department-based (or discipline-based) Programs look mostly to the academic departments across the university to designate honors courses in a wide range of subjects. In these programs, such as Penn State's Schreyer Honors College, the University of Georgia Honors Program, and the University of Arkansas Honors College, the honors administration devotes even more time to coordinating the best possible relationships with Deans and Department Chairs, not to mention Provosts, in order to have as many honors courses as possible.

Now, here are the specific differences between honors colleges and honors programs.

In this edition, honors colleges have an edge over honors programs in most rating categories, but not in some of the most important ones.

Here are the categories in which honors colleges have better overall ratings:

Number of honors classes--honors colleges offer an honors class for every 13.7 students; programs offer an honors class for every 14.9 students.

Number of honors classes in key disciplines—honors colleges offer a class in a key discipline for every 25.6 students; programs offer a class in a key discipline for every 29.6 students.

Extent of honors participation—for each member in good standing in honors colleges, 1.17 honors classroom seats are occupied; for each member in good standing in honors programs, 1.08 honors classroom seats are occupied.

Honors-only class size—the average honors-only class size in honors colleges is 18.2 students; the average honors-only class size in honors programs is 20.2 students.

Overall class size—this measure includes mixed and contract honors classes, both of which have non-honors students. The overall class size in honors colleges, including honors-only classes as well, is 25.2 students. In honors programs, the overall class size is 28.1 students.

Value-added grad rate—this is the difference between the honors grad rate and the grad rate for the university as a whole. Honors colleges have a slight edge, due partly to the greater difference, on average, between honors and non-honors students.

Honors perks (priority registration, dorm features, room availability)—honors colleges all have priority registration in some form; a few honors programs do not. Honors colleges have somewhat higher dorm and availability ratings than honors programs.

Number of students per honors staff member—this is the most significant difference. Honors colleges average 120 students per staff member; honors programs average 161 students per staff member.

On the other hand, honors programs have the edge in three important categories.

Honors curriculum requirements—for honors graduation, honors programs require an average of 1.2 honors credits above the average graduation credit requirements of honors colleges.

Honors graduation rates—as might be expected with several honors programs being affiliated with public elite universities, the six-year honors graduation rate for honors programs (90.6%) averages a significant 4.3 points higher than the rate for honors colleges (86.3%).

Prestigious scholarships (Rhodes, Marshall, Truman, Goldwater, etc.)—the same factor that leads to higher honors graduation rates for honors programs likely contributes to a much higher total of prestigious awards versus those won by students in universities with honors colleges.

Selectivity

Although selectivity is not a rating category, the mean (**new** SAT) admissions score for honors programs is 1440, versus the mean score for honors colleges of 1410. This factor also contributes to the higher graduation rates and a greater success at winning prestigious scholarships on the part of universities with honors programs instead of honors colleges. If we had included the honors programs at the University of Michigan and the University of Virginia, as in previous editions, the differences in test scores would have been even greater.

Size

The difference between the sizes of honors colleges and honors programs is very significant, with honors colleges (in this set of 50 colleges and programs) being 50% larger than honors programs.

The average number of members in good standing in the 31 honors colleges rated in this edition is 2,249. In the 2014 edition, the average size of honors colleges (a somewhat different set, with 21 carrying over to this edition) was 1,900 members. The growth in the size of honors colleges is a definite trend.

- The Barrett Honors College at Arizona State University reported 4,800 members in 2014; the number in this edition is 6,247.
- The approximate number of members in the Hutton Honors College at Indiana University was 4,000; now it is 5,000.
- At the South Carolina Honors College, the 2014 number was approximately 1,400. Now it is 1,620.
- The Commonwealth Honors College at UMass Amherst reported about 3,000 members in 2014, but now has 3,800.
- At Ole Miss, the Sally McDonnell Barksdale Honors College reported 1,123 members in 2014, but the membership listed in this edition is 1,251.
- The Purdue Honors College reported 1,555 members in 2014, a number which has risen to 1,888 members.

The average number of members in good standing in the 19 honors programs rated in this edition is far lower, at 1,496, than the average for honors colleges (2,249). For the 2014 edition, the 25 honors programs (15 carryovers in this edition) had an average membership of 1,492, a difference that is not significantly different from the current average.

The overall average number of members in good standing for all 50 rated colleges and programs in this edition is 1,742.

Given such a difference in the average sizes, at least in this group of honors colleges and programs, the amount of funding and resources involved in establishing and operating an honors college is far greater than the amount needed for most honors programs.

We have noticed that many students apply to prominent public universities and then, almost as an afterthought, begin to wonder if the honors program at University A makes that school a better choice than regular admission to the higher-ranked University B.

A far better way to look at honors is to evaluate programs in some depth at the earliest stages of the college application process. Otherwise, students realize too late that the honors application or scholarship deadlines have already passed, or find themselves searching for anecdotal evidence with little time to spare.

Honors colleges and programs differ greatly in size, quality, curricula, housing, overall philosophy, and financial aid opportunities. Working through the maze of differences can be a daunting prospect, especially when time is an issue. When it comes to honors programs, many of the most important questions can be answered only by consideration of those all-important "details." Below are twenty steps that should be very useful in helping you make the best decision regardless of whether you want a public or private university honors program:

1. Match basic admission requirements with your test scores, GPA, and essays.

2. Request actual average admission statistics. These may vary greatly from basic (minimum) requirements. In general, honors students will have average test scores 6-10% higher than the 25th percentile of accepted students for the university as a whole. The 25th percentile scores are available from *U.S. News* and other sources. If there is a wide gap between the basic and average stats, and your stats are much closer to the basic stats, then you can probably find a better option. That said, if the admissions requirements are more holistic and less stats-driven, you may be fine.

3. Determine the size of the honors program (mean size in major public universities is 1,742, but programs may be as small as 140 or as large as 6,900).

4. Ask the fish-to-pond question: Are honors students big fish in a small pond or is the pond full of sizable fish? The more selective the university as a whole, the bigger all the fish. Some parents and prospective students might prefer an honors program that stands apart on campus, while others might like a program that is more expansive. Perhaps if you are not sold on the overall quality of the university, you might choose the former; if you think the university as a whole has a strong student body or you simply prefer a non-elitist atmosphere, then you might like the latter.

5. Assess the quality of the city, surrounding area, and climate.

6. Determine the curriculum requirements as a percentage of graduation requirements. Generally, the number of honors hours should be at least 25% of the total required for graduation.

7. Determine the number of honors sections per semester/quarter.

8. Evaluate the reputation of university in preferred or likely areas of study.

9. Ask whether there are special research opportunities for undergrads **and if an honors thesis is required.** Some students do not want the extra challenge; others realize how important it can be for attending graduate or professional school, or even for employment opportunities.

10. Ask about staff size, the number of advisers, and availability to students, as well as special freshmen orientation programs.

If the above check out, then:

1. Ask about the number of honors sections, <u>by subject</u>, per semester or quarter and try to verify; determine the average enrollment in honors seminars and sections. The average class size can vary greatly among honors programs, from fewer than 10 students per class to more than 35. Most seminars and all-honors sections should have around 20-25 students or fewer, although in almost every case you will find that there are a few large classes, notably in first-year sciences, business, economics, and political science. Some honors programs have few or no honors courses in certain disciplines.

2. Ask about the <u>types</u> of honors sections: all-honors seminars; all-honors sections offered by honors <u>or</u> a department; "mixed" sections of honors and non-honors students; and the percentage of honors contract/option/conversion courses per average student at time of graduation. <u>Mixed sections</u> may be small or, more often, larger sections that can have more than 100 total students in 3-4 credit hour courses. Of these students, maybe 10-20 could be honors students, who then meet for one hour a week (rarely, two hours a week) in separate "discussion" or "recitation" sections. These sections can be led by tenured professors but are typically led by adjunct faculty or graduate students. Ask how many sections are mixed, and of these, ask how many of the main section classes are large.

<u>Contract courses</u> are regular—and often larger—sections with both honors and non-honors students, mostly the latter, in which honors students do extra work and meet occasionally with the instructor one-on-one. While most programs have some contract courses, they are generally more prevalent in large honors colleges and programs. There are advantages and disadvantages associated with contract courses. They can speed up graduation, offer more flexibility, expand the influence of honors in the university as a whole, and foster contacts with mentoring faculty. But their quality and class size may vary greatly.

3. Ask about tuition discounts, scholarships, continuing financial aid, including special recruitment of National Merit Scholars.

4. Determine if there is priority registration for honors students and, if so, type of priority registration.

5. Research the types of special honors housing for freshmen <u>and</u> upperclassmen, if any, including basic floor plans, on-site laundry, suite or corridor-style rooms, air-conditioning, location of nearest dining hall, proximity of major classroom buildings (especially in preferred subjects), and availability of shuttles and other transportation on campus. <u>If there is no special honors housing, it is often a sign that the honors program does not want to foster an elitist atmosphere. The absence of priority registration may be an additional sign.</u>

6. Research the study-abroad opportunities; some universities have a separate division for study-abroad programs.

7. Ask about the presence and involvement of advisers for prestigious scholarships, such as Goldwater, Rhodes, Marshall, Truman, etc., and program success in achieving these awards.

8. Ask about additional fees for participation in honors **and ask about the percentage of honors "completers."** These are honors students who actually complete all of the honors requirements and graduate with some form of honors. There are some programs that have completion rates as low as 25% and a few with completion rates higher than 80%. (This is different from the graduation rate, which, for freshmen honors entrants, is anywhere from 75%–99% after six years.)

9. Now, try to assess the quality of the honors program versus quality of university as a whole.

10. VISIT the college if you have not done so and try to question current honors students. Some of the information mentioned above can only come from a personal visit or be learned after a student has been accepted.

In each of our profiles of public honors programs in national universities, there is a section titled "Prestigious Awards" that provides a summary of the awards earned by undergraduates and graduates of the universities as a whole. The awards that we track include the Rhodes Scholarship, Marshall Scholarship, Gates Cambridge Scholarship, Truman Scholarship, Churchill Scholarship, National Science Foundation Graduate Research Fellowships, and Fulbright Student Scholarships, most of which are for college upperclassmen or graduates. Undergraduate awards include the Goldwater Scholarships, Udall Scholarships, Boren Scholarships, and Gilman Scholarships. Until readers become familiar with these scholarships, it will be useful to refer to this page when reading the "Prestigious Awards" section in each profile

It is a great honor for an undergraduate or graduate to win a prestigious award, and many of the awards lead to notable success in graduate school and public life. Below are brief descriptions of each award.

Boren Scholarships provide $20,000-$30,000 to U.S. undergraduate students, including freshmen, to study abroad in areas of the world that are critical to U.S. interests and underrepresented in study abroad, including Africa, Asia, Central & Eastern Europe, Eurasia, Latin America, and the Middle East. The countries of Western Europe, Canada, Australia, and New Zealand are excluded. The GPA requirement is 3.50, with a relevant background and language ability.

Churchill Scholarships are valued at approximately $45,000 for 9-12 months of study at Cambridge University. Eligibility requires at least a bachelor's degree and a 3.70 GPA; however, the average GPA is closer to 3.90. Students in the STEM disciplines and public health are eligible. Only 14 scholars are chosen each year.

Fulbright Student Scholarships are for graduating seniors or graduates who are selected to study or teach overseas. The award has a value of up to $25,000 for one year. Depending on whether the recipient is teaching English or conducting research, the GPA requirements vary from 3.40 (English) to 3.90.

Gates Cambridge Scholarships are the most generous awards we track, currently valued at about $84,000 for up to three years of graduate study at Cambridge University. Successful candidates must have at least a 3.80 GPA and be graduating seniors or graduates. Although many Gates Cambridge Scholars are STEM students, the award is not restricted to scholars in the STEM disciplines. About 95 scholars are chosen annually from more than 4,000 candidates.

Gilman Scholarships allow students of limited means and students in underrepresented disciplines to study or participate in internships abroad. The average value is $4,000. Required GPA is 3.20 to 3.50.

Goldwater Scholarships are perhaps the most prestigious undergraduate awards. They are valued at $7,500 per year, and successful candidates are outstanding students in the STEM fields with a GPA of 3.80 and higher. There have been a few two-time winners. A university may nominate up to four candidates a year. About 300 scholars are chosen each year from among thousands of sophomore and junior candidates.

Marshall Scholarships are extremely prestigious awards granted to about 40 American graduating seniors in all majors each year. Scholars currently receive approximately $28,000 per year to study at one of scores of universities in the United Kingdom, usually for two years, but sometimes for three years. A large number of Marshall Scholars study at the universities of Cambridge and Oxford; the University of

London (King's College, University College, Imperial College); and the London School of Economics and Political Studies (LSE). The GPA requirement is 3.80 and higher.

National Science Foundation Graduate Research Fellowships are awarded to 900-1,000 students annually to fund three years of graduate study in a STEM field or a social or behavioral science discipline. Fellows receive $10,500 for each of the three years. A minimum GPA of 3.70 and very high GRE scores are required.

Rhodes Scholarships remain the best-known and most prestigious of all awards, in addition to being the oldest. Each year 32 Americans are chosen to study for two (and sometimes three) years at the University of Oxford, in all majors. The dollar value of the award is similar to the value of the Marshall Scholarship, and the minimum GPA requirement is also 3.80.

Truman Scholarships are awarded to 55-60 juniors at participating U.S. universities who want to go to graduate school in preparation for a career in public service (government or the nonprofit and advocacy sectors). The minimum GPA requirement is 3.80. Awardees receive $2,000 to complete their undergraduate education and $30,000 total for up to three years of postgraduate study.

Udall Scholarships provide $5,000 toward tuition for undergraduates interested in environmental, sustainability, or planning issues, or for Native Americans focusing on health care or tribal policy. Only 50 awards are granted each year.

Although we are not ranking honors colleges and programs in numerical order, the summary below provides average (mean) overall results for the 50 programs that we rated, and additional data.

Size of Honors Colleges/Programs:

Average size of all colleges/programs=1,742
Average size of 31 honors colleges=2,249
Average size of 19 honors programs=1,496
Largest of all 50 colleges/programs=~6,900
Smallest of all 50 colleges/programs=411

Curriculum Requirements:

Average number of honors credit hours required for program completion=29.0 semester credits
Required honors credit hours as a percentage of total credits required for graduation=24.2%
Highest credit hour completion level of the 50 colleges and programs=45 credits
Lowest credit hour completion level of the 50 colleges and programs=18 credits

Honors Enrollment, by Type of Honors Class Section:

Average percentage of honors classroom seats in honors-only sections=81.3%
Average percentage of honors classroom seats in mixed honors sections=13.6%
Average percentage of honors classroom seats in honors contract sections=5.1%

Number and Percentage of Programs with 90%-100% of Honors Classroom Seats in Honors-Only Sections= 22 programs, or 44%

Number of Honors Classes Offered: One honors section for every 14.2 honors individuals enrolled in the term reported.

Number of Honors Classes in Key Disciplines: One honors section in each key discipline for every 26.3 honors individuals enrolled in the term reported.

Average Ratio of Honors Classroom "Seats" to Total Number of Honors Members in Good Standing: 1.13 classroom seats per 1.0 member in good standing. Range=.2.00 to .51.

Average Honors-only Class Size: 19.0 students. Range= 9.1 to 31.7.

Average Honors Overall Class Size, including Mixed and Contract Sections: 26.3 students. The average mixed section had an average 51.1 students in the main course section. The average honors contract section had an average of 60.1 students. Range Overall Class Size= 15.4 to 64.1.

Honors Graduation Rate (6-year), Freshman Entrants, not necessarily Honors "Completers":
Average honors grad rate for programs with SAT requirement of:

>1500= 95.0%.
1400-1499= 92.6%.

1350-1399= 86.2%.
1300-1349= 83.4%. (Minus one outlier of 73.6%=84.6%.)
<1300= 85.6%.

Ratio of Honors Students to Honors Staff:

Average number of honors students to honors staff person=135.6
Highest average number of honors students to staff=403.3
Lowest average number of honors students to staff=52.0

Ratio of Honors Dorm Spaces to total of First- and Second-Year Members of Program:

Average ratio of honors dorm spaces to students=.63
Highest ratio of honors dorm spaces to students=1.30
Lowest ratio of honors dorm spaces to students=.14

Test Scores:

Mean two-part (old) SAT for enrolled students in all 50 programs= 1355; new SAT, 1415
Lowest average (old) SAT score=1240; new SAT, 1310
Highest average (old) SAT score=1505 (estimated); new SAT, 1535

Ranking Data for Academic Departments: For business and engineering, the rankings are of the undergraduate programs; for all other departments, the rankings are of graduate programs.

Much of our data is unique and is therefore not available in any other publication or online. Some of these unique data elements include:

• Comparative statistics on the number of prestigious scholarships won by each national university
• Actual honors class sizes from 100% of the rated 50 public honors programs
• Actual honors graduation rates from 98% of the 50 rated honors programs
• Comparative information about the honors residence halls (or lack thereof) designated by all 50 rated honors programs, including room configurations, amenities, and nearest dining facilities
• Ratios of honors students to administrative staff, 98% of rated programs
• Descriptions of the types of honors courses offered by each program, including the percentage breakdown of honors-only class sections, mixed sections, and contract sections

A list of honors colleges and programs with 5.0 and 4.5 ratings appears at the bottom of page 7.

NAME: UNIVERSITY OF ALABAMA HONORS COLLEGE.

Date Established: 2003.

Location: Tuscaloosa, Alabama.

University Full-time Undergraduate Enrollment (2015): 27,737.

Honors Members in Good Standing: 6,900 *estimated* size; (mean size of all 50 programs is 1,742). This is the largest honors program in the country.

Honors Average Admission Statistics (all Alabama honors programs): Estimated old SAT, 1360; estimated new SAT, 1420. Computer-based honors old SAT, 1450; estimated new SAT, 1490. University Fellows old SAT, 1400; estimated new SAT, 1450.

Average High School GPA/Class Rank: Regular Honors, 3.77, and 84% are in the top 10% of their class. Computer-based Honors, 4.30. University Fellows, 3.8.

Basic Admission Requirements: ACT, 28. Old SAT, 1250; new SAT, 1310. Minimum high school GPA, 3.5.

Application Deadline(s): *Please verify with each program, as some deadlines could change.*

For University Fellows applications, the deadline is December 15, 2016; for other applications there is "no formal deadline," but for housing and orientation purposes, the earlier the better.

Honors Programs with old SAT scores from 1351—1396: Purdue, Oregon, Alabama, Massachusetts, Penn State, Indiana, CUNY Macaulay, Texas A&M, NJIT, Missouri, Oregon State, Delaware, LSU, Vermont, Temple.

Administrative Staff: 19.

RATINGS AT A GLANCE: For all mortarboard ratings immediately below, a score of 5 is the maximum and represents a comparison with all 50 honors colleges and programs. More detailed explanations follow the "mortarboard" ratings.

PERCEPTION* OF UNIVERSITY AS A WHOLE, NOT OF HONORS: 🎓🎓🎓🎓

*Perception is based on the university's ranking among public universities in the 2016 U.S. News Best Colleges report. Please bear in mind that the better the U.S. News ranking, the more difficult it is for an honors college or program to have a rating that equals or improves on the magazine ranking.

OVERALL HONORS RATING: 🎓🎓🎓🎓

Curriculum Requirements: 🎓🎓🎓 **Number of. Honors Classes Offered:** 🎓🎓🎓🎓 1/2

Number of Honors Classes in Key Disciplines: 🎓🎓🎓🎓1/2

Extent of Honors Enrollment: 🎓🎓🎓🎓🎓

Honors-only Class Size: 🎓🎓🎓1/2

Overall Class Size (Honors-only plus mixed, contract): 🎓🎓🎓🎓

Honors Grad Rate: 🎓🎓🎓🎓

Value-Added Grad Rate: 🎓🎓🎓🎓1/2

Ratio of Staff to Students: 🎓🎓🎓1/2

Priority Registration: Yes, honors students register for all courses, honors and otherwise, with the first group of students during each year they are in the program.

Honors Housing Amenities: 🎓🎓🎓🎓1/2

Honors Housing Availability: 🎓🎓🎓🎓

Prestigious Awards: 🎓🎓🎓🎓1/2

RATING SCORES AND EXPLANATIONS:

Curriculum Requirements (3.0): The most important rating category, the curriculum completion requirement (classes required to complete honors) defines not only what honors students should learn but also the extent to which honors students and faculty are connected in the classroom. If there is a thesis or capstone requirement, it reinforces the individual contact and research skills so important to learning.

The average number of honors semester hours required for completion across all 50 programs is 29.0.

For the University Honors Program, students are required to earn at least 18 hours of Honors credit, including at least six hours of Honors Foundation courses, and graduate with an overall GPA of at least 3.3. There is **no thesis requirement.**

The Computer-based Honors Experience requires completion of two specialized honors computer science courses and four 3-credit projects "combining the student's research and computer applications." Students must graduate with an overall GPA of 3.3. **No thesis is required.**

The International Honors Program requires 9 hours of coursework with an international focus along with 12 hours of foreign language. Students must graduate with a 3.3 GPA. **No thesis is required.**

AP/IB credits are **not** counted as replacements for honors courses.

University Fellows:

Freshman year—"Seminars to explore issues of servant leadership, personal development, project development and implementation, and civic engagement; Black Belt Experience in May, wherein Fellows partner with local initiatives, programs, and individuals in Perry County, Alabama and implement projects that address challenges of systemic poverty."

Sophomore year—"Seminars to explore issues of leadership in the community, including a series of exposures to the practical and multi-faceted aspects of being a good citizen; participate in significant contributions both individually and collaboratively in an effort to connect idea development with the creation of positive action."

Junior year—"Receive individualized assistance and support for career options and post-undergraduate opportunities; active and ongoing research and correspondence with key figures in their field of interest, including pertinent professional conferences; peer Mentors and committee chairs for UFE Committees in the planning and implementation of key events, programs and initiatives."

Senior year—"Distinguish themselves in their fields of study through published or presented articles, research, or related productive materials; reflect their work in a four-year culminating Portfolio; teach one-hour Honors College seminar courses on a topic of their choosing. No thesis is required."

Contract courses: Only six credit hours can be earned through honors contract courses, so most honors credits come from all-honors classes.

Number of Honors Classes Offered (4.5): This is a measure of the total **adjusted** honors main sections available in the term reported, not including labs and thesis. An adjusted main section has 3 or more semester credits, or equivalent, and sections with fewer credits receive a lower prorated value.

Alabama honors offered a section for every **11.0** enrolled students. The average for all 50 programs is 14.2. The lower the number, the better.

In the term reported, In the term reported, **94.8%** of honors enrollment was **in honors-only sections; none in mixed honors sections (honors and non-honors students); and 5.2% in contract sections (regular sections in which honors students "contract" to do extra work** The averages for all fifty programs are 81.3% in honors-only sections; 13.6 % in mixed honors sections; and 5.1% in contract sections.

Number of Honors Classes in Key Disciplines (4.5): The 15 "key" disciplines are biological sciences; business (all); chemistry; communications (especially public speaking); computer science; economics; engineering (all); English; history; math (all); philosophy; physics; political science; psychology; and sociology, anthropology, and gender studies. Interdisciplinary sections, such as those often taken for General Education credit in the first two years, do receive a lesser, prorated discipline "credit" because they introduce students to multiple disciplines in an especially engaging way, often with in-depth discussion.

For this measure, mixed and contract sections are not counted as a section in a key discipline unless students taking the sections for honors credit make up at least 10% of the total section enrollment. In the term reported, the honors college offered a section in a key discipline for every **20 honors students.** The average for all 50 programs is 26.3. The lower the number, the better.

The college offered **187 adjusted sections in key disciplines,** and **174 are listed as honors-only sections.** The most sections were in English, engineering, computer science, history, math, and psychology, followed by chemistry, biology, and business. There was one physics section, five in sociology, anthropology, and gender studies combined.

The college offered more than 200 seminars and interdisciplinary classes, including "Faith in Philosophy & Literature"; "Heroes, Faith, and Justice"; and "Machiavelli in History and Politics."

The combination of seminars and courses in the disciplines makes the honors college a **blended** program.

Extent of Honors Enrollment (5.0): Not all honors students take an honors class each term, especially after the first two years. Programs that have fewer honors classes for upper-division honors students will generally have fewer total members in good standing who are actually enrolled in a given term. (Please be aware, however, that honors students not enrolled in a class for a term are still connected to the honors community through residential and extracurricular activities.)

For example, if honors students in a program occupy 1,800 honors classroom seats in a given term, and there are 3,000 honors students in good standing, the extent of enrollment is .67. For programs that require a thesis, the ratio (score) reported below might in fact be somewhat higher, since we only count "regular" class enrollment for this measure, and not thesis enrollment. **Alabama has a ratio of 1.71,** far higher than the average of 1.13 for all 50 programs. The higher the ratio, the better.

Average Class Size, Honors-only Sections (3.5): Offered mostly in the first two years, honors-only classes tend to be smaller and, as the name implies, have no or very few students other than those in the honors program. These class sections are almost always much smaller than mixed or contract sections, or regular non-honors class sections in the university.

The average honors-only class size at the honors college is **22.9 students.** The average for all 50 programs is 19.0 students.

Average Class Size, Overall (4.0): The overall class calculation is based on the *proportion* of honors students in each type of class (honors-only, mixed honors, and honors contract sections). Thus it is not a raw average. The overall honors-credit class size is **26.6 students,** versus the average for all 50 programs, also 26.3 students. It should be noted, however, that the predominance of all-honors sections at the college is a more important factor.

These class size averages also do not correspond to the number of students per honors sections numbers above. The reason is that, in computing average class size metrics, we include enrollment in each 1-2-credit section, not just sections with 3 or more credits.

Along with the honors-only average of 22.9 students, the contract sections with honors credit for individual honors students average **89.3 students.** Across all fifty programs, the average mixed honors section has 51.1 students, and the average contract section has 60.1 students.

Honors Graduation Rate (4.0): The rating is based on the actual grad rate for students who entered the program six years earlier, whether or not the students remained in honors. The **actual rate of 88.4%** is also compared to the rates of other programs with the same test score entry requirement range, and then adjusted to the **score of 88.6.** The average honors graduation rate for all programs with similar test scores required for admission is 86.2%.

Value-Added Grad Rate (4.5): The value-added rate measures the extent to which the adjusted score listed above exceeds the six-year grad rate for the university as a whole. **The university-wide rate is 66%.**

Ratio of Staff to Honors Students (3.5): There is 1 staff member for every 1**74.7** students. (Mean ratio for all 50 programs is 1 staff member for every 135.6 students.)

Honors Residence Halls, Amenities (4.5): Living-Learning Communities allow students to have access to educational programs and extra-curricular activities exclusive to the Honors College. The honors residence community includes Blount and Paty Halls, but almost 60% of honors students living on campus reside in Ridgecrest North and South, while another 28% live in Ridgecrest East and West.

These coed living-learning facilities form the center of the University's tightly-knit Honors community. "These buildings feature 4-bedroom suites with private bedrooms, 2 bathrooms, a living/dining area, and a kitchenette. The kitchenette has a full-size refrigerator, microwave, and cabinet space. The bedrooms feature height-adjustable beds with extended twin mattresses.

"In addition to the benefits of living with other Honors College students, faculty residents in each dormitory further increase the value of such an opportunity." Faculty-in-residence programs offer social events and serve as informal advisors for students living in those dorms.

The rating would have been 5.0 if one or more of the halls had dining on site.

Honors Residence Halls, Availability (4.0): This rating compares the number of places in honors residence halls to the number of honors freshman and sophomore members in good standing, approximately 3,450. The ratio for the college is .**48** rooms for each first- and second-year student, a bit below average. The average for all fifty programs is .63 places.

Prestigious Awards (4.5): The awards that we track and include are listed in the section titled "Prestigious Scholarships." The awards are sometimes won by students who are not in an honors college or program, but increasingly many are enrolled in honors programs. It is also a trend that honors colleges and programs help to prepare their students for the awards competitions.

Alabama students, many of them from the honors college, have had strong success in recent years in winning Goldwater scholarships, the most prestigious undergraduate awards, given to students with outstanding promise in STEM fields. Alabama students have also earned 15 Rhodes scholarships during the entire history of the award, along with an impressive 16 Truman scholarships.

UNRATED FEATURES

Continuation Requirements: 3.30 GPA.

Academic Strengths, National Rankings: This is based on national rankings of *graduate* programs in all but engineering and business, where undergraduate rankings are used.

The average departmental ranking at Alabama is within the top 100 nationwide. Leading departments include business (61), followed by English (91), chemistry, history, and psychology, all 92.

Undergraduate Research: "The College and University have several research programs of interest to prospective students. The Emerging Scholars Program introduces first-time freshmen to research. The Computer-based Honors Program is a four-year program that begins in the first semester of the students' freshman years, and emphasizes collaborative projects and research.

The McNair Program is open to juniors in all fields of study who comply with the admission criteria of the program. McNair assists students in research and in locating and funding graduate education."

The College of Arts and Sciences is beginning a new Research Connections Program, which links scholars who have recently joined the Arts and Sciences faculty and undergraduate students.

"The College of Arts and Sciences has several disciplinary honors programs that are open to current students. Students may or may not be in University Honors to participate in disciplinary honors. Most of the disciplinary honors programs require or recommend that students engage in research and complete theses."

Honors Study Abroad: "The University of Alabama offers a variety of summer and interim overseas study programs that allow you to travel with a group of UA students and study under the direction of a UA professor. UA's summer programs have recently been offered in Australia, Austria, Belgium, China, Dublin, Ecuador, England, France, Ghana, Greece, Guatemala, Iceland, Italy, Japan, Korea, London, Mexico, Oxford, Spain, Sweden, Turkey, Vietnam, and other locations.

"An exchange program is a direct link between The University of Alabama and an overseas partner institution. UA has many exchange programs that allow students to continue their academic courses while studying overseas. These competitive programs are open to all qualified students who have studied on the UA campus for at least one semester. Students chosen as exchange participants pay regular UA tuition and spend one semester or year abroad. UA holds exchange relationships with universities in the following countries: Australia, Austria, Belgium, China, Denmark, England, France, Germany, Italy, Japan, Korea, The Netherlands, and Wales."

Financial Aid: The honors college and university are well-known for their recruitment of National scholars, especially National Merit Finalists, who receive:

--Value of tuition for up to five years or 10 semesters for degree-seeking undergraduate and graduate (or law) studies.

--One year of on-campus housing at regular room rate (based on assignment by Housing and Residential Communities.

--A $3,500 per year Merit Scholarship stipend for four years. A student must maintain at least a 3.3 GPA to continue receiving this scholarship stipend. If a corporate-sponsored scholarship from the National Merit Corporation is received, the total value cannot exceed $3,500. (For example, if you receive a corporate-sponsored scholarship of $2,000 per year, UA will contribute $1,500 per year to reach the total stipend amount of $3,500. There is a one-time allowance of $2,000 for use in summer research or international study (after completing one year of study at UA).

--Technology Enrichment Allowance $1,000.

National Merit Semifinalists are also eligible for extremely generous aid, and eight university fellows receive aid that is competitive with NMS finalists. The term "full ride" is alive at Alabama.

Honors Fees: None.

Degree of Difference: This is based on the differences between (1) the average (2015, two-part) SAT scores for enrolled honors students (estimated 1360) and (2) the average test scores for all students in the university (1220) as a whole. The test scores may be an indication of how "elite" honors students may be perceived as compared to students in the university as a whole. The scores can also provide an indication of how well prepared the non-honors students in the university may be. **Please keep in mind that neither high nor low test scores determine the overall quality of a program.**

NAME: UNIVERSITY OF ARIZONA HONORS COLLEGE.

Date Established: 1999 (Preceded by Honors Program, 1962.)

Location: Tucson, Arizona.

University Full-time Undergraduate Enrollment (2015): 29,529.

Honors Members in Good Standing: 4,572; (mean size of all 50 programs is 1,742).

Honors Average Admission Test Score(s): ACT, 28.9; old SAT, 1282; est. new SAT, 1340.

Average High School GPA/Class Rank: 3.83.

Basic Admission Requirements: The honors college uses an index to predict academic success in the program. The index combines high school GPA, test scores, advanced courses and college-credit classes in high school, etc. "We also use an essay question that taps into motivation. Students can submit a teacher recommendation, 7th semester transcripts, personal statement, and additional information for a more holistic review."

Application Deadline(s): *Please verify with each program, as some deadlines could change.*

May 1, 2017, regular UA application.

Honors Programs with old SAT scores from 1240—1291: Arkansas, Oklahoma State, Texas Tech, Montana, Washington State, New Mexico, South Dakota, Colorado State, Arizona, Montana State, Arizona State.

Administrative Staff: 29, plus 8 interdisciplinary faculty.

RATINGS AT A GLANCE: For all mortarboard ratings immediately below, a score of 5 is the maximum and represents a comparison with all 50 honors colleges and programs. More detailed explanations follow the "mortarboard" ratings.

PERCEPTION* OF UNIVERSITY AS A WHOLE, NOT OF HONORS: 🎓🎓🎓[1/2]

*Perception is based on the university's ranking among public universities in the 2016 U.S. News Best Colleges report. Please bear in mind that the better the U.S. News ranking, the more difficult it is for an honors college or program to have a rating that equals or improves on the magazine ranking.

OVERALL HONORS RATING: 🎓🎓🎓🎓

Curriculum Requirements: 🎓🎓🎓🎓🎓

Number of Honors Classes Offered: 🎓🎓🎓[1/2]

Number of Honors Classes in Key Disciplines: 🎓🎓🎓 1/2

Extent of Honors Enrollment: 🎓🎓🎓🎓 1/2

Honors-only Class Size: 🎓🎓🎓 1/2

Overall Class Size (Honors-only plus mixed, contract): 🎓🎓🎓

Honors Grad Rate: 🎓🎓🎓 1/2

Value-Added Grad Rate: 🎓🎓🎓🎓 1/2

Ratio of Staff to Students: 🎓🎓🎓🎓

Priority Registration: Yes, honors students register for all courses, honors and otherwise, with the first group of students during each year they are in the program.

Honors Housing Amenities: 🎓🎓🎓 1/2

Honors Housing Availability: 🎓🎓🎓 1/2

Prestigious Awards: 🎓🎓🎓 0 🎓🎓

RATING SCORES AND EXPLANATIONS:

Curriculum Requirements (5.0): The most important rating category, the curriculum completion requirement (classes required to complete honors) defines not only what honors students should learn but also the extent to which honors students and faculty are connected in the classroom. If there is a thesis or capstone requirement, it reinforces the individual contact and research skills so important to learning.

The average number of honors semester hours required for completion across all 50 programs is 29.0

The basic completion requirement at the Arizona Honors College is 30 credits, but the average with all completion options and some credits from the unique Honors Minor in Health and Human Values (below) is about **36** credits.

The Da Vinci award and graduation with honors in *three* majors requires 42 credit hours, including 24 honors class credits, 12 of which may be earned in contract courses. The **thesis requirement is 18 credits**, or 6 for each major.

The Da Vinci award and graduation with honors in *two* majors requires 36 credit hours, including 24 honors class credits, 12 of which may be earned in contract courses. The **thesis requirement is 12 credits**, or 6 for each major.

Graduation with honors requires the completion of 30 hours of honors credits. Included in the 30 hours is a **6-hour thesis**. Of the 30 total hours, up to 12 may be earned by taking honors contract courses, which allow honors students in regular sections to contract with the instructor to do extra work.

Graduation with honors as an engaged honors scholar requires 21 honors credits, 12 of which may be by contract, along with 3 credits in an "honors engagement experience" plus a 6-credit thesis. Honors experiences can include professional development and internships, study abroad, research, leadership classes, and civic engagement.

Graduation with honors from the College of Engineering requires the completion of 30 hours, but, of those 30 hours, only 17 hours are in honors courses, including up to six hours by contract. Instead of a thesis, students complete an Honors engineering capstone (6 units) and earn 7 credit hours engineering design courses.

Honors graduation from the Eller College of Management Entrepreneurship requires the completion of 21 credit hours, 12 of which may be earned in contract classes (no more than 6 hours in lower division contract classes). In addition, there is an honors capstone project that counts for another 9 credit hours.

The Honors College also has a First Level Honors Award (essentially for two years of honors work), which requires completion of 15 credit hours and a GPA of 3.50.

"The College offers an interdisciplinary minor in Health and Human Values (18 units). The minor is structured with the Honors faculty team teaching the Methods in Human Health and Values and the capstone course during which students will design a small scale intervention in health care. Students can choose the other four courses from a variety of Honors courses developed across the colleges, including Evidence Based Medicine, History of Epidemics, Bodies and Machines, Introduction to Medical Anthropology, and Medical Science Fiction. *Students can choose to do their Honors thesis in the minor to fulfill the requirement for graduation with Honors.*"

AP/IB credits are **not** counted as replacements for honors courses.

Number of Honors Classes Offered (3.5): This is a measure of the total **adjusted** honors main sections available in the term reported, not including labs and thesis. An adjusted main section has 3 or more semester credits, or equivalent, and sections with fewer credits receive a lower prorated value.

Arizona honors offered a section for every **18.3** enrolled students. The average for all 50 programs is 14.2 The lower the number, the better.

In the term reported, **58.0%** of honors enrollment was **in honors-only sections; 38.5% in mixed honors sections (honors and non-honors students); and 3.5% in contract sections (regular sections in which honors students "contract" to do extra work** The averages for all fifty programs are 81.3% in honors-only sections; 13.6 % in mixed honors sections; and 5.1% in contract sections.

Number of Honors Classes in Key Disciplines (3.5): The 15 "key" disciplines are biological sciences; business (all); chemistry; communications (especially public speaking); computer science; economics;

engineering (all); English; history; math (all); philosophy; physics; political science; psychology; and sociology, anthropology, and gender studies. Interdisciplinary sections, such as those often taken for General Education credit in the first two years, do receive a lesser, prorated discipline "credit" because they introduce students to multiple disciplines in an especially engaging way, often with in-depth discussion.

For this measure, mixed and contract sections are not counted as a section in a key discipline unless students taking the sections for honors credit make up at least 10% of the total section enrollment.

In the term reported, the honors college offered a section in a key discipline for every **41.4 honors students.** The average for all 50 programs is 26.3. The lower the number, the better.

Out of **78 adjusted sections in key disciplines, 29 were honors-only sections.** The most sections by far were in English, and there was a very high number of physics sections, a fact noted in the last review. Business was another key discipline represented strongly. There were no adjusted sections in computer science, philosophy, and psychology, and just a few in math and history.

The college does offer seminars, about 60 1-credit special topics seminars in social sciences and humanities, and another 30 or so with 2-3 credits. Among the latter were "Global Social Entrepreneurism" and "Exploring Electronic Presence." The honors college is a **blended** program, with a significant tilt toward a discipline-based type.

Extent of Honors Enrollment (4.5): Not all honors students take an honors class each term, especially after the first two years. Programs that have fewer honors classes for upper-division honors students will generally have fewer total members in good standing who are actually enrolled in a given term. (Please be aware, however, that honors students not enrolled in a class for a term are still connected to the honors community through residential and extracurricular activities.)

For example, if honors students in a program occupy 1,800 honors classroom seats in a given term, and there are 3,000 honors students in good standing, the extent of enrollment is .67. For programs that require a thesis, the ratio (score) reported below might in fact be somewhat higher, since we only count "regular" class enrollment for this measure, and not thesis enrollment. **Arizona has a ratio of 1.34,** significantly above the average of 1.13 for all 50 programs. The higher the ratio, the better.

Average Class Size, Honors-only Sections (3.5): Offered mostly in the first two years, honors-only classes tend to be smaller and, as the name implies, have no or very few students other than those in the honors program. These class sections always are much smaller than mixed or contract sections, or regular non-honors class sections in the university.

The average honors-only class size at the honors college is **22 students.** The average for all 50 programs is 19.0 students.

Average Class Size, Overall (3.0): The overall class calculation is based on the *proportion* of honors students in each type of class (honors-only, mixed honors, and honors contract sections). Thus it is not a raw average. The overall honors-credit class size is **51.1 students,** versus the average for all 50 programs of 26.3 students.

These class size averages also do not correspond to the number of students per honors sections numbers above. The reason is that, in computing average class size metrics, we include enrollment in each 1-2-credit section, not just sections with 3 or more credits.

Along with the honors-only average of 22 students, at Arizona the mixed honors sections average **81.0 students,** and the contract sections with honors credit for individual honors students average **203.7 students.** Across all fifty programs, the average mixed honors section has 51.1 students, and the average contract section has 61.1 students.

Honors Graduation Rate (3.5): The rating is based on the actual grad rate for students who entered the program six years earlier, whether or not the students remained in honors. The **actual rate of 83.9%** is also compared to the rates of other programs with the same test score entry requirement range, and then adjusted to the **score of 83.7.** The average honors graduation rate for all programs with similar test scores required for admission is 85.6%.

Value-Added Grad Rate (4.5): The value-added rate measures the extent to which the adjusted score listed above exceeds the six-year grad rate for the university as a whole. **The university-wide rate is 60%.**

Ratio of Staff to Honors Students (4.0): There is 1 staff member for every 138.5 students. (Mean ratio for all 50 programs is 1 staff member for every 135.6 students.)

Honors Residence Halls, Amenities (3.5): "Honors students can choose to live in one of two Honors residence halls or from 20 other halls on campus. Statistics show that 90% of Honors students live in a residence hall their first year and almost 40% remain on campus in subsequent years.

"Árbol de la Vida is the largest and newest Honors hall comprised of five buildings connected by bridges. Its green design, cutting edge technology and modern design make it one of the most desired places to live on campus," the Dean reports. "This hall has many smart, sustainable features, like solar-heated water, low-flow water fixtures, smart thermostats, 'green' outlets, and passive water harvesting. Honors classes and Honors advising are also offered on-site." About 80% of honors students living on campus live in Árbol de la Vida. The rooms are traditional rooms with hall baths, and, of course, air-conditioned.

"Yuma Hall is listed on the National Register of Historic Places and features the classic red brick tradition of UA campus. Its location in the historic north area of campus is close to the Eller College of Management, College of Engineering, College of Fine Arts and Memorial Student Union. Inviting community spaces include sunken living room, kitchen, multi-media study space, recreation room and large patio. Yuma hall was the first Honors hall and this close-knit community celebrated its 25th anniversary as Honors housing in 2013."

Honors Residence Halls, Availability (3.5): This rating compares the number of rooms in honors residence halls to the number of honors freshman and sophomore members in good standing, approximately 2,286. The ratio for the college is **.39** rooms for each first- and second-year student. The average for all fifty programs is .63 rooms.

Prestigious Awards (5.0): The awards that we track and include are listed in the section titled "Prestigious Scholarships." The awards are sometimes won by students who are not in an honors college or program, but increasingly many are enrolled in honors programs. It is also a trend that honors colleges and programs help to prepare their students for the awards competitions.

Arizona students, many of them from the honors college, have won a very impressive 24 Rhodes scholarships, 16 Truman awards, six Marshall scholarships, and five Gates Cambridge awards. Arizona students have earned an impressive 44 Goldwater scholarships for undergrads in STEM fields, and the university is a leader in winning Udall awards. It also has a strong record in winning Boren and Gilman foreign study and travel scholarships.

UNRATED FEATURES

Continuation Requirements: 3.20.

Academic Strengths, National Rankings: This is based on national rankings of *graduate* programs in all but engineering and business, where undergraduate rankings are used. One of the weakness of the *U.S. News* rankings is that they focus on too many wealth-related metrics while ignoring their own assessments of academic departments.

The University of Arizona is a prime example. The average national departmental ranking across 15 departments at UA is 39. Leading departments are earth sciences (7), sociology (20), business (22), economics (36), biology (38), physics (39), and computer science (40).

Undergraduate Research: "Spirit of Inquiry Research grant program awards approximately $35,000 to students who work with a faculty mentor. Research can be started in summer and continue during academic year with presentation at Honors Engagement Expo in April.

"Honors College offers small grants to support Honors thesis and travel costs for students presenting research at conferences approximately $10,000 in each category.

"The Honors College sponsors three cash awards at the Student Showcase where undergraduates from across the university can present their research and creative expression. Honors students can win awards for Best Project, Social Responsibility, and Health and Human Values."

Honors Study Abroad: "The Honors College offers five study abroad programs where students can study for a summer, semester or year in another country. The most popular is the Honors Trip, a tale of two cities where students earn 6 units of Honors humanities credits in locations such as London/ Paris or London/ Vienna. Summer study also includes a 4- week archaeology experience on the Greek island of Paros that earns 6 units of anthropology and 6-week adventure in Namibia studying conversation biology and ecology.

"The Honors College offers $90,000 annually in study abroad scholarships to help students from all backgrounds attain international experience. The university also has scholarship opportunities that many Honors students receive; all National Scholars can receive $1,500 toward study abroad.

"The University of Arizona has a total of 220 study abroad programs that students can choose among. 30 are agreements with international universities where the student enrolls directly and credits transfer to UA. 61 are faculty led experiences, many of which are summer programs that span the globe. 34 are agreements with organizations that provide study abroad to a variety of institutions; these programs, like Semester at Sea, typically transfer as elective credit. There are 85 exchange relationships with international universities and 10 other programs that involve international internships."

Financial Aid: "UA offers scholarships for resident and non-resident National Merit Scholars and National Hispanic Scholars."

Arizona National Scholars: $18,000 per academic year + one-time $1,500 Study Abroad Award for UA Study Abroad program.

Non-Arizona National Scholars: $7,000 to $17,000+ $5,000 National Scholar Award +one-time $1,500 Study Abroad Award for UA Study Abroad program

Arizona Semi-Finalists: $12,000 per academic year

Non-Arizona Semi-Finalists: $5,000 to $17,000 + $2,000 National Scholar Award.

"The University of Arizona offers $90.5 million in need based financial aid and $62.5 million in merit-based scholarships annually. Nearly all Honors students receive merit based scholarships and many qualify for need based aid.

"The Honors College provides more than $1.1 million in scholarship support with over $380,000 in need based aid. Honors College scholarships help students make the most of their Honors education by supporting educational costs, study abroad, internships, civic engagement, research experiences, thesis costs, travel to conferences, leadership and professional development. Scholarships awarded in the last year totaled $90,000 study abroad, $45,000 internships, $40,000 research, $25,000 professional development, $10,000 thesis, and $10,000 travel to conferences.

"Twenty-three percent of honors students who attended the U. of A. last year had received Pell grants or other forms of need-based federal support, which may have be combined with merit based awards."

Honors Fees: The Honors College has a special program fee of $500 per year that is charged to students. Approximately $300,000 is set aside for financial aid to assist students with the costs of the fee.

Placement Experiences: In 2015, 33% of Honors graduates were entering the workforce and 24% were taking a gap year, working and traveling before going to graduate or professional school.

Of those entering post-baccalaureate education, 36% were entering Masters programs, 32% were enrolling in Ph.D. programs, 11% had been accepted to medical schools, 9% were going to law school, and 11% were entering professional programs such as Pharmacy, Veterinary, Dental, Physician's Assistant and Physical Therapy schools. A total of 80% of alumni reported completing a post-baccalaureate degree within 5 years of graduating from UA.

Degree of Difference: This is based on the differences between (1) the average (2015, two-part) SAT scores for enrolled honors students (1282) and (2) the average test scores for all students in the university (1100) as a whole. The test scores may be an indication of how "elite" honors students may be perceived as compared to students in the university as a whole. The scores can also provide an indication of how well prepared the non-honors students in the university may be. **Please keep in mind that neither high nor low test scores determine the overall quality of a program.**

NAME: BARRETT, THE HONORS COLLEGE, AT ARIZONA STATE UNIVERSITY.

Date Established: 1988.

Location: Tempe, Arizona.

University <u>Full-time Undergraduate</u> Enrollment (2015): 52,381.

Honors Members in Good Standing: 6,247 (mean size of all 50 programs is 1,742).

Honors <u>Average</u> Admission Statistics: The ACT for first-year entrants is 29; the SAT (old) two-part score 1291; new SAT estimate, 1350.

Average High School GPA/Class Rank: 3.77, and 84% are in the top 10% of their class.

<u>Basic</u> Admission Requirements: "Barrett has no 'basic score or GPA requirement.' We make a *subjective* decision on admissions based on the opinions of a 25-person admissions committee reading 9–page independent admissions applications that students fill out 'after' they are accepted into ASU. In this sense, we are exactly like a private college."

Application Deadline(s): *Please verify with each program, as some deadlines could change.*

Early action deadline I- November 1, 2016 (notification December 15); early action deadline II- January 8, (February 10); regular deadline February 15 (March 17); final deadline April 30 (notification May 26).

Honors Programs with old SAT scores from 1240—1291: Arkansas, Oklahoma State, Texas Tech, Montana, Washington State, New Mexico, South Dakota, Colorado State, Arizona, Montana State, Arizona State.

Administrative Staff: 63, plus 42 full-time faculty.

RATINGS AT A GLANCE: For all mortarboard ratings immediately below, a score of 5 is the maximum and represents a comparison with all 50 honors colleges and programs. More detailed explanations follow the "mortarboard" ratings.

PERCEPTION* OF UNIVERSITY AS A WHOLE, <u>NOT</u> OF HONORS: 🎓🎓🎓^1/2

*Perception is based on the university's ranking among public universities in the 2016 U.S. News Best Colleges report. Please bear in mind that the better the U.S. News ranking, the more difficult it is for an honors college or program to have a rating that equals or improves on the magazine ranking.

OVERALL HONORS RATING: 🎓🎓🎓🎓🎓

Curriculum Requirements: 🎓🎓🎓🎓🎓

Number of Honors Classes Offered: 🎓🎓🎓🎓

Number of Honors Classes in Key Disciplines: 🎓🎓🎓$^{1/2}$

Extent of Honors Enrollment: 🎓🎓🎓🎓$^{1/2}$

Honors-only Class Size: 🎓🎓🎓🎓🎓

Overall Class Size (Honors-only plus mixed, contract): 🎓🎓🎓

Honors Grad Rate: 🎓🎓🎓🎓$^{1/2}$

Value-Added Grad Rate: 🎓🎓🎓🎓$^{1/2}$

Ratio of Staff to Students: 🎓🎓🎓🎓🎓

Priority Registration: Yes, honors students register for all courses, honors and otherwise, with the first group of students during each year they are in the program.

Honors Housing Amenities: 🎓🎓🎓🎓🎓

Honors Housing Availability: 🎓🎓🎓🎓🎓

Prestigious Awards: 🎓🎓🎓🎓🎓

RATING SCORES AND EXPLANATIONS:

Curriculum Requirements (5.0): The most important rating category, the curriculum completion requirement (classes required to complete honors) defines not only what honors students should learn but also the extent to which honors students and faculty are connected in the classroom. If there is a thesis or capstone requirement, it reinforces the individual contact and research skills so important to learning.

The average number of honors semester hours required for completion across all 50 programs is 29.0.

At Barrett, "entrance as a first-year student, four year program, 36 total credits of the 120 required for graduation from ASU are required as honors credits. More may be taken, but the 36 credits are a minimum." An **honors thesis is required,** and *Barrett has one of the highest, if not the highest honors completion rate of any program in the nation, at approximately 85%.*

Honors program courses must account for 12 of the 36 credit hours required. Another 6 hours are for the honors thesis. All first year entrants must take required seminars, especially the "Human Event" course. Up to 24 credit hours may be in honors contract sections. As noted below in explanations related to class type and size, Barrett students make full use of contract classes.

Students can also enter Barrett at the conclusion of a two-year program at a community college or as rising juniors at ASU with appropriate credentials. Such students do not take the "Human Event" course, but they do need to complete 21 credit hours in honors as well as an honors thesis.

AP/IB credits are **not** counted as replacements for honors courses.

Number of Honors Classes Offered (4.0): This is a measure of the total **adjusted** honors main sections available in the term reported, not including labs and thesis. (Please read the section titled "All about Honors Classes".) An adjusted main section has 3 or more semester credits, or equivalent, and sections with fewer credits receive a lower prorated value.

Barrett had a ratio of **14.9** enrolled students per each *adjusted* main section. The mean for all 50 programs is 14.2. The lower the ratio, the better. Here it must be noted that mixed and contract sections only count toward computing main sections in proportion to the Barrett students enrolled in them for honors credit. Please read the very important section titled "All about Honors Classes" in the introductory pages of this book. Barrett has literally hundreds of contract sections—but they are not counted in the rating as full honors sections.

In the term reported, **46.9%** of honors enrollment was **in honors-only sections; 14.5% in mixed honors sections (honors and non-honors students); and 38.6% in contract sections (regular sections in which honors students "contract" to do extra work).** The averages for all fifty programs are 81.3% in honors-only sections; 13.6 % in mixed honors sections; and 5.1% in contract sections.

Number of Honors Classes in Key Disciplines (3.5): The 15 "key" disciplines are biological sciences; business (all); chemistry; communications (especially public speaking); computer science; economics; engineering (all); English; history; math (all); philosophy; physics; political science; psychology; and sociology, anthropology, gender studies as a group. Interdisciplinary sections, such as those often taken for General Education credit in the first two years, do receive a lesser, prorated discipline "credit" because they introduce students to multiple disciplines in an especially engaging way, often with in-depth discussion.

For this measure, mixed and contract sections are not counted as a section in a key discipline unless Barrett students taking the sections for honors credit make up at least 10% of the total section enrollment.

In the term reported, the program had a ratio of **43.6 honors students** per each adjusted main section in some or all "key disciplines." The mean for all 50 programs is 26.3. The lower the ratio, the better. If all contract sections in these disciplines were counted, Barrett would have a much better ratio, probably the best. The large size of the honors college also contributes to somewhat higher ratios and class sizes (see below).

Out of **106 adjusted sections in key disciplines**, the college offered **35 honors-only sections**, and another 39 mixed sections. The most sections were in engineering, biology, math, and English, followed by political science, psychology, and physics. The college also offered more than 180 seminar sections, most of them in the "Human Event" sequence. In these courses, "students examine human thought and imagination from various perspectives, including philosophy, history, literature, religion, science, and art. Coursework emphasizes critical thinking, discussion, and argumentative writing."

The combination of seminars and courses in the disciplines makes the honors college a **blended** program.

Extent of Honors Enrollment (4.5): Not all honors students take an honors class each term, especially after the first two years. Programs that have fewer honors classes for upper-division honors students will generally have fewer total members in good standing who are actually enrolled in a given term. (Please be aware, however, that honors students not enrolled in a class for a term are still connected to the honors community through residential and extracurricular activities.)

For example, if honors students in a program occupy 1,800 honors classroom seats in a given term, and there are 3,000 honors students in good standing, the extent of enrollment is .67. For programs that require a thesis, the ratio (score) reported below might in fact be somewhat higher, since we only count "regular" class enrollment for this measure, and not thesis enrollment. **Barrett has a ratio of 1.27,** significantly higher than the mean of 1.13 for all 50 programs. The higher the ratio, the better.

Average Class Size, Honors-only Sections (5.0): Offered mostly in the first two years, honors-only classes tend to be smaller and, as the name implies, have no or very few students other than those in the honors program. These class sections always are much smaller than mixed or contract sections, or regular non-honors class sections in the university.

The average honors-only class size at Barrett is **15.9 students,** remarkable for such a large program. The average for all 50 programs is 19.0 students.

Average Class Size, Overall (3.0): The overall class calculation is based on the *proportion* of honors students in each type of class (honors-only, mixed honors, and honors contract sections). Thus it is not a raw average. The overall honors-credit class size at Barrett is **64.1 students,** versus the average for all 50 programs of 26.3 students.

These class size averages also do not correspond to the number of students per honors sections numbers above. The reason is that, in computing average class size metrics, we include enrollment in each 1-2-credit section, not just sections with 3 or more credits.

Along with the honors-only average of 15.9 students, at Barrett the mixed honors sections average **81.9 students,** and the contract sections with honors credit for individual honors students average **115.8 students.** Across all fifty programs, the average mixed honors section has 51.1 students, and the average contract section has 60.1 students.

Honors Graduation Rate (4.5): The rating is the based on the actual grad rate for students who entered the program six years earlier, whether or not the students remained in honors. The **actual rate of 89%** is also compared to the rates of other programs with the same test score entry requirement range, and then adjusted to the **score of 89.4.** In some cases this measure favors programs within universities with relatively higher test scores for the student population as a whole. The average honors graduation rate for all programs with similar test scores required for admission is 85.6%.

Value-Added Grad Rate (4.5): The value-added rate measures the extent to which the adjusted score listed above exceeds the six-year grad rate for the university as a whole. **The university-wide rate is 63%.** Note:

This measure generally favors programs within universities with relatively lower test scores for the student population as a whole.

Ratio of Staff to Honors Students (5.0): There is 1 staff member for every **74.4** students. (Mean ratio for all 50 programs is 1 staff member for every 135.6 students.)

Honors Residence Halls, Amenities (5.0): The Dean is understandably proud of the residential and support facilities for Barrett Students: "It is difficult to compare Barrett housing to any other university honors college at the moment. We are the only university in the nation with our own entire 9-acre, $140 million, 600,000 square feet honors campus at Tempe [Barrett Honors Complex], complete with everything a private college campus would have, besides things like the university health service and the student recreation center.

"In addition to this campus, we have added another entire campus at Tempe in the last two years directly across the street from us; it is called the "Vista del Sol" campus and is another 20 acres and 1,800 beds in apartment-style living, with its own community center, swimming pool and retail area. We thus now have 3,500 honors students living in honors-specified spaces on the ASU campus in Tempe alone. On top of this, we have Barrett living communities on each of the other three of ASU's campuses in the Phoenix Valley, though the one described just above is at Tempe, the biggest campus of ASU.

"The other three Barrett communities-- at the ASU West, ASU Downtown Phoenix, and ASU Polytechnic campuses--have honors headquarter space with classrooms, computer labs, advising offices, social lounges, conference rooms and faculty offices. Also at each of the other campuses, there is separate honors residential housing that is usually several floors or wings of a larger residential hall that also houses non-honors students. Each of these housing units has a dining hall, laundry, kitchens at least "down the hall," honors lounges, a choice of suite-like rooms, they are co-ed by room but not by hall and have special honors RAs (or "CAs" as we call them at ASU). *We require honors students to live on campus in honors residences at all four of ASU's Barrett campuses and communities for two years.* Several at each campus stay for all four years, and they are encouraged to do so if they wish."

About 84% of Barrett students in honors housing live in the Barrett Honors Complex and Vista del Sol.

Honors Residence Halls, Availability (5.0): This rating compares the number of places in honors residence halls to the number of honors freshman and sophomore members in good standing, approximately 3,124. The ratio for the college is **1.29** rooms for each first- and second-year student, **one of the top availability scores**. The average for all fifty programs is .63 places.

Prestigious Awards (5.0): The awards that we track and include are listed in the section titled "Prestigious Scholarships." The awards are sometimes won by students who are not in an honors college or program, but increasingly many are enrolled in honors programs. It is also a trend that honors colleges and programs help to prepare their students for the awards competitions.

ASU—and Barrett students, in particular—have an outstanding record of achievement in this category: 57 Goldwater Scholars (one of the most in the nation); 33 Udall Scholars, again one of the best totals; 16 Marshall Scholars, 20 Truman Scholars, 5 Rhodes Scholars; a national leader in Fulbright student awards; high achievement in Boren and Gilman foreign study awards; and a solid, growing number of National \ Science Foundation Graduate Research winners. This kind of success strongly indicates the highest level of Barrett *and* university support for aspiring scholars.

UNRATED FEATURES

Continuation Requirements: 3.25 GPA.

Academic Strengths, National Rankings: This is based on national rankings of *graduate* programs in all but engineering and business, where undergraduate rankings are used. One of the weaknesses of the *U.S. News* rankings is that they focus on too many wealth-related metrics while ignoring their own assessments of academic departments. Based on those rankings alone, how many people would suspect that the *average* ASU department ranking nationwide is in the *top 50?*

Leading departments include education (14), earth sciences (20), business (29), economics (36), psychology (38), engineering (41), and computer science (48).

Undergraduate Research: From the Dean: "Barrett has a full-time person in an office of Internships and Research Experiences that arranges both internships and research experiences for any honors student who asks, and in thirteen years at Barrett and ASU I am not aware of "any" honors student who has wished to do the kind of formal "lab-type" research this kind of question is usually getting at, who has not found that kind of research to do. For this reason, we do not advertise in our admissions material that we "guarantee" a research experience, since every Barrett student who wants one gets anyway!

Honors Study Abroad: "Barrett has its own summer study abroad courses each summer, taking between 150 and 250 students on 3 to 6 trips each summer. The trips go all over the world (Paris and Berlin, London/Dublin/Edinburgh, Spain, Costa Rica, Greece and Italy are the most recent in the last two years). The trips are led by Barrett faculty, take only Barrett students, and the students get credit for one or two full honors courses on each trip since they both take the courses and visit the countries that are the subjects of the courses in each case. In addition to these trips, there are over 30 summer study abroad trips from ASU open to all students each summer, and honors students can take those too, gaining honors credit for courses taught on those trips by completing an honors contract during the trip.

"We have close to $200,000 per year in scholarship funds, given out on a need basis, to help send students on these trips from all socioeconomic backgrounds.

"We have formal exchanges with the National University of Singapore and the University of Groningen in the Netherlands each academic year, and one starting in the coming year with Beihang University in Beijing. During each of these around four students from each institution travel to the other for a semester."

Financial Aid: "The financial aid office of ASU handles all scholarships, including those for honors students," the Dean reports. "ASU gives out many levels of merit aid, and then of course has need-based aid. 95% of Barrett students have merit aid, but 40% also have need-based aid *on top of* their merit aid. The merit aid is dispensed using a formulaic combination of high school GPA, rank in class, and ACT or SAT scores, and is "tiered" as you would expect by decreasing dollar amounts as this combination decreases. **The university also has <u>uncapped</u> national scholar awards that are the same amount for**

National Merit, Hispanic and Achievement Scholars. These are **full out of state tuition** for all OOS national scholars, even if it increases as they are at ASU, and **$16,000 per year** for in-state national scholars. Both in-state and out-of-state national scholars also receive $1,500 towards research costs for research they do, and $1,000 for any honors travel they carry out while at ASU."

Honors Fees: "Each Barrett student pays a fee of $1,500 per year to be an honors student. There is extra financial aid and a fee waiver system set up for financially needy students specifically to address this fee."

Placement Experiences: Barrett students find medical, dental, veterinary, law, and graduate school opportunities at the top institutions in the nation, as well as employment at leading firms in all major industries. The Dean reports that 37% of graduates go to graduate school, not counting business; 33% to direct employment; 10% to medical, dental, or veterinary school; 6% to business school; 4% to law school; and 10% who choose volunteering, travel, or other options.

Degree of Difference: This is based on the differences between (1) the average (old, two-part) SAT scores for enrolled honors students (1291) and (2) the average test scores for all students in the university (1150) as a whole. The test scores may be an indication of how "elite" honors students may be perceived as compared to students in the university as a whole. The scores can also provide an indication of how well prepared the non-honors students in the university may be. **Please keep in mind that neither high nor low test scores determine the overall quality of a program.**

NAME: UNIVERSITY OF ARKANSAS HONORS COLLEGE.

Date Established: 2002 (Preceded by Arts & Sciences honors program (1954) and College of Business honors program (1997).

Location: Fayetteville, Arkansas.

University <u>Full-time Undergraduate</u> Enrollment (2015): 19,243

Honors Members in Good Standing: 3,055; (mean size of all 50 programs is 1,742).

Honors <u>Average</u> Admission Test Score(s): ACT, 30; old SAT, 1268; est. new SAT, 1325.

Average High School GPA/Class Rank: 3.67; 3.79 Walton College of Business.

<u>Basic</u> Admission Requirements: ACT, 28; Old SAT, 1240; estimated new SAT, 1310. High school GPA 3.50 (Walton College of Business, 3.75).

Application Deadline(s): *Please verify with each program, as some deadlines could change.*

For Early admission deadline November 1, 2016 for priority application; for scholarships, priority deadline is November 15, 2016, and the final deadline is February 1, 2017; for other financial aid, March 1, 2017.

Honors Programs with old SAT scores from 1240—1291: Arkansas, Oklahoma State, Texas Tech, Montana, Washington State, New Mexico, South Dakota, Colorado State, Arizona, Montana State, Arizona State.

Administrative Staff: 26

RATINGS AT A GLANCE: For all mortarboard ratings immediately below, a score of 5 is the maximum and represents a comparison with all 50 honors colleges and programs. More detailed explanations follow the "mortarboard" ratings.

PERCEPTION* OF UNIVERSITY AS A WHOLE, <u>NOT</u> OF HONORS: 🎓🎓🎓 1/2

*Perception is based on the university's ranking among public universities in the 2016 U.S. News Best Colleges report. Please bear in mind that the better the U.S. News ranking, the more difficult it is for an honors college or program to have a rating that equals or improves on the magazine ranking.

OVERALL HONORS RATING: 🎓🎓🎓🎓 1/2

Curriculum Requirements: 🎓🎓🎓🎓

Number of Honors Classes Offered: 🎓🎓🎓🎓 1/2

Number of Honors Classes in Key Disciplines: 🎓🎓🎓🎓

Extent of Honors Enrollment: 🎓🎓🎓🎓

Honors-only Class Size: 🎓🎓🎓🎓^{1/2}

Overall Class Size (Honors-only plus mixed, contract): 🎓🎓🎓🎓^{1/2}

Honors Grad Rate: 🎓🎓🎓🎓

Value-Added Grad Rate: 🎓🎓🎓🎓^{1/2}

Ratio of Staff to Students: 🎓🎓🎓🎓^{1/2}

Priority Registration: Honors students do not register before all students, but do register with the class ahead of them.

Honors Housing Amenities: 🎓🎓🎓🎓

Honors Housing Availability: 🎓🎓🎓🎓

Prestigious Awards: 🎓🎓🎓🎓^{1/2}

RATING SCORES AND EXPLANATIONS:

Curriculum Requirements (4.0): The most important rating category, the curriculum completion requirement (classes required to complete honors) defines not only what honors students should learn but also the extent to which honors students and faculty are connected in the classroom. If there is a thesis or capstone requirement, it reinforces the individual contact and research skills so important to learning.

The average number of honors semester hours required for completion across all 50 programs is 29.0.

The honors college coordinates the honors programs in the J. William Fulbright College of Arts and Sciences; the Fay Jones School of Architecture; the College of Education and Health Professions; the Sam M. Walton College of Business; the College of Engineering; and the Dale Bumpers School of Agricultural, Food, and Life Sciences. The credit hours required for honors completion vary significantly, with the College of Arts and Sciences and the School of Architecture having the most extensive requirements, **33-36 hours in Arts and Sciences and 38 hours in Architecture**. Because the college allows AP credits (up to 6) to substitute for honors credits, the total credit "score" is **29.64**.

Business honors requires 17 credit hours, engineering 12 credit hours, and education/health professions 24 hours. The Bumpers School requirement is 15 credit hours. There is an **honors thesis** requirement for **all honors students.**

AP/IB credit is allowed in all honors programs, in substitution for up to six credit hours, and the **AP test score** requirement is 4.5.

Number of Honors Classes Offered (4.5): This is a measure of the total **adjusted** honors main sections available in the term reported, not including labs and thesis. An adjusted main section has 3 or more semester credits, or equivalent, and sections with fewer credits receive a lower prorated value.

Arkansas honors offered a section for every **12.9** enrolled students. The average for all 50 programs is 14.2. The lower the number, the better.

In the term reported, **99.9%** of honors enrollment was **in honors-only sections; 1% in mixed honors sections (honors and non-honors students); and none in contract sections (regular sections in which honors students "contract" to do extra work).** The averages for all fifty programs are 81.3% in honors-only sections; 13.6 % in mixed honors sections; and 5.1% in contract sections.

Number of. Honors Classes in Key Disciplines (4.0): The 15 "key" disciplines are biological sciences; business (all); chemistry; communications (especially public speaking); computer science; economics; engineering (all); English; history; math (all); philosophy; physics; political science; psychology; and sociology, anthropology, and gender studies. Interdisciplinary sections, such as those often taken for General Education credit in the first two years, do receive a lesser, prorated discipline "credit" because they introduce students to multiple disciplines in an especially engaging way, often with in-depth discussion.

For this measure, mixed and contract sections are not counted as a section in a key discipline unless students taking the sections for honors credit make up at least 10% of the total section enrollment.

In the term reported, the honors college offered a section in a key discipline for every **24.6 honors students.** The average for all 50 programs is 26.3. The lower the number, the better.

Out of **86 adjusted sections in key disciplines, all are listed as honors-only sections**. The most sections were in engineering, history, business, English, philosophy, and psychology. There were 3 physics sections, 7 in sociology, anthropology, and gender studies combined. The college offered at least one course, typically more, in all 15 key disciplines. The rating is not a "5" because the total number of sections, while not low, does keep the rating down slightly.

The college does not *at this time (see below)* offer seminars and interdisciplinary sections in any significant number. This virtually total emphasis on classes in the disciplines makes the honors college one of the purest **discipline-based** programs.

But this will change, and soon. According to the Dean, "Beginning in Spring 2017…*we will offer a series of Honors College Signature Seminars on cutting-edge topics taught by top professors*. Students must apply to participate and will be designated Dean's Fellows in the Honors College. There will be two seminars offered each semester. The first two will be Teeth: Evolution's Bite, taught by Peter Ungar, Distinguished Professor and Chairman of the Department of Anthropology in the J. William Fulbright College of Arts and Sciences; and Prosecution: (Un)Making a Murder, taught by Brian Gallini, Associate

Dean for Research and Faculty Development in the University of Arkansas School of Law. Proposed topics for future seminars include Hunger, Cancer, Water, Profit, and Jesus.

"To date the Honors College has provided more than $500,000 in start up funding, on a competitive basis, to faculty teams developing interdisciplinary, problem-focused honors courses for junior and senior honors students." These will be in addition to the seminars listed above. These are very positive developments, indeed.

Extent of Honors Enrollment (4.0): Not all honors students take an honors class each term, especially after the first two years. Programs that have fewer honors classes for upper-division honors students will generally have fewer total members in good standing who are actually enrolled in a given term. (Please be aware, however, that honors students not enrolled in a class for a term are still connected to the honors community through residential and extracurricular activities.)

For example, if honors students in a program occupy 1,800 honors classroom seats in a given term, and there are 3,000 honors students in good standing, the extent of enrollment is .67. For programs that require a thesis, the ratio (score) reported below might in fact be somewhat higher, since we only count "regular" class enrollment for this measure, and not thesis enrollment. **Arkansas has a ratio of 1.01**, a bit below the average of 1.13 for all 50 programs. The higher the ratio, the better.

Average Class Size, Honors-only Sections (4.5): Offered mostly in the first two years, honors-only classes tend to be smaller and, as the name implies, have no or very few students other than those in the honors program. These class sections always are much smaller than mixed or contract sections, or regular non-honors class sections in the university.

The average honors-only class size at the honors college is **17.1 students**. The average for all 50 programs is 19.0 students.

Average Class Size, Overall (4.5): The overall class calculation is based on the *proportion* of honors students in each type of class (honors-only, mixed honors, and honors contract sections). Thus it is not a raw average. The overall honors-credit class size is **20.1 students**, versus the average for all 50 programs of 26.3 students.

These class size averages also do not correspond to the number of students per honors sections numbers above. The reason is that, in computing average class size metrics, we include enrollment in each 1-2-credit section, not just sections with 3 or more credits.

Honors Graduation Rate (4.0): The rating is based on the actual grad rate for students who entered the program six years earlier, whether or not the students remained in honors. The **actual rate of 85%** is also compared to the rates of other programs with the same test score entry requirement range, and then adjusted to the **adjusted score of 84.97.** The average honors graduation rate for all programs with similar test scores required for admission is 85.3%.

Value-Added Grad Rate (4.5): The value-added rate measures the extent to which the adjusted score listed above exceeds the six-year grad rate for the university as a whole. **The university-wide rate is 62%.**

Ratio of Staff to Honors Students (4.5): There is 1 staff member for every 105.3 students. (Mean ratio for all 50 programs is 1 staff member for every 135.6 students.)

Honors Residence Halls, Amenities (4.0): "Hotz Honors Hall, home to Honors College freshmen, is newly renovated and features small study rooms and open study spaces, a home theater, presentation rooms, a kitchen, a covered patio, and a music room. In addition to the communal activities created through the close proximity of the honors students, Honors College graduate assistants initiate special programs and events to enhance the intellectual and social community in the hall. Honors faculty members are invited for monthly programs focusing on undergraduate research and publication. The 'Pizza and Professor on the Patio' sessions cover an eclectic array of topics. Small interest groups and networking opportunities among peers and upper class honors students abound. Recent activities include upper class mentor panels, live streaming of athletic events, a tessellated mural painting, the Olympic Ceremonies celebration with a nod to Russian cuisine and culture, the building of gingerbread structures during the holidays, and many more diverse and unique events specifically targeted to our freshmen."

Most first-year honors students living on campus reside in Hotz Hall, which has traditional rooms and hall baths. Upperclassmen can live in Gatewood Hall, Northwest Quad, or Futrall Hall. Gatewood and Northwest Quad feature suite-style rooms. All are air-conditioned.

Honors Residence Halls, Availability (4.0): This rating compares the number of rooms in honors residence halls to the number of honors freshman and sophomore members in good standing, approximately 1,528. The ratio for the college is **.42** rooms for each first- and second-year student, a bit below average. The average for all fifty programs is .63 rooms.

Prestigious Awards (4.5): The awards that we track and include are listed in the section titled "Prestigious Scholarships." The awards are sometimes won by students who are not in an honors college or program, but increasingly many are enrolled in honors programs. It is also a trend that honors colleges and programs help to prepare their students for the awards competitions.

Arkansas students, many of them from the honors college, are outstanding at winning Goldwater scholarships, the most prestigious undergraduate awards, given to students with outstanding promise in STEM fields. UA students have won 50 Goldwater awards to date. **At least one UA students has won a Goldwater scholarship in each of the last 20 years.** They have also earned 10 Rhodes scholarships during the entire history of the award, along with an impressive 21 Truman scholarships.

UNRATED FEATURES

Continuation Requirements: 3.50; 3.75 in Walton School of Business.

Academic Strengths, National Rankings: This is based on national rankings of *graduate* programs in all but engineering and business, where undergraduate rankings are used. One of the weaknesses of the *U.S. News* rankings is that they focus on too many wealth-related metrics while ignoring their own assessments of academic departments.

Business, located within the Walton School of Business, is the leading program at UA, ranked 43rd in the nation. Education and engineering are also ranked in the top 100 in the nation.

Undergraduate Research: "In 2015, the Honors College provided over $396,227 from our endowment in support of undergraduate research, including over $240,495 in student stipends and $125,000 in faculty mentor funds, and $30,732 in conference travel not covered by other funds, including fellowships and scholarships, State [Arkansas] Undergraduate Research Fellowships, and NSF REU grants." In addition, all honors college students must complete a thesis.

Honors Study Abroad: "Over the past 10 years, the Honors College has awarded more than $4.5 million in study-abroad grants using endowment funds from the 2002 Walton Foundation gift that helped create the Honors College. The Honors College Study Abroad Grants help students pay for international study experiences ranging from two weeks to one year in length. **Last year, 164 students received a total of $545,622 in grant funding.** For many of our students, raised in a poor Southern state, the study abroad grants provide a first chance to see the larger world and experience other cultures in a meaningful way. Of the Honors College students who were awarded a study abroad grant in 2015, 27% had never traveled outside of the United States; 77% had never studied abroad before."

"The University of Arkansas owns the University of Arkansas Rome Center, recently ranked among the 50 Best Study Abroad Programs by Best College Reviews. The U. of A. Rome Center offers courses to our own students in several fields of study and also students from other Southeastern Conference universities. The U. of A. has active exchange programs with 18 universities in Austria, Belgium, Denmark, United Kingdom, France, Germany, Italy, Spain, Sweden, Japan, Hong Kong, South Korea, and Australia, with others in the works in African and Latin American nations. Individual colleges maintain exchanges with additional institutions. Among the strongest of these exchanges are with Gent University, Belgium; Karl - Franzens University, Austria; Politecnico di Torino, Italy; University of Essex and University of Sussex, England; and the University of Regensburg, Germany."

Under the leadership of Dean Lynda Coon, the Honors College has set an ambitious goal to increase the number of honors graduates who have studied abroad from 50 percent (already more than three times the national average) to 70 percent by 2020.

Financial Aid: "Each year the Honors College awards up to 90 fellowships to entering freshmen that provides each student $70,000 over four years, plus non-resident tuition, if applicable," the Dean reports. "For programs with degree plans of more than four years, extra semesters of funding may be available. The fellowships are renewable annually based on academic performance and personal conduct.

"As indicated elsewhere…we provide over $1 million annually to support honors students in studying abroad and conducting faculty-mentored research.

"Most honors students who do not win a fellowship receive other merit-based scholarships offered through the Office of Academic Scholarships. These range from scholarships providing $10,000 per year, renewable for four or five years (depending on course of study), to one-time awards of $1000. Current students who perform well once they arrive on campus can apply for competitive scholarships at the university level and at the college level that are reserved for returning students.

"In addition to fellowships and scholarships awarded through the Honors College and the U. of A. Office of Academic Scholarships, the State of Arkansas awards merit-based scholarships that are available to students who are Arkansas residents. The Arkansas Governor's Distinguished Scholarship provides $10,000 per year, and many of the 375 awarded annually go to U. of A. honors students." Students may also combine awards. "For example, an in-state honors student who receives an Honors College Fellowship and the Arkansas Distinguished Governor's Scholarship has a total scholarship package of $110,000 over four years."

"Twenty-three percent of honors students who attended the U. of A. last year had received Pell grants or other forms of need-based federal support, which may have be combined with merit based awards."

Honors Fees: None.

Placement Experiences: *"Each year we give an exit survey to our graduating honors students. Based on our responses for the years 2013-2015, roughly 92.5% of our students have placement or a path towards placement upon graduation. Key metrics include the following:*

- Have been accepted to graduate or professional school (50.8%)
- Planning to apply to graduate or professional school in the future (13.9%)
- Entering the workforce (26%)
- Working as a volunteer (e.g. Teach for America, AmeriCorps, Peace Corps, etc.) (1.8%)
- Uncertain (7.5%)

Graduates have been accepted by the most prestigious institutions in the nation for graduate and professional study, including all of the Ivies, Stanford, and MIT.

"Over the past 10 years, 90% of our pre-med students, on average, have won acceptance to medical school – more than twice the national average."

Degree of Difference: This is based on the differences between (1) the average (2015, two-part) SAT scores for enrolled honors students (1268) and (2) the average test scores for all students in the university (1160) as a whole. The test scores may be an indication of how "elite" honors students may be perceived as compared to students in the university as a whole. The scores can also provide an indication of how well prepared the non-honors students in the university may be. **Please keep in mind that neither high nor low test scores determine the overall quality of a program.**

NAME: THE HONORS COLLEGE AT AUBURN UNIVERSITY.

Date Established: 1998 (Preceded by Honors Program, 1979.)

Location: Auburn, Alabama.

University <u>Full-time Undergraduate</u> Enrollment (2015): 18,853.

Honors Members in Good Standing: 1,776; (mean size of all 50 programs is 1,742).

Honors <u>Average</u> Admission Test Score(s): ACT, 31.5; old SAT, 1336; est. new SAT, 1395.

Average High School GPA/Class Rank: 4.22.

<u>Basic</u> Admission Requirements: ACT, 29; old SAT, 1290; est. new SAT, 1350. High school GPA, 3.85.

Application Deadline(s): *Please verify with each program, as some deadlines could change.*

January 15, 2017.

Honors Programs with old SAT scores from 1315—1350: Idaho, Georgia State, Virginia Tech, Utah, Iowa, Auburn, Houston, Mississippi, VCU.

Administrative Staff: 11.

RATINGS AT A GLANCE: For all mortarboard ratings immediately below, a score of 5 is the maximum and represents a comparison with all 50 honors colleges and programs. More detailed explanations follow the "mortarboard" ratings.

PERCEPTION* OF UNIVERSITY AS A WHOLE, <u>NOT</u> OF HONORS: 🎓🎓🎓🎓

*Perception is based on the university's ranking among public universities in the 2016 U.S. News Best Colleges report. Please bear in mind that the better the U.S. News ranking, the more difficult it is for an honors college or program to have a rating that equals or improves on the magazine ranking.

OVERALL HONORS RATING: 🎓🎓🎓🎓

Curriculum Requirements: 🎓🎓🎓🎓

Number of Honors Classes Offered: 🎓🎓🎓 1/2

Number of Honors Classes in Key Disciplines: 🎓🎓🎓🎓

Extent of Honors Enrollment: 🎓🎓🎓🎓

Honors-only Class Size: 🎓🎓🎓 1/2

Overall Class Size (Honors-only plus mixed, contract): 🎓🎓🎓🎓

Honors Grad Rate: 🎓🎓🎓🎓

Value-Added Grad Rate: 🎓🎓🎓🎓

Ratio of Staff to Students: 🎓🎓🎓 1/2

Priority Registration: Yes, honors students can register with the class ahead of them.

Honors Housing Amenities: 🎓🎓🎓🎓 1/2

Honors Housing Availability: 🎓🎓🎓🎓 1/2

Prestigious Awards: 🎓🎓🎓 1/2

RATING SCORES AND EXPLANATIONS:

Curriculum Requirements (4.0): The most important rating category, the curriculum completion requirement (classes required to complete honors) defines not only what honors students should learn but also the extent to which honors students and faculty are connected in the classroom. If there is a thesis or capstone requirement, it reinforces the individual contact and research skills so important to learning.

The average number of honors semester hours required for completion across all 50 programs is 29.0.

The completion requirement at Auburn for the University Honors Scholar designation is 30 credits. These must include 3 credits in honors "participation" courses and 6 hours in a "senior experience."

Participation courses include Honors Freshmen Exploration, Honors Lyceum, Honors Book Club and Honors Forum. Honors Freshman Exploration classes provide insights and practical skills related to study abroad, course registration, campus activities and participation, and service learning. The maximum for Honors Lyceum (1 credit each) is two courses. These include spirited discussions of current events, controversial issues, and international affairs. Honors Forum allows honors students to earn up to two credits (1 hour each) by attending 10 lectures, films, or performances pre-approved by the college. Students write reflective essays after each event. Honors Book Club participation is also limited to two total credits and requires reading and detailed discussion of 2-3 books.

Senior experiences, 6 credits, mean the student must complete a **thesis,** capstone project, or three graduate courses. Students must graduate with at least a 3.40 GPA.

To complete requirements for Honors Scholar (different from University Honors Scholar designation, above), the student must complete 27 credits, including 3 honors participation credits. There does not appear to be a thesis requirement. Graduation requires a 3.2 GPA.

Finally, a third option requires 7 credits, including 1 credit in a participation option and 6 credits from a thesis or graduate courses.

AP/IB credits are **not** counted as replacements for honors courses.

Number of Honors Classes Offered (3.5): This is a measure of the total **adjusted** honors main sections available in the term reported, not including labs and thesis. An adjusted main section has 3 or more semester credits, or equivalent, and sections with fewer credits receive a lower prorated value.

Auburn honors offered a section for every **17.9** enrolled students. The average for all 50 programs is 14.2. The lower the number, the better.

In the term reported, **99.5%** of honors enrollment was **in honors-only sections; and .5% in mixed honors sections (honors and non-honors students). No contract sections were reported.** The averages for all fifty programs are 81.3% in honors-only sections; 13.6 % in mixed honors sections; and 5.1% in contract sections.

Number of Honors Classes in Key Disciplines (4.0): The 15 "key" disciplines are biological sciences; business (all); chemistry; communications (especially public speaking); computer science; economics; engineering (all); English; history; math (all); philosophy; physics; political science; psychology; and sociology, anthropology, and gender studies. Interdisciplinary sections, such as those often taken for General Education credit in the first two years, do receive a lesser, prorated discipline "credit" because they introduce students to multiple disciplines in an especially engaging way, often with in-depth discussion.

For this measure, mixed and contract sections are not counted as a section in a key discipline unless students taking the sections for honors credit make up at least 10% of the total section enrollment.

In the term reported, the honors college offered a section in a key discipline for every **25.1 honors students.** The average for all 50 programs is 26.3. The lower the number, the better.

Out of **47 adjusted sections in key disciplines**, **all were honors-only sections**. The most sections were in math (10), English (7), and biology (6), followed by history, philosophy, and physics. There were no adjusted sections in communications, engineering, or computer science.

The college does offer seminars, about 18 honors participation sections with 1 credit, as well as nine 3-credit special topics seminars in social sciences and humanities, including "Genomics and Personalized Medications," and "Technology and Culture." The honors college is a somewhat **blended** program, with a strong tilt toward a discipline-based type.

Extent of Honors Enrollment (4.0): Not all honors students take an honors class each term, especially after the first two years. Programs that have fewer honors classes for upper-division honors students will generally have fewer total members in good standing who are actually enrolled in a given term. (Please be aware, however, that honors students not enrolled in a class for a term are still connected to the honors community through residential and extracurricular activities.)

For example, if honors students in a program occupy 1,800 honors classroom seats in a given term, and there are 3,000 honors students in good standing, the extent of enrollment is .67. For programs that require a thesis, the ratio (score) reported below might in fact be somewhat higher, since we only count "regular" class enrollment for this measure, and not thesis enrollment. **Auburn has a ratio of 1.06,** almost the average of 1.13 for all 50 programs. The higher the ratio, the better.

Average Class Size, Honors-only Sections (3.5): Offered mostly in the first two years, honors-only classes tend to be smaller and, as the name implies, have no or very few students other than those in the honors program. These class sections always are much smaller than mixed or contract sections, or regular non-honors class sections in the university.

The average honors-only class size at the honors college is **24.7 students.** The average for all 50 programs is 19.0 students. Here it should be noted that most programs that have a high percentage of honors-only class sections, those sections tend to be somewhat larger. The all-honors makeup of these sections is more important than the slightly larger class size.

Average Class Size, Overall (4.0): The overall class calculation is based on the *proportion* of honors students in each type of class (honors-only, mixed honors, and honors contract sections). Thus it is not a raw average. The overall honors-credit class size is **24.6 students,** versus the average for all 50 programs of 26.3 students.

These class size averages also do not correspond to the number of students per honors sections numbers above. The reason is that, in computing average class size metrics, we include enrollment in each 1-2-credit section, not just sections with 3 or more credits.

Along with the honors-only average of 24.6 students, the mixed honors sections average **2.75 students,** and the contract sections with honors credit for individual honors students average **(NA)** students. Across all fifty programs, the average mixed honors section has 51.1 students, and the average contract section has 60.1 students.

Honors Graduation Rate (4.0): The rating is the based on the actual grad rate for students who entered the program six years earlier, whether or not the students remained in honors. The **actual rate of 84.5%** is also compared to the rates of other programs with the same test score entry requirement range, and then adjusted to the **score of 84.5%.** The average honors graduation rate for all programs with similar test scores required for admission is 83.4%.

Value-Added Grad Rate (4.0): The value-added rate measures the extent to which the adjusted score listed above exceeds the six-year grad rate for the university as a whole. **The university-wide rate is 71%.**

Ratio of Staff to Honors Students (3.5): There is 1 staff member for every **161.5** students. (Mean ratio for all 50 programs is 1 staff member for every 135.6 students.)

Honors Residence Halls, Amenities (4.5): Almost half of the honors students who live on campus reside in Aubie Hall, which has suite-style rooms and is, of course, air-conditioned. The other honors dorms are on the Quad—Broun, Harper, Little, and Teague—and have double suites with four students sharing a connecting bath. Dining for the Quad dorms is in Foy Hall.

Honors Residence Halls, Availability (4.5): This rating compares the number of places in honors residence halls to the number of honors freshman and sophomore members in good standing, approximately 888. The ratio for the college is **.73** rooms for each first- and second-year student. The average for all fifty programs is .63 places.

Prestigious Awards (3.5): The awards that we track and include are listed in the section titled "Prestigious Scholarships." The awards are sometimes won by students who are not in an honors college or program, but increasingly many are enrolled in honors programs. It is also a trend that honors colleges and programs help to prepare their students for the awards competitions.

Auburn students have won four Rhodes scholarships, four Truman awards, three Marshall scholarships, and three Gates Cambridge awards. Auburn students are increasingly successful in earning Goldwater scholarships for undergrads in STEM fields, with 30 so far.

UNRATED FEATURES

Continuation Requirements: 3.30 for first-year students; 3.20 for others.

Academic Strengths, National Rankings: This is based on national rankings of *graduate* programs in all but engineering and business, where undergraduate rankings are used. One of the weaknesses of the *U.S. News* rankings is that they focus on too many wealth-related metrics while ignoring their own assessments of academic departments.

At Auburn, the average national departmental ranking across 15 departments at UA is just under 100. Leading departments are business and engineering, ranked 50th and 56th respectively. Education (74) and computer science (74) is followed by computer science (90), math (95), and English (96).

Undergraduate Research: No information provided.

Honors Study Abroad: Recent honors study-abroad opportunities include Croatia, Rome, Cuba; and Panama. EuroScholars is a study-abroad program "for advanced students to conduct research at top-rated institutions while taking a language and culture courses. You'll have the option to study at one of nine European Research Universities across Belgium, Finland, Switzerland, Germany, Sweden, and the Netherlands. This research is undertaken over an entire semester (summers are excluded), working one-on-one with faculty and all majors are welcome."

The Oxford Programme includes tutorial-style courses with Oxford faculty. "While there, you will have the same experience as full-time Oxford students by living and taking your tutorials at Christ Church, New College, Trinity or University College. This program will be available all year round. Students must have relevant background in the subjects that they wish to study, so please contact the Honors College for more information."

Financial Aid: (Next page.)

National Merit *Finalists* receive a National Merit Presidential Scholarship:

- Value of resident tuition for four years for Alabama residents, currently $36,288 for four years ($9,072 per year), or $88,000 over four years for non-residents ($22,000 per year);

- On-campus housing for one year, valued at $7,800;

- University stipend for four years at $4,000 to $8,000 ($1,000 to $2,000 per year), depending on eligibility as determined by National Merit Scholarship Corporation and financial need as determined through completion of FAFSA.

National Merit *Semifinalists:*

"Alabama [in-state] National Merit Semifinalists who have a minimum 3.5 high school GPA and meet the January 15 application for admission priority deadline receive a four year, renewable Spirit of Auburn Founders Scholarship in the amount of $32,000 over four years at $8,000 per year, replacing a Freshman Scholarship of lesser value if previously awarded."

Out-of-state NMS Semifinalists who have a minimum 3.5 high school GPA and meet the January 15 application for admission priority deadline "receive a four year, renewable Academic Heritage Scholarship in the amount of $52,000 over four years at $13,000 per year, replacing a Freshman Scholarship of lesser value if previously awarded."

Honors Fees: First-year Honors student - $250/semester; Second-year Honors student - $225/semester; Third-year and beyond Honors student - $200/semester.

Placement Experiences: No information provided.

Degree of Difference: This is based on the differences between (1) the average (2015, two-part) SAT scores for enrolled honors students (1336) and (2) the average test scores for all students in the university (1230) as a whole. The test scores may be an indication of how "elite" honors students may be perceived as compared to students in the university as a whole. The scores can also provide an indication of how well prepared the non-honors students in the university may be. **Please keep in mind that neither high nor low test scores determine the overall quality of a program.**

NAME: CALHOUN HONORS COLLEGE, CLEMSON UNIVERSITY.

Date Established: 1962.

Location: Clemson, South Carolina.

University Full-time Undergraduate Enrollment: 16,572

Honors Members in Good Standing: 1,399 (mean size of all 50 programs is 1,742).

Honors Average Admission Statistics: The ACT for first-year entrants is 33; the old two-part SAT, 1442. Estimated new SAT score, 1482. "We consider applicants with standardized test scores below these typical thresholds provided that the applicant has an otherwise exceptional academic record."

Average High School GPA/Class Rank: Top 10% preferred.

Basic Admission Requirements: ACT 30; old two-part SAT score 1320. Estimated new SAT score, 1380.

Application Deadline(s): *Please verify with each program, as some deadlines could change.*

Clemson Honors (Calhoun): Priority honors deadline December 8, 2016; students must have applied to the university by December 1, 2016 and must have all supporting documentation (transcript, teacher and counselor letters of recommendation) submitted by December 15, 2016); regular deadline March 1, 2017, (transcripts and letters due by March 15, 2017); notification on rolling basis; after that date, space-available only.

Honors Programs with old SAT scores from 1402—1469: UCF, Connecticut, Kentucky, Washington, Maryland, North Carolina, UC Irvine, Kansas, Minnesota, Tennessee, South Carolina, Clemson, UT Austin, Georgia.

Administrative Staff: 10.

RATINGS AT A GLANCE: For all mortarboard ratings immediately below, a score of 5 is the maximum and represents a comparison with all 50 honors colleges and programs. More detailed explanations follow the "mortarboard" ratings.

PERCEPTION* OF UNIVERSITY AS A WHOLE, NOT OF HONORS: 🎓🎓🎓🎓$^{1/2}$

*Perception is based on the university's ranking among public universities in the 2016 U.S. News Best Colleges report. Please bear in mind that the better the U.S. News ranking, the more difficult it is for an honors college or program to have a rating that equals or improves on the magazine ranking.

OVERALL HONORS RATING: 🎓🎓🎓🎓🎓

Curriculum Requirements: 🎓🎓🎓🎓

Number of Honors Classes Offered: 🎓🎓🎓🎓 1/2

Number of Honors Classes in Key Disciplines: 🎓🎓🎓🎓 1/2

Extent of Honors Enrollment: 🎓🎓🎓🎓

Honors-only Class Size: 🎓🎓🎓🎓 1/2

Overall Class Size (Honors-only plus mixed, contract): 🎓🎓🎓🎓

Honors Grad Rate: 🎓🎓🎓🎓🎓

Value-Added Grad Rate: 🎓🎓🎓🎓

Ratio of Staff to Students: 🎓🎓🎓🎓

Priority Registration: Yes, honors students register for all courses, honors and otherwise, with the first group of students during each year they are in the program.

Honors Housing Amenities: 🎓🎓🎓🎓🎓

Honors Housing Availability: 🎓🎓🎓🎓

Prestigious Awards: 🎓🎓🎓 1/2

RATING SCORES AND EXPLANATIONS:

Curriculum Requirements (4.0): The most important rating category, the curriculum completion requirement (classes required to complete honors) defines not only what honors students should learn but also the extent to which honors students and faculty are connected in the classroom. If there is a thesis or capstone requirement, it reinforces the individual contact and research skills so important to learning.

The average number of honors semester hours required for completion across all 50 programs is 29.0.

Clemson honors students who complete only the General Honors curriculum (the majority) typically complete the 18 hours of honors credit in two years. "The main purpose of General Honors is to broaden the student's intellectual perspectives. To this end, students are encouraged to take honors courses in as many different areas of study as possible. Students who successfully complete the requirements for General Honors are awarded the Certificate of Achievement in General Honors." The General Honors option does not have a thesis requirement.

Students who complete both General Honors and Departmental Honors average about **30 credit hours, including an honors thesis**. "Students who successfully complete the requirements for general *and* departmental honors or who complete departmental honors are awarded the B.C. Inabinet medallion and are honored at an awards ceremony the day before commencement."

AP/IB credits are **not** counted as replacements for honors courses.

Number of Honors Classes Offered (4.5): This is a measure of the total **adjusted** honors main sections available in the term reported, not including labs and thesis. (Please read the section titled "All about Honors Classes".) An adjusted main section has 3 or more semester credits, or equivalent, and sections with fewer credits receive a lower prorated value.

The Clemson honors college had a ratio of **12.1** enrolled students per each main section. The mean for all 50 programs is 14.2. The lower the ratio, the better.

In the term reported, the percentage of honors enrollment was **69.6% in honors-only sections; 24.7% in mixed honors sections (honors and non-honors students); and 5.6% in contract sections (regular sections in which honors students "contract" to do extra work** The averages for all fifty programs are 81.3% in honors-only sections; 13.6 % in mixed honors sections; and 5.1% in contract sections.

Number of Honors Classes in Key Disciplines (4.5): The 15 "key" disciplines are biological sciences; business (all); chemistry; communications (especially public speaking); computer science; economics; engineering (all); English; history; math (all); philosophy; physics; political science; psychology; and sociology/anthropology/gender studies. Interdisciplinary sections, such as those often taken for General Education credit in the first two years, do receive a lesser, prorated discipline "credit" because they introduce students to multiple disciplines in an especially engaging way, often with in-depth discussion.

In the term reported, the program had ratio of **19.7 honors students** per each main section in some or all "key disciplines." The mean for all 50 programs is 26.3. The lower the ratio, the better.

Out of **65 adjusted sections in key disciplines**, the college had 39 honors-only sections. Biology, business, chemistry, math, physics, and English accounted for 45 of the 65 sections, 13 in biology alone. Communications, computer science, and engineering were offered in another 13 sections. There was only one section each in economics, philosophy, political science, and psychology. Sociology, anthropology, or gender studies had two sections total. The college also offered about 20 interdisciplinary seminars, among them "The Science of Ethics"; "Who Gets What and Why"; and "World of Ideas."

The combination of seminars and courses in the disciplines makes the honors college a **blended** program.

Extent of Honors Enrollment (4.0): Not all honors students take an honors class each term, especially after the first two years. Programs that have fewer honors classes for upper-division honors students will generally have fewer total members in good standing who are actually enrolled in a given term. (Please be aware, however, that honors students not enrolled in a class for a term are still connected to the honors community through residential and extracurricular activities.)

For example, if honors students in a program occupy 1,800 honors classroom seats in a given term, and there are 3,000 honors students in good standing, the extent of enrollment is .67. For programs that require a thesis, the ratio (score) reported below might in fact be somewhat higher, since we only count "regular" class enrollment for this measure, and not thesis enrollment. **Clemson has a ratio of 1.13**; the mean is also 1.13 for all 50 programs. The higher the ratio, the better.

Average Class Size, Honors-only Sections (4.5): Offered mostly in the first two years, honors-only classes tend to be smaller and, as the name implies, have no or very few students other than those in the honors program. These class sections always are much smaller than mixed or contract sections, or regular non-honors class sections in the university.

The average honors-only class size at Clemson honors college is **16.6 students**. The average for all 50 programs is 19.0 students.

Average Class Size, Overall (4.0): The overall class calculation is based on the *proportion* of honors students in each type of class (honors-only, mixed honors, and honors contract sections). Thus it is not a raw average. The overall honors-credit class size at Clemson is **25.7 students**, versus the average for all 50 programs of 26.3 students.

These class size averages also do not correspond to the number of students per honors sections numbers above. The reason is that, in computing average class size metrics, we include enrollment in each 1-2-credit section, not just sections with 3 or more credits.

Along with the honors-only average of 16.6 students, at Clemson the mixed honors sections average **47.7 students,** and the contract sections with honors credit for individual honors students average **40.6 students.** Across all fifty programs, the average mixed honors section has 51.1 students, and the average contract section has 60.1 students.

Honors Graduation Rate (5.0): The rating is the based on the actual grad rate for students who entered the program six years earlier, whether or not the students remained in honors. The **actual rate of 94%** is also compared to the rates of other programs with the same test score entry requirement range, and then adjusted to the **score of 94.1.** In some cases this measure favors programs within universities with relatively higher test scores for the student population as a whole. The average honors graduation rate for all programs with similar test scores required for admission is 92.6%.

Value-Added Grad Rate (4.0): The value-added rate measures the extent to which the adjusted score listed above exceeds the six-year grad rate for the university as a whole. **The university-wide rate is 82%.** Note: This measure generally favors programs within universities with relatively lower test scores for the student population as a whole.

Ratio of Staff to Honors Students (4.0): There is 1 staff member for every **139.9** students. (Mean ratio for all 50 programs is 1 staff member for every 135.6 students.)

Honors Residence Halls, Amenities (5.0): Prospective applicants should know about the **new honors residence hall, which will open in Fall 2016.** The honors director reports that "we will open the new Honors Center at Core Campus, Clemson's first residential college. The complex will include suite-style housing for [409] Honors students (freshmen and upperclassmen); the Honors College administrative offices; classrooms, study areas, and academic event spaces open to all Honors students (whether or not they live in Core Campus); and a dining hall and other dining options (open to all students on campus)."

The consolidation of honors administrative functions and student housing in residential honors colleges is an important development, though sometimes one that takes a long time to achieve.

Honors Residence Halls, Availability (4.0): This rating compares the number of places in honors residence halls to the number of honors freshman and sophomore members in good standing, just under 700. The ratio for the college is **.59** rooms for each first- and second-year student. The average for all fifty programs is .63 places.

Prestigious Awards (3.5): The awards that we track and include are listed in the section titled "Prestigious Scholarships." The awards are sometimes won by students who are not in an honors college or program, but increasingly many are enrolled in honors programs. It is also a trend that honors colleges and programs help to prepare their students for the awards competitions. In the case of Clemson, achievement in winning major national postgraduate awards, such as Rhodes, Marshall, and Truman scholarships, has been minimal. On the other hand, Clemson students have won 35 Goldwater scholarships, awarded for undergraduate promise in the STEM disciplines. This is above the median for all 50 programs.

UNRATED FEATURES

Continuation Requirements: 3.40 GPA.

Academic Strengths, National Rankings: This is based on national rankings of *graduate* programs in all but engineering and business, where undergraduate rankings are used. At Clemson, engineering and business are the strongest departments, ranked 56 and 61, respectively. Other departments in the top 100 nationwide are education, economics, computer science, chemistry, and math.

Undergraduate Research: In addition to the thesis requirement for students who complete the departmental honors option, the director reports that "many Honors students participate in undergraduate research through Clemson's Creative Inquiry Program; some of these creative inquiry groups consist wholly or predominantly of Honors students." He also confirms that 46% of honors students participate in formal research activities.

Honors Study Abroad: "We offer Educational Enrichment Travel Grants to approximately 100 students every year (up to $3000 each) for research, internship, or other educational experiences," the director reports. "We offer a five-week summer Honors-only program in Europe focusing on the history and politics of the European Union, and an innovative online program linking Honors students studying in Europe during the Spring semester. In addition, two students are selected each year for a full scholarship to the St. Peter's Summer School at Oxford University, Oxford, England."

Financial Aid: Clemson's National Scholars Program is the university's premier undergraduate scholarship program, and it is independent of the National Merit Scholars Program. The Clemson National Scholars Program provides full scholarship equal to the cost of tuition, fees, room, board and books to approximately 12 students a year. Honors students at Clemson University are eligible for numerous additional merit scholarships," the director says. "In-state students in Honors who are also designated as Palmetto Fellows by the state of South Carolina receive the $2,500 Palmetto Pact

Scholarship, and many receive the prestigious $2,500 Presidential Scholarship as well. **Out-of-state Honors students usually qualify for an award of between $7,500 and $17,500 annually**--depending on test scores, high school performance and financial need."

Honors Fees: $500 per semester (Fall 2016).

Placement Experiences: "Our graduates enroll in a wide range of graduate and professional schools and are employed by large and small corporations, government agencies, and non-profit organizations. Professional schools include the Harvard Medical School, the Harvard Business School, Yale Law School, Berkeley Law School, the Johns Hopkins Medical School, Emory University School of Medicine, Duke University School of Medicine, the University of South Carolina School of Medicine, and the Medical University of South Carolina. Graduate schools include Stanford, MIT, the University of Michigan, the Georgia Institute of Technology, Harvard, Yale, and many others. Corporations include Goldman Sachs, Boeing, Michelin, BMW, BB&T Bank, Adidas, General Electric, and many more."

Degree of Difference: This is based on the differences between (1) the average (2015, two-part) SAT scores for enrolled honors students (1442) and (2) the average test scores for all students in the university (1260) as a whole. This may be an indication of how "elite" honors students may be perceived as compared to students in the university as a whole. The test scores can also provide an indication of how well prepared the non-honors students in the university may be. **Please keep in mind that neither high nor low test scores determine the overall quality of a program.**

NAME: COLORADO STATE UNIVERSITY HONORS PROGRAM.

Date Established: 1957.

Location: Fort Collins, Colorado.

University Full-time Undergraduate Enrollment: 21,253.

Honors Members in Good Standing: 1,563 (mean size of all 50 programs is 1,742).

Honors Average Admission Statistics: ACT, 30; old two-part SAT, 1280. Est. new SAT score, 1340.

Average High School GPA/Class Rank: 4.15.

Basic Admission Requirements: ACT, 27; old SAT, 1200. Est. new SAT score, 1270. High school GPA, 3.70, usually in the top 10%.

Application Deadline(s): *Please verify with each program, as some deadlines could change.*

December 1, 2016.

Honors Programs with old SAT scores from 1240—1291: Arkansas, Oklahoma State, Texas Tech, Montana, Washington State, New Mexico, South Dakota, Colorado State, Arizona, Montana State, Arizona State.

Administrative Staff: 5.

RATINGS AT A GLANCE: For all mortarboard ratings immediately below, a score of 5 is the maximum and represents a comparison with all 50 honors colleges and programs. More detailed explanations follow the "mortarboard" ratings.

PERCEPTION* OF UNIVERSITY AS A WHOLE, NOT OF HONORS: 🎓🎓🎓$^{1/2}$

*Perception is based on the university's ranking among public universities in the 2016 U.S. News Best Colleges report. Please bear in mind that the better the U.S. News ranking, the more difficult it is for an honors college or program to have a rating that equals or improves on the magazine ranking.

OVERALL HONORS RATING: 🎓🎓🎓

Curriculum Requirements: 🎓🎓🎓$^{1/2}$

Number of Honors Classes Offered: 🎓🎓🎓

Number of Honors Classes in Key Disciplines: 🎓🎓🎓$^{1/2}$

Extent of Honors Enrollment: 🎓🎓🎓$^{1/2}$

Honors-only Class Size: 🎓🎓🎓🎓 1/2

Overall Class Size (Honors-only plus mixed, contract): 🎓🎓🎓 1/2

Honors Grad Rate: 🎓🎓🎓 1/2

Value-Added Grad Rate: 🎓🎓🎓🎓

Ratio of Staff to Students: 🎓🎓🎓

Priority Registration: Yes, students have priority registration for all four years.

Honors Housing Amenities: 🎓🎓🎓🎓

Honors Housing Availability: 🎓🎓🎓🎓🎓

Prestigious Awards: 🎓🎓🎓

RATING SCORES AND EXPLANATIONS:

Curriculum Requirements (3.5): The most important rating category, the curriculum completion requirement (classes required to complete honors) defines not only what honors students should learn but also the extent to which honors students and faculty are connected in the classroom. If there is a thesis or capstone requirement, it reinforces the individual contact and research skills so important to learning.

The average number of honors semester hours required for completion across all 50 programs is 29.0.

The average completion for CSU Honors is **26** semester hours, as follows.

Track 1 (Entering First-year students) requires 17 credits in honors seminars, 6 credits in honors departmental courses/honors options, and a 3-credit **thesis.**

Track 2 (Transfers, Continuing Students) requires 19 credits in departmental honors courses/honors options, 4 credits in honors seminars, and a 3-credit **thesis.**

AP/IB credits are **not** counted as replacements for honors courses

Number of Honors Classes Offered (3.0): This is a measure of the total **adjusted** honors main sections available in the term reported, not including labs and thesis. (Please read the section titled "All about Honors Classes".) An adjusted main section has 3 or more semester credits, or equivalent, and sections with fewer credits receive a lower prorated value.

The honors program had a ratio of **25.4** enrolled students per each main section. The mean for all 50 programs is 14.2. The lower the ratio, the better.

In the term reported, an estimated **72.9%** of honors enrollment was **in honors-only sections; 9.8% in mixed sections with honors and non-honors students; and 17.3% in contract (option) sections (regular sections in which honors students "contract" to do extra work.** The averages for all fifty programs are 81.3% in honors-only sections; 13.6 % in mixed honors sections; and 5.1% in contract sections.

Number of Honors Classes in Key Disciplines (3.5): The 15 "key" disciplines are biological sciences; business (all); chemistry; communications (especially public speaking); computer science; economics; engineering (all); English; history; math (all); philosophy; physics; political science; psychology; and sociology/anthropology/gender studies. Interdisciplinary sections, such as those often taken for General Education credit in the first two years, do receive a lesser, prorated discipline "credit" because they introduce students to multiple disciplines in an especially engaging way, often with in-depth discussion.

For this measure, mixed and contract sections are not counted as a section in a key discipline unless students taking the sections for honors credit make up at least 10% of the total section enrollment.

In the term reported, the program had ratio of **50.4 honors students** per each main section in some or all "key disciplines." The mean for all 50 programs is 26.3. The lower the ratio, the better.

Out of **18 adjusted sections in key disciplines**, the program had sections in business (5), history (4), biology, philosophy, psychology,(3) each, and math ,(2).

The program also offered more than 35 excellent seminar sections, all with 3-4 credits. Among the many interesting course titles are "What We Can Learn from the Ancient Greeks about Women, Men, and Human Behavior?"; "Darwin, Marx, Mill, Freud, and Nietzsche: How Five 19th Century Thinkers Shaped 20th Century Thought and Events. Are Their Ideas Relevant Today?"; and "Why Do They Hate Us? Understanding the Myths, Realities and Limits of the American Empire."

The combination of seminars and courses in the disciplines makes the program an example of a **blended** program.

Extent of Honors Enrollment (3.5): Not all honors students take an honors class each term, especially after the first two years. Programs that have fewer honors classes for upper-division honors students will generally have fewer total members in good standing who are actually enrolled in a given term. (Please be aware, however, that honors students not enrolled in a class for a term are still connected to the honors community through residential and extracurricular activities.)

For example, if honors students in a program occupy 1,800 honors classroom seats in a given term, and there are 3,000 honors students in good standing, the extent of enrollment is .67. For programs that require a thesis, the ratio (score) reported below might in fact be somewhat higher, since we only count "regular" class enrollment for this measure, and not thesis enrollment. The program **has a ratio of .83**; the mean is 1.13 for all 50 programs. The higher the ratio, the better.

Average Class Size, Honors-only Sections (4.5): Offered mostly in the first two years, honors-only classes tend to be smaller and, as the name implies, have no or very few students other than those in the

honors program. These class sections are almost always much smaller than mixed or contract sections, or regular non-honors class sections in the university. The average honors-only class size in the honors program is **16.9 students**. The average for all 50 programs is 19.0 students.

Average Class Size, Overall (3.5): The overall class calculation is based on the *proportion* of honors students in each type of class (honors-only, mixed honors, and honors contract sections). Thus it is not a raw average. The overall honors-credit class size is **31.4 students**, versus the average for all 50 programs of 26.3 students.

These class size averages also do not correspond to the number of students per honors sections numbers above. The reason is that, in computing average class size metrics, we include enrollment in each 1-2-credit section, not just sections with 3 or more credits.

Along with the honors-only average of 17.3 students, mixed sections averaged **51.7**, and the contract sections with honors credit for individual honors students were not reported. Across all fifty programs, the average mixed honors section has 51.1 students, and the average contract section has 60.1 students.

Honors Graduation Rate (3.5): The rating is the based on the actual grad rate for students who entered the program six years earlier, whether or not the students remained in honors. The **actual rate of 84.1%** is also compared to the rates of other programs with the same test score entry requirement range, and then adjusted to the **score of 83.9%.** In some cases this measure favors programs within universities with relatively higher test scores for the student population as a whole. The average honors graduation rate for all programs with similar test scores required for admission is 83.4%.

Value-Added Grad Rate (4.0): The value-added rate measures the extent to which the adjusted score listed above exceeds the six-year grad rate for the university as a whole. **The university-wide rate is 66%.** Note: This measure generally favors programs within universities with relatively lower test scores for the student population as a whole.

Ratio of Staff to Honors Students (3.0): There is 1 staff member for every **312.6** students. (Mean ratio for all 50 programs is 1 staff member for every 135.6 students.)

Honors Residence Halls, Amenities (4.0): About 200 first-year honors students live in the Academic Village Residence Hall, with air-conditioned suite-style rooms with shared baths. The nearest dining facility is the Rams Horn located within the Academic Village complex.

The remaining 26% of honors students in honors housing reside in Edwards Residence Hall. The hall has traditional double rooms and hall baths for freshmen and upperclassmen, and does not have air-conditioning. The closest dining is also at the Rams Horn in the Academic Village. Edwards provides students with a more economical housing option.

Honors Residence Halls, Availability (5.0): This rating compares the number of places in honors residence halls to the number of honors freshman and sophomore members in good standing, just under 2,000. The ratio for the honors program is **1.00** rooms for each first-year students. The average for all fifty programs is .63 places.

Prestigious Awards (3.0): The awards that we track and include are listed in the section titled "Prestigious Scholarships." The awards are sometimes won by students who are not in an honors college or program, but increasingly many are enrolled in honors programs. It is also a trend that honors colleges and programs help to prepare their students for the awards competitions.

CSU students have won 8 Udall scholarships and 15 Goldwater awards, both awarded to undergraduates, the latter for outstanding promise in STEM fields. CSU students have also won an impressive 5 Marshall scholarships for postgraduate study in the U.K.

UNRATED FEATURES

Continuation Requirements: 3.00 GPA, to stay in the program and 3.50 overall to graduate with honors.

Academic Strengths, National Rankings: This is based on national rankings of *graduate* programs in 15 disciplines, except engineering and business, where undergraduate rankings are used.

Most academic departments at CSU are ranked better than 100 in the nation among all universities. The most recognized department is chemistry (49), followed by computer science, engineering, and physics, (70) each. Other leading departments are math (73) and biology (75).

Undergraduate Research: "…57% of honors students participate in undergraduate research."

Honors Study Abroad: "We created summer Honors seminars and courses as 3- to 5-week Study Abroad experiences," the director tells us. "In summer 2016, we are offering Honors seminars in Oxford and Rome and Honors sections of English and Business courses in Zambia and Europe (Stockholm, London, and Budapest), respectively. These will be offered every summer. We plan to increase the number of such courses.

"Enrichment Awards (up to $400) and the Spot's Scholarship ($1,250) can be used for Study Abroad. A focus of our fundraising is focused on assisting students in paying for these experiences."

Financial Aid: "In addition to other merit and need-based scholarships offered by the University, the University Honors Program awards entering first-year students a $1,000 per year Honors scholarship, renewable each year, for 4 years. There are donor-endowed scholarships awarded to ~10 students per year. Students can receive Enrichment Awards and Thesis Improvement Grants each year ($400 per award)."

Resident Merit Scholarships:

- For 2016-2017: $16,000 to $4,000 ($4,000 to $1,000 per year) may be awarded to Colorado-resident first-time freshmen who meet [certain] criteria by the previously stated February 1 Application for Admission due date. Admitted students (who met the Feb 1 date) can submit additional academic work (test scores, transcripts) by March 1 to strengthen their application for scholarship eligibility. *The best awards required a high GPA and minimum old SAT of 1440 (ACT 33 and higher:*

- Boettcher Scholarship recipients, finalists and semifinalists, National Merit finalists who list CSU as their first-choice institution with the National Merit Scholarship Corporation, National Hispanic Scholars, and National Achievement Scholars who do not fall into the above chart, will receive a Ram Recognition Award of $1,000-$2,000 per year.

- Scholarship awarding will start early-October and continue through March. Only students who are awarded will receive notification.

Non-Resident Merit Scholarships:

For 2016-2017, $40,000 - $24,000 ($10,000 to $6,000 per year) may be awarded to non-resident first-time freshmen who meet the criteria in the below listed chart, by the previously stated February 1 complete Application for Admission due date. Admitted students (who met the Feb 1 date) can submit additional academic work (test scores, transcripts) by March 1 to strengthen their application for scholarship eligibility. *National Merit Finalists who list CSU as their first-choice institution with the National Merit Scholarship Corporation will automatically receive the [highest award level], as will National Hispanic Scholars and National Achievement Scholars.*

Honors Fees: None.

Placement Experiences: "In graduate surveys, About half (50%) were planning to enter post-graduate professional or graduate programs; about 36% had jobs after graduation, and 14% did not specify any plans."

Degree of Difference: This is based on the differences between (1) the average (2015, two-part) SAT scores for enrolled honors students (1280) and (2) the average test scores for all students in the university (1120) as a whole. The test scores may be an indication of how "elite" honors students may be perceived as compared to students in the university as a whole. The scores can also provide an indication of how well prepared the non-honors students in the university may be. **Please keep in mind that neither high nor low test scores determine the overall quality of a program.**

NAME: UNIVERSITY OF CONNECTICUT HONORS PROGRAM.

Date Established: 1964.

Location: Storrs, Connecticut.

University Full-time Undergraduate Enrollment: 17,677.

Honors Members in Good Standing: 2,113 (mean size of all 50 programs is 1,742).

Honors Average Admission Statistics: ACT, 32; old two-part SAT, 1406. Est. new SAT score, 1455.

Average High School GPA/Class Rank: 96th percentile.

Basic Admission Requirements: None listed.

Application Deadline(s): *Please verify with each program, as some deadlines could change.*

Deadline is January 15, 2017, but for full consideration for scholarships apply by December 1, 2016.

Honors Programs with old SAT scores from 1402—1469: UCF, Connecticut, Kentucky, Washington, Maryland, North Carolina, UC Irvine, Kansas, Minnesota, Tennessee, South Carolina, Clemson, UT Austin, Georgia.

Administrative Staff: 19.

RATINGS AT A GLANCE: For all mortarboard ratings immediately below, a score of 5 is the maximum and represents a comparison with all 50 honors colleges and programs. More detailed explanations follow the "mortarboard" ratings.

PERCEPTION* OF UNIVERSITY AS A WHOLE, NOT OF HONORS: 🎓🎓🎓🎓[1/2]

*Perception is based on the university's ranking among public universities in the 2016 U.S. News Best Colleges report. Please bear in mind that the better the U.S. News ranking, the more difficult it is for an honors college or program to have a rating that equals or improves on the magazine ranking.

OVERALL HONORS RATING: 🎓🎓🎓🎓

Curriculum Requirements: 🎓🎓🎓🎓

Number of Honors Classes Offered: 🎓🎓🎓🎓

Number of Honors Classes in Key Disciplines: 🎓🎓🎓🎓[1/2]

Extent of Honors Enrollment: 🎓🎓🎓🎓[1/2]

Honors-only Class Size: 🎓🎓🎓🎓

Overall Class Size (Honors-only plus mixed, contract): 🎓🎓🎓

Honors Grad Rate: 🎓🎓🎓🎓🎓

Value-Added Grad Rate: 🎓🎓🎓¹/²

Ratio of Staff to Students: 🎓🎓🎓🎓

Priority Registration: Yes, honors students have priority registration for all courses, in the form of being able to register with the class ahead of them.

Honors Housing Amenities: 🎓🎓🎓¹/²

Honors Housing Availability: 🎓🎓🎓🎓🎓

Prestigious Awards: 🎓🎓🎓

RATING SCORES AND EXPLANATIONS:

Curriculum Requirements (4.0): The most important rating category, the curriculum completion requirement (classes required to complete honors) defines not only what honors students should learn but also the extent to which honors students and faculty are connected in the classroom. If there is a thesis or capstone requirement, it reinforces the individual contact and research skills so important to learning.

The average number of honors semester hours required for completion across all 50 programs is 29.0.

To complete *both* honors options requires at least **28** semester hours.

Sophomore Honors requires 16-18 credit hours within the student's first two years, the higher number being required for honors students who do not take a 1-credit First Year Experience Seminar. Of the required hours, at least three honors credits must be earned in an Honors Core course. Students must also attend an honors thesis/research preparation workshop; attend at least five honors events and submit journal information on time; have a cumulative GPA of 3.40 or higher; and earn a grade of B- or better in any honors course or honors conversion (contract) to receive honors credit.

Graduation as an **Honors Scholar** requires completion of 12 credits at the 2000 level or above in departmental honors coursework, research, and thesis, plus an additional 3 credits that may be in any department at any level. At least three of these 15 credits must be in an honors or graduate course (not conversion, independent study, or thesis). Honors credit is only awarded when students earn a B- or better in an honors course or an honors conversion. Students must have earned a cumulative GPA of at least 3.40.

Up to 3 credits may apply to both Sophomore Honors and Honors Scholar completion.

AP/IB credits are **not** counted as replacements for honors courses

Number of Honors Classes Offered (4.0): This is a measure of the total **adjusted** honors main sections available in the term reported, not including labs and thesis. (Please read the section titled "All about Honors Classes".) An adjusted main section has 3 or more semester credits, or equivalent, and sections with fewer credits receive a lower prorated value.

The honors program had a ratio of **14.5** enrolled students per each main section. The mean for all 50 programs is 14.2. The lower the ratio, the better.

In the term reported, the percentage of honors enrollment was an estimated **72.0% in honors-only sections; 17.0% in mixed sections with honors and non-honors students; and 11.0% reported in contract sections (regular sections in which honors students "contract" to do extra work.** The averages for all fifty programs are 81.3% in honors-only sections; 13.6 % in mixed honors sections; and 5.1% in contract sections.

Number of Honors Classes in Key Disciplines (4.5): The 15 "key" disciplines are biological sciences; business (all); chemistry; communications (especially public speaking); computer science; economics; engineering (all); English; history; math (all); philosophy; physics; political science; psychology; and sociology/anthropology/gender studies. Interdisciplinary sections, such as those often taken for General Education credit in the first two years, do receive a lesser, prorated discipline "credit" because they introduce students to multiple disciplines in an especially engaging way, often with in-depth discussion.

For this measure, mixed and contract sections are not counted as a section in a key discipline unless students taking the sections for honors credit make up at least 10% of the total section enrollment.

In the term reported, the program had a ratio of **20.0 honors students** per each main section in some or all "key disciplines." The mean for all 50 programs is 26.3. The lower the ratio, the better.

Out of **86 adjusted sections in key disciplines**, the program offered **55 honors-only sections.** Math (17—a very high number), English (14), and biology (11) had the most sections, followed by engineering (8), political science (7), and psychology (4). Sociology, anthropology, and gender studies had 6 sections combined.

The program also offered more than 40 excellent seminar sections, most with 3-4 credits. Among the many interesting course titles are "Other People's Worlds"; "Privacy in the Information Age"; "Gender and War"; and the "Sociology of Anti-Semitism."

The combination of seminars and courses in the disciplines makes the program an example of a large **blended** program.

Extent of Honors Enrollment (4.5:): Not all honors students take an honors class each term, especially after the first two years. Programs that have fewer honors classes for upper-division honors students will generally have fewer total members in good standing who are actually enrolled in a given term. (Please be

aware, however, that honors students not enrolled in a class for a term are still connected to the honors community through residential and extracurricular activities.)

For example, if honors students in a program occupy 1,800 honors classroom seats in a given term, and there are 3,000 honors students in good standing, the extent of enrollment is .67. For programs that require a thesis, the ratio (score) reported below might in fact be somewhat higher, since we only count "regular" class enrollment for this measure, and not thesis enrollment. The program **has a ratio of 1.28**; the mean is 1.13 for all 50 programs. The higher the ratio, the better.

Average Class Size, Honors-only Sections (4.0): Offered mostly in the first two years, honors-only classes tend to be smaller and, as the name implies, have no or very few students other than those in the honors program. These class sections are almost always much smaller than mixed or contract sections, or regular non-honors class sections in the university.

The average honors-only class size in the honors program is **18.9 students**. The average for all 50 programs is 19.0 students.

Average Class Size, Overall (3.0): The overall class calculation is based on the *proportion* of honors students in each type of class (honors-only, mixed honors, and honors contract sections). Thus it is not a raw average. The overall honors-credit class size is **49.8 students**, versus the average for all 50 programs of 26.3 students.

These class size averages also do not correspond to the number of students per honors sections numbers above. The reason is that, in computing average class size metrics, we include enrollment in each 1-2-credit section, not just sections with 3 or more credits.

Along with the honors-only average of 18.9 students, mixed sections averaged **183.9**, and the contract sections with honors credit for individual honors students averaged **61.2**. Across all fifty programs, the average mixed honors section has 51.1 students, and the average contract section has 60.1 students.

Honors Graduation Rate (4.5): The rating is based on the actual grad rate for students who entered the program six years earlier, whether or not the students remained in honors. The **actual rate of 92.0%** is also compared to the rates of other programs with the same test score entry requirement range, and then adjusted to the **score of 92.0%.** In some cases this measure favors programs within universities with relatively higher test scores for the student population as a whole. Impressively, **85% graduated in four years.** The average honors graduation rate for all programs with similar test scores required for admission is 92.6%.

Value-Added Grad Rate (3.5): The value-added rate measures the extent to which the adjusted score listed above exceeds the six-year grad rate for the university as a whole. **The university-wide rate is 81%.** Note: This measure generally favors programs within universities with relatively lower test scores for the student population as a whole.

Ratio of Staff to Honors Students (4.0): There is 1 staff member for every **111.2** students. (Mean ratio for all 50 programs is 1 staff member for every 135.6 students.)

Honors Residence Halls, Amenities (3.5): "UConn has among the highest percentage of students living on campus of any public university in the nation," the director reports. "Almost all Honors freshmen live in the Honors First Year Honors Residential Community in the Buckley-Shippee Complex, which also contains the Honors Programming and Events Office. After the first year, many (43%) Honors students choose to remain in Honors housing and participate in events and community activities at the other halls. We have continued to expand our upper-class Honors housing options to respond to this demand.

"We attribute much of our success in building the Honors community through our *intentional* selection of traditional corridor-style rooms, particularly for first-year students. This community promotes academic success and retention. Suites are available for upper-class students."

About two-thirds of the honors students in honors housing live in Buckley and Shippee Halls. The residences houses mostly first-year honors students and some upperclassmen..

"Buckley Hall is also home to our Honors Programming & Events office, providing first-year Honors students easy access to staff members. Buckley Hall includes one seminar room used for several Honors First Year Experience courses."

Now housing 126 honors students, Shippee in Fall 2016 will be home to 290 honors students, including some upperclassmen.

Both dorms have traditional rooms and hall baths, and do not have room air-conditioning. But they do have on-site dining.

"Other housing options for Fall 2016 are Brock Hall (increasing from 90 to 230); Snow Hall (310), replacing Wilson Hall; and Next Gen (110)." Next Gen will house multiple learning communities, including Women in Math, Science, and Engineering; Innovation House; and Engineering House. Other amenities include study spaces, classrooms, computer lab, and an Innovation Zone / Maker Space including 3D printers.

Honors Residence Halls, Availability (5.0): This rating compares the number of rooms in honors residence halls to the number of honors freshman and sophomore members in good standing, just under 1,057. The ratio for the honors program is **.96** rooms for each first- and second-year student. The average for all fifty programs is .63 rooms.

Prestigious Awards (3.0): The awards that we track and include are listed in the section titled "Prestigious Scholarships." The awards are sometimes won by students who are not in an honors college or program, but increasingly many are enrolled in honors programs. It is also a trend that honors colleges and programs help to prepare their students for the awards competitions.

Like one of its neighbors, UMass Amherst, UConn competes for prestigious scholarships with both Ivy League institutions and highly-ranked liberal arts colleges; but rapid improvement is at hand.

"The Office of National Scholarships and Fellowships (ONS&F), also part of Enrichment Programs, has been in operation for only ten years. ONS&F serves all UConn students, and many nominees and recipients of major awards have been Honors students. Since 2005, UConn Honors students have received three Marshall scholarships, fifteen Goldwater scholarships, four Udall scholarships, two Truman scholarships, and a Mitchell scholarship. During the same period, we have also had twelve Goldwater honorable mentions, eight Truman finalists, six Marshall finalists, three Rhodes finalists, two Udall honorable mentions, one Mitchell finalist, one Gates Cambridge finalist, and one Carnegie Junior Fellow finalist and who were Honors students.

"ONS&F also supports students applying for a variety of other scholarships and awards. In the past ten years, honors students have been awarded 8 NSF Graduate Research Fellowships, one DOE SCGF, one Pickering Undergraduate Fellowship, one NSEP Boren, two Critical Language Scholarships, and several U.S. Student Fulbright Grants (including one UK Fulbright Summer Institute grant) among other prestigious national awards. (The Fulbright competition is only recently being administrated by ONS&F beginning in 2014, so our institutional data is inexact.) For example, UConn is eligible to nominate one honors project proposal each year for the National Collegiate Honors Council Portz Fellowship, and our students have won this national competition in four of the last five years. Students are encouraged to work with ONS&F throughout their collegiate careers for mentorship, advice, and application assistance."

UNRATED FEATURES

Continuation Requirements: 3.40 GPA, and completion of at least 6 honors credits each year.

Academic Strengths, National Rankings: This is based on national rankings of *graduate* programs in 15 disciplines, except engineering and business, where undergraduate rankings are used.

Most academic departments at UConn are ranked better than 70th in the nation among all universities. The most recognized department is education (26), followed by business (50), and psychology and sociology (52 each). History and English are ranked 60 and 63, respectively. Engineering and physics are each ranked 70th in the nation.

Undergraduate Research: "Undergraduate research is a key aspect of UConn Honors, as all Honors graduates must complete an independent thesis project. The Honors Program works closely with the Office of Undergraduate Research (OUR), also part of Enrichment Programs, to develop our students' skills and opportunities in research, scholarship, and creative activity. OUR sponsors regular workshops, information sessions, seminars, and exhibitions of student work in order to engage the UConn community as a whole in conversations about undergraduate research.

"Honors students are encouraged to plan their undergraduate research careers early, starting with a thesis workshop within their first two years. In addition to the resources and opportunities offered to all undergraduate researchers through [the Office of Undergraduate Research], Honors students may participate in programs like the ISA Honors Awards for Undergraduate International Studies Research or Holster Scholars.

"ISA Honors Awards…support social science projects that spans across countries, regions, or the globe…[T]hese awards offer up to $1,000 per student to cover travel costs and other expenses associated with research projects in international studies.

Inspired by Robert Holster's own experiences as a member of the inaugural class of UConn Honors, the Holster First Year Project supports a small number of motivated Honors students in independent study projects during the summer following their first year."

Honors Study Abroad: "Through its Office of Study Abroad, UConn offers over 300 programs for students seeking international experiences to enrich their education. Some of these are especially geared toward Honors students and earn Honors credit, including exchanges with University College Maastricht and University College Utrecht, both in the Netherlands, and National University of Singapore, as well as UConn faculty-led experiences in South Africa (includes NGO internship), Spain (advanced neuroscience study), Guatemala (social entrepreneurship), Armenia (archeology field school), and London (global commerce).

"Honors students may also earn Honors credits through course conversion contracts while studying abroad. The contract may be between the student and the instructor at the international institution or between the student and a faculty advisor in the relevant UConn department. This allows Honors students to participate in any UConn Study Abroad experience—including over 20 exchanges through the Universitas 21 network of international research universities—without interrupting their Honors plans of study."

Financial Aid: "A large majority (96%) of Honors first-year students at UConn receive at least one renewable merit scholarship. These scholarships are administered through the Office of Undergraduate Admissions.

"All Connecticut semifinalists and finalists in the National Achievement Scholarship Program, the National Hispanic Recognition Program, and the National Merit Semifinalist Competition, in addition to outstanding students from every Connecticut high school may be nominated to apply for the Nutmeg Scholarship (full tuition, housing, and meal plan).

"A few scholarship programs are specifically connected to the Honors Program, including automatic Honors admission for award winners. This includes the Stamps Scholars Award, which connects recipients to a national network through the Stamps Family Charitable Foundation; the John and Valerie Rowe Health Professions Scholars, which provides opportunities to students from backgrounds underrepresented in the health fields; and the STEM Scholars, part of the state of Connecticut's revolutionary investment in STEM education."

Honors Fees: None.

Placement Experiences: UConn honors grads in recent years have pursued graduate or professional studies at all Ivy League universities, MIT, Caltech, Cambridge University, the University of London, UC Berkeley, Michigan, Virginia, and Georgetown, among many others.

Degree of Difference: This is based on the differences between (1) the average (2015, two-part) SAT scores for enrolled honors students (1406) and (2) the average test scores for all students in the university (1250) as a whole. The test scores may be an indication of how "elite" honors students may be perceived as compared to students in the university as a whole. The scores can also provide an indication of how well prepared the non-honors students in the university may be. **Please keep in mind that neither high nor low test scores determine the overall quality of a program.**

NAME: WILLIAM E. MACAULAY HONORS COLLEGE AT THE CITY UNIVERSITY OF NEW YORK.

Date Established: 2001.

Location: New York, New York.

University Full-time Undergraduate Enrollment: Est. 83,809.

Honors Members in Good Standing: 2,144 (mean size of all 50 programs is 1,742).

Honors Average Admission Statistics: Old two-part SAT, 1372. Est. new SAT score, 1420.

Average High School GPA/Class Rank: Top 6.6%.

Basic Admission Requirements: Old SAT, 1200. Est. new SAT, 1270. At least a 90 numerical average.

Application Deadline(s): *Please verify with each program, as some deadlines could change.*

December 1, 2016; notification of Macaulay acceptance, March 15, 2017.

Honors Programs with old SAT scores from 1351—1396: Purdue, Oregon, Alabama, Massachusetts, Penn State, Indiana, CUNY Macaulay, Texas A&M, NJIT, Missouri, Oregon State, Delaware, LSU, Vermont, Temple.

Administrative Staff: 32 FTEs.

RATINGS AT A GLANCE: For all mortarboard ratings immediately below, a score of 5 is the maximum and represents a comparison with all 50 honors colleges and programs. More detailed explanations follow the "mortarboard" ratings.

PERCEPTION* OF UNIVERSITY AS A WHOLE, NOT OF HONORS: 🎓🎓🎓 1/2

*Perception is based on the university's ranking among public universities in the 2016 U.S. News Best Colleges report. Please bear in mind that the better the U.S. News ranking, the more difficult it is for an honors college or program to have a rating that equals or improves on the magazine ranking.

OVERALL HONORS RATING: 🎓🎓🎓🎓🎓

Curriculum Requirements: 🎓🎓🎓🎓 1/2

Number of Honors Classes Offered: 🎓🎓🎓🎓 1/2

Number of Honors Classes in Key Disciplines: 🎓🎓🎓🎓 1/2

Extent of Honors Enrollment: 🎓🎓🎓🎓

Honors-only Class Size: 🎓🎓🎓¹ᐟ²

Overall Class Size (Honors-only plus mixed, contract): 🎓🎓🎓🎓

Honors Grad Rate: 🎓🎓🎓🎓

Value-Added Grad Rate: 🎓🎓🎓🎓¹ᐟ²

Ratio of Staff to Students: 🎓🎓🎓🎓🎓

Priority Registration: Yes, honors students register for all courses, honors and otherwise, with the first group of students during each year they are in the program.

Honors Housing Amenities: 🎓🎓🎓🎓

Honors Housing Availability: 🎓🎓🎓¹ᐟ²

Prestigious Awards: 🎓🎓🎓🎓¹ᐟ²

RATING SCORES AND EXPLANATIONS:

Curriculum Requirements (4.5): The most important rating category, the curriculum completion requirement (classes required to complete honors) defines not only what honors students should learn but also the extent to which honors students and faculty are connected in the classroom. If there is a thesis or capstone requirement, it reinforces the individual contact and research skills so important to learning.

The average number of honors semester hours required for completion across all 50 programs is 29.0.

Graduation and completion of honors at Macaulay requires a *minimum* of about **34** credits. Students must have four 3-credit honors seminars; four 3-credit honors courses; 3 credits in an honors experience, such as an internship or studying abroad; 30 hours (no credits) of community service; and a 6-credit honors **thesis**. Students must also complete departmental honors courses if offered in their major.

AP/IB credits are **not** counted as replacements for honors.

Number of Honors Classes Offered (4.5): This is a measure of the total **adjusted** honors main sections available in the term reported, not including labs and thesis. (Please read the section titled "All about Honors Classes".) An adjusted main section has 3 or more semester credits, or equivalent, and sections with fewer credits receive a lower prorated value.

The honors program had a ratio of **10.3** enrolled students per each main section. The mean for all 50 programs is 14.2. The lower the ratio, the better.

In the term reported, **100.0%** of honors enrollment was **in honors-only sections.** The averages for all fifty programs are 81.3% in honors-only sections; 13.6 % in mixed honors sections; and 5.1% in contract sections.

Number of Honors Classes in Key Disciplines (4.5): The 15 "key" disciplines are biological sciences; business (all); chemistry; communications (especially public speaking); computer science; economics; engineering (all); English; history; math (all); philosophy; physics; political science; psychology; and sociology/anthropology/gender studies. Interdisciplinary sections, such as those often taken for General Education credit in the first two years, do receive a lesser, prorated discipline "credit" because they introduce students to multiple disciplines in an especially engaging way, often with in-depth discussion.

In the term reported, the program had a ratio of **16.9 honors students** per each main section in some or all "key disciplines." The mean for all 50 programs is 26.3. The lower the ratio, the better.

Out of **78 adjusted sections in key disciplines, all were honors-only sections.** The most sections were in English (17), business (16), history (7), math and philosophy (5), economics, political science, and psychology (4 each), biology and communications (3 each), and chemistry (2). Sociology, anthropology, and gender studies combined (5).

The program also offered an impressive 67 seminars, 3 credits each, on multiple CUNY campuses. About 16 of these were Honors in the Humanities, Honors in the Social Sciences, or Honors in Math and Natural Sciences. About 114-15 were titled "Arts in New York City." Several more were titled "Science Forward," and another was "What Is the Common Good?"

Extent of Honors Enrollment (5.0): Not all honors students take an honors class each term, especially after the first two years. Programs that have fewer honors classes for upper-division honors students will generally have fewer total members in good standing who are actually enrolled in a given term. (Please be aware, however, that honors students not enrolled in a class for a term are still connected to the honors community through residential and extracurricular activities.)

For example, if honors students in a program occupy 1,800 honors classroom seats in a given term, and there are 3,000 honors students in good standing, the extent of enrollment is .67. For programs that require a thesis, the ratio (score) reported below might in fact be somewhat higher, since we only count "regular" class enrollment for this measure, and not thesis enrollment. The college **has a ratio of 1.90**; the mean is 1.13 for all 50 programs. The higher the ratio, the better.

Average Class Size, Honors-only Sections (3.5): Offered mostly in the first two years, honors-only classes tend to be smaller and, as the name implies, have no or very few students other than those in the honors program. These class sections are almost always much smaller than mixed or contract sections, or regular non-honors class sections in the university.

The average honors-only class size in the honors program is **24.6 students**. The average for all 50 programs is 19.0 students.

Average Class Size, Overall (4.0): The overall class calculation is based on the *proportion* of honors students in each type of class (honors-only, mixed honors, and honors contract sections). Thus it is not a raw average. The overall honors-credit class size is **24.6 students**, versus the average for all 50 programs of 26.3 students.

These class size averages also do not correspond to the number of students per honors sections numbers above. The reason is that, in computing average class size metrics, we include enrollment in each 1-2-credit section, not just sections with 3 or more credits.

Honors Graduation Rate (4.0): The rating is based on the actual grad rate for students who entered the program six years earlier, whether or not the students remained in honors. The **actual rate of 86.4%** is also compared to the rates of other programs with the same test score entry requirement range, and then adjusted to the **score of 86.5%.** In some cases this measure favors programs within universities with relatively higher test scores for the student population as a whole. The average honors graduation rate for all programs with similar test scores required for admission is 86.2%.

Value-Added Grad Rate (4.5): The value-added rate measures the extent to which the adjusted score listed above exceeds the six-year grad rate for the university as a whole. **The estimated university-wide rate is 64%.** Note: This measure generally favors programs within universities with relatively lower test scores for the student population as a whole.

Ratio of Staff to Honors Students (5.0): There is 1 staff member for every **67.0** students. (Mean ratio for all 50 programs is 1 staff member for every 135.6 students.)

Honors Residence Halls, Amenities (4.0): Macaulay has five residence halls, one each at Baruch College, Brooklyn College, Hunter College, Lehman College, and Queens College.

By far, the Brookdale Residence at Hunter College, in Manhattan, has the most Macaulay students who live in honors housing, more than 600. Almost all the rooms at Brookdale, a Health Sciences community, are singles, but with hall baths. The facility houses both freshmen and upperclassmen. The rooms are not air-conditioned. Brookdale is less than three miles northeast of Greenwich Village, and near the East River. **Rooms are "offered free or at major discounts for honors students."** [Emphasis added.]

Only 27 Macaulay students live in the Baruch College Residence, located at 1760 Third Avenue, upper east side near Central Park. The rooms are doubles and triples; they are air-conditioned. There are no Macaulay discounts, but honors students have priority.

Only 5 Macaulay students live in the Brooklyn College Residence. Room configurations vary; rooms are air-conditioned.

The honors residence at Lehman College, in the Bronx, is an off-campus townhouse, housing 20 students.

About 60 Macaulay upperclassmen live at the Summit Residence at Queens College. The rooms are not air-conditioned.

Honors Residence Halls, Availability (3.5): This rating compares the number of rooms in honors residence halls to the number of honors freshman and sophomore members in good standing, about 1,072. The ratio for the honors program is **.39** rooms for each first- and second-year student. The average for all fifty programs is .63 rooms.

Prestigious Awards (4.5): The awards are sometimes won by students who are not in an honors program. The awards that we track and include are listed in the section titled "Prestigious Scholarships." The awards are sometimes won by students who are not in an honors college or program, but increasingly many are enrolled in honors programs. It is also a trend that honors colleges and programs help to prepare their students for the awards competitions.

CUNY students have won 7 Rhodes scholarships, 5 Marshall scholarships, and 11 Truman scholarships. They have also won 36 Goldwater scholarships. CUNY students also have a solid record of winning NSF graduate fellowships and have been very successful in winning Fulbright Student scholarships.

UNRATED FEATURES

Continuation Requirements: 3.30 GPA for first three semesters, then 3.50 going forward.

Academic Strengths, National Rankings: This is based on national rankings of *graduate* programs in 15 disciplines, except engineering and business, where undergraduate rankings are used.

As for CUNY, City College is strongest in physics, engineering, and psychology; Baruch for business, especially accounting; Brooklyn for its coordinated engineering program, with transfer opportunities to Michigan, Wisconsin, and MIT, and for its graduate program in cinema; Hunter, creative writing and psychology; Queens for psychology, and the Aaron Copland School of Music. Most campuses also have notable programs in the fine arts, as well as solid programs in nursing and health care.

Undergraduate Research: "Macaulay students have a 100% record of being accepted to present at the National Conferences on Undergraduate Research (NCUR) meetings every year. In addition, we offer the following special programs in undergraduate research:

"1. Macaulay Honors College Research Assistantship Program--The Macaulay Honors College Research Assistantship Program matches CUNY faculty members pursuing original research in their various disciplines with Macaulay Honors College students who are eager to learn more about a given intellectual field of inquiry. These pairings of faculty and students work together to create new knowledge in a discipline, affording students an opportunity make valuable contributions to the work of their faculty mentors.

"Everyone will participate in a Macaulay Research Expo at which faculty and students will present the results of the work done together.

"Through the Macaulay Research Assistantship Program, Macaulay students have worked on microfluidic systems for cell migration, assessed lead exposure from air particulates in city gardens, explored the relationship between New York City Mayoral approval ratings and historical events, and helped make a documentary film about a gangsta surfer in Far Rockaway. Others have become co-authors of scientific publications. One student changed his major to chemistry because of his research in nanotechnology.

"2. Macaulay Springboard--The Macaulay Springboard represents an effort at Macaulay Honors College to work with students to redefine the capstone project.

For seniors who are interested in fulfilling their capstone project requirement in a new way, this course will be offered to all graduating students as a six-credit, two-semester, yearlong guided workshop in preparing springboard projects, an alternative to the traditional capstone or honors thesis. Students will design and create springboard projects, which will be launched at graduation (and eligible for Capstone Reimagined Awards).

Study Abroad: "A Macaulay grant from the Opportunities Fund will provide financial support for any credit-bearing study abroad program. Students can request to use the Opportunities Fund to cover program costs--including airfare, housing, and meals, up to the limit of $7,500, if the student attends a semester long or yearlong study abroad program.

"Macaulay Honors College has cooperative ties to several international universities who sponsor Macaulay students in customized learning environments." These include:

Cuba--Partnering with the University of Havana Faculty 3-credit course offers marine and terrestrial fieldwork course in the Peninsula de Zapata National Park.

Dominican Republic--Partnering with CIEE, a 3-credit course offers an introduction to public health practice and its particular manifestations in the Dominican Republic, and more generally, the Caribbean and Latin America.

Galapagos--Partnering with Universidad San Francisco de Quito in Ecuador, 3-credit course examines theories that have shaped the concept of evolution, and how Darwin's experience in the Galapagos Islands influenced his ideas.

Israel--In partnership with Tel Aviv University's Porter School of Environmental Sciences the program consists of two courses and a carefully planned live and learn program of trips and cultural experiences. All participants take **Israel and Sustainability**, then will add a second course of their choosing.

Indonesia--Coming summer of 2017, in partnership with the Institut Pertanian Bogor, a credit-bearing course on tropical insect biodiversity and ecology, to be followed by a field component in Indonesia.

Spain--Offered in partnership with CIEE in Barcelona, students studied one of three 3-credit tracks in business, global architecture or the arts.

Financial Aid: Financial Aid available to Macaulay Honors College students:

- Federal PELL Grant
- TAP
- HESC Scholarships/Grants (E.g. NYS Scholarships for Academic Excellence)

- SEOG
- New York City Council Scholarship
- The Dream. US Scholarship

Students accepted into the Macaulay Honors College are automatically considered for all scholarships.

Honors Fees: None.

Placement Experiences: "70% of Macaulay alumni work in New York City, 86% in New York State.

"31% of alumni are working within 2 years after graduation. Selected employers include: BBC Worldwide Americas, Bloomberg, Boeing, Booz Allen, CitiGroup, General Electric, Goldman Sachs, Google, J.P. Morgan Stanley, and The Metropolitan Opera.

"46% of alumni are attending graduate or professional school within 2 years after graduation. Of those attending graduate and professional schools, 10% attend medical school and 9% attend law school. Selected graduate and professional schools include: Harvard Law School, Harvard Medical School, Howard University, MIT, NYU Law School, Oxford University, and Stanford Law School."

Degree of Difference: This is based on the differences between (1) the average (2015, two-part) SAT scores for enrolled honors students (1372) and (2) the average test scores for all students in the university (1150) as a whole. The test scores may be an indication of how "elite" honors students may be perceived as compared to students in the university as a whole. The scores can also provide an indication of how well prepared the non-honors students in the university may be. **Please keep in mind that neither high nor low test scores determine the overall quality of a program.**

NAME: UNIVERSITY OF DELAWARE HONORS PROGRAM.

Date Established: 1976.

Location: Newark, Delaware.

University <u>Full-time Undergraduate</u> Enrollment: 17,458.

Honors Members in Good Standing: 1,872 (mean size of all 50 programs is 1,742).,

Honors <u>Average</u> Admission Statistics: ACT, 30; old two-part SAT, 1388. Est. new SAT score, 1440. (For the class entering Fall 2015, the two part SAT average was 1450 and ACT average was 31.)

Average High School GPA/Class Rank: 4.05; top 8.4% of class.

<u>Basic</u> Admission Requirements: None listed.

Application Deadline(s): *Please verify with each program, as some deadlines could change.*

January 15, 2017, including honors essay; (notification mid-March 2017).

Honors Programs with old SAT scores from 1351—1396: Purdue, Oregon, Alabama, Massachusetts, Penn State, Indiana, CUNY Macaulay, Texas A&M, NJIT, Missouri, Oregon State, Delaware, LSU, Vermont, Temple.

Administrative Staff: 10.

RATINGS AT A GLANCE: For all mortarboard ratings immediately below, a score of 5 is the maximum and represents a comparison with all 50 honors colleges and programs. More detailed explanations follow the "mortarboard" ratings.

PERCEPTION* OF UNIVERSITY AS A WHOLE, <u>NOT</u> OF HONORS: 🎓🎓🎓🎓$^{1/2}$

*Perception is based on the university's ranking among public universities in the 2016 U.S. News Best Colleges report. Please bear in mind that the better the U.S. News ranking, the more difficult it is for an honors college or program to have a rating that equals or improves on the magazine ranking.

OVERALL HONORS RATING: 🎓🎓🎓🎓$^{1/2}$

Curriculum Requirements: 🎓🎓🎓🎓

Number of Honors Classes Offered: 🎓🎓🎓🎓🎓

Number of Honors Classes in Key Disciplines: 🎓🎓🎓🎓🎓

Extent of Honors Enrollment: 🎓🎓🎓🎓 1/2

Honors-only Class Size: 🎓🎓🎓🎓 1/2

Overall Class Size (Honors-only plus mixed, contract): 🎓🎓🎓🎓

Honors Grad Rate: 🎓🎓🎓🎓🎓

Value-Added Grad Rate: 🎓🎓🎓 1/2

Ratio of Staff to Students: 🎓🎓🎓 1/2

Priority Registration: "Honors Program students register in the first group for their class year (i.e. Honors seniors by credit are first to register before all other seniors, Honors juniors by credit are first to register before all other juniors, and so forth). They can register for Honors courses and all other courses at that time."

Honors Housing Amenities: 🎓🎓🎓

Honors Housing Availability: 🎓🎓🎓🎓 1/2

Prestigious Awards: 🎓🎓🎓🎓 1/2

RATING SCORES AND EXPLANATIONS:

Curriculum Requirements (4.0): The most important rating category, the curriculum completion requirement (classes required to complete honors) defines not only what honors students should learn but also the extent to which honors students and faculty are connected in the classroom. If there is a thesis or capstone requirement, it reinforces the individual contact and research skills so important to learning.

The average number of honors semester hours required for completion across all 50 programs is 29.0.

The *Honors Degree with Distinction* requires at least **30 credits** earned in Honors courses, including a 6-credit **thesis**. A minimum of 12 credits in 300-level courses or higher are required, not including the first-year interdisciplinary Honors colloquium.

In addition, at least 12 credits must be in the major department or in courses in collateral disciplines specifically required for the major.

For graduation, a successful oral presentation of an acceptable thesis or project must be presented to a committee of faculty approved by the major department and the University of Delaware Honors Program.

The *Honors Degree* has the same basic requirements as the Honors Degree with Distinction, but instead of the thesis, students are required to have 3 credits in an Honors Degree seminar or Honors Capstone

Course, or comparable senior experience approved by the major and the Honors Program, to be completed in one of the last two semesters of the student's degree program.

The *General Honors Award* does not result in an honors degree, but an honors award granted after the sophomore year and completion of 18 honors credits, including the 3-credit colloquium and English honors composition course. To earn the General Honors Award, students must also participate in the Honors Freshman Living Learning Community. "Honors students typically complete 12 credits of Honors coursework in the first year, including a 3-credit Honors Colloquium and a 3-credit Honors freshman composition course. The General Honors Award requires an additional 6 credits of Honors in the 2nd year and a minimum GPA of 3.3 at the end of the 2nd year."

The *Honors Foreign Language Certificate* honors program "is unique in awarding an honors certificate to students who complete 12 credit hours of honors foreign language offered by the Department of Foreign Languages and Literatures."

AP/IB credits are not counted as replacements for honors courses.

Number of Honors Classes Offered (5.0): This is a measure of the total **adjusted** honors main sections available in the term reported, not including labs and thesis. (Please read the section titled "All about Honors Classes".) An adjusted main section has 3 or more semester credits, or equivalent, and sections with fewer credits receive a lower prorated value.

The program offered an adjusted section for every **6.55** enrolled students. The average for all 50 programs is 14.2 students . The lower the number, the better.

In the term reported, **70.4% of honors enrollment was in honors-only sections; 28.8% in mixed honors sections (honors and non-honors students); and .8% reported in contract sections (regular sections in which honors students "contract" to do extra work).** The averages for all fifty programs are 81.3% in honors-only sections; 13.6 % in mixed honors sections; and 5.1% in contract sections.\

Number of Honors Classes in Key Disciplines (5.0): The 15 "key" disciplines are biological sciences; business (all); chemistry; communications (especially public speaking); computer science; economics; engineering (all); English; history; math (all); philosophy; physics; political science; psychology; and sociology/anthropology/gender studies. Interdisciplinary sections, such as those often taken for General Education credit in the first two years, do receive a lesser, prorated discipline "credit" because they introduce students to multiple disciplines in an especially engaging way, often with in-depth discussion.

For this measure, mixed and contract sections are not counted as a section in a key discipline unless students taking the sections for honors credit make up at least 10% of the total section enrollment.

In the term reported, the program had a ratio of **12.9 honors students** per each main section in some or all "key disciplines." The mean for all 50 programs is 26.3. The lower the ratio, the better.

Out of **92 adjusted sections in key disciplines**, the program had **59 honors-only sections.** The most sections were in English (13), business (11), economics (10), and engineering and history (9 each). Biology, computer science, and psychology (6 each). There were only 2 sections in math. Sociology, anthropology, and gender studies combined has 5 sections.

The program also offered 2 seminar sections for seniors only. Another 12 sections in honors colloquia for freshmen are offered each semester.

With the combination of seminars, colloquia, and a large number of classes in the academic disciplines the program is a **blended program,** but with a strong emphasis on department-based courses.

Extent of Honors Enrollment (4.5:): Not all honors students take an honors class each term, especially after the first two years. Programs that have fewer honors classes for upper-division honors students will generally have fewer total members in good standing who are actually enrolled in a given term. (Please be aware, however, that honors students not enrolled in a class for a term are still connected to the honors community through residential and extracurricular activities.)

For example, if honors students in a program occupy 1,800 honors classroom seats in a given term, and there are 3,000 honors students in good standing, the extent of enrollment is .67. For programs that require a thesis, the ratio (score) reported below might in fact be somewhat higher, since we only count "regular" class enrollment for this measure, and not thesis enrollment. The program **has a ratio of 1.37**; the mean is 1.13 for all 50 programs. The higher the ratio, the better.

Average Class Size, Honors-only Sections (4.5): Offered mostly in the first two years, honors-only classes tend to be smaller and, as the name implies, have no or very few students other than those in the honors program. These class sections are almost always much smaller than mixed or contract sections, or regular non-honors class sections in the university.

The average honors-only class size in the honors program is **16.9 students**. The average for all 50 programs is 19.0 students.

Average Class Size, Overall (4.0): The overall class calculation is based on the *proportion* of honors students in each type of class (honors-only, mixed honors, and honors contract sections). Thus it is not a raw average. The overall honors-credit class size is **24.3 students**, versus the average for all 50 programs of 26.3 students.

These class size averages also do not correspond to the number of students per honors sections numbers above. The reason is that, in computing average class size metrics, we include enrollment in each 1-2-credit section, not just sections with 3 or more credits.

Along with the honors-only average of 16.9 students, the mixed honors sections average **42.3 students,** and the contract sections with honors credit for individual honors students average **23.9 students**. Across all fifty programs, the average mixed honors section has 51.1 students, and the average contract section has 60.1 students.

Honors Graduation Rate (5.0): The rating is based on the actual grad rate for students who entered the program six years earlier, whether or not the students remained in honors. The **actual rate of 91.3%** is also compared to the rates of other programs with the same test score entry requirement range, and then adjusted to the **score of 91.9%.** In some cases this measure favors programs within universities with relatively higher test scores for the student population as a whole. The average honors graduation rate for all programs with similar test scores required for admission is 86.2%.

Value-Added Grad Rate (3.5): The value-added rate measures the extent to which the adjusted score listed above exceeds the six-year grad rate for the university as a whole. **The university-wide rate is 81%.** Note: This measure generally favors programs within universities with relatively lower test scores for the student population as a whole.

Ratio of Staff to Honors Students (3.5): There is 1 staff member for every **187.2** students. (Mean ratio for all 50 programs is 1 staff member for every 135.6 students.)

Honors Residence Halls, Amenities (3.0): About 600 honors students living in honors housing, all freshmen, are in Redding Hall. The residence has traditional double rooms and hall baths. The location is quite good. The nearest dining is in Russell Hall.

"All freshman Honors students are required to live in Honors housing during their first year unless they are living at home with a parent/guardian. Freshman Honors Housing is important because it gives students an opportunity to study together, share their talents and interests with each other, and also have upper-division Honors peer mentors (Munson Fellows) who guide them through their first year. The Munson Fellows are specially trained to assist with academic questions and registration, but are also event planners and community builders to give the freshmen a complete living/learning experience."

As for upperclassmen in honors housing, about 100 of them, Harter and Sharp Halls are the honors residences. Sharp is air-conditioned, while Harter is not. The most convenient dining for both is the Caesar Rodney Dining Complex.

Honors Residence Halls, Availability (4.5): This rating compares the number of rooms in honors residence halls to the number of honors freshman and sophomore members in good standing, about 936. The ratio for the honors program is **.75** rooms for each first- and second-year student. The average for all fifty programs is .63 rooms.

Prestigious Awards (4.5): The awards that we track and include are listed in the section titled "Prestigious Scholarships." The awards are sometimes won by students who are not in an honors college or program, but increasingly many are enrolled in honors programs. It is also a trend that honors colleges and programs help to prepare their students for the awards competitions.

UD students have won 10 Rhodes scholarships, 1 Gates Cambridge scholarship, 3 Marshall scholarships, and 20 Truman awards. They have also won a total of 46 Goldwater scholarships. Of importance is that the trend is upward: Since 1990, UD students have won half the Rhodes total, all of the Gates Cambridge and Marshall scholarships, 39 of the Goldwater awards, and 14 of the Truman scholarships. UD Honors students alone have won about 90% of these.

UNRATED FEATURES

Continuation Requirements: After completion of freshman year, a cumulative GPA of 3.20. After completion of sophomore and junior years, a cumulative GPA of 3.30. For graduation with honors or honors distinction, 3.40 GPA.

Academic Strengths, National Rankings: This is based on national rankings of *graduate* programs in 15 disciplines, except engineering and business, where undergraduate rankings are used.

The average departmental rank at UD is in the low 70's nationwide. Leading departments are education (35), engineering (56), chemistry (60), English (63), history and sociology (64), psychology (67), earth sciences (69), and computer science (70). The graduate programming in chemical engineering is ranked 9th in the nation.

Undergraduate Research: "As of graduation this upcoming spring 2016, we have approximately 85 students conducting undergraduate research with a thesis on track to complete an Honors Degree with Distinction. We also have approximately 115 students that conducted undergraduate research this past summer with our Summer Scholars Program."

Study Abroad: "The University of Delaware was the first institution to have a study abroad trip (the 1923 trip to Paris). Since then, UD has been a leader in Study Abroad. One reason for UD's success is our winter session (optional 5-week term in January through early February). We have a large variety of study abroad programs in the winter session, allowing our students to travel even if their majors are structured so that they cannot be away for an entire semester. In our study abroad history, we have been to all 7 continents. There are merit-based and need-based scholarships for study abroad, ranging from $500 to $4,000.

"UD semester study abroad programs are available in Japan, Argentina, Spain, England, France, and Austria. Semester exchange programs are available with Bond University, Australia; The German American Federation; Hong Kong Polytechnic, Lisbon University, Portugal; Lyon, France; Seinan, Japan; Soka, Japan; the Swiss School of Tourism and Hospitality; and the University of Pretoria, South Africa.

"The UD Honors Program just completed its third winter session Honors-only Study Abroad trip to Italy this year. Students must apply for this trip through a competitive selection process. They take two 300-level Honors courses: one content course and one service learning course that they plan together as a group the semester before the trip.

"The Honors Program also coordinates the only international Alternative Spring Break Trip to the Dominican Republic. The trip cost is subsidized by the Honors Program.

"Students can also apply for Honors Enrichment Awards to participate in individual non-credit-bearing opportunities, including experiences that require travel abroad."

Financial Aid: "All freshmen admitted to the University of Delaware's Honors Program are also offered a merit scholarship. *These awards vary from $1,000 a year to a **full ride** that covers tuition, room, board and fees. Merit Awards are offered irrespective of financial need. Awards for non-residents are larger than residents as a result of the tuition difference.* The University also sponsors the Distinguished Scholars program, which allows the strongest Honors applicants each year to compete for named awards.

These awards range in amounts that cover tuition to those that provide funding for all expenses including a stipend for an enrichment activity.

"All admitted freshmen are also eligible for need-based aid with need determined by the EFC on the FAFSA. Students are eligible for federal funding including the Pell grant, work study, and both subsidized and unsubsidized loans. UD also has institutional aid and provides need-based grants to eligible Honors students. UD will meet the cost for all in-state Honors students up to the cost of the bill minus all federal aid including loans. Total loan costs for a resident will not exceed 25% of total cost of a degree.

"Several departments may also have institutional aid available, which is distributed based on talent or academic interest. Music scholarships require an audition."

Honors Fees: None.

Placement Experiences: 2015 graduates:

Post-Graduate Education--Carnegie Mellon University; Columbia University; Duke University; Harvard Law School; Harvard University; Johns Hopkins University; The London School of Economics and Political Science; MIT; Stanford University; Texas A&M College of Veterinary Medicine; Tulane University Law School; UCLA Law School; University of California, Davis; University of Massachusetts Medical School; University of North Carolina Chapel Hill; University of Pennsylvania; University of Pennsylvania Law School; University of Virginia School of Medicine; Villanova School of Law; Yale University.

Employers--Amazon; Deloitte Consulting; DuPont; Ernst and Young; Food and Drug Administration; Goldman Sachs; Google; JPMorgan Chase; McKinsey and Company; Microsoft; Peace Corps; Spanish Government Ministry of Education and Culture; Teach for America; The Boeing Company; W.L. Gore and Associates; University Massy Cancer Center.

Degree of Difference: This is based on the differences between (1) the average (2015, two-part) SAT scores for enrolled honors students (1388) and (2) the average test scores for all students in the university (1200) as a whole. The test scores may be an indication of how "elite" honors students may be perceived as compared to students in the university as a whole. The scores can also provide an indication of how well prepared the non-honors students in the university may be. **Please keep in mind that neither high nor low test scores determine the overall quality of a program.**

NAME: UNIVERSITY OF GEORGIA HONORS PROGRAM.

Date Established: 1960.

Location: Athens, Georgia.

University Full-time Undergraduate Enrollment: 25,371.

Honors Members in Good Standing: 2,390 (mean size of all 50 programs is 1,742).,

Honors Average Admission Statistics: ACT, 33; old two-part SAT, 1469. Est. new SAT score, 1510. UGA is among the top three most selective programs under review.

Average High School GPA/Class Rank: None listed.

Basic Admission Requirements: "UGA Honors does not have a set minimum for board scores or HS GPA."

Application Deadline(s): *Please verify with each program, as some deadlines could change.*

February 1, 2017; (notification April 1, 2017).

Honors Programs with old SAT scores from 1402—1469: UCF, Connecticut, Kentucky, Washington, Maryland, North Carolina, UC Irvine, Kansas, Minnesota, Tennessee, South Carolina, Clemson, UT Austin, Georgia.

Administrative Staff: 19 FTEs.

RATINGS AT A GLANCE: For all mortarboard ratings immediately below, a score of 5 is the maximum and represents a comparison with all 50 honors colleges and programs. More detailed explanations follow the "mortarboard" ratings.

PERCEPTION* OF UNIVERSITY AS A WHOLE, NOT OF HONORS: 🎓🎓🎓🎓 1/2

*Perception is based on the university's ranking among public universities in the 2016 U.S. News Best Colleges report. Please bear in mind that the better the U.S. News ranking, the more difficult it is for an honors college or program to have a rating that equals or improves on the magazine ranking.

OVERALL HONORS RATING: 🎓🎓🎓🎓🎓

Curriculum Requirements: 🎓🎓🎓🎓🎓

Number of Honors Classes Offered: 🎓🎓🎓🎓 1/2

Number of Honors Classes in Key Disciplines: 🎓🎓🎓🎓

Extent of Honors Enrollment: 🎓🎓🎓 1/2

Honors-only Class Size: 🎓🎓🎓🎓 1/2

Overall Class Size (Honors-only plus mixed, contract): 🎓🎓🎓🎓

Honors Grad Rate: 🎓🎓🎓🎓🎓

Value-Added Grad Rate: 🎓🎓🎓 1/2

Ratio of Staff to Students: 🎓🎓🎓🎓

Priority Registration: Yes, honors students register for all courses, honors and otherwise, with the first group of students during each year they are in the program.

Honors Housing Amenities: 🎓🎓🎓🎓

Honors Housing Availability: 🎓🎓🎓

Prestigious Awards: 🎓🎓🎓🎓🎓

RATING SCORES AND EXPLANATIONS:

Curriculum Requirements (5.0): The most important rating category, the curriculum completion requirement (classes required to complete honors) defines not only what honors students should learn but also the extent to which honors students and faculty are connected in the classroom. If there is a thesis or capstone requirement, it reinforces the individual contact and research skills so important to learning.

The average number of honors semester hours required for completion across all 50 programs is 29.0.

For Graduation with Highest Honors, students must complete at least **36** credits, including 9 courses of honors credit (about 30 semester hours). These must include at least 1 honors seminar and at least 3 upper-division honors courses. Students must also complete a **6-credit thesis, OR a 6-credit internship with a research component, OR 9-12 credits in graduate courses.** Finally, students must finish with a very high GPA, 3.90.

For Graduation with High Honors, students must complete the same requirements as above, but the GPA requirement is 3.70.

For Graduation with Honors, the 30-credit course requirement listed above applies but students do not complete the 6-credit thesis/internship or the 9-12 credits of graduate work. The final GPA must be at least 3.40.

AP/IB credits are not counted as replacements for honors courses.

Number of Honors Classes Offered (4.5): This is a measure of the total **adjusted** honors main sections available in the term reported, not including labs and thesis. (Please read the section titled "All about Honors Classes".) An adjusted main section has 3 or more semester credits, or equivalent, and sections with fewer credits receive a lower prorated value.

The honors program offered an adjusted section for every **10.4** enrolled students. The average for all 50 programs is 14.2 students . The lower the number, the better.

In the term reported, **75.4%** of honors enrollment was **in honors-only sections; 2.0% in mixed honors sections (honors and non-honors students); and 22.6% in contract sections (regular sections in which honors students "contract" to do extra work).** The averages for all fifty programs are 81.3% in honors-only sections; 13.6 % in mixed honors sections; and 5.1% in contract sections.

Number of Honors Classes in Key Disciplines (4.0): The 15 "key" disciplines are biological sciences; business (all); chemistry; communications (especially public speaking); computer science; economics; engineering (all); English; history; math (all); philosophy; physics; political science; psychology; and sociology/anthropology/gender studies. Interdisciplinary sections, such as those often taken for General Education credit in the first two years, do receive a lesser, prorated discipline "credit" because they introduce students to multiple disciplines in an especially engaging way, often with in-depth discussion.

For this measure, mixed and contract sections are not counted as a section in a key discipline unless students taking the sections for honors credit make up at least 10% of the total section enrollment.

In the term reported, the program had a ratio of **22.9 honors students** per each main section in some or all "key disciplines." The mean for all 50 programs is 26.3. The lower the ratio, the better.

Out of **72 adjusted sections in key disciplines**, the program had **58 honors-only sections.** The most sections were in English and psychology (12 each), business and political science (7 each), history and philosophy (6 apiece), economics and math (4 each), chemistry and communications (2 each), and biology (1). Sociology, anthropology, or gender studies had a combined total of 6 sections. There were no sections in physics or computer science.

Although there are a few seminars offered, UGA honors is an outstanding example of a **discipline-based program.**

Extent of Honors Enrollment (3.5:): Not all honors students take an honors class each term, especially after the first two years. Programs that have fewer honors classes for upper-division honors students will generally have fewer total members in good standing who are actually enrolled in a given term. (Please be aware, however, that honors students not enrolled in a class for a term are still connected to the honors community through residential and extracurricular activities.)

For example, if honors students in a program occupy 1,800 honors classroom seats in a given term, and there are 3,000 honors students in good standing, the extent of enrollment is .67. For programs that require a thesis, the ratio (score) reported below might in fact be somewhat higher, since we only count "regular" class enrollment for this measure, and not thesis enrollment. The program **has a ratio of .93**; the mean is 1.13 for all 50 programs. The higher the ratio, the better.

Average Class Size, Honors-only Sections (4.5): Offered mostly in the first two years, honors-only classes tend to be smaller and, as the name implies, have no or very few students other than those in the honors program. These class sections are almost always much smaller than mixed or contract sections, or regular non-honors class sections in the university.

The average honors-only class size in the honors program is **18.0 students**. The average for all 50 programs is 19.0 students.

Average Class Size, Overall (4.0): The overall class calculation is based on the *proportion* of honors students in each type of class (honors-only, mixed honors, and honors contract sections). Thus it is not a raw average. The overall honors-credit class size is **23.6 students**, versus the average for all 50 programs of 26.3 students.

These class size averages also do not correspond to the number of students per honors sections numbers above. The reason is that, in computing average class size metrics, we include enrollment in each 1-2-credit section, not just sections with 3 or more credits.

Along with the honors-only average of 18.0 students, the mixed honors sections average **5.6 students,** and the contract sections with honors credit for individual honors students average **43.8 students.** Across all fifty programs, the average mixed honors section has 51.1 students, and the average contract section has 60.1 students.

Honors Graduation Rate (5.0): The rating is based on the actual grad rate for students who entered the program six years earlier, whether or not the students remained in honors. The **actual rate of 96.7%** is also compared to the rates of other programs with the same test score entry requirement range, and then adjusted to the **score of 97.1%.** In some cases this measure favors programs within universities with relatively higher test scores for the student population as a whole. The average honors graduation rate for all programs with similar test scores required for admission is 92.6%.

Value-Added Grad Rate (3.5): The value-added rate measures the extent to which the adjusted score listed above exceeds the six-year grad rate for the university as a whole. **The university-wide rate is 85%.** Note: This measure generally favors programs within universities with relatively lower test scores for the student population as a whole.

Ratio of Staff to Honors Students (4.0): There is 1 staff member for every **125.8 students**. (Mean ratio for all 50 programs is 1 staff member for every 135.6 students.)

Honors Residence Halls, Amenities (4.0): "Myers Hall serves as the Honors magnet residence hall at UGA. This beautifully renovated hall is home to 250 first-year Honors students, affording them the opportunity to live and study in a learning community of like-minded peers. An Honors satellite advising office is also conveniently located in Myers Hall."

Myers has 85% corridor rooms and hall baths, along with 15% suite-style rooms with connecting baths. The residence hall is air-conditioned, has on-site laundry on every floor, and is notable for having a kitchen area on each floor. The Myers location is excellent—and the dining options are remarkable. Snelling and Oglethorpe are convenient, yes, but here's the best news: "UGA Food Services has participated in the Loyal E. Horton Dining Awards program (the gold standard for national recognition in this area) for 25 years, receiving a national record of 68 Horton awards since 1987."

Honors Residence Halls, Availability (3.0): This rating compares the number of rooms in honors residence halls to the number of honors freshman and sophomore members in good standing, about 1195. The ratio for the honors program is **.21** rooms for each first- and second-year student. The average for all fifty programs is .63 rooms.

Prestigious Awards (5.0): The awards that we track and include are listed in the section titled "Prestigious Scholarships." The awards are sometimes won by students who are not in an honors college or program, but increasingly many are enrolled in honors programs. It is also a trend that honors colleges and programs help to prepare their students for the awards competitions.

UGA students have an outstanding record of earning prestigious awards and consistently win a lot of awards to undergraduates, including 17 Udall scholarships, 49 Goldwater scholarships, and 11 Boren scholarships. The UGA record of winning other prestigious scholarships is equally impressive: 23 Rhodes scholarships; 6 Gates Cambridge awards; 7 Marshall scholarships; and 18 Truman awards. UGA honors students have won an extremely high percentage of total awards in this category.

UNRATED FEATURES

Continuation Requirements: 3.40.

Academic Strengths, National Rankings: This is based on national rankings of *graduate* programs in 15 disciplines, except engineering and business, where undergraduate rankings are used.

The average national departmental ranking at UGA is about 65th in the nation, lead by business (29), education (34), biology (42), sociology (46), psychology (48), math and psychology (both 52), chemistry (56), and economics (64).

Undergraduate Research: An outstanding feature of honors at UGA is The Center for Undergraduate Research Opportunities (CURO), a faculty-mentored undergraduate research initiative.

"Though it is still administered through the Honors Program, today CURO is open to all undergraduates at UGA without regard to discipline, major, or GPA.

"CURO research courses are faculty-mentored, and individualized syllabi are facilitated for each student. Students can become involved with an existing research project, or they can ask faculty mentors to oversee projects of their own design. Thus, students can choose their own research agenda to fit their own professional and academic goals, yet pursue it under faculty guidance.

"Through CURO, students can begin faculty-mentored undergraduate research as early as their first semester and can continue for up to four full years. In 2014-15, 488 unique students completed 704 CURO courses with 302 faculty members from 83 academic departments for a total of 2253 credit hours. *Of those 488 students, 380 (78%) were in the Honors Program.* [Emphasis added.]

"CURO also offers a range of other opportunities, including a summer research fellowship program; an undergraduate research symposium; an online student research journal; and a specialized undergraduate research scholarship to support students from underrepresented groups.

"Participation in CURO coursework and programming has been linked to two important indicators of student success: higher GPAs and increased 4- and 6-year graduation rates. Since the inception of CURO, every recipient from UGA of a Udall or Goldwater scholarship has participated in CURO research coursework, as is the case with recipients of Rhodes, Marshall, and Gates Cambridge scholarships." [Emphasis added.]

Study Abroad: "During the academic year 2014-15, 379 unique honors students earned credit for 411 study abroad experiences – about 15% of our student population. Of the 665 Honors students who graduated in academic year 2014-2015, 383 (or **57%**) report having completed some form of travel study while at UGA.

"The Honors International Scholars Program supports second- and third-year honors students engaging in overseas opportunities. In 2015, this program gave **58** students a total of **$215,500** to participate in traditional university-sponsored study abroad programs, university-to-university exchanges, intensive language-training institutes, internships, and public service projects.

"UGA has year-round residential centers in Oxford, England; Cortina, Italy; and in the Monteverde region of Costa Rica. (All first-year Foundation Fellows study at Oxford University and live in the UGA house there.) Others enroll in semester or year-round exchanges at one of UGA's 50 exchange partners abroad."

Financial Aid: From the 2014 response: "Approximately 85% of UGA students are in-state and are eligible for the HOPE Scholarship. A full 100% of in-state Honors students carry this scholarship ([the very high] selection criteria ensure this).

"In addition to these broad scholarships, the Honors Program administers three internal scholarship programs: (1) the Foundation Fellowship (which approximates the full cost of attendance and supplies a generous set of enrichment funds to support study abroad, internships, undergraduate research, etc.), awarded to a total of about 90 Honors students; (2) the Ramsey Honors Scholarship (which offers approximately 75% of the financial support of the Foundation Fellowship), awarded to between 20 and 30 total Honors students; and (3) the CURO Honors Scholarship, which supplies a $2,000 annual stipend (on top of other awards) to 40 Honors students from underrepresented groups, who specialize in undergraduate research.

"In addition to these scholarships, there are several other funding opportunities for students through the Honors Program, including the HISP awards mentioned above, as well as Honors Internship programs in New York City, Washington, DC, and Savannah, GA (which supply stipends of $3,000 to $4,000); the Ash Service Award (a $3,000 stipend); and the Crane Leadership Scholarship (a $1,000 award).

"It should be noted that the majority of these funding opportunities are directly attributable to the fact that the Honors Program has its own, very active fundraising office."

Honors Fees: None.

Placement Experiences: None listed.

Degree of Difference: This is based on the differences between (1) the average (2015, two-part) SAT scores for enrolled honors students (1469) and (2) the average test scores for all students in the university (1235) as a whole. The test scores may be an indication of how "elite" honors students may be perceived as compared to students in the university as a whole. The scores can also provide an indication of how well prepared the non-honors students in the university may be. **Please keep in mind that neither high nor low test scores determine the overall quality of a program.**

NAME: GEORGIA STATE UNIVERSITY HONORS COLLEGE.

Date Established: 2011.

Location: Atlanta, Georgia.

University Full-time Undergraduate Enrollment: 18,976.

Honors Members in Good Standing: 1,602 (mean size of all 50 programs is 1,742).

Honors Average Admission Statistics: Fall 2015: ACT, 29; old two-part SAT, 1320. Est. new SAT score, 1380. Fall 2016: ACT, 30-31; old two-part SAT, 1360; est. new SAT, 1420.

Average High School GPA/Class Rank: Fall 2015, 3.80; Fall 2016, 3.85.

Basic Admission Requirements: ACT, 28. Old SAT, 1250; est. new score, 1310. High school GPA, 3.5.

Application Deadline(s): *Please verify with each program, as some deadlines could change.*

"Admission is limited to approximately the top 5-7% of the incoming first-year students each year. For best consideration for the Honors College and merit scholarships please apply by the Early Action Deadline (November 15, 2016)."

Honors Programs with old SAT scores from 1315—1350: Idaho, Georgia State, Virginia Tech, Utah, Iowa, Auburn, Houston, Mississippi, VCU.

Administrative Staff: 12.

RATINGS AT A GLANCE: For all mortarboard ratings immediately below, a score of 5 is the maximum and represents a comparison with all 50 honors colleges and programs. More detailed explanations follow the "mortarboard" ratings.

PERCEPTION* OF UNIVERSITY AS A WHOLE, NOT OF HONORS: 🎓🎓🎓

*Perception is based on the university's ranking among public universities in the 2016 U.S. News Best Colleges report. Please bear in mind that the better the U.S. News ranking, the more difficult it is for an honors college or program to have a rating that equals or improves on the magazine ranking.

OVERALL HONORS RATING: 🎓🎓🎓 1/2

Curriculum Requirements: 🎓🎓🎓 1/2

Number of Honors Classes Offered: 🎓🎓🎓🎓🎓

Number of Honors Classes in Key Disciplines: 🎓🎓🎓🎓🎓

Extent of Honors Enrollment:

Honors-only Class Size:

Overall Class Size (Honors-only plus mixed, contract):

Honors Grad Rate: 1/2

Value-Added Grad Rate:

Ratio of Staff to Students:

Priority Registration: Yes, honors students register for all courses, honors and otherwise, with the first group of students during each year they are in the program.

Honors Housing Amenities:

Honors Housing Availability:

Prestigious Awards:

RATING SCORES AND EXPLANATIONS:

Curriculum Requirements (3.5): The most important rating category, the curriculum completion requirement (classes required to complete honors) defines not only what honors students should learn but also the extent to which honors students and faculty are connected in the classroom. If there is a thesis or capstone requirement, it reinforces the individual contact and research skills so important to learning.

The average number of honors semester hours required for completion across all 50 programs is 29.0.

Completion of the Advanced and Research Honors level requires a total of **24** honors credits. This includes 18 course credits (including 6 credits in colloquia), and a 6-credit honors **thesis.** A maximum of 9 course credits may be in the form of honors contract courses.

Completion of Advanced Honors is the same as above, minus the thesis requirement.

General Honors requires 13 credits, six of which must be in honors colloquia.

AP/IB credits are not counted as replacements for honors courses.

Number of Honors Classes Offered (5.0): This is a measure of the total **adjusted** honors main sections available in the term reported, not including labs and thesis. (Please read the section titled "All about

Honors Classes".) An adjusted main section has 3 or more semester credits, or equivalent, and sections with fewer credits receive a lower prorated value.

The college offered a section for every **8.5** enrolled students. The average for all 50 programs is 14.2. The lower the number, the better.

In the term reported, **54.0%** of honors enrollment was **in honors-only sections; 41.0% in mixed honors sections (honors and non-honors students); and 5.0% in contract sections (regular sections in which honors students "contract" to do extra work).** The averages for all fifty programs are 81.3% in honors-only sections; 13.6 % in mixed honors sections; and 5.1% in contract sections.

Number of Honors Classes in Key Disciplines (5.0): The 15 "key" disciplines are biological sciences; business (all); chemistry; communications (especially public speaking); computer science; economics; engineering (all); English; history; math (all); philosophy; physics; political science; psychology; and sociology/anthropology/gender studies. Interdisciplinary sections, such as those often taken for General Education credit in the first two years, do receive a lesser, prorated discipline "credit" because they introduce students to multiple disciplines in an especially engaging way, often with in-depth discussion.

For this measure, mixed and contract sections are not counted as a section in a key discipline unless students taking the sections for honors credit make up at least 10% of the total section enrollment.

In the term reported, the program had a ratio of **12.8 honors students** per each main section in some or all "key disciplines." The mean for all 50 programs is 26.3. The lower the ratio, the better.

Out of **50 adjusted sections in key disciplines**, the Honors College had **22** that were **honors-only sections.** The most sections were in biology (12), philosophy and psychology (6 each), communications, economics, math, and political science (4 each), and business, chemistry, and history (2 each). The only subjects missing were computer science and engineering, the latter not being a department at Georgia State.

The college also offered about 25 sections in 1-credit seminars in the Fall, and another four or so 3-credit seminars, including "Motivations of Terrorists and Terrorist Groups" and "Youth Development in Context: The Immigrant Experience."

Although there are a few seminars offered, the Georgia State Honors College is mostly a **discipline-based program.**

Extent of Honors Enrollment (3.0): Not all honors students take an honors class each term, especially after the first two years. Programs that have fewer honors classes for upper-division honors students will generally have fewer total members in good standing who are actually enrolled in a given term. (Please be aware, however, that honors students not enrolled in a class for a term are still connected to the honors community through residential and extracurricular activities.)

For example, if honors students in a program occupy 1,800 honors classroom seats in a given term, and there are 3,000 honors students in good standing, the extent of enrollment is .67. For programs that require a thesis, the ratio (score) reported below might in fact be somewhat higher, since we only count

"regular" class enrollment for this measure, and not thesis enrollment. The college **has a ratio of .76**; the mean is 1.13 for all 50 programs. The higher the ratio, the better.

Average Class Size, Honors-only Sections (4.0): Offered mostly in the first two years, honors-only classes tend to be smaller and, as the name implies, have no or very few students other than those in the honors program. These class sections are almost always much smaller than mixed or contract sections, or regular non-honors class sections in the university.

The average honors-only class size in the honors program is **18.0 students**. The average for all 50 programs is 19.0 students.

Average Class Size, Overall (4.0): The overall class calculation is based on the *proportion* of honors students in each type of class (honors-only, mixed honors, and honors contract sections). Thus it is not a raw average. The overall honors-credit class size is **25.3 students**, versus the average for all 50 programs of 26.3 students.

These class size averages also do not correspond to the number of students per honors sections numbers above. The reason is that, in computing average class size metrics, we include enrollment in each 1-2-credit section, not just sections with 3 or more credits.

Along with the honors-only average of 18.0 students, the mixed honors sections average **34.7 students,** and the contract sections with honors credit for individual honors students average **25.2 students.** Across all fifty programs, the average mixed honors section has 51.1 students, and the average contract section has 60.1 students.

Honors Graduation Rate (3.5): The rating is based on the actual grad rate for students who entered the program six years earlier, whether or not the students remained in honors. The **actual rate of 81%** is also compared to the rates of other programs with the same test score entry requirement range, and then adjusted to the **score of 80.6%.** In some cases this measure favors programs within universities with relatively higher test scores for the student population as a whole. The average honors graduation rate for all programs with similar test scores required for admission is 83.4%.

Value-Added Grad Rate (5.0): The value-added rate measures the extent to which the adjusted score listed above exceeds the six-year grad rate for the university as a whole. The university-wide rate is 54%. Note: This measure generally favors programs within universities with relatively lower test scores for the student population as a whole.

Ratio of Staff to Honors Students (4.0): There is 1 staff member for every **133.5** students. (Mean ratio for all 50 programs is 1 staff member for every 135.6 students.)

Honors Residence Halls, Amenities (4.0): University Commons is the honors residence, featuring four-bedroom, two-bath apartments. The residence houses about 170 freshmen and upperclassmen. It is air-conditioned. The most convenient dining is in Piedmont North.

Honors Residence Halls, Availability (5.0): This rating compares the number of rooms in honors residence halls to the number of honors freshman and sophomore members in good standing, about 801.

The ratio for the honors program is **1.00** rooms for each first- and second-year student. The average for all fifty programs is .63 rooms.

"Honors housing placement is actually guaranteed to ALL entering freshmen who complete the housing application and pay the application fee on or before May 1st; returning upperclassmen are also guaranteed Honors housing placement when they apply and pay by their required dates."

Prestigious Awards (3.0): The awards that we track and include are listed in the section titled "Prestigious Scholarships." The awards are sometimes won by students who are not in an honors college or program, but increasingly many are enrolled in honors programs. It is also a trend that honors colleges and programs help to prepare their students for the awards competitions.

"Georgia State has produced 24 Fulbright Scholars, 10 Boren Scholars, and 42 Gilman Scholars. Georgia State undergraduates have also won 2 prestigious Goldwater Scholarships, the ThinkSwiss Scholarship, the Mellon Undergraduate Curatorial Fellowship, and the Kernan Social Justice Fellowship. Since its inception three years ago, the Honors College has advanced finalists for several competitive national scholarships including the Marshall Scholarship and the Mitchell Scholarship."

UNRATED FEATURES

Continuation Requirements: 3.30.

Academic Strengths, National Rankings: This is based on national rankings of *graduate* programs in 15 disciplines, except engineering and business, where undergraduate rankings are used.

The information systems specialty in the Robinson College of Business is ranked 12th in the nation. The Education School is 59th. Among the other leading departments are economics (72), sociology (76), and political science (83). English (98), psychology (101), physics (112), computer science (113), history (116), and chemistry (117) are among other departments ranked nationally.

Undergraduate Research: Honors College Undergraduate Research Program is called "Discover with Honors."

The Dean reports that the "Honors College offers several signature research experiences for students within the college: the University Assistantship Program, the annual Georgia State Undergraduate Research Conference, the Honors Thesis Project, and Discovery, the Honors College Undergraduate Research Journal.

"The University Assistantship Program offers students the opportunity to be matched with a faculty member to work on research, scholarship, or creative work. Its mission is to involve students from all disciplines in an experiential learning opportunity that is in alignment with their career interests. Through the UAP, students are offered stipends in the amount of $2,500/year for their work.

"The Georgia State Undergraduate Research Conference is held annually and hosted by the Honors College. Students have the opportunity to present their work in the form of a poster, an oral, artistic, or musical display. Annually, about 150 students, sponsored by a faculty mentor, participate in this conference. The top three winners in each of four categories are awarded cash prizes.

"The Honors Thesis Project is a curricular (six semester hours) opportunity for students to work on an independent study. Sponsored by a faculty mentor, students from all disciplines are able to complete critical literature reviews, empirically-based studies, and creative projects.

"*Discovery*, the Honors College research journal, offers Honors students the opportunity to submit their work for peer-review and publication. Published electronically by BePress, as well as in printed format, Discovery is a showcase for undergraduate research. "Finally, all Honors students in good standing may apply to the college for travel and research grants to present their undergraduate research in local, regional, national and international disciplinary conferences."

Study Abroad: "Honors students regularly register for study abroad experiences led by Georgia State University professors in the May and summer semesters, and earn honors credit. Several faculty affiliates who teach seminars in the college conduct a related student abroad experience; for example, a seminar on Human Rights in Argentina precedes a Maymester study abroad.

"The Honors College also has a summer research intensive exchange program with Hong Kong Baptist University in chemistry. Students in this program are matched with research mentors, complete a research project, and present it to the host country and their own when they return.

"Study abroad and exchange programs require financial resources. The Office of International Initiatives offers a large number of scholarships; other awards are available through departments and research centers. For students who have never traveled outside of the United States, the OII offers full scholarship is available for any study abroad or exchange program of any length. In addition, the OII offers a larger number of smaller scholarships to defray expenses."

Financial Aid: "The Presidential Scholarship provides eight semesters of full tuition and fees, housing, living and textbook expenses, as well as a University Assistantship and a study abroad stipend. The Presidential Scholarship, the most prestigious scholarship offered to entering Georgia State freshmen, was offered to ten outstanding students in fall 2015.

"The University Assistantship, available to both entering freshmen and, by recommendation, to enrolled Honors students, provides $2,500 per academic year to students conducting mentored research.

"Georgia State Foundation scholarships, awarded at admission to all Honors students who are admitted Early Action, provide up to $3,000 per academic year to offset the cost of attendance.

"The Honors College also offers scholarship support to enrolled students:

- Dugald-Hudson Memorial Scholarship – provides $1,000 per semester to rising juniors;
- Kirkland-Sattelmeyer Scholarship – provides $1,000 per semester to rising juniors;
- Mary Grabbe Memorial fund – provides $1,000 grants for study abroad;
- Apperson Family Scholarship – provides $500 per semester for Honors students not admitted as entering freshmen;

- Madison Roarabaugh Scholarship – provides $500 per semester;
- Alonzo B. and Norris F. Herndon Human Rights Scholarships – provides grants of $500 per semester, for up to six semesters;
- Honors College Excellence Awards – provides varying awards for outstanding scholarship and research."

Honors Fees: None.

Placement Experiences: Honors grads are studying law at Emory, Notre Dame, UC Berkeley, Georgia, Michigan, Virginia, Washington University in St. Louis, and Yale, among others. They are studying medicine at Duke, George Washington, Harvard, Georgia, among others. Among the grad schools they are attending are Brown, Carnegie-Mellon, Columbia, Cornell, Emory, Georgetown, Johns Hopkins, Harvard, London School of Economics and Political Science, NYU, Stanford, UC Berkeley, Michigan, UT Austin, UW Madison, Washington University St. Louis, Yale, and many others.

Honors college grads are employed at Emory, Federal Reserve Bank of Atlanta, Ernst & Young, Office of the Governor of Georgia, and Proctor and Gamble, among many more.

Degree of Difference: This is based on the differences between (1) the average (2015, two-part) SAT scores for enrolled honors students (1320) and (2) the average test scores for all students in the university (1070) as a whole. The test scores may be an indication of how "elite" honors students may be perceived as compared to students in the university as a whole. The scores can also provide an indication of how well prepared the non-honors students in the university may be. **Please keep in mind that neither high nor low test scores determine the overall quality of a program.**

NAME: THE HONORS COLLEGE, UNIVERSITY OF HOUSTON.

Date Established: 1958.

Location: Houston, Texas.

University Full-time Undergraduate Enrollment: 23,973.

Honors Members in Good Standing: 1,951 (mean size of all 50 programs is 1,742).

Honors Average Admission Statistics: ACT, 29.5. Old SAT, 1337; est. new SAT, 1400.

Average High School GPA/Class Rank: 3.75; top 10% of high school class.

Basic Admission Requirements: "The Honors College application process does not employ minimum requirements in the admissions review process. Applicants are holistically evaluated – academics (grades, types of classes taken, trend in grades, test scores), writing, and leadership/involvement are considered by the admissions committee. Academically talented students who can add to the vibrant Honors community are sought. The admissions committee consists of Honors administrators, deans, faculty, and staff."

Application Deadline(s): *Please verify with each program, as some deadlines could change.*

December 1, 2016, for priority consideration; final deadline April 1, 2017.

Honors Programs with old SAT scores from 1315—1350: Idaho, Georgia State, Virginia Tech, Utah, Iowa, Auburn, Houston, Mississippi, VCU.

Administrative Staff: 29 FTEs.

RATINGS AT A GLANCE: For all mortarboard ratings immediately below, a score of 5 is the maximum and represents a comparison with all 50 honors colleges and programs. More detailed explanations follow the "mortarboard" ratings.

PERCEPTION* OF UNIVERSITY AS A WHOLE, NOT OF HONORS: 🎓🎓🎓

*Perception is based on the university's ranking among public universities in the 2016 U.S. News Best Colleges report. Please bear in mind that the better the U.S. News ranking, the more difficult it is for an honors college or program to have a rating that equals or improves on the magazine ranking.

OVERALL HONORS RATING: 🎓🎓🎓🎓🎓

Curriculum Requirements: 🎓🎓🎓🎓🎓

Number of Honors Classes Offered: 🎓🎓🎓🎓🎓

Number of Honors Classes in Key Disciplines: 🎓🎓🎓🎓🎓

Extent of Honors Enrollment: 🎓🎓🎓🎓🎓

Honors-only Class Size: 🎓🎓🎓^1/2

Overall Class Size (Honors-only plus mixed, contract): 🎓🎓🎓🎓

Honors Grad Rate: 🎓🎓🎓

Value-Added Grad Rate: 🎓🎓🎓🎓🎓

Ratio of Staff to Students: 🎓🎓🎓🎓🎓

Priority Registration: Yes, honors students register for all courses, honors and otherwise, immediately after athletes and veterans (the first group), during each year they are in the program.

Honors Housing Amenities: 🎓🎓🎓🎓🎓

Honors Housing Availability: 🎓🎓🎓🎓^1/2

Prestigious Awards: 🎓🎓🎓

RATING SCORES AND EXPLANATIONS:

Curriculum Requirements (5.0): The most important rating category, the curriculum completion requirement (classes required to complete honors) defines not only what honors students should learn but also the extent to which honors students and faculty are connected in the classroom. If there is a thesis or capstone requirement, it reinforces the individual contact and research skills so important to learning.

The average number of honors semester hours required for completion across all 50 programs is 29.0.

The honors college requires a minimum of **36 credits** to complete the University Honors with Honors in the Major. A 6-credit **thesis** is required.

Graduation with University Honors requires 33 total credits, including a 3-credit capstone.

Completion of Collegiate Honors requires 18 credits, including a 3-credit capstone.

Collegiate Honors in the Major requires 15 credits, including a 6-credit thesis.

Membership in the Honors College requires the completion of 12 honors credits.

Finally, Membership in the Honors College with Honors in the Major requires a 6-credit thesis.

AP/IB credits are not counted as replacements for honors courses.

Number of Honors Classes Offered (5.0): This is a measure of the total **adjusted** honors main sections available in the term reported, not including labs and thesis. (Please read the section titled "All about Honors Classes".) An adjusted main section has 3 or more semester credits, or equivalent, and sections with fewer credits receive a lower prorated value.

The college offered a section for every **7.7** enrolled students. The average for all 50 programs is 14.2. The lower the number, the better.

In the term reported, **78.6%** of honors enrollment was **in honors-only sections; 20.1% in mixed honors sections (honors and non-honors students); and 1.3% in contract sections (regular sections in which honors students "contract" to do extra work).** The averages for all fifty programs are 81.3% in honors-only sections; 13.6 % in mixed honors sections; and 5.1% in contract sections.

Number of Honors Classes in Key Disciplines (5.0): The 15 "key" disciplines are biological sciences; business (all); chemistry; communications (especially public speaking); computer science; economics; engineering (all); English; history; math (all); philosophy; physics; political science; psychology; and sociology/anthropology/gender studies. Interdisciplinary sections, such as those often taken for General Education credit in the first two years, do receive a lesser, prorated discipline "credit" because they introduce students to multiple disciplines in an especially engaging way, often with in-depth discussion.

For this measure, mixed and contract sections are not counted as a section in a key discipline unless students taking the sections for honors credit make up at least 10% of the total section enrollment.

In the term reported, the program had a ratio of **11.2 honors students** per each main section in some or all "key disciplines." The mean for all 50 programs is 26.3. The lower the ratio, the better.

Out of **113 adjusted sections in key disciplines**, the program had **85 honors-only sections.** The most sections were in English (42, the highest of any program), biology, business, and political science (10 each), engineering (9), history (8), psychology (5), computer science and math (4 each), and chemistry and communications (3 each). There was at least one section in all 15 disciplines.

The college also offered 24 sections of the "Human Situation," the gateway course to the honors college. The title for Fall 2015 was "Human Situation: Antiquity."

"This is a 10-hour sequence that helps you hone your critical thinking and writing skills while reading great religious, literary, philosophical and political texts. It is interdisciplinary to the core, team-taught in lecture and student-driven in discussion. You will emerge from it a fearless reader, confident in your ability to talk with professors and others about major aspects of being human. You will also be a much stronger writer and critical thinker — skills that transfer to any area of study."

The Honors College combines the Human Situation interdisciplinary classes with extensive departmental honors classes, but it is essentially a **discipline-based honors program.**

Extent of Honors Enrollment (5.0): Not all honors students take an honors class each term, especially after the first two years. Programs that have fewer honors classes for upper-division honors students will generally have fewer total members in good standing who are actually enrolled in a given term. (Please be aware, however, that honors students not enrolled in a class for a term are still connected to the honors community through residential and extracurricular activities.)

For example, if honors students in a program occupy 1,800 honors classroom seats in a given term, and there are 3,000 honors students in good standing, the extent of enrollment is .67. For programs that require a thesis, the ratio (score) reported below might in fact be somewhat higher, since we only count "regular" class enrollment for this measure, and not thesis enrollment. The college **has a ratio of 2.00**; the mean is 1.13 for all 50 programs. The higher the ratio, the better.

Average Class Size, Honors-only Sections (3.5): Offered mostly in the first two years, honors-only classes tend to be smaller and, as the name implies, have no or very few students other than those in the honors program. These class sections are almost always much smaller than mixed or contract sections, or regular non-honors class sections in the university.

The average honors-only class size in the honors program is **23.6 students**. The average for all 50 programs is 19.0 students.

Average Class Size, Overall (4.0): The overall class calculation is based on the *proportion* of honors students in each type of class (honors-only, mixed honors, and honors contract sections). Thus it is not a raw average. The overall honors-credit class size is **24.6 students**, versus the average for all 50 programs of 26.3 students.

These class size averages also do not correspond to the number of students per honors sections numbers above. The reason is that, in computing average class size metrics, we include enrollment in each 1-2-credit section, not just sections with 3 or more credits.

Along with the honors-only average of 23.6 students, the mixed honors sections average **27.2 students,** and the contract sections with honors credit for individual honors students average **43.5 students.** Across all fifty programs, the average mixed honors section has 51.1 students, and the average contract section has 60.1 students.

Honors Graduation Rate (3.0): The rating is based on the actual grad rate for students who entered the program six years earlier, whether or not the students remained in honors. The **actual rate of 74.5%** is also compared to the rates of other programs with the same test score entry requirement range, and then adjusted to the **score of 73.5%.** In some cases this measure favors programs within universities with relatively higher test scores for the student population as a whole. The average honors graduation rate for all programs with similar test scores required for admission is 83.4%.

Value-Added Grad Rate (5.0): The value-added rate measures the extent to which the adjusted score listed above exceeds the six-year grad rate for the university as a whole. **The university-wide rate is 48%.** Note: This measure generally favors programs within universities with relatively lower test scores for the student population as a whole.

Ratio of Staff to Honors Students (5.0): There is 1 staff member for every **52.0** students. (Mean ratio for all 50 programs is 1 staff member for every 135.6 students.)

Honors Residence Halls, Amenities (5.0): About 560 honors students, freshmen and upperclassmen, live in Cougar Village I. The residence has air-conditioned, suite-style rooms, and "neighborhood themes" matching scholarships students have received (e.g., National Merit, Tier One, Terry)." The nearest dining is at the Fresh Food Company.

An additional 172 honors upperclassmen live in Cougar Place, which has features similar to those in Cougar Village. Cougar Woods dining hall is nearby.

Honors Residence Halls, Availability (4.5): This rating compares the number of rooms in honors residence halls to the number of honors freshman and sophomore members in good standing, about 975. The ratio for the honors program is .75 rooms for each first- and second-year student. The average for all fifty programs is .63 rooms.

Prestigious Awards (3.0): The awards that we track and include are listed in the section titled "Prestigious Scholarships." The awards are sometimes won by students who are not in an honors college or program, but increasingly many are enrolled in honors programs. It is also a trend that honors colleges and programs help to prepare their students for the awards competitions.

U of H students have won 7 Goldwater scholarships, 2 Marshall scholarships, and 1 Truman scholarship.

"The scholarship program is housed within the Office of Undergraduate Research, which is located physically and administratively in the Honors College. This office recently welcomed a new staff member to its team. This full-time staff member assists students with major award applications, manages the campus nomination process, and coordinates the submission of all supporting documents for a wide range of national and international scholarships. Since the addition of this staff member, the total number of students applying for competitive scholarships and internships has increased."

UNRATED FEATURES

Continuation Requirements: 3.25, and the same for graduation.

Academic Strengths, National Rankings: This is based on national rankings of *graduate* programs in 15 disciplines, except engineering and business, where undergraduate rankings are used.

U of H has several departments ranked in the top 100 in the nation, including earth sciences (64), political science (68), economics (72), engineering-graduate school (73, and chemical engineering 33, chemistry (84), math (87), English (91), and business (92).

Undergraduate Research: "112 Honors students participated in organized mentored undergraduate research in the last year. This is 49.8% of the total number of participants in organized mentored undergraduate research. This is 5.7% of the number of students in the Honors College. Since mentored research usually happens in the senior year, it would be fair to say that about four times this, or about a quarter of each class of Honors students, participate in some kind of mentored research during their four years.

Study Abroad: "University of Houston Honors College faculty have led study abroad tours for three decades, but our focus on international education has grown in frequency, range, and focus over the past 10 years. We typically sponsor two to three cultural excursions a year to destinations such as the UK, France, Spain, Italy, Germany, Greece, Turkey, Ecuador, Peru, and Israel, which represents a greater variety of options than any other academic unit on our campus. We have also begun regular clinical service-learning trips, particularly to our partner 'Shoulder to Shoulder' clinic in Santa Ana, Honduras, and life science travel to the Galapagos Islands. In the last three years we have also sponsored clinical trips to Haiti and rural India, and are currently helping to support a campus initiative for travel to Cuba combining honors undergraduates and graduate students from the College of Social Work.

"We lead travel for a select few students to special programs in Human Rights at the UN and Oxford University, in conjunction with the Hobby Center for Public Policy. Lastly, our view of international education is that it should be connected to the total trajectory of the student's career, so we regularly advise and encourage students to apply for major competitive awards such as the Critical Language Scholarship (Department of State), the Fulbright, and the Boren Awards, among others. *Each Honors College student who studies abroad receives at least $500 in scholarship support, and many receive $2,000 or more.*"[Emphasis added.]

Financial Aid: Students are guaranteed to be reviewed for academic/merit scholarships if they have a completed University of Houston application by December 1:

Academic Excellence Scholarship—"The Academic Excellence Scholarship is for students who have a competitive academic profile – typically a score of 1200 on the critical reading and math sections of the SAT (26 ACT composite) with a class rank in the top 20 percent. The amount awarded varies from $2,500 to $8,500 per year.

Tier One Scholarship—"The UH Tier One Scholarships were established by President Renu Khator to attract highly qualified students to the University of Houston by funding four years of tuition and mandatory fees, two years of on-campus room and board, and stipends for research ($1,000) and study abroad ($2,000). Students must have a score of 1300 on the SAT (critical reading and math) or 29 on the ACT and a rank in the top 10% in order to be nominated for the Tier One Scholarship. If nominated, students must submit a structured resume and attend a Tier One Scholarship Invitational Event (where they will participate in a group interview) to be considered for the award. *The Tier One class for fall 2015 consisted of 41 first-year students, who will be receiving approximately $866,834 in scholarship awards.*"[Emphasis added.]

National Merit Scholarship—"The University of Houston awards scholarship support covering the entire cost of tuition, required fees, room and board, including stipends for research ($1,000) and study abroad ($2,000) to National Merit Scholarship Finalists who select the University of Houston as their first-choice institution in accordance with the rules and deadlines established by the National Merit Scholarship Corporation. *In 2015, 29 new National Merit Scholars joined the University of Houston's class of 2019 and will receive approximately $613,126 in scholarship awards.*" [Emphasis added.]

Provost Service Learning Scholarship—"The Provost Service Learning Scholarship is awarded contingent upon service completed through the Bonner Program, which supports not only students, but also the University's efforts to serve the community. Academically excellent incoming students are invited to apply, and in 2015, 36 students were awarded $61,000 in PSLS funds."

Honors Fees: FTIC (First Time In College) Fee= $200 (one time only)

Academic Support Fee= $125 (fall and spring semesters)

Activities and Materials Fee= $125 (fall and spring semesters)

No fee associated with Honors Residence Halls.

Placement Experiences: "For the 2015 graduating class of the Honors College at the University of Houston, approximately 35% of graduating students planned to immediately enter a graduate or professional school program and 55% of graduating students planned to immediately enter the workforce (with 10% undecided on their plans at time of survey).

"A partial list of graduate and professional schools that the 2015 graduating class of the Honors College at the University of Houston were accepted to includes: Baylor College of Medicine, Boston University, College of William and Mary, George Washington University, John Hopkins University, Texas A&M Health Science Center- College of Medicine, Texas Tech School of Law, University of California, San Diego, University of California, Berkeley, University of Colorado, University of Essex, University of Houston Law Center, University of Nottingham, University of Texas Medical Branch – Galveston, University of Texas School of Dentistry, University of Texas Southwestern Medical School, Wake Forest University, Washington and Lee University, Washington University St. Louis, and Yale University.

"For students entering the workforce in 2015, the top industries included: Accounting, Arts/Non-profit, Community/Public Health, Education, Engineering, Logistics, Marketing/Sales, Music, Oil & Gas, Programming, Project Management, Research, Risk Management, and Supply Chain Management."

Degree of Difference: This is based on the differences between (1) the average (2015, two-part) SAT scores for enrolled honors students (1337) and (2) the average test scores for all students in the university (1150) as a whole. The test scores may be an indication of how "elite" honors students may be perceived as compared to students in the university as a whole. The scores can also provide an indication of how well prepared the non-honors students in the university may be. **Please keep in mind that neither high nor low test scores determine the overall quality of a program.**

NAME: UNIVERSITY HONORS PROGRAM, UNIVERSITY OF IDAHO.

Date Established: 1983.

Location: Moscow, Idaho.

University Full-time Undergraduate Enrollment: 7,824.

Honors Members in Good Standing: 516 (mean size of all 50 programs is 1,742).

Honors Average Admission Statistics: ACT, 29; Old SAT, 1315; est. new SAT, 1380.

Average High School GPA/Class Rank: 3.93; class rank is not considered.

Basic Admission Requirements: "The University Honors Program (UHP) encourages all qualified applicants to apply for admission. Initial admission decisions are based on a correlation between their cumulative, unweighted high school GPA and their highest ACT composite score or the highest SAT critical reading and math scores. Applicants who meet the initial admission index are invited to submit four short compositions (one to two double-spaced paragraphs) which describe significant learning experiences and perspectives.

"If students do not meet the admission criteria, they may apply through an exception application which requires two letters of recommendation from teachers and a description of why they want to be in the program and any special circumstances that should be considered.

"Current UI students with a 3.5 or higher UI cumulative GPA, after completion of 15 or more credits and a grade of B or better in English 102 are encouraged to apply for admission to the UHP."

Application Deadline(s): *Please verify with each program, as some deadlines could change.*

Priority application deadline for the university is December 1, 2016.

Honors Programs with old SAT scores from 1315—1350: Idaho, Georgia State, Virginia Tech, Utah, Iowa, Auburn, Houston, Mississippi, VCU.

Administrative Staff: 4.

RATINGS AT A GLANCE: For all mortarboard ratings immediately below, a score of 5 is the maximum and represents a comparison with all 50 honors colleges and programs. More detailed explanations follow the "mortarboard" ratings.

PERCEPTION* OF UNIVERSITY AS A WHOLE, NOT OF HONORS: 🎓🎓🎓

*Perception is based on the university's ranking among public universities in the 2016 U.S. News Best Colleges report. Please bear in mind that the better the U.S. News ranking, the more difficult it is for an honors college or program to have a rating that equals or improves on the magazine ranking.

OVERALL HONORS RATING: 🎓🎓🎓1/2

Curriculum Requirements: 🎓🎓🎓1/2

Number of Honors Classes Offered: 🎓🎓🎓🎓

Number of Honors Classes in Key Disciplines: 🎓🎓🎓🎓

Extent of Honors Enrollment: 🎓🎓🎓

Honors-only Class Size: 🎓🎓🎓

Overall Class Size (Honors-only plus mixed, contract): 🎓🎓🎓🎓

Honors Grad Rate: 🎓🎓🎓🎓

Value-Added Grad Rate: 🎓🎓🎓🎓🎓

Ratio of Staff to Students: 🎓🎓🎓🎓

Priority Registration: Yes, honors students register for all courses during each year they are in the program.

Honors Housing Amenities: 🎓🎓🎓🎓1/2

Honors Housing Availability: 🎓🎓🎓🎓

Prestigious Awards: 🎓🎓🎓1/2

RATING SCORES AND EXPLANATIONS:

Curriculum Requirements (3.5): The most important rating category, the curriculum completion requirement (classes required to complete honors) defines not only what honors students should learn but also the extent to which honors students and faculty are connected in the classroom. If there is a thesis or capstone requirement, it reinforces the individual contact and research skills so important to learning.

The average number of honors semester hours required for completion across all 50 programs is 29.0.

The Honors Certificate requires **27 credits**, as below:

- Three honors humanities credits;
- Three honors social science credits;
- Three honors science credits;
- Three honors analytical and quantitative reasoning credits;
- Additional honors elective credits to total 27 credits, with at least six upper-division credits.

"Students must complete courses from at least three different disciplines within the social sciences and humanities. An honors Integrated Seminar may count toward the three discipline requirement. Up to 12 honors contract credits, including Honors Research credits, may be applied toward the Certificate. Students who participate in a one-semester study abroad experience may receive an Honors Certificate by completing 24 credits rather than the required 27 honors credits. Students who participate in a two-semester study abroad experience may receive an Honors Certificate by completing 21 rather than the required 27 honors credits.

"The University Honors Program Core Award is the second highest distinction an honors student can earn at the University of Idaho. Students must complete 19 total honors-designated credits. Up to 9 honors contract credits, including Honors Research, may be applied toward the Core Award. Students who participate in a semester-long study abroad experience may receive an Honors Core Award by completing 16 rather than the required 19 honors credits."

AP/IB credits are not counted as replacements for honors courses.

Number of Honors Classes Offered (4.0): This is a measure of the total **adjusted** honors main sections available in the term reported, not including labs and thesis. (Please read the section titled "All about Honors Classes".) An adjusted main section has 3 or more semester credits, or equivalent, and sections with fewer credits receive a lower prorated value.

The program offered a section for every **15.9** students. The average for all 50 programs is 14.2. The lower the number, the better.

In the term reported, **96.2%** of honors enrollment was **in honors-only sections; 2% in mixed honors sections (honors and non-honors students); and 1.8% in contract sections (regular sections in which honors students "contract" to do extra work).** The averages for all fifty programs are 81.3% in honors-only sections; 13.6 % in mixed honors sections; and 5.1% in contract sections.

Number of Honors Classes in Key Disciplines (4.0): The 15 "key" disciplines are biological sciences; business (all); chemistry; communications (especially public speaking); computer science; economics; engineering (all); English; history; math (all); philosophy; physics; political science; psychology; and sociology/anthropology/gender studies. Interdisciplinary sections, such as those often taken for General Education credit in the first two years, do receive a lesser, prorated discipline "credit" because they introduce students to multiple disciplines in an especially engaging way, often with in-depth discussion.

For this measure, mixed and contract sections are not counted as a section in a key discipline unless students taking the sections for honors credit make up at least 10% of the total section enrollment.

In the term reported, the program had a ratio of **17.7 honors students** per each main section in some or all "key disciplines." The mean for all programs is 26.3. The lower the ratio, the better.

Out of **11 adjusted sections in key disciplines offered in Fall 2015**, the program had **10 honors-only sections.** The most sections were in English (4), and chemistry (2), with the remaining sections being in math, philosophy, and psychology.

The program also offered five signature Integrated Seminars: "Sacred Journeys"—two sections; "Globalization"; "Love and Happiness"; and "Future Agriculture: Promise or Peril?"

The program combines interdisciplinary classes with several departmental honors classes, and is an example of a **small blended program.**

Extent of Honors Enrollment (3.0): Not all honors students take an honors class each term, especially after the first two years. Programs that have fewer honors classes for upper-division honors students will generally have fewer total members in good standing who are actually enrolled in a given term. (Please be aware, however, that honors students not enrolled in a class for a term are still connected to the honors community through residential and extracurricular activities.)

For example, if honors students in a program occupy 1,800 honors classroom seats in a given term, and there are 3,000 honors students in good standing, the extent of enrollment is .67. For programs that require a thesis, the ratio (score) reported below might in fact be somewhat higher, since we only count "regular" class enrollment for this measure, and not thesis enrollment. The program **has a ratio of .76**; the mean is 1.13 for all 50 programs. The higher the ratio, the better.

Average Class Size, Honors-only Sections (3.0): Offered mostly in the first two years, honors-only classes tend to be smaller and, as the name implies, have no or very few students other than those in the honors program. These class sections are almost always much smaller than mixed or contract sections, or regular non-honors class sections in the university.

The average honors-only class size in the honors program is **25.1 students**. The average for all 50 programs is 19.0 students.

Average Class Size, Overall (4.0): The overall class calculation is based on the *proportion* of honors students in each type of class (honors-only, mixed honors, and honors contract sections). Thus it is not a raw average. The overall honors-credit class size is **24.7 students**, versus the average for all 50 programs of 26.3students.

These class size averages also do not correspond to the number of students per honors sections numbers above. The reason is that, in computing average class size metrics, we include enrollment in each 1-2-credit section, not just sections with 3 or more credits.

Along with the honors-only average of 25.1 students, the mixed honors sections average **8.0 students,** and the contract sections with honors credit for individual honors students average **22.2 students.** Across all fifty programs, the average mixed honors section has 51.1 students, and the average contract section has 60.1 students.

Honors Graduation Rate (4.0): The rating is based on the actual grad rate for students who entered the program six years earlier, whether or not the students remained in honors. The **actual rate of 85%** is also compared to the rates of other programs with the same test score entry requirement range, and then adjusted to the **score of 85%.** In some cases this measure favors programs within universities with relatively higher test scores for the student population as a whole. The average honors graduation rate for all programs with similar test scores required for admission is 83.4%.

Value-Added Grad Rate (5.0): The value-added rate measures the extent to which the adjusted score listed above exceeds the six-year grad rate for the university as a whole. **The university-wide rate is 58%.** Note: This measure generally favors programs within universities with relatively lower test scores for the student population as a whole.

Ratio of Staff to Honors Students (4.0): There is 1 staff member for every **129.0** students. (Mean ratio for all 50 programs is 1 staff member for every 135.6 students.)

Honors Residence Halls, Amenities (4.5): Honors freshmen, 76 in all, live in McCoy Honors Hall on two concurrent floors. The air-conditioned rooms are traditional doubles with hall baths. An especially convenient feature is that Bob's Dining Hall is only 100 yards from McCoy.

Upperclassmen, about 75, live in the Scholars Living/Learning Community. Scholars has the same features as McCoy—but Bob's is 200 yards away.

Honors Residence Halls, Availability (4.0): This rating compares the number of rooms in honors residence halls to the number of honors freshman and sophomore members in good standing, about 258. The ratio for the honors program is **.59** rooms for each first- and second-year student. The average for all fifty programs is .63 rooms.

Prestigious Awards (3.5): The awards that we track and include are listed in the section titled "Prestigious Scholarships." The awards are sometimes won by students who are not in an honors college or program, but increasingly many are enrolled in honors programs. It is also a trend that honors colleges and programs help to prepare their students for the awards competitions.

"The UI Distinguished Scholarships Office, housed in the Honors Program, advises and assists students who are interested in applying for national scholarships and fellowships. UI students have been successful in many of the award competitions including Goldwater (28), awarded to outstanding students in the STEM fields; Gilman (62) awarded to support academic studies abroad; and Udall (15) awarded to students committed to careers in the environment, tribal policy, or Native American health care. UI students consistently win prestigious National Science Foundation Graduate Research Fellowships, and have also been successful with the Fulbright US Student Program and Fulbright UK Summer Institutes, and the Boren Scholarship. The university has had 7 Truman and 20 Rhodes [scholars]."

UNRATED FEATURES

Continuation Requirements: 3.30, and the same for graduation.

Academic Strengths, National Rankings: This is based on national rankings of *graduate* programs in 15 disciplines, except engineering and business, where undergraduate rankings are used.

UI has ranked programs in earth sciences, business, chemistry, engineering, physics, and education.

Undergraduate Research: "Honors Thesis: Encouraged but not required in either of our graduating distinctions (Certificate or Core Award).

"The honors thesis provides an opportunity for honors students to have a challenging capstone experience that encourages diligent and creative work in collaboration with a faculty mentor over an extended period of time. Thesis projects challenge students to draw on knowledge and abilities that they have developed throughout the course of their education and to apply them to an in-depth investigation of a chosen topic. Students develop their research, critical thinking, writing, and oral presentation skills through the thesis process, which in turn prepares students for their professional career as well as for graduate school.

"The Honors Thesis distinction and the project title are included on the transcript. Projects may take a wide variety of forms and culminate in a creative work, a performance or exhibit, an original scientific manuscript or report, etc."

Study Abroad: "The UI is affiliated with over 370 universities in 69 countries including 29 partnership universities and affiliations with five study abroad program providers. The UI offers faculty-led programs, study abroad programs, exchange programs, and overseas experiential programs including internships and volunteer assignments over the summer, fall and spring semester, and winter break. The UI is one of a handful of universities in the U.S. that have a student fee-funded study abroad International Experience Grant, and it provides $157,000 in study abroad scholarships each year.

"In 2015, the Honors Program sponsored a faculty-led summer study abroad program to Ecuador. Students explored the Ecuador and Andean culture both in the classroom and in the field, going to Quito, the Amazon Rainforest and the Galapagos Islands. In Quito, students lived with a host family and took classes at the local university, studying the history, politics, economics, art, language, music, dance and archaeology of the country. In the Amazon Rainforest and the Galapagos Islands, students learned through a variety of field experiences even visiting a native village in the Amazon.

Financial Aid: *"The UI National Merit Scholar program guarantees a full-ride scholarship that covers university-defined educational costs for basic tuition and fees and room and board in a UI residence hall for four years.* UI enrolled 23 National Merit Scholars in the fall 2015 semester, bringing the total overall National Merit Scholar enrollment to 78 students, surpassing last year's record number. *UI now enrolls more National Merit scholars than any public university in the Northwest.*[Emphasis added.]

"The UI provides automatic scholarships for incoming students based on their high school GPA which range up to $4,000 for in-state students and up to $8,000 for out-of-state students.

"The Honors Program automatically considers all admitted honors students for scholarships. Ten Honors Presidential Scholars and ten Honors Fellows are selected each year based on academic record, test scores and evidence of leadership, service, and involvement in high school. The Honors Program also awards approximately twenty-five Western Undergraduate Exchange (WUE) scholarships. Recipients pay 150% of Idaho resident tuition and basic registration fees; and the award is renewable for up to four years for first-year recipients.

"The Honors Program and the Office of Undergraduate Research provide funding to students to assist with costs of undergraduate research and to support travel to meetings."

Honors Fees: None.

Placement Experiences: None listed.

Degree of Difference: This is based on the differences between (1) the average (2015, two-part) SAT scores for enrolled honors students (1315) and (2) the average test scores for all students in the university (1050) as a whole. The test scores may be an indication of how "elite" honors students may be perceived as compared to students in the university as a whole. The scores can also provide an indication of how well prepared the non-honors students in the university may be. **Please keep in mind that neither high nor low test scores determine the overall quality of a program.**

NAME: CAMPUS HONORS PROGRAM, UNIVERSITY OF ILLINOIS.

Date Established: 1986.

Location: Urbana-Champaign, Illinois.

University Full-time Undergraduate Enrollment: 31,742.

Honors Members in Good Standing: 500 (mean size of all 50 programs is 1,742).

Honors Average Admission Statistics: ACT, 34; old SAT equivalent, 1500-1510; est. new SAT, 1540.

Average High School GPA/Class Rank: 3.79.

Basic Admission Requirements: "The Campus Honors programs has minimum ACT and UI's Academic Index (Academic Index is an assessment of high school grades and other factors) that vary for each college….The CHP minimum ACT Composite Score generally begins in the low-30's for ACT, yet the minimum ACT Composite Score in certain majors may be closer to 35 (such as Computer Science)…

"In our admissions process, we look for genuine enthusiasm and a wide array of interests, as shown by the personal statement and high school activities (both breadth and depth, as well as leadership); we also conduct a limited reference check. Each application is pre-screened (a student application with a perfect ACT or SAT but with limited or no engagement in high school activities does not move forward), and each remaining application is subsequently reviewed holistically.

"Students not initially admitted to the CHP have an additional chance to be admitted to the program during the 'Off-cycle admissions process' which occurs after the first semester of the freshman year."

Application Deadline(s): *Please verify with each program, as some deadlines could change.*

Priority deadline November 1, 2016 preferably earlier; final deadline December 15, 2016.

Honors Programs with old SAT scores (or ACT equivalent) of 1500 or higher: Oklahoma, Illinois.

Administrative Staff: 4.5 FTEs.

RATINGS AT A GLANCE: For all mortarboard ratings immediately below, a score of 5 is the maximum and represents a comparison with all 50 honors colleges and programs. More detailed explanations follow the "mortarboard" ratings.

PERCEPTION* OF UNIVERSITY AS A WHOLE, NOT OF HONORS:

*Perception is based on the university's ranking among public universities in the 2016 U.S. News Best Colleges report. Please bear in mind that the better the U.S. News ranking, the more difficult it is for an honors college or program to have a rating that equals or improves on the magazine ranking.

OVERALL HONORS RATING: 🎓🎓🎓🎓[1/2]

Curriculum Requirements: 🎓🎓🎓

Number of Honors Classes Offered: 🎓🎓🎓🎓[1/2]

Number of Honors Classes in Key Disciplines: 🎓🎓🎓🎓

Extent of Honors Enrollment: 🎓🎓🎓🎓🎓

Honors-only Class Size: 🎓🎓🎓🎓

Overall Class Size (Honors-only plus mixed, contract): 🎓🎓🎓🎓[1/2]

Honors Grad Rate: 🎓🎓🎓🎓🎓

Value-Added Grad Rate: 🎓🎓🎓[1/2]

Ratio of Staff to Students: 🎓🎓🎓🎓

Priority Registration: Chancellor's Scholars register first (with students with disabilities and athletes), by order of number of hours previously earned, followed by the James Scholars from each college. "Incoming first year students must register on their orientation date with all other incoming students (so are advised to get as early an orientation date as possible), and this is the only time they will not have registration priority; to accommodate these students' needs, a percentage of CHP class spots are held for incoming first-year students, and waitlists are maintained when necessary."

Honors Housing Amenities: 🎓🎓🎓🎓[1/2]

Honors Housing Availability: 🎓🎓🎓🎓🎓

Prestigious Awards: 🎓🎓🎓🎓🎓

RATING SCORES AND EXPLANATIONS:

Curriculum Requirements (3.0): The most important rating category, the curriculum completion requirement (classes required to complete honors) defines not only what honors students should learn but also the extent to which honors students and faculty are connected in the classroom. If there is a thesis or capstone requirement, it reinforces the individual contact and research skills so important to learning.

The average number of honors semester hours required for completion across all 50 programs is 29.0.

Enrolled students in the CHP are referred to as Chancellor's Scholars. "There are also honors programs in every college (these individuals are referred to as 'James Scholars'), and in many departments. The James Scholar Programs range from a few dozen students (for example, the College of Media and the College of Fine and Applied Arts) up to the College of Engineering and College of Liberal Arts James Scholar Programs, which usually number more than 1,000. *Students can be Chancellor's Scholars and James Scholars if they are accepted by both programs.*

CHP completion requires about **18 credits.** Chancellor's Scholars must take at least four "regular" CHP classes, or 12-13 credits. They must also complete a 3-credit capstone seminar. "We also have co-curricular requirements: Over their undergraduate career, Chancellor's Scholars must participate in 4 "Scholar Adventurers Series" programs which range from 1.5-3 hours, and 1 Krannert Dress Rehearsal (this fine and applied arts event usually 1 hour of lecture, and up to 3 hours of performance)."

AP/IB credits are not counted as replacements for honors courses.

Number of Honors Classes Offered (4.5): This is a measure of the total **adjusted** honors main sections available in the term reported, not including labs and thesis. (Please read the section titled "All about Honors Classes".) An adjusted main section has 3 or more semester credits, or equivalent, and sections with fewer credits receive a lower prorated value.

The program offered a section for every **11.8** students. The average for all 50 programs is 14.2. The lower the number, the better.

In the term reported, **100.0%** of honors class enrollment was **in honors-only sections; none in mixed honors sections (honors and non-honors students); and none in contract sections (regular sections in which honors students "contract" to do extra work).** The averages for all fifty programs are 81.3% in honors-only sections; 13.6 % in mixed honors sections; and 5.1% in contract sections.

Number of Honors Classes in Key Disciplines (4.0): The 15 "key" disciplines are biological sciences; business (all); chemistry; communications (especially public speaking); computer science; economics; engineering (all); English; history; math (all); philosophy; physics; political science; psychology; and sociology/anthropology/gender studies. Interdisciplinary sections, such as those often taken for General Education credit in the first two years, do receive a lesser, prorated discipline "credit" because they introduce students to multiple disciplines in an especially engaging way, often with in-depth discussion.

For this measure, mixed and contract sections are not counted as a section in a key discipline unless students taking the sections for honors credit make up at least 10% of the total section enrollment.

In the term reported, the program had a ratio of **21.7 honors students** per each main section in some or all "key disciplines." The mean for all programs is 26.3. The lower the ratio, the better.

In the term reported, the program offered **23 adjusted sections in key disciplines**, and **all were honors-only sections.** The sections were in math (7), biology (4), business, economics, English, and physics (2 each), and philosophy and psychology (1 each). Sociology, anthropology, and gender studies combined have 2 sections.

The program also offered about ten 1- and 2-credit sections, including "Exploring General Studies" and "Leadership and Professional Development." The James Scholars series of 35 one-credit sections was called "Leadership and Society."

The program combines leadership classes with several honors classes in the disciplines, and is an example of a small **discipline-based program.** At the same time, however, the "Campus Honors Program is the only option that brings in students from all colleges at Illinois."

Extent of Honors Enrollment (5.0): Not all honors students take an honors class each term, especially after the first two years. Programs that have fewer honors classes for upper-division honors students will generally have fewer total members in good standing who are actually enrolled in a given term. (Please be aware, however, that honors students not enrolled in a class for a term are still connected to the honors community through residential and extracurricular activities.)

For example, if honors students in a program occupy 1,800 honors classroom seats in a given term, and there are 3,000 honors students in good standing, the extent of enrollment is .67. For programs that require a thesis, the ratio (score) reported below might in fact be somewhat higher, since we only count "regular" class enrollment for this measure, and not thesis enrollment. The program **has an *estimated* ratio of 1.78**; the mean is 1.13 for all 50 programs. The higher the ratio, the better.

Average Class Size, Honors-only Sections (4.0): Offered mostly in the first two years, honors-only classes tend to be smaller and, as the name implies, have no or very few students other than those in the honors program. These class sections are almost always much smaller than mixed or contract sections, or regular non-honors class sections in the university.

The average honors-only class size in the honors program is **18.4 students**. The average for all 50 programs is 19.0 students.

Average Class Size, Overall (4.5): The overall class calculation is based on the *proportion* of honors students in each type of class (honors-only, mixed honors, and honors contract sections). Thus it is not a raw average. The overall honors-credit class size is **18.4 students**, versus the average for all 50 programs of 26.3 students.

These class size averages also do not correspond to the number of students per honors sections numbers above. The reason is that, in computing average class size metrics, we include enrollment in each 1-2-credit section, not just sections with 3 or more credits.

Honors Graduation Rate (5.0): The rating is based on the actual grad rate for students who entered the program six years earlier, whether or not the students remained in honors. The **actual rate of 94.9%** is also compared to the rates of other programs with the same test score entry requirement range, and then adjusted to the **score of 95.1%.** In some cases this measure favors programs within universities with relatively higher test scores for the student population as a whole. The average honors graduation rate for all programs with similar test scores required for admission is 95.0%. **Note:** *The CHP rate is based on 4.5-5 years, rather than 6, so it is even more impressive.*

Value-Added Grad Rate (3.5): The value-added rate measures the extent to which the adjusted score listed above exceeds the six-year grad rate for the university as a whole. **The university-wide rate is**

84%. Note: This measure generally favors programs within universities with relatively lower test scores for the student population as a whole.

Ratio of Staff to Honors Students (4.0): There is 1 staff member for every **111.1** students. (Mean ratio for all 50 programs is 1 staff member for every 135.6 students.)

Honors Residence Halls, Amenities (4.5): A new feature for the CHP is an honors residence, Nugent Hall. "Approximately 180 beds are reserved for freshmen and the remaining 60 beds for returning honors students. Based on student interest, the honors residence hall will likely be expanded."

Nugent has coed floors with single-gender rooms. The residence is air-conditioned and has traditional double rooms with hall baths. Ikenberry Dining Hall is attached to Nugent Hall.

"The residence has an honors theme with three pillars that define its emphasis (Inquiry, Civic Engagement, Leadership)."

Honors Residence Halls, Availability (5.0): This rating compares the number of rooms in honors residence halls to the number of honors freshman and sophomore members in good standing, about 250. The ratio for the honors program is **.96** rooms for each first- and second-year student. The average for all fifty programs is .63 rooms.

Prestigious Awards (5.0): The awards that we track and include are listed in the section titled "Prestigious Scholarships." The awards are sometimes won by students who are not in an honors college or program, but increasingly many are enrolled in honors programs. It is also a trend that honors colleges and programs help to prepare their students for the awards competitions.

"The University of Illinois has more Churchill Scholars [20] than any other public institution, and is sixth overall after Princeton, Harvard, Yale, Cornell, and Duke.

"Four Marshall Scholars in the past 6 years. Illinois' 25 scholars overall rank #2 among public institutions (after Berkeley) and 13th among all institutions.

"Luce Scholars: 5 recipients in the past 8 years.

"Gates-Cambridge: 9 scholars since 2000.

"Fulbright: Illinois has been listed as a 'US Student Top Producer' of Fulbright awards for each of the past 6 years and in 2015, was the #5 public university in the country for number of Fulbright recipients.

"Goldwater: 69 recipients—on average, nearly three of our four nominees win!

"Udall: winners or honorable mentions each of the past 7 years, including 4 recipients."
UIUC also has 9 Rhodes scholars and 11 Truman scholars.

UNRATED FEATURES

Continuation Requirements: 3.30, and the same for graduation. For James Scholars, the GPA requirements vary according to departmental requirements.

Academic Strengths, National Rankings: This is based on national rankings of *graduate* programs in 15 disciplines, except engineering and business, where undergraduate rankings are used.

UIUC has an outstanding faculty, among the top 20 or so in the nation among major universities, public or private. Among the many excellent departments are computer science and engineering (both 5), chemistry (6), psychology (7), physics (9), business (15), math (17), history (20), English (22), and education and political science (both 23).

Undergraduate Research: "We estimate that at any one time 25-30% of our students are participating in research in an official/supervised setting, and that before our students graduate, at least 65-70% of our students have done some form of research. This does not take into account independent research and/or performance-based research.

"The University of Illinois does have a relatively new Office of Undergraduate Research (OUR), which began offering a Certificate in Undergraduate Research last year. The OUR is also working on systematizing all research course numbers to be consistent, though if course credit is not sought, their position is that a student should be paid for their work.

"The Campus Honors Program offers CHP Summer Research grants (up to $2,000), sponsors students to present their work at conferences, and schedules two co-curricular events per year for research."

Study Abroad: "The CHP awards between $10,000 - $15,000 in CHP Summer Travel grants on an annual basis (up to $1,000 per student).

"Budget permitting, the CHP also hosts students on a CHP Summer Intercultural Tour to a variety of locations, including Peru, Japan, Ecuador and the Galapagos, and Curacao; the amount required for each student is heavily subsidized by the CHP, so the student only covers up to half of the cost.

"Field trips are fully or partially covered for students for CHP classes, which may range from visits to the Art Institute in Chicago to a research study tour to Yellowstone."

Financial Aid: "Chancellor's Scholars in the Campus Honors Program are supported by a small stipend ($1,500) for their first year if they are in-state.

"Chancellor's Scholars who are domestic out of state (5-8 per year) and incoming first year students who are selected for a merit scholarship (2 per year) receive a partial tuition waiver that is guaranteed for their first four semesters (as long as they remain in good standing), and which may be renewed at a smaller amount in subsequent semesters if the budget allows."

Honors Fees: None.

Placement Experiences: CHP graduates go on to win prestigious fellowships, attend leading graduate and professional schools, and find employment with major employers. Many also spend some time in public service endeavors before moving on to other employment or postgraduate work.

Degree of Difference: This is based on the differences between (1) the average (2015, two-part) SAT scores for enrolled honors students (1500-1510=ACT equivalent) and (2) the average test scores for all s students in the university (1300 ACT equivalent) as a whole. The test scores may be an indication of how "elite" honors students may be perceived as compared to students in the university as a whole. The scores can also provide an indication of how well prepared the non-honors students in the university may be. **Please keep in mind that neither high nor low test scores determine the overall quality of a program.**

NAME: HUTTON HONORS COLLEGE.

Date Established: 1965.

Location: Bloomington, Indiana.

University Full-time Undergraduate Enrollment: 31,370.

Honors Members in Good Standing: 5,000 (mean size of all 50 programs is 1,742).

Honors Average Admission Statistics: ACT, 32; old SAT equivalent, 1370; est. new SAT, 1420.

Average High School GPA/Class Rank: 3.98; top 6%.

Basic Admission Requirements: 31 ACT or 1360-1380 SAT and 3.95 or top 5% class rank.

32-33 ACT or 1390-1460 SAT and 3.90 GPA or top 7.5% class rank;

34-36 ACT or 1470+ SAT and 3.85 GPA or top 10% class rank.

Application Deadline(s): *Please verify with each program, as some deadlines could change.*

Deadline for Hutton scholarships November 1, 2016.

Honors Programs with old SAT scores from 1351—1396: Purdue, Oregon, Alabama, Massachusetts, Penn State, Indiana, CUNY Macaulay, Texas A&M, NJIT, Missouri, Oregon State, Delaware, LSU, Vermont, Temple.

Administrative Staff: 14.

RATINGS AT A GLANCE: For all mortarboard ratings immediately below, a score of 5 is the maximum and represents a comparison with all 50 honors colleges and programs. More detailed explanations follow the "mortarboard" ratings.

PERCEPTION* OF UNIVERSITY AS A WHOLE, NOT OF HONORS: 🎓🎓🎓🎓$^{1/2}$

*Perception is based on the university's ranking among public universities in the 2016 U.S. News Best Colleges report. Please bear in mind that the better the U.S. News ranking, the more difficult it is for an honors college or program to have a rating that equals or improves on the magazine ranking.

OVERALL HONORS RATING: 🎓🎓🎓$^{1/2}$

Curriculum Requirements: 🎓🎓🎓

Number of Honors Classes Offered: 🎓🎓🎓🎓🎓

Number of Honors Classes in Key Disciplines: 🎓🎓🎓🎓🎓

Extent of Honors Enrollment: 🎓🎓🎓

Honors-only Class Size: 🎓🎓🎓🎓🎓🎓

Overall Class Size (Honors-only plus mixed, contract): 🎓🎓🎓🎓

Honors Grad Rate: 🎓🎓🎓🎓 1/2

Value-Added Grad Rate: 🎓🎓🎓🎓

Ratio of Staff to Students: 🎓🎓🎓

Priority Registration: No.

Honors Housing Amenities: 🎓🎓🎓🎓

Honors Housing Availability: 🎓🎓🎓

Prestigious Awards: 🎓🎓🎓🎓🎓

RATING SCORES AND EXPLANATIONS:

Curriculum Requirements (3.0): The most important rating category, the curriculum completion requirement (classes required to complete honors) defines not only what honors students should learn but also the extent to which honors students and faculty are connected in the classroom. If there is a thesis or capstone requirement, it reinforces the individual contact and research skills so important to learning.

The average number of honors semester hours required for completion across all 50 programs is 29.0.

For the General Honors Notation (GHN), "students must complete a minimum of **21 credit hours** of honors courses, or a combination of honors courses and study abroad (6 credit hours for one year abroad, 3 credit hours for one semester, and 1 credit hour for a summer program of at least 4 weeks' duration). The only requirement we impose for fulfillment of the 21 hours is that at least 6 hours must be from courses with the HON-H prefix; the remaining 15 hours may be fulfilled with additional HON-H courses, with departmental or school honors courses, and/or with study abroad."

AP/IB credits are not counted as replacements for honors courses.

Number of Honors Classes Offered (5.0): This is a measure of the total **adjusted** honors main sections available in the term reported, not including labs and thesis. (Please read the section titled "All about Honors Classes".) An adjusted main section has 3 or more semester credits, or equivalent, and sections with fewer credits receive a lower prorated value.

The program offered a section for every **9.7** students. The average for all 50 programs is 14.2. The lower the number, the better.

In the term reported, **36.3%** of honors class enrollment was **in honors-only sections; 63.7% in mixed honors sections (honors and non-honors students); and none in contract sections (regular sections in which honors students "contract" to do extra work).** The averages for all fifty programs are 81.3% in honors-only sections; 13.6 % in mixed honors sections; and 5.1% in contract sections.

Number of Honors Classes in Key Disciplines (5.0): The 15 "key" disciplines are biological sciences; business (all); chemistry; communications (especially public speaking); computer science; economics; engineering (all); English; history; math (all); philosophy; physics; political science; psychology; and sociology/anthropology/gender studies. Interdisciplinary sections, such as those often taken for General Education credit in the first two years, do receive a lesser, prorated discipline "credit" because they introduce students to multiple disciplines in an especially engaging way, often with in-depth discussion.

For this measure, mixed and contract sections are not counted as a section in a key discipline unless students taking the sections for honors credit make up at least 10% of the total section enrollment.

In the term reported, the program had a ratio of **16.0 honors students** per each main section in some or all "key disciplines." The mean for all programs is 26.3. The lower the ratio, the better.

In the term reported, the program offered **129 adjusted sections in key disciplines**, and **40 were honors-only sections.** Business had 48 sections, the most of any program. Other key disciplines included computer science (18), communications (15), psychology (10), chemistry, English, and math (8 each), and economics (2). Sociology, anthropology, and gender studies combined had 8 sections.

The program also offered more than 35 interdisciplinary classes, including 3 sections in "Ideas and Experience"; 4 sections in "Great Authors, Composers, and Artists"; and 5 titled "The Intricate Human."

The program combines interdisciplinary classes with a very large number of honors classes in the disciplines, and is an example of a large **blended program.**

Extent of Honors Enrollment (3.0): Not all honors students take an honors class each term, especially after the first two years. Programs that have fewer honors classes for upper-division honors students will generally have fewer total members in good standing who are actually enrolled in a given term. (Please be aware, however, that honors students not enrolled in a class for a term are still connected to the honors community through residential and extracurricular activities.)

For example, if honors students in a program occupy 1,800 honors classroom seats in a given term, and there are 3,000 honors students in good standing, the extent of enrollment is .67. For programs that require a thesis, the ratio (score) reported below might in fact be somewhat higher, since we only count "regular" class enrollment for this measure, and not thesis enrollment. The program **has an *estimated* ratio of .70**; the mean is 1.13 for all 50 programs. The higher the ratio, the better.

Average Class Size, Honors-only Sections (5.0): Offered mostly in the first two years, honors-only classes tend to be smaller and, as the name implies, have no or very few students other than those in the honors program. These class sections are almost always much smaller than mixed or contract sections, or regular non-honors class sections in the university.

The average honors-only class size in the honors program is **12.2 students**. The average for all 50 programs is 19.0 students.

Average Class Size, Overall (4.0): The overall class calculation is based on the *proportion* of honors students in each type of class (honors-only, mixed honors, and honors contract sections). Thus it is not a raw average. The overall honors-credit class size is **25.4 students**, versus the average for all 50 programs of 26.3 students.

These class size averages also do not correspond to the number of students per honors sections numbers above. The reason is that, in computing average class size metrics, we include enrollment in each 1-2-credit section, not just sections with 3 or more credits.

Along with the honors-only average of 12.2 students, the mixed honors sections average **32.9 students,** and the contract sections with honors credit for individual honors students average **(NA)** students. Across all fifty programs, the average mixed honors section has 51.1 students, and the average contract section has 60.1 students.

Honors Graduation Rate (4.5): The rating is based on the actual grad rate for students who entered the program six years earlier, whether or not the students remained in honors. The **actual rate of 89%** is also compared to the rates of other programs with the same test score entry requirement range, and then adjusted to the **score of 89.3%.** In some cases this measure favors programs within universities with relatively higher test scores for the student population as a whole. The average honors graduation rate for all programs with similar test scores required for admission is 86.2%.

Value-Added Grad Rate (4.0): The value-added rate measures the extent to which the adjusted score listed above exceeds the six-year grad rate for the university as a whole. **The university-wide rate is 78%.** Note: This measure generally favors programs within universities with relatively lower test scores for the student population as a whole.

Ratio of Staff to Honors Students (3.0): There is 1 staff member for every **357.1** students. (Mean ratio for all 50 programs is 1 staff member for every 135.6 students.)

Honors Residence Halls, Amenities (4.0): Hutton assigns honors students to four residence halls, with most students, about 200, living in Teter. The other residences are Forest, Briscoe, and Union Street. All residences are air-conditioned. Forest and Teter have traditional rooms with hall baths; Briscoe and Union Street have suite-style rooms. The dining hall closest to Forest and Union Street halls is Woodlands; dining closest to Teter is Wright Cafeteria; and the most convenient dining hall for Briscoe is Gresham.

Honors Residence Halls, Availability (3.0): This rating compares the number of rooms in honors residence halls to the number of honors freshman and sophomore members in good standing, about 2,500. The ratio for the honors program is **.18** rooms for each first- and second-year student. The average for all fifty programs is .63 rooms.

Prestigious Awards (5.0): The awards that we track and include are listed in the section titled "Prestigious Scholarships." The awards are sometimes won by students who are not in an honors college or program, but increasingly many are enrolled in honors programs. It is also a trend that honors colleges and programs help to prepare their students for the awards competitions.

IU students have an excellent all-around record of winning these awards: Truman scholars, 20; Marshall scholars, 17; Rhodes scholars, 16; Churchill scholars, 5; and Gates Cambridge, 2. University grads also win a high number of Fulbright Student scholarships and NSF Graduate Research fellowships.

IU students also have a very strong record of winning Goldwater scholarships for undergraduates in the STEM fields, 45 to date.

UNRATED FEATURES

Continuation Requirements: 3.30 for continuation, and 3.40 for graduation with the General Honors Notation.

Academic Strengths, National Rankings: This is based on national rankings of *graduate* programs in 15 disciplines, except engineering and business, where undergraduate rankings are used.

IU has one of the nation's leading faculties, with an average departmental ranking of about 30 among all universities public or private. The many strong departments are business (10), sociology (12), English (22), history (23), chemistry (24), political science (25), psychology (26), education (28), and biology and math (34 each).

Undergraduate Research: "The Cox Research Scholars Program is a merit- and need-based scholarship program open to Indiana residents of exemplary achievement and scholarly curiosity. The Cox Research Scholars Program offers recipients the unique opportunity to participate in meaningful research or creative activity under the mentorship of a faculty member. Each recipient is required to work an average of 10 hours per week over all four years on a scholarly, research-based project related to his or her academic interests. The Cox Research scholarship covers four years (eight semesters) of up to the total cost of attendance as determined by the Office of Student Financial Assistance. About 25 Cox Research Scholarships are offered each year to incoming freshmen."

Study Abroad: "The Hutton Honors Program is the proud home of the Edward L. Hutton International Experiences Program (HIEP). *The HIEP is the single largest source of funding for Indiana University Bloomington undergraduate students participating in an international experience.* Support is available for a variety of activities, including study abroad, overseas research, international internships, student teaching in another country, and volunteer service abroad. During 2014-15, the HIEP awarded over $800,000 in grants to 484 students." [Emphasis added.]

Financial Aid: "Honors students who submit a complete admissions *application to Indiana University by November 1 receive an automatic IU Achievement Scholarship from the university.* The amount of the award is based on academic information provided at the time of admission. Amounts range from $1,000-$8,000 for resident students and $1,000-$11,000 for non-resident students.

"Indiana University offers scholarships in recognition of student success in a variety of national scholar programs. National Merit Finalists, National Achievement Finalists, and National Hispanic Recognition students each receive a $1,000 renewal scholarship from IU.

"Additionally, honors students who submit a complete admission application by November 1 are invited to complete the Selective Scholarship Application (SSA) to apply for additional merit scholarship funding from the Hutton Honors College as well as other departmental scholarship programs.

"A committee of Honors College faculty carefully reads each SSA application. "We are particularly interested in the quality of your high school program, the courses you have taken, the quality of your writing, and the nature of your extracurricular activities.

"Approximately *25 percent of honors applicants are awarded an additional $1,000 to $8,000* from the HHC based on the SSA application. HHC Scholarships are renewable for four years (eight semesters) by maintaining a 3.4 or above GPA, completing a minimum of three graded honors courses during the first two years, and attending at least one approved cultural/educational event each year." [Emphases added.]

Honors Fees: $7.00/year.

Placement Experiences: None reported.

Degree of Difference: This is based on the differences between (1) the average (2015, two-part) SAT scores for enrolled honors students (1370) and (2) the average test scores for all students in the university (1175) as a whole. The test scores may be an indication of how "elite" honors students may be perceived as compared to students in the university as a whole. The scores can also provide an indication of how well prepared the non-honors students in the university may be. **Please keep in mind that neither high nor low test scores determine the overall quality of a program.**

NAME: UNIVERSITY OF IOWA HONORS PROGRAM.

Date Established: 1958.

Location: Iowa City, Iowa.

University Full-time Undergraduate Enrollment: 19,546.

Honors Members in Good Standing: 3,226 (mean size of all 50 programs is 1,742).

Honors Average Admission Statistics: ACT, 30; old SAT equivalent, 1340; est. new SAT, 1400.

Average High School GPA/Class Rank: 4.00; top 6%.

Basic Admission Requirements: 30 ACT; old SAT, 1340; est. new SAT, 1400; 3.80 GPA.

Application Deadline(s): *Please verify with each program, as some deadlines could change.*

Some scholarship deadlines are in late November 2016; final deadline May 1, 2017.

Honors Programs with old SAT scores from 1315—1350: Idaho, Georgia State, Virginia Tech, Utah, Iowa, Auburn, Houston, Mississippi, VCU.

Administrative Staff: 8.

RATINGS AT A GLANCE: For all mortarboard ratings immediately below, a score of 5 is the maximum and represents a comparison with all 50 honors colleges and programs. More detailed explanations follow the "mortarboard" ratings.

PERCEPTION* OF UNIVERSITY AS A WHOLE, NOT OF HONORS: 🎓🎓🎓🎓

*Perception is based on the university's ranking among public universities in the 2016 U.S. News Best Colleges report. Please bear in mind that the better the U.S. News ranking, the more difficult it is for an honors college or program to have a rating that equals or improves on the magazine ranking.

OVERALL HONORS RATING: 🎓🎓🎓 1/2

Curriculum Requirements: 🎓🎓🎓 1/2

Number of Honors Classes Offered: 🎓🎓🎓🎓

Number of Honors Classes in Key Disciplines: 🎓🎓🎓🎓

Extent of Honors Enrollment: 🎓🎓🎓🎓 1/2

Honors-only Class Size: 🎓🎓🎓¹/²

Overall Class Size (Honors-only plus mixed, contract): 🎓🎓🎓

Honors Grad Rate: 🎓🎓🎓🎓

Value-Added Grad Rate: 🎓🎓🎓🎓

Ratio of Staff to Students: 🎓🎓🎓

Priority Registration: "Students who automatically qualify for membership in the Honors program via the high school grade point average and ACT score are also qualified for the Old Gold scholarship, which offers priority registration for all semesters after the first one. The Honors Program advocated for this priority registration for our students, but it is administered through the scholarship rather than through Honors. Students who enter the program through our Selective Admissions [transfer] process would not qualify."

Honors Housing Amenities: 🎓🎓🎓🎓¹/²

Honors Housing Availability: 🎓🎓🎓¹/²

Prestigious Awards: 🎓🎓🎓🎓¹/²

RATING SCORES AND EXPLANATIONS:

Curriculum Requirements (3.5): The most important rating category, the curriculum completion requirement (classes required to complete honors) defines not only what honors students should learn but also the extent to which honors students and faculty are connected in the classroom. If there is a thesis or capstone requirement, it reinforces the individual contact and research skills so important to learning.

The average number of honors semester hours required for completion across all 50 programs is 29.0.

Completion of the General Honors requirements requires a total of **24 credits,** including 12 credits in honors courses and 12 credits in honors experiences. These experiences may include honors in the major, internships, study abroad, the Writing Fellows program, work for the Iowa Policy Research Organization, and Engaged Social Innovation. Up to 6 credits may be in approved honors experiential courses. Completing departmental honors often requires up to 12 credits, including a **thesis/capstone,** and these may be used to satisfy the honors experience requirement.

The University Honors for Engineering option requires 24 credits as well, including 6 credits in honors courses and up to 18 credits in honors experiences. Completing departmental honors often requires up to 12 credits, including a thesis/capstone, and these may be used to satisfy part of the honors experience requirement.

AP/IB credits are not counted as replacements for honors courses.

Number of Honors Classes Offered (4.0): This is a measure of the total **adjusted** honors main sections available in the term reported, not including labs and thesis. (Please read the section titled "All about Honors Classes".) An adjusted main section has 3 or more semester credits, or equivalent, and sections with fewer credits receive a lower prorated value.

The program offered a section for every **13.8** students. The average for all 50 programs is 14.2. The lower the number, the better.

In the term reported, **63.0%** of honors class enrollment was **in honors-only sections; 36.0% in mixed honors sections (honors and non-honors students); and 3% in contract sections (regular sections in which honors students "contract" to do extra work).** The averages for all fifty programs are 81.3% in honors-only sections; 13.6 % in mixed honors sections; and 5.1% in contract sections.

Number of Honors Classes in Key Disciplines (4.0): The 15 "key" disciplines are biological sciences; business (all); chemistry; communications (especially public speaking); computer science; economics; engineering (all); English; history; math (all); philosophy; physics; political science; psychology; and sociology/anthropology/gender studies. Interdisciplinary sections, such as those often taken for General Education credit in the first two years, do receive a lesser, prorated discipline "credit" because they introduce students to multiple disciplines in an especially engaging way, often with in-depth discussion.

For this measure, mixed and contract sections are not counted as a section in a key discipline unless students taking the sections for honors credit make up at least 10% of the total section enrollment.

In the term reported, the program had a ratio of **22.0 honors students** per each main section in some or all "key disciplines." The mean for all programs is 26.3 The lower the ratio, the better.

In the term reported, the program offered **82 adjusted sections in key disciplines**, and **63 were honors-only sections.** After deciding to place more than 25 sections of the excellent "Rhetoric" course in the discipline category, we counted about 35 sections in English, appropriate for the university with the best creative writing program in the nation. Other key disciplines were communications (13), engineering (7), philosophy (5), history (4), economics (3), and biology, chemistry, and math (2 each). Sociology, anthropology, and gender studies combined had another 6 sections.

The program also offered 10 sections titled "The Interpretation of Literature" and another 2 sections in creative writing. There were 43 sections of the "Honors First-Year Seminar," with variable titles, such as "Victorian Medical Mysteries and Their Modern Counterparts"; "Volcanic Eruptions: How They Work"; "Different Views of the Sky: Astronomy in Non-Western and Western Cultures"; and "Sex, Politics, and the Bible." An additional six 3-credit seminars were offered, including *Don Quixote:* Contemporary Readings and Artistic Viewpoints."

The program combines seminars with a very large number of honors classes in the disciplines, and is an example of a large **blended program.**

Extent of Honors Enrollment (4.5): Not all honors students take an honors class each term, especially after the first two years. Programs that have fewer honors classes for upper-division honors students will

generally have fewer total members in good standing who are actually enrolled in a given term. (Please be aware, however, that honors students not enrolled in a class for a term are still connected to the honors community through residential and extracurricular activities.)

For example, if honors students in a program occupy 1,800 honors classroom seats in a given term, and there are 3,000 honors students in good standing, the extent of enrollment is .67. For programs that require a thesis, the ratio (score) reported below might in fact be somewhat higher, since we only count "regular" class enrollment for this measure, and not thesis enrollment. Iowa Honors has a ratio of **1.22**; the mean is 1.13 for all 50 programs. The higher the ratio, the better.

Average Class Size, Honors-only Sections (3.5): Offered mostly in the first two years, honors-only classes tend to be smaller and, as the name implies, have no or very few students other than those in the honors program. These class sections are almost always much smaller than mixed or contract sections, or regular non-honors class sections in the university.

The average honors-only class size in the honors program is **23.0 students**. The average for all 50 programs is 19.0 students.

Average Class Size, Overall (3.0): The overall class calculation is based on the *proportion* of honors students in each type of class (honors-only, mixed honors, and honors contract sections). Thus it is not a raw average. The overall honors-credit class size is **68.7 students**, versus the average for all 50 programs of 26.3 students.

These class size averages also do not correspond to the number of students per honors sections numbers above. The reason is that, in computing average class size metrics, we include enrollment in each 1-2-credit section, not just sections with 3 or more credits.

Along with the honors-only average of 23.0 students, the mixed honors sections average **158.1 students**, and the contract sections with honors credit for individual honors students average **48.8 students**. Across all fifty programs, the average mixed honors section has 51.1 students, and the average contract section has 60.1 students.

Honors Graduation Rate (4.0): The rating is based on the actual grad rate for students who entered the program six years earlier, whether or not the students remained in honors. The **actual rate of 85%** is also compared to the rates of other programs with the same test score entry requirement range, and then adjusted to the **score of 85%**. In some cases this measure favors programs within universities with relatively higher test scores for the student population as a whole. The average honors graduation rate for all programs with similar test scores required for admission is 83.8%.

Value-Added Grad Rate (4.0): The value-added rate measures the extent to which the adjusted score listed above exceeds the six-year grad rate for the university as a whole. **The university-wide rate is 70%.** Note: This measure generally favors programs within universities with relatively lower test scores for the student population as a whole.

Ratio of Staff to Honors Students (3.0): There is 1 staff member for every **403.3 students**. (Mean ratio for all 50 programs is 1 staff member for every 135.6 students.)

Honors Residence Halls, Amenities (4.5): Almost 75% of honors students in honors housing are freshmen, most of whom reside in Datum Hall. The residence has a variety of traditional rooms and pod-style bathrooms. It is air-conditioned and has an excellent location for honors students: a tunnel connects Daum to the dining hall in neighboring Burge Hall, and a covered skywalk connects Daum to the Blank Honors Center, which is the administrative home of the program.

Another 25% of honors students in honors housing—all upperclassmen—live in the nearby Cornerstone residence. Cornerstone has air-conditioned, apartment-style rooms. The closest dining is also at Burge Hall.

Finally, about 30 first-year honors students reside in Petersen Hall, home to a STEM Scholars program. Petersen features traditional rooms and hall baths. It is air-conditioned, and the nearest dining is at Hillcrest Hall. STEM students involved in research in the first year can receive $500 of funding to present at a research conference.

Honors Residence Halls, Availability (3.5): This rating compares the number of rooms in honors residence halls to the number of honors freshman and sophomore members in good standing, about 1,613. The ratio for the honors program is **.31** rooms for each first- and second-year student. The average for all fifty programs is .63 rooms.

Prestigious Awards (4.5): The awards that we track and include are listed in the section titled "Prestigious Scholarships." The awards are sometimes won by students who are not in an honors college or program, but increasingly many are enrolled in honors programs. It is also a trend that honors colleges and programs help to prepare their students for the awards competitions.

Iowa students have an excellent record in this category: 20 Rhodes scholarships; 5 Gates Cambridge scholarships; 3 Marshall scholarships; 4 Churchill awards; and 14 Truman scholars.

Iowa students also have an excellent record in achieving undergraduate awards, including 5 Udall scholarships and 49 prestigious Goldwater scholarships. The university is well above the mean in the number of recent Fulbright Student scholars.

UNRATED FEATURES

Continuation Requirements: 3.33 cumulative GPA for continuation, and for honors graduation.

Academic Strengths, National Rankings: This is based on national rankings of *graduate* programs in 15 disciplines, except engineering and business, where undergraduate rankings are used.

Iowa has an excellent faculty, with an average departmental ranking of about 50th among all universities public or private. Especially strong departments are psychology (30), English and political science (32), business (34), sociology (35), economics (40), education and history (both 42), biology (55), and math (56).

Undergraduate Research: "The Iowa Center for Research by Undergraduates, or ICRU, promotes and provides oversight for undergraduate research at the University of Iowa. To promote research ICRU works directly with faculty, research staff, and students to foster mentoring relationships. The center provides nearly $350,000 annually in funding for undergraduates to work with faculty, and this is principally as stipend support although travel support is also available for students to perform and present their work. ICRU also supports annual opportunities for undergraduates to present their work on campus at events such as the Spring Undergraduate Research Festival and Summer Research Conference and off campus at Research in the Capitol, where a group of undergraduate researchers present their work at the Iowa Statehouse. Students and mentors who have excelled in their efforts are recognized by ICRU on behalf of the University through the Excellence in Undergraduate Research and ICRU Distinguished Mentor awards."

Study Abroad: "The Honors program has travel grants available, including those set aside for Honors students participating in the India Winterim program. The India Winterim study-abroad program, which marked its 10th anniversary in 2016, received the 2016 Andrew Heiskell Award for Innovation in International Education from the Institute of International Education."

Financial Aid: "99.8% of the incoming class of Honors students in Fall 2015 received at least one merit scholarship. *Note that the requirements for admissions to Honors for Fall 2016 match those for the Old Gold Scholarship, giving all in-state Honors students (admitted in Fall 2016 and later) $8,500 per year in scholarships automatically, and out of state students $10,000 per year.* [Emphasis added.] The only exception to this would be students who enter the program through the selective admissions process or as transfer students. Most of the latter group will typically qualify for the Iowa Scholars Award (Iowa residents, $3,500 per year) or the National Scholars Award (out of state residents , $5,000 per year). There are also many other scholarships that students can qualify for based on more specific criteria within departments.

"Admitted high school seniors who accept membership in the Honors program and earn at least a 32 ACT composite and a 3.85 GPA on a 4.0 scale are also eligible to apply for a Presidential Scholarship. This scholarship awards $18,500 per year to Iowa residents and $20,000 per year to out of state residents. The program is highly competitive, and no more than 20 first-year students will enroll as Presidential Scholars each year. These scholars are also part of a cohort program that includes social events, leadership opportunities, interactions with the President of the University, and many other benefits.

"All students enrolling as new freshmen also receive a Summer Hawk Tuition Grant, which pays tuition for a full summer of enrollment for in-state students, or the difference between resident and non-resident tuition for out-of-state students.

"All Iowa residents are eligible for a $1,000 study abroad scholarship.

"The Provost Scholarship is available for National Merit finalists, National Achievement finalists and National Hispanic Scholars. It is $3,000 a year for four years and stacks on top of the above scholarships.

"The Honors Program provides over $110,000 per year to currently enrolled honors students."

Honors Fees: None.

Placement Experiences: "67% of 2015 Honors graduates reported pursuing a graduate or professional degree, with another 29% considering the option. Several recent graduates are pursuing law school, medical school, or PhD programs at prestigious institutions such as Harvard and Stanford as well as the University of Iowa's own highly-ranked College of Law and Carver College of Medicine. *One 2016 graduate will join the Rhodes Class of 2016 after having previously compiled Udall, Truman, and Boren scholarships during his time as a University of Iowa Honors student.* [Emphasis added.]

Degree of Difference: This is based on the differences between (1) the average (2015, two-part) SAT scores for enrolled honors students (1335-ACT equivalent) and (2) the average test scores for all students in the university (1150-ACT equivalent) as a whole. The test scores may be an indication of how "elite" honors students may be perceived as compared to students in the university as a whole. The scores can also provide an indication of how well prepared the non-honors students in the university may be. **Please keep in mind that neither high nor low test scores determine the overall quality of a program.**

NAME: UNIVERSITY HONORS PROGRAM AT THE UNIVERSITY OF KANSAS.

Date Established:1956.

Location: Lawrence, Kansas.

University Full-time Undergraduate Enrollment: 17,335.

Honors Members in Good Standing: 1,400 (mean size of all 50 programs is 1,742).

Honors Average Admission Statistics: Est. ACT, 32; old SAT, 1420; est. new SAT, 1470.

Average High School GPA/Class Rank: 3.94 unweighted; top 6%.

Basic Admission Requirements: "There are no minimum GPA or test score requirements. We utilize holistic admissions, examining a student's entire profile in making admissions decisions. We equally weigh all five of the following in making admissions decisions: ACT/SAT composite, unweighted GPA, strength of curriculum, extra-curricular activities, and critical writing skills."

Application Deadline(s): *Please verify with each program, as some deadlines could change.*

November 1, 2016.

Honors Programs with old SAT scores from 1402—1469: UCF, Connecticut, Kentucky, Washington, Maryland, North Carolina, UC Irvine, Kansas, Minnesota, Tennessee, South Carolina, Clemson, UT Austin, Georgia.

Administrative Staff: 14 FTEs.

RATINGS AT A GLANCE: For all mortarboard ratings immediately below, a score of 5 is the maximum and represents a comparison with all 50 honors colleges and programs. More detailed explanations follow the "mortarboard" ratings.

PERCEPTION* OF UNIVERSITY AS A WHOLE, NOT OF HONORS: 🎓🎓🎓🎓

*Perception is based on the university's ranking among public universities in the 2016 U.S. News Best Colleges report. Please bear in mind that the better the U.S. News ranking, the more difficult it is for an honors college or program to have a rating that equals or improves on the magazine ranking.

OVERALL HONORS RATING: 🎓🎓🎓🎓🎓

Curriculum Requirements: 🎓🎓🎓🎓1/2

Number of Honors Classes Offered: 🎓🎓🎓🎓🎓

Number of Honors Classes in Key Disciplines: 🎓🎓🎓🎓🎓

Extent of Honors Enrollment: 🎓🎓🎓🎓$^{1/2}$

Honors-only Class Size: 🎓🎓🎓🎓$^{1/2}$

Overall Class Size (Honors-only plus mixed, contract): 🎓🎓🎓🎓$^{1/2}$

Honors Grad Rate: 🎓🎓🎓🎓$^{1/2}$

Value-Added Grad Rate: 🎓🎓🎓🎓🎓

Ratio of Staff to Students: 🎓🎓🎓🎓$^{1/2}$

Priority Registration: "Honor Students enroll first in all courses. The exception is that first semester freshmen enrollment is based on the Orientation date selected by the student. From second semester onward, Honors Students enroll before the seniors, the athletes, and everyone else at KU."

Honors Housing Amenities: 🎓🎓🎓🎓$^{1/2}$

Honors Housing Availability: 🎓🎓🎓🎓

Prestigious Awards: 🎓🎓🎓🎓🎓

RATING SCORES AND EXPLANATIONS:

Curriculum Requirements (4.5): The most important rating category, the curriculum completion requirement (classes required to complete honors) defines not only what honors students should learn but also the extent to which honors students and faculty are connected in the classroom. If there is a thesis or capstone requirement, it reinforces the individual contact and research skills so important to learning.

The average number of honors semester hours required for completion across all 50 programs is 29.0.

Effective Fall 2016, the program requires about **31 credits** for completion, up from 25 credits in previous years.

Students must complete six honors courses (18 credits), which may also be counted toward KU core, major, or elective requirements, and complete a 1-credit freshman honors seminar (please see below). At least 12 more credits, on average, are earned by completing at least four Honors Enhanced Learning Experiences.

The honors experience requirement can include courses and activities focusing on leadership, public service, research skills, professional development and social entrepreneurship, social justice, aesthetic engagement, global citizenship, and interdisciplinary studies.

Honors Seminar: "In their first semester, all students are required to enroll in a 1-credit-hour freshman honors seminar that serves as an introduction to the Honors Program, the resources offered by the University of Kansas, and one of their academic areas of interest. While closely examining a specific topic, students develop their skills in research, reading, writing, and in-depth discussion. The instructor of the student's seminar also serves as the academic honors advisor for the enrolled students."

AP/IB credits are not counted as replacements for honors courses.

Number of Honors Classes Offered (5.0): This is a measure of the total **adjusted** honors main sections available in the term reported, not including labs and thesis. (Please read the section titled "All about Honors Classes".) An adjusted main section has 3 or more semester credits, or equivalent, and sections with fewer credits receive a lower prorated value.

The program offered a section for every **7.8** students. The average for all 50 programs is 14.2. The lower the number, the better.

In the term reported, **93.1%** of honors class enrollment was **in honors-only sections; 6.9% in mixed honors sections (honors and non-honors students); and none reported in contract sections (regular sections in which honors students "contract" to do extra work).** The averages for all fifty programs are 81.3% in honors-only sections; 13.6 % in mixed honors sections; and 5.1% in contract sections.

Number of Honors Classes in Key Disciplines (5.0): The 15 "key" disciplines are biological sciences; business (all); chemistry; communications (especially public speaking); computer science; economics; engineering (all); English; history; math (all); philosophy; physics; political science; psychology; and sociology/anthropology/gender studies. Interdisciplinary sections, such as those often taken for General Education credit in the first two years, do receive a lesser, prorated discipline "credit" because they introduce students to multiple disciplines in an especially engaging way, often with in-depth discussion.

For this measure, mixed and contract sections are not counted as a section in a key discipline unless students taking the sections for honors credit make up at least 10% of the total section enrollment.

In the term reported, the program had a ratio of **13.1 honors students** per each main section in some or all "key disciplines." The mean for all programs is 26.3. The lower the ratio, the better.

Out of **58 adjusted sections in key disciplines**, the program offered about **52 honors-only sections.** English had the most sections (14), followed by business (9), history and math (5 each), communications and computer science (4 each), biology and chemistry (3 each), and physics, political science, and psychology (2 each). Sociology, anthropology, and/or gender studies had a total of 4 sections. Philosophy was the only discipline that was not represented.

The program also offered almost 40 sections of the 1-credit Freshman Honors Seminar. Essentially, however, the program is an excellent example of a **discipline-based honors program.**

Extent of Honors Enrollment (4.5): Not all honors students take an honors class each term, especially after the first two years. Programs that have fewer honors classes for upper-division honors students will generally have fewer total members in good standing who are actually enrolled in a given term. (Please be aware, however, that honors students not enrolled in a class for a term are still connected to the honors community through residential and extracurricular activities.)

For example, if honors students in a program occupy 1,800 honors classroom seats in a given term, and there are 3,000 honors students in good standing, the extent of enrollment is .67. For programs that require a thesis, the ratio (score) reported below might in fact be somewhat higher, since we only count "regular" class enrollment for this measure, and not thesis enrollment. The program **has a ratio of 1.38**; the mean is 1.13 for all 50 programs. The higher the ratio, the better.

Average Class Size, Honors-only Sections (4.5): Offered mostly in the first two years, honors-only classes tend to be smaller and, as the name implies, have no or very few students other than those in the honors program. These class sections are almost always much smaller than mixed or contract sections, or regular non-honors class sections in the university.

The average honors-only class size in the honors program is **16.3 students**. The average for all 50 programs is 19.0 students.

Average Class Size, Overall (4.5): The overall class calculation is based on the *proportion* of honors students in each type of class (honors-only, mixed honors, and honors contract sections). Thus it is not a raw average. The overall honors-credit class size is **18.7 students**, versus the average for all 50 programs of 26.3 students.

These class size averages also do not correspond to the number of students per honors sections numbers above. The reason is that, in computing average class size metrics, we include enrollment in each 1-2-credit section, not just sections with 3 or more credits.

Along with the honors-only average of 16.3 students, the mixed honors sections average **50.3 students,** and the contract sections with honors credit for individual honors students were not reported. Across all fifty programs, the average mixed honors section has 51.1 students, and the average contract section has 60.1 students.

Honors Graduation Rate (4.5): The rating is based on the actual grad rate for students who entered the program six years earlier, whether or not the students remained in honors. The **actual rate of 91%** is also compared to the rates of other programs with the same test score entry requirement range, and then adjusted to the **score of 90.8%.** In some cases this measure favors programs within universities with relatively higher test scores for the student population as a whole. The average honors graduation rate for all programs with similar test scores required for admission is 92.6%.

Value-Added Grad Rate (5.0): The value-added rate measures the extent to which the adjusted score listed above exceeds the six-year grad rate for the university as a whole. **The university-wide rate is 60%.** Note: This measure generally favors programs within universities with relatively lower test scores for the student population as a whole.

Ratio of Staff to Honors Students (4.5): There is 1 staff member for every **100.0** students. (Mean ratio for all 50 programs is 1 staff member for every 135.6 students.)

Honors Residence Halls, Amenities (4.5): "Templin Hall is the most popular dorm on campus for Honors Students for its renovated, suite-style rooms [air-conditioned] and location. Beginning in 2012, the Department of Housing agreed to turn over the entire hall to the University Honors Program for its student, due to its immediate proximity to Nunemaker Center, the University Honors Program's unique, full-service home. Students are NOT required to live in the Honors hall, but it is recommended." The most convenient dining is at Mrs. E's.

"Many Honor Students also chose to live in a Scholarship Hall. Students complete 4-6 hours of weekly duties, such as cooking or cleaning for the 50-person community. Students apply to live in the scholarship hall and selection is based on financial need, academic merit and essays demonstrating commitment to the cooperative philosophy and diverse community."

There are 12 Scholarship Halls, and they are listed below along with the number of honors students in each:

Men--Battenfield 18, Grace Pearson 15, KK Amini 16, Krehbiel 18, Pearson 8, Stephenson 12.

Women--Dennis E. Rieger 22, Douthart 22, Margaret Amini 16, Miller 15, Sellards 16, Watkins 21.

About half the rooms in the Scholarship Halls are traditional doubles with hall baths, while the other half are suite-style rooms with shared baths. The residence is air-conditioned. "Student residents prepare the meals in their scholarship hall's kitchen for the 50-person community."

Honors Residence Halls, Availability (4.0): This rating compares the number of rooms in honors residence halls to the number of honors freshman and sophomore members in good standing, about 700. The ratio for the honors program is **.57** rooms for each first- and second-year student. The average for all fifty programs is .63 rooms.

Prestigious Awards (5.0): The awards that we track and include are listed in the section titled "Prestigious Scholarships." The awards are sometimes won by students who are not in an honors college or program, but increasingly many are enrolled in honors programs. It is also a trend that honors colleges and programs help to prepare their students for the awards competitions.

This category is a definite area of strength for KU and KU Honors. The director reports that the "majority of National Scholarship nominees and winners have been in the University Honors Program. Every Rhodes Scholar at KU has been an Honors student since the inception of the program. We have had two Gates Cambridge Scholars (all 3 of KU's GC scholars have been in Honors) in the past two years, and two Udall Scholars in one year (out of only about 50 nationally). In addition, we were recently named a participating institution in the Astronaut Scholarship Program."

KU students have won 26 Rhodes scholarships, 9 Marshall scholarships, 18 Truman awards, 3 Gates Cambridge scholarships, and a Churchill scholarship. KU students are also among the national leaders in Udall scholarships (18) and Goldwater scholarships (60), both awarded to undergraduates.

UNRATED FEATURES

Continuation Requirements: For continuation and for graduation, a 3.25 GPA is required.

Academic Strengths, National Rankings: This is based on national rankings of *graduate* programs in 15 disciplines, except engineering and business, where undergraduate rankings are used.

Academic departments at KU have an average ranking of about 60-65 in the nation. Leading departments are education (15), psychology (40), history (50), earth sciences (54), business (61), English (63), sociology (64), and math (68).

Undergraduate Research: "The Honors Program cultivated a university-wide program for undergraduate research until 2012. The program included the Undergraduate Research Symposium, a journal for undergraduate research, and research grants for independent student research. Due to the success of this program, it was spun off as the Center for Undergraduate Research in Fall 2012. Honors students still benefit broadly from the expanded program, which has grown in scope, resources and reach.

"At the University of Kansas, honors research and theses are integral to departmental honors. Many University Honors Program students pursue departmental honors in their major(s) and completion of departmental honors is one pathway for completion of the University Honors Program honors experiences."

Study Abroad: "The University of Kansas is a world leader in study abroad. There are over 130 programs plus an additional 200 ISEP & MAUI consortium sites in over 70 countries. The University Honors Program, however, sends students to far more destinations than the standard Office of Study Abroad offerings. *Essentially, if there is an academic benefit to be gleaned, we will help students coordinate and fund the study abroad destination they might choose.*"[Emphasis added.]

Financial Aid: "By dint of the University's scholarship structure, virtually all Honors students will receive a 4-year, renewable scholarship. All in-state students will receive packages ranging from $4,000 to approximately $80,000 (full tuition, room and board, fees, etc.). Out of state students virtually all have their tuition reduced to a rate of 1.5 times that of in-state students."

Honors Fees: None.

Placement Experiences: Post-Graduation Survey of Spring 2014 Graduates (6 months after graduation):

I have Employment= 43.48%.
I am attending Graduate School= 27.94%.
I am attending Medical School= 14.71%.
I am attending Law School= 4.41%.
I am doing Social/Public Service (e.g. Peace Corp, Teach for America)= 4.41%.
Other Pursuits= 4.41%.

Degree of Difference: This is based on the differences between (1) the average (2015, two-part) SAT scores for enrolled honors students (est. 1420) and (2) the average test scores for all students in the university (1150) as a whole. The test scores may be an indication of how "elite" honors students may be perceived as compared to students in the university as a whole. The scores can also provide an indication of how well prepared the non-honors students in the university may be. **Please keep in mind that neither high nor low test scores determine the overall quality of a program.**

NAME: UNIVERSITY OF KENTUCKY HONORS PROGRAM (transitioning to the new, generously endowed Lewis Honors College). This will be a major boost to honors education at UKY, although the changes cannot be reviewed until the new honors college is fully operational.

Date Established: 1961.

Location: Lexington, Kentucky.

University Full-time Undergraduate Enrollment: 20,690.

Honors Members in Good Standing: 1,615 (mean size of all 50 programs is 1,742).

Honors Average Admission Statistics: ACT, 31.58; old SAT equivalent, 1410; est. new SAT, 1460.

Average High School GPA/Class Rank: 3.90.

Basic Admission Requirements: ACT, 28. Old SAT, 1250; est. new SAT, 1310.

Application Deadline(s): *Please verify with each program, as some deadlines could change.*

December 1, 2016.

Honors Programs with old SAT scores from 1402—1469: UCF, Connecticut, Kentucky, Washington, Maryland, North Carolina, UC Irvine, Kansas, Minnesota, Tennessee, South Carolina, Clemson, UT Austin, Georgia.

Administrative Staff: 7.

RATINGS AT A GLANCE: For all mortarboard ratings immediately below, a score of 5 is the maximum and represents a comparison with all 50 honors colleges and programs. More detailed explanations follow the "mortarboard" ratings.

PERCEPTION* OF UNIVERSITY AS A WHOLE, NOT OF HONORS: 🎓🎓🎓$^{1/2}$

*Perception is based on the university's ranking among public universities in the 2016 U.S. News Best Colleges report. Please bear in mind that the better the U.S. News ranking, the more difficult it is for an honors college or program to have a rating that equals or improves on the magazine ranking.

OVERALL HONORS RATING: 🎓🎓🎓

Curriculum Requirements: 🎓🎓🎓🎓

Number of Honors Classes Offered: 🎓🎓🎓

Number of Honors Classes in Key Disciplines: 🎓🎓🎓

Extent of Honors Enrollment: 🎓🎓🎓

Honors-only Class Size: 🎓🎓🎓🎓$^{1/2}$

Overall Class Size (Honors-only plus mixed, contract): 🎓🎓🎓🎓$^{1/2}$

Honors Grad Rate: 🎓🎓🎓🎓$^{1/2}$

Value-Added Grad Rate: 🎓🎓🎓🎓🎓

Ratio of Staff to Students: 🎓🎓🎓

Priority Registration: Yes, honors students register for all courses, honors and otherwise, with the first group of students during each year they are in the program.

Honors Housing Amenities: 🎓🎓🎓🎓$^{1/2}$

Honors Housing Availability: 🎓🎓🎓🎓

Prestigious Awards: 🎓🎓🎓🎓

RATING SCORES AND EXPLANATIONS:

Curriculum Requirements (4.0): The most important rating category, the curriculum completion requirement (classes required to complete honors) defines not only what honors students should learn but also the extent to which honors students and faculty are connected in the classroom. If there is a thesis or capstone requirement, it reinforces the individual contact and research skills so important to learning.

The average number of honors semester hours required for completion across all 50 programs is 29.0.

Although the completion requirement for the main program, University Honors, at UKY is 21 credits, the program also offers four "Pathway" completion options for Global Scholars, Social Enterprise, Scholars in Engineering and Management, and Scholars in Nursing. The estimate for average completion when all options are included is about **28-29 credits.**

The 21-credit requirement for University Honors includes 9 honors program credits, 6 credits in honors experiences, 3 credits in departmental honors, and a 3-credit capstone or **thesis.**

The Global Scholars completion requirement is 36 credits, including 24 credits in departmental honors, 6 credits in honors experiences, 3 credits in an honors program course, and a 3-credit capstone/**thesis.**

The Social Enterprise option requirements are essentially the same as those for Global Scholars, though with a different emphasis in departmental honors courses.

The Scholars in Engineering and Management (SEAM) option requires 25 total credits, including 13 credits in departmental honors courses, 6 credits in honors experiences, 3 credits in an honors program course, and a 3-credit capstone.

The Scholars in Nursing option requirement is the same as the SEAM requirement above, except for a different emphasis in departmental honors. This program option is unique among all programs under review.

AP/IB credits are not counted as replacements for honors courses.

Number of Honors Classes Offered (3.0): This is a measure of the total **adjusted** honors main sections available in the term reported, not including labs and thesis. (Please read the section titled "All about Honors Classes".) An adjusted main section has 3 or more semester credits, or equivalent, and sections with fewer credits receive a lower prorated value.

The program offered a section for every **30.1** students. The average for all 50 programs is 14.2. The lower the number, the better.

In the term reported, **71.5%** of honors class enrollment was **in honors-only sections; 24.8% in mixed honors sections (honors and non-honors students); and 3.7% in contract sections (regular sections in which honors students "contract" to do extra work).** The averages for all fifty programs are 81.3% in honors-only sections; 13.6 % in mixed honors sections; and 5.1% in contract sections.

Number of Honors Classes in Key Disciplines (3.0): The 15 "key" disciplines are biological sciences; business (all); chemistry; communications (especially public speaking); computer science; economics; engineering (all); English; history; math (all); philosophy; physics; political science; psychology; and sociology/anthropology/gender studies. Interdisciplinary sections, such as those often taken for General Education credit in the first two years, do receive a lesser, prorated discipline "credit" because they introduce students to multiple disciplines in an especially engaging way, often with in-depth discussion.

For this measure, mixed and contract sections are not counted as a section in a key discipline unless students taking the sections for honors credit make up at least 10% of the total section enrollment.

In the term reported, the program had a ratio of **60.9 honors students** per each main section in some or all "key disciplines." The mean for all programs is 26.3
. The lower the ratio, the better.

In the term reported, the program offered **21 adjusted sections in key disciplines**, and **11 honors-only sections.** The most sections were in English (6), math (3), and biology, history, philosophy, and psychology (2 each).

The program also offered about 34 excellent 3-credit honors interdisciplinary sections, including "Music and War in the Twentieth Century"; "Getting at Life's Mechanisms"; "Parallel Visions in the Arts, Sciences, and Literature"; and "Acts of Violence Through the Lens of Social Science."

The program combines interdisciplinary classes with several departmental honors classes, and is an example of a **blended program.**

Extent of Honors Enrollment (3.0): Not all honors students take an honors class each term, especially after the first two years. Programs that have fewer honors classes for upper-division honors students will generally have fewer total members in good standing who are actually enrolled in a given term. (Please be aware, however, that honors students not enrolled in a class for a term are still connected to the honors community through residential and extracurricular activities.)

For example, if honors students in a program occupy 1,800 honors classroom seats in a given term, and there are 3,000 honors students in good standing, the extent of enrollment is .67. For programs that require a thesis, the ratio (score) reported below might in fact be somewhat higher, since we only count "regular" class enrollment for this measure, and not thesis enrollment. The program **has a ratio of .52**; the mean is 1.13 for all 50 programs. The higher the ratio, the better.

Average Class Size, Honors-only Sections (4.5): Offered mostly in the first two years, honors-only classes tend to be smaller and, as the name implies, have no or very few students other than those in the honors program. These class sections are almost always much smaller than mixed or contract sections, or regular non-honors class sections in the university.

The average honors-only class size in the honors program is **17.7 students**. The average for all 50 programs is 19.0 students.

Average Class Size, Overall (4.5): The overall class calculation is based on the *proportion* of honors students in each type of class (honors-only, mixed honors, and honors contract sections). Thus it is not a raw average. The overall honors-credit class size is **20.6 students**, versus the average for all 50 programs of 26.3 students.

These class size averages also do not correspond to the number of students per honors sections numbers above. The reason is that, in computing average class size metrics, we include enrollment in each 1-2-credit section, not just sections with 3 or more credits.

Along with the honors-only average of 17.7 students, the mixed honors sections average **26.3 students**, and the contract sections with honors credit for individual honors students average **38.5 students**. Across all fifty programs, the average mixed honors section has 51.1 students, and the average contract section has 60.1 students.

Honors Graduation Rate (4.5): The rating is based on the actual grad rate for students who entered the program six years earlier, whether or not the students remained in honors. The **actual rate of 90.4%** is also compared to the rates of other programs with the same test score entry requirement range, and then adjusted to the **score of 90.2%.** In some cases this measure favors programs within universities with relatively higher test scores for the student population as a whole. The average honors graduation rate for all programs with similar test scores required for admission is 92.6%.

Value-Added Grad Rate (5.0): The value-added rate measures the extent to which the adjusted score listed above exceeds the six-year grad rate for the university as a whole. **The university-wide rate is 60%.** Note: This measure generally favors programs within universities with relatively lower test scores for the student population as a whole.

Ratio of Staff to Honors Students (3.0): There is 1 staff member for every **230.7** students. (Mean ratio for all 50 programs is 1 staff member for every 135.6 students.)

Honors Residence Halls, Amenities (4.5): Almost 75% of honors students, freshmen and upperclassmen, who reside in honors housing live in Central Residence Hall II and Johnson Hall (formerly Central Residence Hall I). This residence features suite-style, air-conditioned rooms with shared baths. The nearest dining is at K-Lair or The 90.

About a quarter of honors students in honors housing live in Haggin Hall, which has features and dining similar to Central Residence Hall II.

Honors Residence Halls, Availability (4.0): This rating compares the number of rooms in honors residence halls to the number of honors freshman and sophomore members in good standing, about 807. The ratio for the honors program is **.56** rooms for each first- and second-year student. The average for all fifty programs is .63 rooms.

Prestigious Awards (4.0): The awards that we track and include are listed in the section titled "Prestigious Scholarships." The awards are sometimes won by students who are not in an honors college or program, but increasingly many are enrolled in honors programs. It is also a trend that honors colleges and programs help to prepare their students for the awards competitions.

"The Honors Program at the University of Kentucky has a very deliberate connection to the university's Office of Nationally Competitive Awards. We manage invitations to Honors faculty to identify and recommend potential competitive scholarship applicants in their Honors seminars from students' first semesters on campus; those students are then worked with on an individual basis in the Office of Nationally Competitive Awards to lay the groundwork for successful competitive scholarship applications. Additionally, all first-year Honors students are required to attend a mandatory competitive scholarships information session in their first year at the university. Further, the Office of Undergraduate Research works individually with Honors students who engage in research to connect them with the Office of Nationally Competitive Awards staff for consultation and direction."

UKY students have won 9 Rhodes scholarships, 2 Gates Cambridge scholarships, 5 Marshall scholarships, and 13 Truman scholarships. They have also won 5 Udall awards and 19 Goldwater scholarships.

UNRATED FEATURES

Continuation Requirements: 3.00, and the same for graduation.

Academic Strengths, National Rankings: This is based on national rankings of *graduate* programs in 15 disciplines, except engineering and business, where undergraduate rankings are used.

The academic departments at UKY average around 85th in the nation. Among the most recognized are education (58), earth sciences (59), business (61), math (73), political science (76), and psychology (78).

Undergraduate Research: "Students in Honors have the option to complete undergraduate research as part of the Honors experience requirement in the curriculum. Additionally, all Honors students complete a capstone project which, though it may be a creative or performative work, is based fundamentally in undergraduate research."

Study Abroad: "Honors offers a variety of scholarship opportunities for Education Abroad, including the Student Skills Development Award, the Journal-Journey Scholarship, and the Kate Johnson Scholarship. The Program typically offers 3-5 Honors-sponsored education abroad courses in an academic year, all in the summer or winter intersessions. Finally, Honors at UK gives students the option to complete Honors curricular requirements by completing education abroad programs."

Financial Aid: "While most Honors students receive some kind of merit and need-based financial aid from university-wide and external sources, Honors offers a four-year scholarship for tuition: The T.W. Lewis Scholarship Fund provides up to 10 new scholarships in the amount of $5,000 per year for eligible Honors Program students. Up to five scholarships are awarded to applicants from a 10-county region in Eastern Kentucky, including Breathitt, Clay, Floyd, Harlan, Jackson, Knott, Leslie, Letcher, Perry and Wolfe counties. Up to five scholarships are awarded to applicants from Fayette County. Additionally, the Singletary Scholarship is the most prestigious academic scholarship at the university, and all recipients of that award are members of the Honors Program. *Finally, National Merit Scholars who list the University of Kentucky as their first choice are awarded a full tuition, room and board, and stipend package through the Office of Academic Scholarships.* [Emphasis added.]

Honors Fees: None.

Placement Experiences: "Our 2015 Honors graduates were placed in the following sectors (multiple students at some institutions; only a partial report of our graduates):

"**PhD Programs** – UC Berkeley, UC San Francisco, UC Irvine, Georgia Tech, Michigan State, Eastern Kentucky, University of Kentucky; **Pharmacy School** – University of Kentucky; **Medical School** – Emory, Washington University St. Louis, Ohio State University, Tennessee, Kentucky, Louisville; **Law School** – NYU, Virginia, Emory; **MBA Programs** – University of Kentucky; **Veterinary School** – Purdue; **Masters Programs** – MIT, Xavier, Columbia, University of Glasgow, Virginia Commonwealth, Kentucky, Louisville; **Job Placements** – Capital One, Farm Credit Administration, Tennessee Department of Transportation, Teach for America, Hemlock Semiconductor Corporation, Lockheed Martin, PriceWaterhouseCooper, Altec, GE Appliances, Duke Energy, Tempur Sealy International, Deloitte, Kentucky Children's Hospital, Enterprise Holdings, American Woodmark, Flatirons Solutions."

Degree of Difference: This is based on the differences between (1) the average (2015, two-part) SAT scores for enrolled honors students (1410=ACT equivalent) and (2) the average test scores for all students in the university (1150) as a whole. The test scores may be an indication of how "elite" honors students may be perceived as compared to students in the university as a whole. The scores can also provide an indication of how well prepared the non-honors students in the university may be. **Please keep in mind that neither high nor low test scores determine the overall quality of a program.**

NAME: LSU ROGER HADFIELD OGDEN HONORS COLLEGE.

Date Established: 1999.

Location: Baton Rouge, Louisiana.

University <u>Full-time Undergraduate</u> Enrollment: 23,195.

Honors Members in Good Standing: 1,399 (mean size of all 50 programs is 1,742).

Honors <u>Average</u> Admission Statistics: ACT, 31.3; old two-part SAT, 1390. Est. new SAT score, 1440.

Average High School GPA/Class Rank: 3.79 GPA.

<u>Basic</u> Admission Requirements: ACT, 30 (30 Composite with 30 English subscore, or 29 Composite with 31 English subscore); old SAT 1330; new SAT, 1390. High school GPA, 3.5.

Application Deadline(s): *Please verify with each program, as some deadlines could change.*

November 15, 2016; notification mid-December, 2016, onward, on a rolling basis.

Honors Programs with old SAT scores from 1351—1396: Purdue, Oregon, Alabama, Massachusetts, Penn State, Indiana, CUNY Macaulay, Texas A&M, NJIT, Missouri, Oregon State, Delaware, LSU, Vermont, Temple.

Administrative Staff: 13.

RATINGS AT A GLANCE: For all mortarboard ratings immediately below, a score of 5 is the maximum and represents a comparison with all 50 honors colleges and programs. More detailed explanations follow the "mortarboard" ratings.

PERCEPTION* OF UNIVERSITY AS A WHOLE, <u>NOT</u> OF HONORS: 🎓🎓🎓$^{1/2}$

*Perception is based on the university's ranking among public universities in the 2016 U.S. News Best Colleges report. Please bear in mind that the better the U.S. News ranking, the more difficult it is for an honors college or program to have a rating that equals or improves on the magazine ranking.

OVERALL HONORS RATING: 🎓🎓🎓🎓

Curriculum Requirements: 🎓🎓🎓🎓

Number of Honors Classes Offered: 🎓🎓🎓🎓

Number of Honors Classes in Key Disciplines: 🎓🎓🎓$^{1/2}$

Extent of Honors Enrollment: 🎓🎓🎓🎓🎓

Honors-only Class Size: 🎓🎓🎓^{1/2}

Overall Class Size (Honors-only plus mixed, contract): 🎓🎓🎓^{1/2}

Honors Grad Rate: 🎓🎓🎓^{1/2}

Value-Added Grad Rate: 🎓🎓🎓🎓

Ratio of Staff to Students: 🎓🎓🎓🎓^{1/2}

Priority Registration: Yes, honors students register for all courses, honors and otherwise, with the first group of students during each year they are in the program.

Honors Housing Amenities: 🎓🎓🎓🎓^{1/2}

Honors Housing Availability: 🎓🎓🎓🎓^{1/2}

Prestigious Awards: 🎓🎓🎓🎓

RATING SCORES AND EXPLANATIONS:

Curriculum Requirements (4.0): The most important rating category, the curriculum completion requirement (classes required to complete honors) defines not only what honors students should learn but also the extent to which honors students and faculty are connected in the classroom. If there is a thesis or capstone requirement, it reinforces the individual contact and research skills so important to learning.

The average number of honors semester hours required for completion across all 50 programs is 29.0.

The average completion at LSU is about 32 hours, but because of some AP credits being allowed (for introductory chemistry), the number of honors credits needed for completion has been adjusted to 29 credits.

The College Honors option requires 32 total credits, including a **6-credit thesis** and up to 6 credits in honors contract classes.

Sophomore Honors (a "mid-point" level of completion) requires 20 honors credits.

Upper Division Honors Distinction is essentially the same as completing departmental honors requires, usually 12-18 credits, depending on the department, including a 6-credit thesis.

AP/IB credits are **not** counted as replacements for honors courses *except* for the 6-credit chemistry sequence, which requires an AP score of 4 or higher.

Number of Honors Classes Offered (4.0): This is a measure of the total **adjusted** honors main sections available in the term reported, not including labs and thesis. (Please read the section titled "All about Honors Classes".) An adjusted main section has 3 or more semester credits, or equivalent, and sections with fewer credits receive a lower prorated value.

The honors program had a ratio of **14.1** enrolled students per each main section. The mean for all 50 programs is 14.2. The lower the ratio, the better.

In the term reported, an estimated **53.8 %** of honors enrollment was **in honors-only sections; 32.4% in mixed sections with honors and non-honors students; and 13.8% reported in contract sections (regular sections in which honors students "contract" to do extra work**. The averages for all fifty programs are 81.3% in honors-only sections; 13.6 % in mixed honors sections; and 5.1% in contract sections.

Number of Honors Classes in Key Disciplines (3.5): The 15 "key" disciplines are biological sciences; business (all); chemistry; communications (especially public speaking); computer science; economics; engineering (all); English; history; math (all); philosophy; physics; political science; psychology; and sociology/anthropology/gender studies. Interdisciplinary sections, such as those often taken for General Education credit in the first two years, do receive a lesser, prorated discipline "credit" because they introduce students to multiple disciplines in an especially engaging way, often with in-depth discussion.

In the term reported, the program had ratio of **32.5 honors students** per each main section in some or all "key disciplines." The mean for all 50 programs is 26.3. The lower the ratio, the better.

Out of **36 adjusted sections in key disciplines**, about half were **honors-only sections.** The most sections were in communications and history (6 each) math (5), and biology, chemistry, and political science (3 each).

The program also offered more than 20 excellent seminar sections, all with 3 credits. Most of these were in a course titled "Critical Analysis and Social Responsibility: Why War?" Another interesting seminar in Life Sciences was "Natural Disturbances & Society."

The combination of seminars and courses in the disciplines makes the program an example of a **blended** program.

Extent of Honors Enrollment (5.0): Not all honors students take an honors class each term, especially after the first two years. Programs that have fewer honors classes for upper-division honors students will generally have fewer total members in good standing who are actually enrolled in a given term. (Please be aware, however, that honors students not enrolled in a class for a term are still connected to the honors community through residential and extracurricular activities.)

For example, if honors students in a program occupy 1,800 honors classroom seats in a given term, and there are 3,000 honors students in good standing, the extent of enrollment is .67. For programs that require a thesis, the ratio (score) reported below might in fact be somewhat higher, since we only count

"regular" class enrollment for this measure, and not thesis enrollment. The college **has a ratio of 1.41**; the mean is 1.13 for all 50 programs. The higher the ratio, the better.

Average Class Size, Honors-only Sections (3.5): Offered mostly in the first two years, honors-only classes tend to be smaller and, as the name implies, have no or very few students other than those in the honors program. These class sections are almost always much smaller than mixed or contract sections, or regular non-honors class sections in the university.

The average honors-only class size in the honors program is **21.6 students**. The average for all 50 programs is 19.0 students.

Average Class Size, Overall (3.5): The overall class calculation is based on the *proportion* of honors students in each type of class (honors-only, mixed honors, and honors contract sections). Thus it is not a raw average. The overall honors-credit class size is **36.5 students**, versus the average for all 50 programs of 26.3 students.

These class size averages also do not correspond to the number of students per honors sections numbers above. The reason is that, in computing average class size metrics, we include enrollment in each 1-2-credit section, not just sections with 3 or more credits.

Along with the honors-only average of 21.6 students, mixed sections averaged **58.0**, and the contract sections with honors credit for individual honors students averaged **44.2**. Across all fifty programs, the average mixed honors section has 51.1 students, and the average contract section has 60.1 students. Even though the college has a high number of mixed sections, their average class size is quite low.

Honors Graduation Rate (3.5): The rating is the based on the actual grad rate for students who entered the program six years earlier, whether or not the students remained in honors. The **actual rate of 83.4%** is also compared to the rates of other programs with the same test score entry requirement range, and then adjusted to the **score of 83.2%.** In some cases this measure favors programs within universities with relatively higher test scores for the student population as a whole. The average honors graduation rate for all programs with similar test scores required for admission is 86.2%.

Value-Added Grad Rate (4.0): The value-added rate measures the extent to which the adjusted score listed above exceeds the grad rate for the university as a whole. **The university-wide rate is 67%.** Note: This measure generally favors programs within universities with relatively lower test scores for the student population as a whole.

Ratio of Staff to Honors Students (4.5): There is 1 staff member for every **107.6** students. (Mean ratio for all 50 programs is 1 staff member for every 135.6 students.)

Honors Residence Halls, Amenities (4.5): Laville Honors House features traditional double rooms for the most part, with shared hall baths. It is home to more than 600 honors students, making it one of the largest all-honors residence halls. All rooms are air-conditioned with room controls. Although the building is coed, men and women are assigned to separate floors. Laville has two kitchens and two laundry rooms. The building has two large lounge/study areas on the first floor and additional study lounges on each floor. In addition, there is a large public lounge area at the entrance to the building, and an outdoor patio/grove that is enclosed on three sides by the building and on the fourth side by the dining hall. Very convenient dining is adjacent, at The 459.

The Ogden Honors College also occupies The French House--La Maison Française--a Renaissance-style Normandy château built in 1935 as a center for intense study of French language, culture, and literature. The French House remains the only non-Quadrangle LSU structure on the National Register of Historic Places. In its prime, the facility was host to formal entertainment and distinguished visitors to campus. Since 1999, it has housed the daily administrative and student life functions of the LSU Honors College. The 16,000 square foot structure currently houses 4 classrooms, 12 administrative offices, a student lounge, and a large public space--The Grand Salon--which is used for events, receptions, concerts, ceremonies, and performances.

Honors Residence Halls, Availability (4.5): This rating compares the number of places in honors residence halls to the number of honors freshman and sophomore members in good standing, just under 700. The ratio for the honors program is **.88** rooms for each first- and second-year student. The average for all fifty programs is .63 places.

Prestigious Awards (4.0): The awards that we track and include are listed in the section titled "Prestigious Scholarships." The awards are sometimes won by students who are not in an honors college or program, but increasingly many are enrolled in honors programs. It is also a trend that honors colleges and programs help to prepare their students for the awards competitions.

LSU students have won 14 Rhodes scholarships, 4 Marshall scholarships, and 11 Truman scholarships. In addition, LSU students have earned 29 Goldwater scholarships, awarded for undergraduate excellence in the STEM disciplines.

UNRATED FEATURES

Continuation Requirements: 3.00 GPA for good standing, and 3.50 for honors graduation.

Academic Strengths, National Rankings: This is based on national rankings of *graduate* programs in 15 disciplines, except engineering and business, where undergraduate rankings are used.

The average national departmental ranking for LSU is about 85-90. Leading departments are political science (68), earth sciences (69), physics (70), math (73), chemistry and sociology (76), business (80), and English (82). Engineering is ranked 87th in the nation.

Undergraduate Research: "The Honors College does not track all the ways in which students are involved in undergraduate research (independent study courses, [Research Experiences for Undergraduates], research internships, campus jobs, etc.); however, students in the Ogden Honors College are encouraged to participate in a variety of research opportunities:

--Over 110 are current members in LSU's Chancellor's Future Leaders in Research Program, which partners students with faculty research mentors as early as the freshman year.

--Over 80% of Honors College graduating seniors are currently enrolled in thesis coursework. The Honors Thesis is expected to reflect graduate-level research and must be defended before a committee towards the end of the second semester of enrollment. "The Ogden Honors College awards special funds towards completing their Honors Thesis in order to pay for supplies, travel, and reimbursement for research participants.

"Additionally, Ogden Honors students present their thesis research at the LSU Discover Day, a conference open to the campus community."

Honors Study Abroad: "Honors College students comprise the largest number of LSU students participating in study abroad opportunities including summer trips, one semester, and full year programs. The Honors College provides scholarships for students participating in semester and year-long academic programs abroad.

"The Honors College offers special summer programs for Honors students and from 2006-2010, ran the Gateway to China Program fully funded by the university. This program led to LSU's exchange agreement with Tongji University in Shanghai. In Summer 2011, the Honors College led a service learning trip to South Africa in partnership with the University of California (UCLA, UCSB, UCSD, UC Berkeley). From 2014-2016, the Ogden Honors College has led a summer program in Cuba. In summer 2016 an Ogden Honors summer program in Greece will be offered as well."

Financial Aid: "LSU freshman scholarship programs are purposefully aligned with Ogden Honors College admission requirements. While Honors admission is not required for these programs, the design ensures a comprehensive overlap with the Honors entering population.

"Louisiana resident students who meet Honors College criteria receive the state's TOPS scholarship that provides full tuition. These students also receive a $1,500 - $2,500 per year stipend at graduated levels, beginning slightly below standardized test score requirements for Honors admission and rising at tiers above that level. A large majority of students also receive a campus job award of $1,550 per year, which may be used for research employment, a distinct academic advantage.

"Non-resident students receive $7,500 – $20,500 per year stipends at levels that mirror the in-state student program outlined above. A large majority of non-resident students also receive the campus job award of $1,550 per year.

"LSU is a participating institution with the Stamps Foundation Leadership Scholars Award program. Five incoming students each year receive full cost of attendance for four years as well as $14,000 of enrichment funding and guidance from our Ogden Honors College Office of Fellowship Advising in the beneficial use of these funds.

"The Ogden Honors College also offers several distinct scholarship programs:

- direct support for up to five special projects per year at $5,000 each through our Roger Hadfield Ogden Honors Leaders program:
- support for thesis research at $500 - $1,000;
- support for study abroad activity with $500 - $2,000;

- scholarships for underrepresented groups in Engineering and in Business with $4,000 over four years;
- scholarships through the Shell Honors Student Leaders program at $3,500 over four years including interaction with this major energy company."

Honors Fees: None.

Placement Experiences: "Recent Ogden Honors graduates pursue advanced degrees in prestigious programs at Cambridge University, Harvard Law School, Stanford University, MIT, Columbia, Cornell, University of Bristol, Johns Hopkins, UC Berkeley, Vanderbilt University, Texas A&M, University of Texas, Rice, Notre Dame, Northwestern University Medical School, Baylor College of Medicine, Tulane Medical School, University of Texas Health Sciences Center, and George Washington University Law School.

"Our recent alumni work for Apple, Amazon, Google, GE, Chevron, JPMorgan Chase, Shell, Price Waterhouse Coopers, Nestle, ExxonMobil, and eBay. They work for the US Senate and in federal agencies such as the Department of Health and Human Services, the Library of Congress, and the Federal Trade Commission, as well as in service in the Peace Corps and US military. Ogden Honors graduates are influential contributors across a range of industries and comprise a network of passionate alumni."

Degree of Difference: This is based on the differences between (1) the average (2015, two-part) SAT scores for enrolled honors students (1390) and (2) the average test scores for all students in the university (1170) as a whole. The test scores may be an indication of how "elite" honors students may be perceived as compared to students in the university as a whole. The scores can also provide an indication of how well prepared the non-honors students in the university may be. **Please keep in mind that neither high nor low test scores determine the overall quality of a program.**

NAME: HONORS COLLEGE, UNIVERSITY OF MARYLAND.

Date Established: 2009; the University Honors Program was founded in 1966.

Location: College Park, Maryland.

University Full-time Undergraduate Enrollment: 25,027.

Honors Members in Good Standing: 4,000 (mean size of all 50 programs is 1,742).

Honors Average Admission Statistics: Old two-part SAT, 1450. Est. new SAT score, 1490.

Average High School GPA/Class Rank: 4.5.

Basic Admission Requirements: None listed.

Application Deadline(s): *Please verify with each program, as some deadlines could change.*

November 1, 2016; notification late January 2017.

Honors Programs with old SAT scores from 1402—1469: UCF, Connecticut, Kentucky, Washington, Maryland, North Carolina, UC Irvine, Kansas, Minnesota, Tennessee, South Carolina, Clemson, UT Austin, Georgia.

Administrative Staff: 33, across seven distinct living/learning communities.

RATINGS AT A GLANCE: For all mortarboard ratings immediately below, a score of 5 is the maximum and represents a comparison with all 50 honors colleges and programs. More detailed explanations follow the "mortarboard" ratings.

PERCEPTION* OF UNIVERSITY AS A WHOLE, NOT OF HONORS: 🎓🎓🎓🎓🎓

*Perception is based on the university's ranking among public universities in the 2016 U.S. News Best Colleges report. Please bear in mind that the better the U.S. News ranking, the more difficult it is for an honors college or program to have a rating that equals or improves on the magazine ranking.

OVERALL HONORS RATING: 🎓🎓🎓🎓1/2

Curriculum Requirements: 🎓🎓🎓🎓

Number of Honors Classes Offered: 🎓🎓🎓🎓🎓

Number of Honors Classes in Key Disciplines: 🎓🎓🎓🎓1/2

Extent of Honors Enrollment: 🎓🎓🎓🎓

Honors-only Class Size: 🎓🎓🎓🎓🎓

Overall Class Size (Honors-only plus mixed, contract): 🎓🎓🎓🎓🎓

Honors Grad Rate: 🎓🎓🎓🎓🎓

Value-Added Grad Rate: 🎓🎓🎓$^{1/2}$

Ratio of Staff to Students: 🎓🎓🎓🎓$^{1/2}$

Priority Registration: "We hold 50% of seats in Honors Seminars open for matriculating students."

Honors Housing Amenities: 🎓🎓🎓$^{1/2}$

Honors Housing Availability: 🎓🎓🎓🎓🎓

Prestigious Awards: 🎓🎓🎓🎓🎓

RATING SCORES AND EXPLANATIONS:

Curriculum Requirements (4.0): The most important rating category, the curriculum completion requirement (classes required to complete honors) defines not only what honors students should learn but also the extent to which honors students and faculty are connected in the classroom. If there is a thesis or capstone requirement, it reinforces the individual contact and research skills so important to learning.

The average number of honors semester hours required for completion across all 50 programs is 29.0.

The college has seven different completion options; the estimated average credit hours for completion across all options is about **28 credits**. Below is a summary from the executive director of the college:

"The Honors College at UMD is comprised of 7 distinct living-and-learning programs:

1. University Honors: 4 years, = 2000 students;
2. Gemstone: 4 years, = 500 students;
3. Integrated Life Sciences: 2 years, =150 students;
4. Design Cultures Creativity: 2 years, = 140 students;
5. Entrepreneurship & Innovation: 2 years; = 140 students;
6. Advanced Cybersecurity Experience for Students: 2 years; = 150 students (new minor for 3rd and 4th year in Spring 2016);
7. Honors Humanities: 2 years; = 75 students.

"University Honors Program (UH); program course hours = 16.

"Gemstone (GEMS); program course hours = 37.

"This [Gemstone] program is unique; students work in teams of between 10 and 25 students on a single research project of their own design, under the mentorship of a full-time faculty member. So, it is difficult to parcel out the course hours from the capstone hours. At each stage of their project, the team gives a public presentation, and the final results of the project are presented publically and examined by a panel of 'outside' experts."

"Advanced Cybersecurity Experience for Students (ACES); program hours = 14.

"In Spring 2016, the ACES Minor went live. Juniors and Seniors who did not matriculate into the Honors College may, through a competitive application process, become members of ACES (thus, of the Honors College). And, students who were admitted into the Honors College as ACES Freshmen can turn their experience from a 2-year one into a 4-year one."

Entrepreneurship & Innovation; program hours = 15.

Design Cultures & Creativity; program hours = 16.

Honors Humanities; program hours = 16.

All students enrolled in a departmental **or** college honors program are by definition members of the Honors College, and may register for honors courses, whether or not they were admitted to the Honors College at the time of matriculation. Students in University Honors or Honors Humanities, for example, can move on to a departmental honors option in, say, history, which requires an additional 12 credits, including an **honors thesis**. The credits required for departmental vary by department.

AP/IB credits are **not** counted as replacements for honors courses

Number of Honors Classes Offered (5.0): This is a measure of the total **adjusted** honors main sections available in the term reported, not including labs and thesis. (Please read the section titled "All about Honors Classes".) An adjusted main section has 3 or more semester credits, or equivalent, and sections with fewer credits receive a lower prorated value.

The honors program had a ratio of **7.8** enrolled students per each main section. The mean for all 50 programs is 14.2. The lower the ratio, the better.

In the term reported, **96.6 %** of honors enrollment was **in honors-only sections; an estimated 3.4%** **were in contract sections (regular sections in which honors students "contract" to do extra work).** The averages for all fifty programs are 81.3% in honors-only sections; 13.6 % in mixed honors sections; and 5.1% in contract sections.

Number of Honors Classes in Key Disciplines (4.5): The 15 "key" disciplines are biological sciences; business (all); chemistry; communications (especially public speaking); computer science; economics; engineering (all); English; history; math (all); philosophy; physics; political science; psychology; and sociology/anthropology/gender studies. Interdisciplinary sections, such as those often taken for General

Education credit in the first two years, do receive a lesser, prorated discipline "credit" because they introduce students to multiple disciplines in an especially engaging way, often with in-depth discussion.

In the term reported, the program had a ratio of **17.5 honors students** per each main section in some or all "key disciplines." The mean for all 50 programs is 26.3. The lower the ratio, the better.

Out of **79 adjusted sections in key disciplines**, the college had 79 honors-only sections. In Fall 2015, there were 21 sections in English, 16 in computer science (an extremely high number), 12 in business, 10 in math, 3 in engineering, and 3 in physics. In that term, there were no sections in communications or political science. The college also offered more than 175 seminars, including more than 65 for Gemstone students, 6 in Cybersecurity, and 5 in Digital Design, and almost 60 interdisciplinary seminars.

The combination of seminars and courses in the disciplines makes the honors college an outstanding **blended** program, with living/learning themes directly related to honors completion options.

Extent of Honors Enrollment (4.0): Not all honors students take an honors class each term, especially after the first two years. Programs that have fewer honors classes for upper-division honors students will generally have fewer total members in good standing who are actually enrolled in a given term. (Please be aware, however, that honors students not enrolled in a class for a term are still connected to the honors community through residential and extracurricular activities.)

For example, if honors students in a program occupy 1,800 honors classroom seats in a given term, and there are 3,000 honors students in good standing, the extent of enrollment is .67. For programs that require a thesis, the ratio (score) reported below might in fact be somewhat higher, since we only count "regular" class enrollment for this measure, and not thesis enrollment. **UMD has a ratio of .99**; the mean is 1.13 for all 50 programs. The higher the ratio, the better.

Average Class Size, Honors-only Sections (5.0): Offered mostly in the first two years, honors-only classes tend to be smaller and, as the name implies, have no or very few students other than those in the honors program. These class sections are almost always much smaller than mixed or contract sections, or regular non-honors class sections in the university.

The average honors-only class size in the honors program is **15.3 students**. The average for all 50 programs is 19.0 students.

Average Class Size, Overall (5.0): The overall class calculation is based on the *proportion* of honors students in each type of class (honors-only, mixed honors, and honors contract sections). Thus it is not a raw average. The overall honors-credit class size at UMD is **16.8 students**, versus the average for all 50 programs of 26.3 students.

These class size averages also do not correspond to the number of students per honors sections numbers above. The reason is that, in computing average class size metrics, we include enrollment in each 1-2-credit section, not just sections with 3 or more credits.

Along with the honors-only average of 15.3 students, mixed sections averaged (not applicable), and the contract sections with honors credit for individual honors students averaged about **60.0 students.** Across all fifty programs, the average mixed honors section has 51.1 students, and the average contract section has 60.1 students.

Honors Graduation Rate (5.0): The rating is based on the actual grad rate for students who entered the program six years earlier, whether or not the students remained in honors. The **actual rate of 93.5%** is also compared to the rates of other programs with the same test score entry requirement range, and then adjusted to the **score of 93.6.** In some cases this measure favors programs within universities with relatively higher test scores for the student population as a whole. The average honors graduation rate for all programs with similar test scores required for admission is 92.6%.

Value-Added Grad Rate (3.5): The value-added rate measures the extent to which the adjusted score listed above exceeds the six-year grad rate for the university as a whole. **The university-wide rate is 85%.** Note: This measure generally favors programs within universities with relatively lower test scores for the student population as a whole.

Ratio of Staff to Honors Students (4.5): There is 1 staff member for every **93.3** students. (Mean ratio for all 50 programs is 1 staff member for every 135.6 students.)

Honors Residence Halls, Amenities (3.5): Of the approximately 1,910 honors "beds" on campus, about 34% are in Hagerstown Hall, site of the University Honors LLC. The hall features traditional corridor rooms and hall baths almost exclusively, and is air-conditioned only in the halls. Dining is nearby in Ellicott Hall.

Home to the Gemstone LLC, Ellicott has about 18% of the students in honors housing. The facility has the same basic features as Hagerstown, including no air-conditioning in the rooms. Ellicott does have its own dining hall.

Prince Frederick Hall is home to the Cybersecurity (ACES) and Digital Cultures LLCs, with features similar to the facilities listed above, except it does have air-conditioning. While for all other honors residences the closest dining is Ellicott Hall, for Prince Frederick the nearest location is South Dining Hall. About 18% of the students in honors housing live in Prince Frederick.

About 6.5% of honors students in honors housing reside in Anne Arundel Hall, home of the Humanities LLC. The residence is air-conditioned, but laundry is not in the building but in an adjacent location. Rooms are traditional with hall baths.

Students in the Integrated Life Sciences and Design Cultures LLCs live in La Plata Hall—a little more than 2% of students living in honors dorms. La Plata rooms are the same as above residences, and it is air-conditioned.

Honors Residence Halls, Availability (5.0): This rating compares the number of places in honors residence halls to the number of honors freshman and sophomore members in good standing, just under 2,000. The ratio for the honors program is **.91** rooms for each first- and second-year student. The average for all fifty programs is .63 places.

Prestigious Awards (5.0): The awards that we track and include are listed in the section titled "Prestigious Scholarships." The awards are sometimes won by students who are not in an honors college or program, but increasingly many are enrolled in honors programs. It is also a trend that honors colleges and programs help to prepare their students for the awards competitions.

Maryland students have not won many of the most glamorous postgraduate awards, although UM students have earned 9 Truman scholarships, awarded to rising seniors. But UMD is a national leader in Fulbright Student awards and in NSF fellowship grants for graduate study, both of which are strongly indicative of overall excellence. In addition, UM students have won 12 Udall scholarships, 53 Goldwater scholarships, and 31 Boren scholarships for overseas study—the highest number of any program under review.

"UMD's National Scholarships Office is housed in the same main administrative unit as the Honors College (the Office of Undergraduate Studies), but not *in* the Honors College itself. Under new leadership, we are building a wider-diameter pipeline from Honors to prestigious scholarships," the executive director reports.

UNRATED FEATURES

Continuation Requirements: 3.00 GPA, to stay in the program and 3.20 to graduate.

Academic Strengths, National Rankings: This is based on national rankings of *graduate* programs in 15 disciplines, except engineering and business, where undergraduate rankings are used.

Undergraduate Research: At UMD, undergraduate research is department-specific.

Honors Study Abroad: None listed, but UMD as a whole is a leader in study-abroad programs.

Financial Aid: "UMD offers approximately 125 Banneker/Key Scholarships annually. These range from full scholarship (covering full tuition, room & board, and a book allowance) to partial (offering $8K towards tuition and book allowance for in-state students and $12K towards tuition and a book allowance for out-of-state students)."

Honors Fees: None.

Placement Experiences:

Joining the workforce (job in hand) at graduation = 48%;
Enrolling in graduate or professional school = 45%;
(9% to Medical School; 6% to Law School; 1% to Vet School; 1% to Dental School);
Research/internship = 2%;
Travel = 3%;
Unsure = 4%.

"Graduate and professional school destinations of recent graduates: Brown; Carnegie Mellon; College of William & Mary; Columbia; Georgetown; Georgia Tech; Harvard; Johns Hopkins; MIT; NYU; Northwestern; Notre Dame; Ohio State; Princeton; Rice; Stanford; Tulane; University of Chicago; University of Maryland; University of Michigan; University of North Carolina; University of Pennsylvania; University of Texas at Austin; University of Wisconsin; and Yale."

Degree of Difference: This is based on the differences between (1) the average (2015, two-part) SAT scores for enrolled honors students (1450) and (2) the average test scores for all students in the university (1315) as a whole. The test scores may be an indication of how "elite" honors students may be perceived as compared to students in the university as a whole. The scores can also provide an indication of how well prepared the non-honors students in the university may be. **Please keep in mind that neither high nor low test scores determine the overall quality of a program.**

NAME: COMMONWEALTH HONORS COLLEGE.

Date Established: 1998.

Location: Amherst, Massachusetts.

University <u>Full-time Undergraduate</u> Enrollment: 20,684.

Honors Members in Good Standing: 3,800 (mean size of all 50 programs is 1,742)

Honors <u>Average</u> Admission Statistics: Est. ACT, 31; old two-part SAT, 1359. Est. new SAT score, 1420.

Average High School GPA/Class Rank: Est. 4.28, top GPA, top 4%.

<u>Basic</u> **Admission Requirements:** "If you are entering UMass Amherst with an exemplary high school record then you may be considered for admission to the Commonwealth Honors College. There is no separate application process; students are notified of their selection with their general letter of admission.

"Note that the number and quality of applications for freshman admission affect the selectivity of the Commonwealth Honors College review process. If you are not admitted as an incoming freshman, you may apply online as a current UMass Amherst student after you have completed one full-time semester with 12 or more graded credits at UMass Amherst. This online application process uses different criteria for acceptance, which are based on your college career at UMass Amherst."

Application Deadline(s): *Please verify with each program, as some deadlines could change.* Early action

November 1, 2016; regular deadline January 15, 2017.

Honors Programs with old SAT scores from 1351—1396: Purdue, Oregon, Alabama, Massachusetts, Penn State, Indiana, CUNY Macaulay, Texas A&M, NJIT, Missouri, Oregon State, Delaware, LSU, Vermont, Temple.

Administrative Staff: 24.

RATINGS AT A GLANCE: For all mortarboard ratings immediately below, a score of 5 is the maximum and represents a comparison with all 50 honors colleges and programs. More detailed explanations follow the "mortarboard" ratings.

PERCEPTION* OF UNIVERSITY AS A WHOLE, <u>NOT</u> OF HONORS: 🎓 🎓 🎓 🎓 1/2

*Perception is based on the university's ranking among public universities in the 2016 U.S. News Best Colleges report. Please bear in mind that the better the U.S. News ranking, the more difficult it is for an honors college or program to have a rating that equals or improves on the magazine ranking.

OVERALL HONORS RATING: 🎓🎓🎓🎓

Curriculum Requirements: 🎓🎓🎓🎓

Number of Honors Classes Offered: 🎓🎓🎓🎓

Number of Honors Classes in Key Disciplines: 🎓🎓🎓 1/2

Extent of Honors Enrollment: 🎓🎓🎓 1/2

Honors-only Class Size: 🎓🎓🎓🎓

Overall Class Size (Honors-only plus mixed, contract): 🎓🎓🎓🎓 1/2

Honors Grad Rate: 🎓🎓🎓🎓

Value-Added Grad Rate: 🎓🎓🎓🎓

Ratio of Staff to Students: 🎓🎓🎓🎓

Priority Registration: "Many honors sections of courses are restricted to honors students during the pre-registration period, but may be opened to non-honors students when the semester begins on a space available basis with permission of instructor. Approximately 20% of honors freshmen enter with sufficient college credits to give them sophomore standing. By second semester of freshmen year, 70% of honors students have sufficient credits to give them sophomore or junior standing. Because student registration is prioritized by class standing, most honors students are able to register earlier."

Honors Housing Amenities: 🎓🎓🎓🎓🎓

Honors Housing Availability: 🎓🎓🎓🎓 1/2

Prestigious Awards: 🎓🎓🎓🎓

RATING SCORES AND EXPLANATIONS:

Curriculum Requirements (4.0): The most important rating category, the curriculum completion requirement (classes required to complete honors) defines not only what honors students should learn but also the extent to which honors students and faculty are connected in the classroom. If there is a thesis or capstone requirement, it reinforces the individual contact and research skills so important to learning.

The average number of honors semester hours required for completion across all 50 programs is 29.0.

Honors completion at the highest level (Commonwealth Honors College Scholar, with Departmental Honors) requires a minimum of about 28.5 hours of honors credit, of which 5 credits must be honors college classes 6-8 credits in departmental honors course work, 9-12 credits in Gen Ed honors courses, and **6 hours for thesis research and thesis**.

A similar completion option is Commonwealth Honors College Scholar, with Multidisciplinary Honors. The option requires a minimum of about 28.5 credit hours as well, with 5 credits of honors college work, and 15-20 credit hours of departmental honors credits. **There is also a 6-credit thesis requirement**.

Two less demanding options are Departmental Honors, with completion requiring 6-8 credits of *departmental* honors courses along **with a 6-hour thesis**; and Multidisciplinary Honors, which requires 9-12 hours of *interdisciplinary* honors courses **plus a 6-hour thesis.**

AP/IB credits are **not** counted as replacements for honors courses. Note: "Students who complete some or all of their General Education coursework through AP scores must take other honors courses in place of their Honors College Writing or other honors General Education courses they would otherwise take. Alternative honors coursework must be negotiated with an Honors Advisor and entered as an exception in the student's Academic Requirements Report."

Number of Honors Classes Offered (4.0): This is a measure of the total **adjusted** honors main sections available in the term reported, not including labs and thesis. (Please read the section titled "All about Honors Classes".) An adjusted main section has 3 or more semester credits, or equivalent, and sections with fewer credits receive a lower prorated value.

The honors program had a ratio of **14.5** enrolled students per each main section. The mean for all 50 programs is 14.2. The lower the ratio, the better.

In the term reported, In the term reported, **96.7%** of honors enrollment was **in honors-only sections and mixed sections, the latter of which were mostly honors; 3.4% were in contract sections (regular sections in which honors students "contract" to do extra work.** The averages for all fifty programs are 81.3% in honors-only sections; 13.6 % in mixed honors sections; and 5.1% in contract sections.

Number of Honors Classes in Key Disciplines (3.5): The 15 "key" disciplines are biological sciences; business (all); chemistry; communications (especially public speaking); computer science; economics; engineering (all); English; history; math (all); philosophy; physics; political science; psychology; and sociology/anthropology/gender studies. Interdisciplinary sections, such as those often taken for General Education credit in the first two years, do receive a lesser, prorated discipline "credit" because they introduce students to multiple disciplines in an especially engaging way, often with in-depth discussion.

In the term reported, the program had ratio of **30.1 honors students** per each main section in some or all "key disciplines." The mean for all 50 programs is 26.3 The lower the ratio, the better.

Out of **80 adjusted sections in key disciplines**, the college had 68 honors-only sections. Some 22 sections were in English, 11 in math, 8 in economics (a large number), and 6 in biology and history. There were five more in psychology, and sociology, anthropology, and gender studies had 4 sections total. The college also offered about 75 1-and 2-credit interdisciplinary seminars, and about 40 seminars in the "Ideas that Changed the World" series that requires students "to examine texts and works of art that have profoundly shaped the world we live in."

The combination of seminars and courses in the disciplines makes the honors college a strong **blended** program, though with a departmental emphasis.

Extent of Honors Enrollment (3.5): Not all honors students take an honors class each term, especially after the first two years. Programs that have fewer honors classes for upper-division honors students will generally have fewer total members in good standing who are actually enrolled in a given term. (Please be aware, however, that honors students not enrolled in a class for a term are still connected to the honors community through residential and extracurricular activities.)

For example, if honors students in a program occupy 1,800 honors classroom seats in a given term, and there are 3,000 honors students in good standing, the extent of enrollment is .67. For programs that require a thesis, the ratio (score) reported below might in fact be somewhat higher, since we only count "regular" class enrollment for this measure, and not thesis enrollment. **UMass has a ratio of .89**; the mean is 1.13 for all 50 programs. The higher the ratio, the better.

Average Class Size, Honors-only Sections (4.0): Offered mostly in the first two years, honors-only classes tend to be smaller and, as the name implies, have no or very few students other than those in the honors program. These class sections are almost always much smaller than mixed or contract sections, or regular non-honors class sections in the university.

The average honors-only class size in the honors program is **18.3 students**. The average for all 50 programs is 19.0 students.

Average Class Size, Overall (4.5): The overall class calculation is based on the *proportion* of honors students in each type of class (honors-only, mixed honors, and honors contract sections). Thus it is not a raw average. The overall honors-credit class size at the CHC is **20.3 students**, versus the average for all 50 programs of 26.3 students.

These class size averages also do not correspond to the number of students per honors sections numbers above. The reason is that, in computing average class size metrics, we include enrollment in each 1-2-credit section, not just sections with 3 or more credits.

Along with the honors-only average of 18.3 students, the contract sections with honors credit for individual honors students average about **76.9 students**. Across all fifty programs, the average mixed honors section has 51.1 students, and the average contract section has 60.1 students.

Honors Graduation Rate (4.0): The rating is the based on the actual grad rate for students who entered the program six years earlier, whether or not the students remained in honors. The **actual rate of 87.6%** is also compared to the rates of other programs with the same test score entry requirement range, and then adjusted to the **score of 87.8**. In some cases this measure favors programs within universities with relatively higher test scores for the student population as a whole. The average honors graduation rate for all programs with similar test scores required for admission is 86.2%.

Value-Added Grad Rate (4.0): The value-added rate measures the extent to which the adjusted score listed above exceeds the six-year grad rate for the university as a whole. **The university-wide rate is 76%.** Note: This measure generally favors programs within universities with relatively lower test scores for the student population as a whole.

Ratio of Staff to Honors Students (4.0): There is 1 staff member for every **140.7** students. (Mean ratio for all 50 programs is 1 staff member for every 135.6 students.)

Honors Residence Halls, Amenities (5.0): The college has five residence hall options for honors students--two for freshmen and three for upperclassmen. All are part of the new Honors Residential Community that opened in 2013.

About 47% of honors students living in honors housing are freshmen residing in Sycamore Hall (294 students) and Oak Hall (334 students). Both residences have traditional double rooms with corridor baths on the floors. This configuration is thought by many to promote more interactions among new students, and thereby enhance their first year experience. Both dorms are air conditioned with on-site laundry. Living/learning themes in Sycamore are Health Sciences, Leadership, Ideas, Isenberg, and Biology Majors.

Oak Hall has living/learning themes in Creativity, Global Learning, Ideas, Engineering Majors, and Nursing Majors.

Upperclassmen can choose to live in Birch, Linden, Maple, and Elm Halls, and in two floors in Melville Hall, about .2 miles from the CHC residential center. Birch, Linden, Maple, and Elm all have a mix of apartment and suite-style rooms, the latter with shared baths.

This CHC residential community features:

Easy Access to Honors faculty and staff:

• Two Faculty in Residence
• Honors Advising Center
• The Dean's Office and all honors administrative offices
• Faculty offices
• Nine classrooms

Additional features:

• Wi-Fi throughout

• Roots Café - open 24/7--the café continues the campus' reputation for creating and serving healthy, sustainable food. (Recently, UMass Amherst was ranked the 9th healthiest college in the U.S.--and second healthiest public university--according to Greatlist.com. The *Princeton Review* has ranked UMass Amherst second nationally for best campus food.

• A uniquely designed events hall offers flexible seating for small, intimate gatherings or large honors programs. The full space seats up to 290 audience style. When the moveable wall is closed, the west side, with floor to ceiling windows, has a barn door that can be opened to the café providing lounge space with upholstered furniture and additional study space with tables and chairs. The east side can be set up audience style for 120 or with tables and chairs for up to 72. Both sides have full A/V capability.

• Gallery space (current exhibit, "The Student Experience: 150 Years of Living and Learning at UMass Amherst," curated by honors students guided by Art History faculty).

• Located in the campus core, on Commonwealth Avenue.

• Near the Recreation Center and the main library.

• Short distance to other classrooms and facilities on campus.

Honors Residence Halls, Availability (4.5): This rating compares the number of places in honors residence halls to the number of honors freshman and sophomore members in good standing, just under 1,900. The ratio for the honors program is **.82** rooms for each first- and second-year student. The average for all fifty programs is .63 places.

Prestigious Awards (4.0): The awards that we track and include are listed in the section titled "Prestigious Scholarships." The awards are sometimes won by students who are not in an honors college or program, but increasingly many are enrolled in honors programs. It is also a trend that honors colleges and programs help to prepare their students for the awards competitions.

As noted in past editions, UMass faces the toughest competition there is when it comes to winning Rhodes, Marshall, Truman, Goldwater, and other prestigious awards. Many of these awards have to be won by going through regional competitions—and for UMass that competition includes not only Harvard but also MIT, Amherst, and Williams, just to name a few. Nevertheless, the university excels in winning Fulbright student awards and also makes a strong showing in winning NSF graduate research fellowships. To date, UMass students have also won 21 Goldwater scholarships, given to outstanding undergraduates in the STEM disciplines.

UNRATED FEATURES

Continuation Requirements: 3.40 GPA, to stay in the program and to graduate.

Academic Strengths, National Rankings: This is based on national rankings of *graduate* programs in 15 disciplines, except engineering and business, where undergraduate rankings are used.

UMass has a strong faculty reputation in the nation, with the average ranking of departments across all disciplines at about 50th among all universities public or private. Among the many excellent departments are computer science (25), sociology (31), education (42), psychology (46), earth sciences and chemistry (49), and business, English, and physics (50).

Undergraduate Research: "The Commonwealth Honors College (CHC) Fellowship and Grant program provides up to $1,000 per student per semester to support honors student research. Research Assistant Fellowships support students assisting faculty on research projects, while Honors Research Grants support students' own research.

"In Academic Year 2014-2015, CHC awarded $133,635 in research fellowships and grants to 174 honors students.

"All students who complete Departmental Honors or Multidisciplinary Honors and all those who graduate as Commonwealth Honors College Scholars must complete honors research and thesis/project. In AY2014-2015 that included 70% (465) of honors college graduates.

"CHC sponsors the annual Massachusetts statewide Undergraduate Research Conference in which undergraduate students from any of the 28 undergraduate campuses in the Massachusetts Public System of Higher Education may participate. Nearly 1,000 students presented their research at the 21st annual conference in April 2015, and more than 1,000 have registered to present at the 22nd annual conference on April 22, 2016."

Honors Study Abroad: "Commonwealth Honors College (CHC) provides scholarships for honors students participating in the Oxford Summer Program, the Alternative Theaters summer honors program in Edinburgh, and the Grahamstown Theater Festival summer program in South Africa.

"The honors college also offers a special 3-year academic program, the International Scholars Program, which combines academic learning with a period of study abroad in order to provide students with the global competencies they will need to become informed and effective citizens of our ever-expanding world. The program invites all honors students, regardless of major, to develop a concentration in international studies and cross-cultural communication as a supplement to their regular disciplinary work. Students complete two preparatory classes in their sophomore year and a re-entry seminar in their senior year.

"ISP students receive a scholarship from CHC in support of their study abroad.

"ISP students may also complete the **International Scholars Program Certificate**. This undergraduate certificate builds on ISP, adding a three-course supplemental curriculum that students design to meet their personal, academic and professional goals. Students who complete the certificate receive an official designation on their final UMass Amherst transcript.

"CHC also offers Honors 295C, a seminar that assists students in preparation for study abroad by helping them clarify their study abroad goals, choose the best program to meet those goals, and develop a plan."

Financial Aid: The University offers merit scholarships to all entering first-year students accepted to Commonwealth Honors College (CHC); $2,000 for Massachusetts residents and approximately $6,000 for out of state students.

CHC administers Commonwealth Talent Awards academic tuition credits of $1,714 per year for up to 94 students each year.

Additionally, in Academic Year 2015-2016 CHC awarded $259,100 in primarily donor-funded scholarships to 114 students.

Honors Fees: $300 each semester.

Placement Experiences: None listed.

Degree of Difference: This is based on the differences between (1) the average (2015, two-part) SAT scores for enrolled honors students (1359) and (2) the average test scores for all students in the university (1215) as a whole. The test scores may be an indication of how "elite" honors students may be perceived as compared to students in the university as a whole. The scores can also provide an indication of how well prepared the non-honors students in the university may be. **Please keep in mind that neither high nor low test scores determine the overall quality of a program.**

NAME: UNIVERSITY HONORS PROGRAM—UNIVERSITY OF MINNESOTA-TWIN CITIES.

Date Established: 2008 (Collegiate-based Honors prior to 2008).

Location: Minneapolis/St. Paul Minnesota.

University <u>Full-time Undergraduate</u> Enrollment: 28,904.

Honors Members in Good Standing: 2,239 (mean size of all 50 programs is 1,742).

Honors <u>Average</u> Admission Statistics: Est. ACT for first-year entrants is at least 32; est. old two-part SAT, at least 1420. Estimated new SAT score, 1460-1490. Averages vary across colleges, so for College of Biological Sciences and College of Engineering, the SAT scores are likely 40-50 points higher than the overall average. The ACT is likely 33-34. Averages for Carlson School of Management are probably almost as high.

Average High School GPA/Class Rank: Est. 4.1 GPA, top 3-5%.

<u>Basic</u> **Admission Requirements:** "Honors admission is offered to the overall most competitive applicants from each freshman-admitting college."

Application Deadline(s): *Please verify with each program, as some deadlines could change.*

Priority application deadline November 1, 2016 (notification by end of February, 2017); Applications received by December 15, 2016, will receive full consideration for general admission. Honors admission is on a space-available basis, and scholarship consideration is on a funds-available basis.

Honors Programs with old SAT scores from 1402—1469: UCF, Connecticut, Kentucky, Washington, Maryland, North Carolina, UC Irvine, Kansas, Minnesota, Tennessee, South Carolina, Clemson, UT Austin, Georgia.

Administrative Staff: Approximately 21.

RATINGS AT A GLANCE: For all mortarboard ratings immediately below, a score of 5 is the maximum and represents a comparison with all 50 honors colleges and programs. More detailed explanations follow the "mortarboard" ratings.

PERCEPTION* OF UNIVERSITY AS A WHOLE, <u>NOT</u> OF HONORS: 🎓🎓🎓🎓^{1/2}

*Perception is based on the university's ranking among public universities in the 2016 U.S. News Best Colleges report. Please bear in mind that the better the U.S. News ranking, the more difficult it is for an honors college or program to have a rating that equals or improves on the magazine ranking.

OVERALL HONORS RATING: 🎓🎓🎓^{1/2}

Curriculum Requirements: 🎓🎓🎓🎓^{1/2}

Number of Honors Classes Offered: 🎓🎓🎓

Number of Honors Classes in Key Disciplines: 🎓🎓🎓

Extent of Honors Enrollment: 🎓🎓🎓🎓

Honors-only Class Size: 🎓🎓🎓

Overall Class Size (Honors-only plus mixed, contract): 🎓🎓🎓^{1/2}

Honors Grad Rate: 🎓🎓🎓🎓🎓

Value-Added Grad Rate: 🎓🎓🎓🎓

Ratio of Staff to Students: 🎓🎓🎓🎓^{1/2}

Priority Registration: No.

Honors Housing Amenities: 🎓🎓🎓🎓^{1/2}

Honors Housing Availability: 🎓🎓🎓

Prestigious Awards: 🎓🎓🎓🎓🎓

RATING SCORES AND EXPLANATIONS:

Curriculum Requirements (4.5): The most important rating category, the curriculum completion requirement (classes required to complete honors) defines not only what honors students should learn but also the extent to which honors students and faculty are connected in the classroom. If there is a thesis or capstone requirement, it reinforces the individual contact and research skills so important to learning.

The average number of honors semester hours required for completion across all 50 programs is 29.0.

"The UMTC University Honors Program requires one set of requirements for all students in any major. This set of requirements is, however, flexible enough to accommodate all majors. Students work with their honors advisor to determine how they can accomplish the requirements through their particular major or lens. Please keep in mind that these are minimum requirements."

The estimated minimum number of credit hours for completion is **30.5.**

The requirements are based on the accumulation of a minimum number of "honors experiences" during each academic year. The honors experiences can be honors course work, learning abroad (maximum of two experiences for honors credit), research, significant internship or service experience, national conference presentations, or a creative project.

In the **freshman year**, four honors experiences are required, including two from one of the following: honors seminars, departmental honors courses, or freshman seminars, totaling at least 6 credit hours. The other two experiences in the freshman year most often are in honors coursework, but they can be one of the other types listed above.

Sophomores must also meet the four-experience requirement and the same credit hour total, though of course with different courses and seminars.

In the **junior year,** students must take at least one honors course with a minimum of 3 credits. Two non-course experiences are also required: "Students engage in research, scholarship, or creative activity with a faculty mentor—an important step toward the development of a project for the **honors thesis**—while deepening and broadening their knowledge and skill base. They are also encouraged to consider research abroad, service in concert with their research where appropriate, and internships."

Seniors must take at least one 3-credit course, **complete a thesis**, and complete one more honors experience, either a course or one of the other experiences listed above. "Research/scholarship is done prior to and many times during the final writing. Creative projects are presented in the final term with a written document supporting their works."

AP/IB credits are **not** counted as replacements for honors courses.

Number of Honors Classes Offered (3.0): This is a measure of the total **adjusted** honors main sections available in the term reported, not including labs and thesis. (Please read the section titled "All about Honors Classes".) An adjusted main section has 3 or more semester credits, or equivalent, and sections with fewer credits receive a lower prorated value.

The honors program had a ratio of **22.8** enrolled students per each main section. The mean for all 50 programs is 14.2. The lower the ratio, the better.

In the term reported, **89.1%** of honors enrollment was **in honors-only sections; 4.4% in mixed honors sections (honors and non- honors students); and 6.5% in contract sections (regular sections in which honors students "contract" to do extra work** The averages for all fifty programs are 81.3% in honors-only sections; 13.6 % in mixed honors sections; and 5.1% in contract sections.

Number of Honors Classes in Key Disciplines (3.0): The 15 "key" disciplines are biological sciences; business (all); chemistry; communications (especially public speaking); computer science; economics; engineering (all); English; history; math (all); philosophy; physics; political science; psychology; and sociology/anthropology/gender studies. Interdisciplinary sections, such as those often taken for General Education credit in the first two years, do receive a lesser, prorated discipline "credit" because they introduce students to multiple disciplines in an especially engaging way, often with in-depth discussion.

In the term reported, the program had a ratio of **52.7 honors students** per each main section in some or all "key disciplines." The mean for all 50 programs is 26.3. The lower the ratio, the better.

Out of **41 adjusted sections in key disciplines**, the college had 38 honors-only sections. Math, biology, chemistry, physics, psychology, and sociology/anthropology accounted for 28 of the 41 sections, 8 in math alone. Communications, computer science, and engineering were offered in another 13 sections. There was only one section each in communications, English, philosophy, and political science. Sociology, anthropology, or gender studies had 5 sections total.

The program also offered about 20 interdisciplinary seminars, among them "Adventures with the Enemies of Science"; "The Neuroscience of Music and Language"; and "War Makes Worlds: How Today's 'Perpetual War' Shapes Our Lives."

The combination of seminars and courses in the disciplines makes the honors college a **blended** program, though with a departmental emphasis.

Extent of Honors Enrollment (4.0): Not all honors students take an honors class each term, especially after the first two years. Programs that have fewer honors classes for upper-division honors students will generally have fewer total members in good standing who are actually enrolled in a given term. (Please be aware, however, that honors students not enrolled in a class for a term are still connected to the honors community through residential and extracurricular activities.)

For example, if honors students in a program occupy 1,800 honors classroom seats in a given term, and there are 3,000 honors students in good standing, the extent of enrollment is .67. For programs that require a thesis, the ratio (score) reported below might in fact be somewhat higher, since we only count "regular" class enrollment for this measure, and not thesis enrollment. **UMTC has a ratio of 1.03**; the mean is 1.13 for all 50 programs. The higher the ratio, the better.

Average Class Size, Honors-only Sections (3.0): Offered mostly in the first two years, honors-only classes tend to be smaller and, as the name implies, have no or very few students other than those in the honors program. These class sections are almost always much smaller than mixed or contract sections, or regular non-honors class sections in the university.

The average honors-only class size in the honors program is **31.7 students**. The average for all 50 programs is 19.0 students.

Average Class Size, Overall (3.5): The overall class calculation is based on the *proportion* of honors students in each type of class (honors-only, mixed honors, and honors contract sections). Thus it is not a raw average. The overall honors-credit class size at UMTC is **35.1 students**, versus the average for all 50 programs of 26.3 students.

These class size averages also do not correspond to the number of students per honors sections numbers above. The reason is that, in computing average class size metrics, we include enrollment in each 1-2-credit section, not just sections with 3 or more credits.

Along with the honors-only average of 35.1 students, the mixed honors sections average **68.2 students,** and the contract sections with honors credit for individual honors students average about **60 students.**

Across all fifty programs, the average mixed honors section has 51.1 students, and the average contract section has 60.1 students.

Honors Graduation Rate (5.0): This rating is based on the actual grad rate for students who entered the program six years earlier, whether or not the students remained in honors. The **actual rate of 98.6%** is also compared to the rates of other programs with the same test score entry requirement range, and then adjusted to the **score of 99.2.** In some cases this measure favors programs within universities with relatively higher test scores for the student population as a whole. The average honors graduation rate for all programs with similar test scores required for admission is 92.6%.

Value-Added Grad Rate (4.0): The value-added rate measures the extent to which the adjusted score listed above exceeds the grad rate for the university as a whole. **The university-wide rate is 78%.** Note: This measure generally favors programs within universities with relatively lower test scores for the student population as a whole.

Ratio of Staff to Honors Students (4.5): There is 1 staff member for every **110.6** students. (Mean ratio for all 50 programs is 1 staff member for every 135.6 students.)

Honors Residence Halls, Amenities (4.5): Some honors freshmen and some upperclassmen live in Middlebrook Hall. Middlebrook is almost all suite-style--two rooms sharing a bath. The residence hall is air conditioned with a kitchen, on-site laundry, and a lounge on each floor. One great feature is that Middlebrook has its own dining hall and music rooms.

"[Middlebrook] is located adjacent to the west bank of the Mississippi River, Ted Mann Concert Hall, Wilson Library, and is near downtown Minneapolis. The west bank Riverside area offers a variety of music clubs, coffee shops, co-ops, historical buildings, and ethnic and vegetarian restaurants. Middlebrook is easily accessible by foot, bike, free campus connector and shuttle system, and light rail. Most west bank classroom buildings are connected by underground tunnels. Middlebrook Tower was built in 1969, and the east wing expansion (where second-year honors students live) was added in 2001."

Honors Residence Halls, Availability (3.0): This rating compares the number of places in honors residence halls to the number of honors freshman and sophomore members in good standing, just under 1,120. The ratio for the honors program is **.29** rooms for each first- and second-year student. The average for all fifty programs is .63 places. "All freshmen have the option to live in Middlebrook. The number in residence reflects those who have chosen to live there. Approximately half of the freshmen remain after their first year."

Prestigious Awards (5.0): The awards that we track and include are listed in the section titled "Prestigious Scholarships." The awards are sometimes won by students who are not in an honors college or program, but increasingly many are enrolled in honors programs. It is also a trend that honors colleges and programs help to prepare their students for the awards competitions.

UMTC students have an outstanding record of winning prestigious awards, including 24 Rhodes scholarships, 3 Marshall and 4 Gates Cambridge awards, and 20 Truman scholarships. Perhaps the most impressive accomplishment is the 10 Churchill scholarships won by UMTC students, fourth-highest among all public universities. The 55 Goldwater scholarships won by undergraduates in the STEM fields also ranks very high among all public universities. University grads also earn a high number of NSF grants for graduate school and Fulbright student awards.

UNRATED FEATURES

Continuation Requirements: 3.50 GPA. Graduation with honors:

3.50 in last 60 credits, with qualified juried thesis completion = cum laude
3.66 in last 60 credits, with qualified juried thesis completion = magna cum laude
3.75 in last 60 credits, with qualified juried thesis completion = summa cum laude

Academic Strengths, National Rankings: This is based on national rankings of *graduate* programs in 15 disciplines, except engineering and business, where undergraduate rankings are used.

UMTC has one of the best faculty reputations in the nation, with the average ranking of departments across all disciplines about 23rd in the nation. Among the many excellent departments are psychology (9), economics (11), business (15), math (17), political science (19), education and sociology (20), chemistry and history (24), earth sciences (25), and physics (26).

Undergraduate Research: "Eventually all Honors students will complete at least one research or creative expression experience. These experiences lead to the development of the thesis, required of all Latin Honors graduates."

Honors Study Abroad: "Eventually 60% of our students will have a study abroad experience on average."

Financial Aid: Most students invited into the University Honors Program are eligible for some form of merit-based scholarships.

Merit scholarships at UMTC that give preference to National Merit Finalists include the Gold Scholar Award of up to $10,000 per year for four years, and the Cyrus Northrop Scholarship, valued at $5,000 a year for four years. *To qualify for either of these, applicants must list UMTC as their first-choice college by the National Merit Scholarship Corporation deadline.*

The Gold National Scholarship covers the full difference between resident and non-resident tuition rates each year for 4 years.

National Excellence Scholarship covers 50 percent of the difference between resident and non-resident tuition rates each year for 4 years.

Both the Gold National and National Excellence awards are *not* available to applicants from Minnesota, North Dakota, South Dakota, and Wisconsin.

The Bentson/Niblick Scholarship likewise gives preference to National Merit Finalists, and awards up to $2,500 a year for four years. (There is no requirement that applicants list UMTC as their first-choice college.)

Honors Fees: None.

Placement Experiences: None listed.

Degree of Difference: This is based on the differences between (1) the average (2015, two-part) SAT scores for enrolled honors students (1420) and (2) the average test scores for all students in the university (1260) as a whole. The test scores may be an indication of how "elite" honors students may be perceived as compared to students in the university as a whole. The scores can also provide an indication of how well prepared the non-honors students in the university may be. **Please keep in mind that neither high nor low test scores determine the overall quality of a program.**

NAME: SALLY MCDONNELL BARKSDALE HONORS COLLEGE

Date Established: 1997; preceded by honors program established in 1952.

Location: Oxford, Mississippi.

University <u>Full-time Undergraduate</u> Enrollment: 16,665.

Honors Members in Good Standing: 1,251 (mean size of all 50 programs is 1,742).

Honors Programs with old SAT scores from 1315—1350: Idaho, Georgia State, Virginia Tech, Utah, Iowa, Auburn, Houston, Mississippi, VCU.

Average High School GPA/Class Rank: 3.96 GPA.

<u>Basic</u> Admission Requirements: ACT, 28; old SAT, 1250; est. new SAT, 1310.

Application Deadline(s): *Please verify with each program, as some deadlines could change.* Early action

November 1, 2016, notification December 20, 2016; regular deadline is January 5, 2017, notification by early March 2017.

Honors Programs with old SAT scores from 1315—1350: Idaho, Georgia State, Virginia Tech, Utah, Iowa, Auburn, Houston, Mississippi, VCU.

Administrative Staff: 10.

RATINGS AT A GLANCE: For all mortarboard ratings immediately below, a score of 5 is the maximum and represents a comparison with all 50 honors colleges and programs. More detailed explanations follow the "mortarboard" ratings.

PERCEPTION* OF UNIVERSITY AS A WHOLE, <u>NOT</u> OF HONORS: 🎓🎓🎓 1/2

*Perception is based on the university's ranking among public universities in the 2016 U.S. News Best Colleges report. Please bear in mind that the better the U.S. News ranking, the more difficult it is for an honors college or program to have a rating that equals or improves on the magazine ranking.

OVERALL HONORS RATING: 🎓🎓🎓🎓 1/2

Curriculum Requirements: 🎓🎓🎓🎓

Number of Honors Classes Offered: 🎓🎓🎓🎓 1/2

Number of Honors Classes in Key Disciplines: 🎓🎓🎓🎓 1/2

Extent of Honors Enrollment: 🎓🎓🎓🎓

Honors-only Class Size: 🎓🎓🎓🎓🎓

Overall Class Size (Honors-only plus mixed, contract): 🎓🎓🎓🎓$^{1/2}$

Honors Grad Rate: 🎓🎓🎓🎓

Value-Added Grad Rate: 🎓🎓🎓🎓$^{1/2}$

Ratio of Staff to Students: 🎓🎓🎓🎓

Priority Registration: Yes, honors students register for all courses, honors and otherwise, with the first group of students during each year they are in the program.

Honors Housing Amenities: 🎓🎓🎓🎓

Honors Housing Availability: 🎓🎓🎓🎓$^{1/2}$

Prestigious Awards: 🎓🎓🎓$^{1/2}$

RATING SCORES AND EXPLANATIONS:

Curriculum Requirements (4.0): The most important rating category, the curriculum completion requirement (classes required to complete honors) defines not only what honors students should learn but also the extent to which honors students and faculty are connected in the classroom. If there is a thesis or capstone requirement, it reinforces the individual contact and research skills so important to learning.

The average number of honors semester hours required for completion across all 50 programs is 29.0.

The honors completion requirement at SMBHC is 29 credit hours, **including a thesis of 3-6 hours of credit.** All honors students must take the Honors 101-Honors 102 Freshman Honors seminars, both of which meet the composition requirement for the university.

Junior-entry students complete approximately 12 credits, 3-6 of which are an honors thesis. At least 3 of the total credits must be from a non-research honors course.

AP/IB credits are **not** counted as replacements for honors courses.

Number of Honors Classes Offered (4.5): This is a measure of the total **adjusted** honors main sections available in the term reported, not including labs and thesis. (Please read the section titled "All about Honors Classes".) An adjusted main section has 3 or more semester credits, or equivalent, and sections with fewer credits receive a lower prorated value.

The honors college had a ratio of **10.3** enrolled students per each main section. The mean for all 50 programs is 14.2. The lower the ratio, the better.

In the term reported, In the term reported, **88.3 %** of honors enrollment was **in honors-only sections; 11.7% in mixed honors sections (honors and non-honors students); and none reported in contract sections (regular sections in which honors students "contract" to do extra work.** The averages for all fifty programs are 81.3% in honors-only sections; 13.6 % in mixed honors sections; and 5.1% in contract sections.

Number of Honors Classes in Key Disciplines (4.5): The 15 "key" disciplines are biological sciences; business (all); chemistry; communications (especially public speaking); computer science; economics; engineering (all); English; history; math (all); philosophy; physics; political science; psychology; and sociology/anthropology/gender studies. Interdisciplinary sections, such as those often taken for General Education credit in the first two years, do receive a lesser, prorated discipline "credit" because they introduce students to multiple disciplines in an especially engaging way, often with in-depth discussion.

In the term reported, the program had ratio of **20.6 honors students** per each main section in some or all "key disciplines." The mean for all 50 programs is 26.3. The lower the ratio, the better.

Out of **40 adjusted sections in key disciplines**, the college had 35 honors-only sections. Math (8), English (6), biology (6), history (5), and chemistry (4) were offered. There were no sections in communications, computer science, or engineering. The college had also almost 30 interdisciplinary freshman seminars, all of which emphasize rhetoric and writing while studying great works.

The combination of seminars and courses in the disciplines makes the honors college a **blended** program.

Extent of Honors Enrollment (4.0): Not all honors students take an honors class each term, especially after the first two years. Programs that have fewer honors classes for upper-division honors students will generally have fewer total members in good standing who are actually enrolled in a given term. (Please be aware, however, that honors students not enrolled in a class for a term are still connected to the honors community through residential and extracurricular activities.)

For example, if honors students in a program occupy 1,800 honors classroom seats in a given term, and there are 3,000 honors students in good standing, the extent of enrollment is .67. For programs that require a thesis, the ratio (score) reported below might in fact be somewhat higher, since we only count "regular" class enrollment for this measure, and not thesis enrollment. **The college has a ratio of 1.10**, versus the mean of 1.13 for all 50 programs. The higher the ratio, the better.

Average Class Size, Honors-only Sections (5.0): Offered mostly in the first two years, honors-only classes tend to be smaller and, as the name implies, have no or very few students other than those in the honors program. These class sections always are much smaller than mixed or contract sections, or regular non-honors class sections in the university.

The average honors-only class size at the honors college is **15.0 students**. The average for all 50 programs is 19.0 students.

Average Class Size, Overall (4.5): The overall class calculation is based on the *proportion* of honors students in each type of class (honors-only, mixed honors, and honors contract sections). Thus it is not a raw average. The overall honors-credit class size at the college is **22.1 students**, versus the average for all 50 programs of 26.3 students.

These class size averages also do not correspond to the number of students per honors sections numbers above. The reason is that, in computing average class size metrics, we include enrollment in each 1-2-credit section, not just sections with 3 or more credits.

Along with the honors-only average of 15.0 students, the small number mixed honors sections average **75.7 students.** No contract enrollment was reported. Across all fifty programs, the average mixed honors section has 51.1 students.

Honors Graduation Rate (4.0): The rating is based on the actual grad rate for students who entered the program six years earlier, whether or not the students remained in honors. The **actual rate of 85.2%** is also compared to the rates of other programs with the same test score entry requirement range, and then adjusted to the **score of 85.2.** The average honors graduation rate for all programs with similar test scores required for admission is 83.8%.

Value-Added Grad Rate (4.5): The value-added rate measures the extent to which the adjusted score above exceeds the six-year grad rate for the university as a whole. **The university-wide rate is 61%.**

Ratio of Staff to Honors Students (4.0): There is 1 staff member for every **125.1** students. (Mean ratio for all 50 programs is 1 staff member for every 135.6 students.)

Honors Residence Halls, Amenities (4.0): Most first-year honors students live in Pittman Hall, and they account for about 87% of places in honors dorms. Pittman is air-conditioned and features suite-style rooms with shared baths. The nearest dining is at the Rebel Market.

The remainder of honors students who live in honors housing reside in Residential College South. The residence also has air-conditioned, suite-style rooms—and has on-site dining. This residence is for both freshmen and upperclassmen.

Honors Residence Halls, Availability (4.5): This rating compares the number of places in honors residence halls to the number of honors freshman and sophomore members in good standing, just under 625. The ratio for the college is **.63 rooms** for each first- and second-year student. The average for all fifty programs is also .63 places.

"No residence halls are co-ed, although the floors in Pittman and other contemporary residence halls have women at one end and men at the other. Some honors freshmen will choose to live in other residence halls. Housing has arranged for honors students who want to remain on campus to live in clusters in the South Residential College."

Prestigious Awards (3.5): The awards that we track and include are listed in the section titled "Prestigious Scholarships." The awards are sometimes won by students who are not in an honors college or program, but increasingly many are enrolled in honors programs. It is also a trend that honors colleges and programs help to prepare their students for the awards competitions.

Ole Miss students have won 25 Rhodes scholarships and 14 Truman scholarships, to go along with 14 Goldwater awards to undergraduate students in the STEM disciplines. Ole Miss students also earn a significant number of Gilman awards for studying abroad.

UNRATED FEATURES

Continuation Requirements: 3.20 by the end of the freshman year, 3.40 by the end of the sophomore year, 3.50 by the end of the junior year and in senior year.

Academic Strengths, National Rankings: This is based on national rankings of *graduate* programs in all but engineering and business, where undergraduate rankings are used.

The strongest departments at Ole Miss are history, English, business, and education, all ranked in the top 100 in the nation.

Undergraduate Research: "Honors students, both SMBHC Scholars and Junior-Entry students, must complete a research project and senior thesis in order to graduate from the Honors College. Typically, the work done in the research project feeds into the thesis. Unless, the student successfully petitions to do something else, the work is performed in the student's major. The length and content of the thesis is based on the type of work each discipline expects."

Honors Study Abroad: "Most students study abroad in the junior year; 22% of the Honors College juniors studied abroad for a full summer or longer. Honors students comprised 7% of the undergraduate student body in 2014-2015, but made up 38% of those who studied abroad a full summer, semester or a year.

"The SMBHC has Honors Fellowships, which we award to support study abroad or internship opportunities. The amount we award is based on duration of the program."

Financial Aid: "Most students entering the Honors College as freshmen are eligible for University Academic Excellence awards based on their test scores and high school GPAs. These awards can reach $7,644 per year for in-state students and more than $21,000 for out-of-state students. Below are specific awards for National Scholars:

National Merit Semifinalist/Finalist Award

- **Award Amount:** Currently valued at $50,156 ($12,539 per year–includes a full-tuition scholarship, currently valued at $7,644 per year and the standard cost of double-occupancy room in a campus residence hall currently valued at $4,895 per year). Non-Resident students will also receive a full non-resident scholarship currently valued at $14,268 per year. Finalists may receive additional awards. This scholarship is awarded in lieu of the Academic Excellence Scholarship.

- **Eligibility:** Entering freshmen with National Merit Semifinalist/Finalist status and a 3.0 or higher GPA.

National Merit Finalist Award (if no corporate award)

- **Award Amount:** $4,000 ($1,000 per year)
- **Eligibility:** Entering freshmen with finalist status and selection of Ole Miss as first choice *and who are not receiving a National Merit Corporate award.*

National Hispanic Recognition Award

- **Award Amount:** $8,000 ($2,000/year)
- **Eligibility:** Entering freshmen who are named to the College Board's National Hispanic Recognition Program after taking the PSAT/NMSQT. This award can be stacked with Academic Excellence unless a student is designated a National Merit Semi-Finalist or Finalist, in which case the upgraded Finalist/Semi-finalist packages apply instead.

Barnard Scholarship

- **Award Amount:** $20,000 ($5,000 / year)
- **Eligibility:** Entering freshmen who have achieved National Merit Finalist status and have a 3.0 or higher high school GPA.

"In addition to the Academic Excellence awards, entering honors freshmen are competitive for scholarships awarded by the University or by specific departments, like the Croft Institute for International Studies, the Lott Leadership Institute, the School of Accountancy, the School of Business, the School of Engineering, and the Center for Manufacturing Excellence. The SMBHC awards 12-13 scholarships worth $8,000 a year and 2 scholarships worth $6,250 a year. Our selection is based on the application for admission to the Honors College."

Honors Fees: None.

Placement Experiences: None listed.

Degree of Difference: This is based on the differences between (1) the average (2015, two-part) SAT scores for enrolled honors students (1340) and (2) the average test scores for all students in the university (1110) as a whole. The test scores may be an indication of how "elite" honors students may be perceived as compared to students in the university as a whole. The scores can also provide an indication of how well prepared the non-honors students in the university may be. **Please keep in mind that neither high nor low test scores determine the overall quality of a program.**

NAME: UNIVERSITY OF MISSOURI HONORS COLLEGE.

Date Established: 1958.

Location: Columbia, Missouri.

University Full-time Undergraduate Enrollment: 25,859.

Honors Members in Good Standing: 2,550 (mean size of all 50 programs is 1,742).

Honors Average Admission Statistics: The ACT, 31; the old two-part SAT, 1380. Estimated new SAT score, 1430.

Average High School GPA/Class Rank: 3.98 GPA; top 8%.

Basic Admission Requirements: Direct eligibility for admission to the Honors College is met if a prospective student satisfies any one of the following inverse scale criteria:

1. An ACT score of 31 (old SAT 1360, new 1420) AND either a top 15% class rank OR a high school core GPA of 3.58
2. An ACT score of 30 (old SAT 1330, new SAT 1390) AND either a top 10% class rank OR a high school core GPA of 3.74
3. An ACT score of 29 (old SAT 1290, new SAT 1350) AND either a top 5% class rank OR a high school core GPA of 3.91

Application Deadline(s): *Please verify with each program, as some deadlines could change.*

Applications open on August 15 of each academic year. Priority deadlines for applying to Mizzou and the Honors College for scholarship eligibility is December 1. Deadline for applying to the Honors College is March 1.

Honors Programs with old SAT scores from 1351—1396: Purdue, Oregon, Alabama, Massachusetts, Penn State, Indiana, CUNY Macaulay, Texas A&M, NJIT, Missouri, Oregon State, Delaware, LSU, Vermont, Temple.

Administrative Staff: 13.

RATINGS AT A GLANCE: For all mortarboard ratings immediately below, a score of 5 is the maximum and represents a comparison with all 50 honors colleges and programs. More detailed explanations follow the "mortarboard" ratings.

PERCEPTION* OF UNIVERSITY AS A WHOLE, NOT OF HONORS:

*Perception is based on the university's ranking among public universities in the 2016 U.S. News Best Colleges report. Please bear in mind that the better the U.S. News ranking, the more difficult it is for an honors college or program to have a rating that equals or improves on the magazine ranking.

OVERALL HONORS RATING:

Curriculum Requirements:

Number of Honors Classes Offered: 1/2

Number of Honors Classes in Key Disciplines:

Extent of Honors Enrollment:

Honors-only Class Size: 1/2

Overall Class Size (Honors-only plus mixed, contract): 1/2

Honors Grad Rate: 1/2

Value-Added Grad Rate:

Ratio of Staff to Students:

Priority Registration: At MU, priority registration is reserved only for those with legislative or required designations (currently limited to athletes, veterans, and students who are differently-abled). The Honors College gives a form of priority registration as follows:

1. All Honors students receive priority registration *only* for Honors courses—General Honors and Departmental Honors sections.
2. First-year, first-time college students, are pre-populated into both Honors and non-Honors courses during the Summer Welcome process, when we register them in [Freshman Interest Groups, FIGs] and into courses that are reserved for students with specified ACT and high school GPA levels of achievement.
3. All students who are enrolled in FIGs in the Fall Semester have the opportunity to co-enroll in a common Spring Semester course with their FIG members prior to the start of early registration.

Honors Housing Amenities:

Honors Housing Availability:

Prestigious Awards: 1/2

RATING SCORES AND EXPLANATIONS:

Curriculum Requirements (3.0): The most important rating category, the curriculum completion requirement (classes required to complete honors) defines not only what honors students should learn but also the extent to which honors students and faculty are connected in the classroom. If there is a thesis or capstone requirement, it reinforces the individual contact and research skills so important to learning.

The average number of honors semester hours required for completion across all 50 programs is 29.0.

"To receive the Honors Certificate, which signifies completion of all MU Honors College requirements, students must have at least **20 credit hours** of Honors courses.

"Beginning in Fall 2017, newly enrolled students will be required to earn 24 credit hours of Honors courses in order to complete the certificate.

"The Honors credit hours (MU is on a semester system) may include any number of General Honors and Departmental Honors course credits, but no more than eight hours of Honors Learning-by-Contract credit, eight hours of approved graduate credit, and/or six hours of Honors transfer credits. Students must achieve a C or better for regular Honors credit or graduate courses and a B or better for Honors Learning-by-Contract courses.

"Students are encouraged to take at least one Honors course a semester and to design their individualized Honors Certificate program of study using a mix of both General Honors and Departmental Honors courses." There is **no thesis** requirement.

"One of the most distinctive elements of the Honors College at MU is the MedOpp Program, serving as MU's only Pre-Med Advising and Medical/Dental School Entrance Program" according to the director.

"With the assistance of a Program Coordinator and one Advisor, students who declare Pre-Med as a focus will be invited to participate in the Program's series of workshops, student groups, application assistance process (including the possibility of a practice interview by a faculty panel), and placement program.

"This broad range of programming is available to more than 200 students per year. And MedOpp also coordinates three Freshman Interest Groups (FIGs) each year, two honors-only and one for underrepresented students, to help extend students' exposure.

"Those who participate, fully, in the MedOpp Program increase their chances of acceptance into medical school by over 50% (when compared to other MU students), which is also above the national average by more than 30%."

AP/IB credits are **not** counted as replacements for honors courses.

Number of Honors Classes Offered (3.5): This is a measure of the total **adjusted** honors main sections available in the term reported, not including labs and thesis. (Please read the section titled "All about

Honors Classes".) An adjusted main section has 3 or more semester credits, or equivalent, and sections with fewer credits receive a lower prorated value.

The honors college had a ratio of **19.0** enrolled students per each main section. The mean for all 50 programs is 14.2. The lower the ratio, the better.

In the term reported, **67.5%** of honors enrollment was **in honors-only sections; 27.3% in mixed honors sections (honors and non-honors students); and 5.2% reported in contract sections (regular sections in which honors students "contract" to do extra work).** The averages for all fifty programs are 81.3% in honors-only sections; 13.6 % in mixed honors sections; and 5.1% in contract sections.

Number of Honors Classes in Key Disciplines (3.0): The 15 "key" disciplines are biological sciences; business (all); chemistry; communications (especially public speaking); computer science; economics; engineering (all); English; history; math (all); philosophy; physics; political science; psychology; and sociology/anthropology/gender studies. Interdisciplinary sections, such as those often taken for General Education credit in the first two years, do receive a lesser, prorated discipline "credit" because they introduce students to multiple disciplines in an especially engaging way, often with in-depth discussion.

In the term reported, the program had a ratio of **50.8 honors students** per each main section in some or all "key disciplines." The mean for all 50 programs is 26.3. The lower the ratio, the better.

Out of **34 adjusted sections in key disciplines**, the college had 21 honors-only sections. English and business had 6 each, philosophy (4), history 3 and math (2). There were no sections in biology, communications, computer science, or engineering, political science, or psychology.

The college had also had about 28 interdisciplinary tutorial sections, 1 credit each. Eleven more sections, 3 credits each, were titled "The Ancient World." Six more interesting interdisciplinary sections combined disciplines within the sciences, social sciences, and humanities, including "Human Sciences Sequence I: Personal Identity"; "Finding the Story in Science"; and "Environment: from Molecules to the Cosmos."

The combination of seminars and courses in the disciplines makes the honors college a **blended** program.

Extent of Honors Enrollment (3.0): Not all honors students take an honors class each term, especially after the first two years. Programs that have fewer honors classes for upper-division honors students will generally have fewer total members in good standing who are actually enrolled in a given term. (Please be aware, however, that honors students not enrolled in a class for a term are still connected to the honors community through residential and extracurricular activities.)

For example, if honors students in a program occupy 1,800 honors classroom seats in a given term, and there are 3,000 honors students in good standing, the extent of enrollment is .67. For programs that require a thesis, the ratio (score) reported below might in fact be somewhat higher, since we only count "regular" class enrollment for this measure, and not thesis enrollment. **The college has a ratio of .78**, versus the mean of 1.13 for all 50 programs. The higher the ratio, the better.

Average Class Size, Honors-only Sections (4.5): Offered mostly in the first two years, honors-only classes tend to be smaller and, as the name implies, have no or very few students other than those in the

honors program. These class sections always are much smaller than mixed or contract sections, or regular non-honors class sections in the university.

The average honors-only class size at the honors college is **17.2 students**. The average for all 50 programs is 19.0 students.

Average Class Size, Overall (3.5): The overall class calculation is based on the *proportion* of honors students in each type of class (honors-only, mixed honors, and honors contract sections). Thus it is not a raw average. The overall honors-credit class size at the college is **36.1 students**, versus the average for all 50 programs of 26.3 students.

These class size averages also do not correspond to the number of students per honors sections numbers above. The reason is that, in computing average class size metrics, we include enrollment in each 1-2-credit section, not just sections with 3 or more credits.

Along with the honors-only average of 17.2 students, the number mixed honors sections average **73.3** students. Contract enrollment average was **88.0**. Across all fifty programs, the average mixed honors section has 51.1 students, and the average contract section has 60.1.

Honors Graduation Rate (4.5): The rating is based on the actual grad rate for students who entered the program six years earlier, whether or not the students remained in honors. The **actual rate of 89.0%** is also compared to the rates of other programs with the same test score entry requirement range, and then adjusted to the **score of 89.3%**. The average honors graduation rate for all programs with similar test scores required for admission is 86.2%.

Value-Added Grad Rate (4.0): The value-added rate measures the extent to which the adjusted score listed above exceeds the grad rate for the university as a whole. **The university-wide rate is 69%.**

Ratio of Staff to Honors Students (3.0): There is 1 staff member for every **212.5** students. (Mean ratio for all 50 programs is 1 staff member for every 135.6 students.)

Honors Residence Halls, Amenities (4.0): More than two-thirds of honors students living in honors housing reside in Schurz Hall, only for first-year students. Schurz is air-conditioned, with traditional double rooms and hall baths. "Schurz has the highest GPA of any residence hall on campus," the director tells us. It houses "two Honors Experience FIGs, an Honors Scholars & Fellows FIG, and two Pre-Medicine Honors FIGs." The most convenient dining options include Baja Grill, Plaza 900, and Mizzou Market/Pershing Commons.

Mark Twain Hall (West Campus): "Remodeled and reopened in 2013, Mark Twain Hall houses 80 Honors students out of a total of 380 residents; all rooms are suite style; co-ed by suites; The MARK on 5th Street dining facility is located within Mark Twain; air-conditioned, on-site laundry, Honors lounges by floors and FIGs; houses the Walter Williams Journalism Scholars FIGs and the Kinder Institute's Constitutionalism & Democracy Honors FIG."

College Avenue Residence Hall (Central Campus): "Built in 2006, College Ave. houses 40 Honors students out of a total of 215 residents; all rooms are suite style; co-ed by suites; close to Baja Grill, Plaza

900 and Mizzou Market/Pershing Commons; air-conditioned, on-site laundry; houses the Honors and Journalism Social Justice FIG."

Mark Twain and College Avenue provide housing for honors upperclassmen.

Honors Residence Halls, Availability (3.0): This rating compares the number of places in honors residence halls to the number of honors freshman and sophomore members in good standing, just under 1,275. The ratio for the college is **.30 rooms** for each first- and second-year student. The average for all fifty programs is .63 places.

Prestigious Awards (4.5): The awards that we track and include are listed in the section titled "Prestigious Scholarships." The awards are sometimes won by students who are not in an honors college or program, but increasingly many are enrolled in honors programs. It is also a trend that honors colleges and programs help to prepare their students for the awards competitions.

Mizzou students have won 18 Rhodes scholarships, four Marshall and four Gates Cambridge awards, and 17 Truman scholarships, to go along with 26 Goldwater awards to undergraduate students in the STEM disciplines. Especially noteworthy is that a Mizzou scholar is in the inaugural class of Schwarzman Scholars, a new and very prestigious award designed "to give the world's best and brightest students the opportunity to develop their leadership skills and professional networks through a one-year Master's Degree at Tsinghua University in Beijing – one of China's most prestigious universities."

UNRATED FEATURES

Continuation Requirements: 3.50 to remain in the program and graduate with honors.

Academic Strengths, National Rankings: This is based on national rankings of *graduate* programs in all but engineering and business, where undergraduate rankings are used.

Missouri academic departments rank among the top 75 or so in the nation across the 15 disciplines that we track. In addition to having one of the nation's best journalism schools, MU is strong in education (45) business (50), psychology (52), political science (61), English (63), history (64), and math (65).

Undergraduate Research: "We believe that research and artistry is one of the highest-impact practices that a student can undertake **Discovery Fellows** work collaboratively with …[and] gain insight into the professional world of their field, enhance their knowledge base and critical thinking skills, and better prepare for graduate studies."

Eligibility--First-year students with a 33 ACT composite (or better), who have applied to and been accepted by MU and the Honors College by January 15 of their senior year, who complete the application, and who are selected by their respective major College Dean and faculty. All Discovery Fellows receive a $2,000 scholarship. Students for this and other research programs listed below must work 8-10 hours/week, participate in workshops, and remain enrolled in the Honors College.

Show Me Scholars "participate in a four-year sequence of high-impact practices designed to expose them to the full spectrum of academic life and provide them with a solid grounding for graduate study or competitive employment.

"Eligibility--The SMS program is open to Missouri residents who have a 33 ACT or higher and who have applied to and been accepted by the Honors College by October 15 of their senior year, who complete the application, and is selected by the Honors College.

"Scholarship: All Show-Me Scholars receive at least a $500 scholarship in their junior year (or associated summer semester).

"ASH (Arts, Social Sciences, & Humanities) Scholars work collaboratively with a team of two faculty and between six and eight students on a specific research or artistry project designed and led by the faculty.... The program seeks to replicate the 'lab' experience of the STEM fields for students in other disciplines.

"Eligibility: Any active Honors student, enrolled in a major that is classified as one of the ASH disciplines, as selected by the faculty and the ASH Advisory Team.

"Scholarship: All ASH Scholars receive a $2,000 scholarship.

"In addition to these formal programs, students who are engaged in other programs or projects can apply for the **Honors College Student Experiential Learning Award (HC-SELA)** to support pursuing supplemental research learning opportunities such as presenting at a conference, publication, archival research, or attending a professional development workshop. These awards are between $100 and $500 each."

Honors Study Abroad: "The Honors College sponsors three Honors-only Study Abroad Programs and partners with thirty-three other MU programs to offer Honors credit for a study abroad learning experience.

1. **Accra, GHANA** | *Advocacy and Internship in Ghana.* Students participate in an internship in international development and human rights as they simultaneously explore how to alleviate poverty and public health crises, and work with NGOs on communicating the needs and policies that impact Sub-Saharan Africa. Twelve students.
2. **The Hague, NETHERLANDS** | *Peace, Justice, and the International Courts.* Participants will interact with jurists, investigators, diplomats, and NGO leaders while also witnessing on-going trials at the ICC, ICTY, and ICJ (among others). A side-trip to study the effects of the Holocaust on Amsterdam is included. Twelve students; in partnership with LeMoyne College, NY.
3. **Quito, ECUADOR** | *Biology, Culture, and Sustainability.* A multiple-location program that explores the biodiversity in Ecuador's costal lowlands, the Andes mountains, and Amazon basin. Participants engage with local sustainable development projects and learn about many of the indigenous peoples and their efforts to confront ever-changing realities. Twelve students.

"The Honors College allows students to turn any MU study-abroad program into an honors experience through an Honors Learning-by-Contract or Independent Study credit agreement. Discussions are currently underway to add four more Honors-only programs to South Africa, Costa Rica, China, and Australia.

"The Honors College also offers scholarship support for students who participate in our programs, most often in the amount of full tuition. Additionally, students can apply for the **Honors College Student Experiential Learning Award (HC-SELA)** to support a portion of their study abroad if they plan on producing a presentable academic project upon their return."

Financial Aid: "National Merit Scholars' support varies between $750 and $2,000 awards and is given to as many as twenty entering students each year."

"There are numerous scholarships offered by the University of Missouri for which students are considered automatically, given that we are a land-grant institution, when they are admitted to MU. Candidates for the Honors College are among the most common recipients and many of the criteria coincide with the admissions criteria for the College."

"The **Mizzou Scholars Award**, which requires at least a 33 ACT (1450, old SAT) and an application to MU by December 1 of a student's high school senior year, is an award of $10,000 and is renewable for three additional years if Honors College status is maintained. The **Chancellor's Award**, requiring at least a 31 ACT (1360, old SAT) and a high school class rank in the top 10%, provides $6,500 a year and is also renewable for up to three additional years. The **Curators Scholarship** requires a 28ACT (1250, old ACT) and high school rank in the top 5%, and like the other two, is renewable for a period of three additional years.

"*Out-of-state students* can also qualify for the **Mark Twain Non-Resident Scholarship**. Minimum requirements are a 27 ACT (1210, old SAT) and top 50% of high school class, but as this is a very competitive award, the higher your ACT score and class rank, the more competitive you will be. The top value for the Mark Twain Scholarship is $10,000, renewable for up to three additional years, for students in the top 25% of their class, and $8,500 for those in the top half. Some lesser amounts are also available for students in the lower ACT score ranges. A very select few students may be eligible for the **Mizzou**

Heritage Scholarship if they are both out-of-state and the child of a Mizzou alumnus. It waives the non-resident portion of tuition (approximately $14,500 per year) and requires at least a 27 ACT (1210 SAT) and top 25% class rank."

Honors Fees: None.

Placement Experiences: None listed.

Degree of Difference: This is based on the differences between (1) the average (2015, two-part) SAT scores for enrolled honors students (1380) and (2) the average test scores for all students in the university (1170) as a whole. The test scores may be an indication of how "elite" honors students may be perceived as compared to students in the university as a whole. The scores can also provide an indication of how well prepared the non-honors students in the university may be. **Please keep in mind that neither high nor low test scores determine the overall quality of a program.**

NAME: DAVIDSON HONORS COLLEGE.

Date Established: 1991.

Location: Missoula, Montana.

University <u>Full-time Undergraduate</u> Enrollment: 8,089.

Honors Members in Good Standing: 650 (mean size of all 50 programs is 1,742).

Honors <u>Average</u> Admission Statistics: ACT, 28; old two-part SAT, 1265. Est. new SAT score, 1325.

Average High School GPA/Class Rank: 3.85.

<u>Basic</u> Admission Requirements: ACT, 27; old SAT, 1200. Est. new SAT score, 1270.

Application Deadline(s): *Please verify with each program, as some deadlines could change.*

December 2, 2016, for scholarships; after that date, on a rolling admissions basis.

Honors Programs with old SAT scores from 1240—1291: Arkansas, Oklahoma State, Texas Tech, Montana, Washington State, New Mexico, South Dakota, Colorado State, Arizona, Montana State, Arizona State.

Administrative Staff: 7.

RATINGS AT A GLANCE: For all mortarboard ratings immediately below, a score of 5 is the maximum and represents a comparison with all 50 honors colleges and programs. More detailed explanations follow the "mortarboard" ratings.

PERCEPTION* OF UNIVERSITY AS A WHOLE, <u>NOT</u> OF HONORS: 🎓🎓🎓

*Perception is based on the university's ranking among public universities in the 2016 U.S. News Best Colleges report. Please bear in mind that the better the U.S. News ranking, the more difficult it is for an honors college or program to have a rating that equals or improves on the magazine ranking.

OVERALL HONORS RATING: 🎓🎓🎓$^{1/2}$

Curriculum Requirements: 🎓🎓🎓$^{1/2}$

Number of Honors Classes Offered: 🎓🎓🎓🎓🎓

Number of Honors Classes in Key Disciplines: 🎓🎓🎓🎓

Extent of Honors Enrollment: 🎓🎓🎓🎓

Honors-only Class Size: 🎓🎓🎓🎓

Overall Class Size (Honors-only plus mixed, contract): 🎓🎓🎓🎓$^{1/2}$

Honors Grad Rate: 🎓🎓🎓

Value-Added Grad Rate: 🎓🎓🎓🎓🎓

Ratio of Staff to Students: 🎓🎓🎓🎓$^{1/2}$

Priority Registration: Honors students have priority registration for all all-honors sections and mixed-honors sections that are offered.

Honors Housing Amenities: 🎓🎓🎓

Honors Housing Availability: 🎓🎓🎓🎓

Prestigious Awards: 🎓🎓🎓🎓$^{1/2}$

RATING SCORES AND EXPLANATIONS:

Curriculum Requirements (3.5): The most important rating category, the curriculum completion requirement (classes required to complete honors) defines not only what honors students should learn but also the extent to which honors students and faculty are connected in the classroom. If there is a thesis or capstone requirement, it reinforces the individual contact and research skills so important to learning.

The average number of honors semester hours required for completion across all 50 programs is 29.0.

The average completion at the honors college is **24** semester hours, as follows.

To become a University Scholar, an honors student can earn up to 19 credit hours of the total in honors courses; up to 8 credit hours each in contract courses or honors experiences; and up to 3 credit hours in a *required* capstone project.

"Although it was not offered during the Fall 2015 semester, the Davidson Honors College has established an Honors Seminar on 'Leadership: Mind, Heart, and Spine' that is designed specifically to help students think about personal development toward their scholarship, graduate school, and professional goals," according to the Dean.

"Beginning in the Fall 2016 semester, the DHC has also announced a series of 'Davidson Honors College Launch Awards' that are earmarked for incoming students to use (after satisfactory completion of their first year in the College) to offset the costs of undertaking unpaid professional internship opportunities or other experiential learning opportunities such as undergraduate research or study abroad.

"Experiential Learning is increasingly emphasized at the Davidson Honors College. We encourage our students to use up to two 'out-of-class' experiences (e.g. research assistantships, study abroad, career development internships, service learning) toward their University Scholar designation. The Davidson Honors College is extremely proud to be a hub for Civic Engagement at the University of Montana. Our Office for Civic Engagement has led the successful university effort to achieve the Carnegie Foundation's Community Engagement Classification, and every year the Honors College offers over 10 Service-Learning Designated Courses at the University (among more than 90 across the entire campus)."

AP/IB credits are **not** counted as replacements for honors courses.

Number of Honors Classes Offered (5.0): This is a measure of the total **adjusted** honors main sections available in the term reported, not including labs and thesis. (Please read the section titled "All about Honors Classes".) An adjusted main section has 3 or more semester credits, or equivalent, and sections with fewer credits receive a lower prorated value.

The honors program had a ratio of **8.7** enrolled students per each main section. The mean for all 50 programs is 14.2. The lower the ratio, the better.

In the term reported, the percentage of honors enrollment was an estimated **66.1% in honors-only sections; 32% in mixed sections with honors and non-honors students; and 1.9% were in contract sections (regular sections in which honors students "contract" to do extra work** The averages for all fifty programs are 81.3% in honors-only sections; 13.6 % in mixed honors sections; and 5.1% in contract sections.

Number of Honors Classes in Key Disciplines (4.0): The 15 "key" disciplines are biological sciences; business (all); chemistry; communications (especially public speaking); computer science; economics; engineering (all); English; history; math (all); philosophy; physics; political science; psychology; and sociology/anthropology/gender studies. Interdisciplinary sections, such as those often taken for General Education credit in the first two years, do receive a lesser, prorated discipline "credit" because they introduce students to multiple disciplines in an especially engaging way, often with in-depth discussion.

In the term reported, the program had ratio of **21.3 honors students** per each main section in some or all "key disciplines." The mean for all 50 programs is 26.3. The lower the ratio, the better.

Out of **18 adjusted sections in key disciplines**, the college had 1 honors-only section. There were 5 sections in English, 4 in biology, 3 in history, and 1 each in math and philosophy. In sociology, anthropology, and gender studies combined there were 2 sections. The college also offered 19 1-credit seminars, including more than 8 titled "Ways of Knowing."

The combination of seminars and courses in the disciplines makes the honors college an example of a small **blended** program, with an emphasis on mixed departmental courses in the key disciplines.

Extent of Honors Enrollment (4.0): Not all honors students take an honors class each term, especially after the first two years. Programs that have fewer honors classes for upper-division honors students will

generally have fewer total members in good standing who are actually enrolled in a given term. (Please be aware, however, that honors students not enrolled in a class for a term are still connected to the honors community through residential and extracurricular activities.)

For example, if honors students in a program occupy 1,800 honors classroom seats in a given term, and there are 3,000 honors students in good standing, the extent of enrollment is .67. For programs that require a thesis, the ratio (score) reported below might in fact be somewhat higher, since we only count "regular" class enrollment for this measure, and not thesis enrollment.. The college **has a ratio of 1.11**; the mean is 1.13 for all 50 programs. The higher the ratio, the better.

Average Class Size, Honors-only Sections (4.0): Offered mostly in the first two years, honors-only classes tend to be smaller and, as the name implies, have no or very few students other than those in the honors program. These class sections are almost always much smaller than mixed or contract sections, or regular non-honors class sections in the university.

The average honors-only class size in the honors program is **19.1 students**. The average for all 50 programs is 19.0 students.

Average Class Size, Overall (4.5): The overall class calculation is based on the *proportion* of honors students in each type of class (honors-only, mixed honors, and honors contract sections). Thus it is not a raw average. The overall honors-credit class size at the college is **18.3 students**, versus the average for all 50 programs of 26.3 students.

These class size averages also do not correspond to the number of students per honors sections numbers above. The reason is that, in computing average class size metrics, we include enrollment in each 1-2-credit section, not just sections with 3 or more credits.

Along with the honors-only average of 19.1 students, mixed sections averaged 15.9, and the contract sections with honors credit for individual honors students averaged about **32.6** students. Across all fifty programs, the average mixed honors section has 51.1 students, and the average contract section has 60.1 students. Even though the college has a high number of mixed sections, their average class size is quite low.

Honors Graduation Rate (3.0): The rating is based on the actual grad rate for students who entered the program six years earlier, whether or not the students remained in honors. The **actual rate of 79.5%** is also compared to the rates of other programs with the same test score entry requirement range, and then adjusted to the **score of 78.9**. In some cases this measure favors programs within universities with relatively higher test scores for the student population as a whole. The average honors graduation rate for all programs with similar test scores required for admission is 85.6%.

Value-Added Grad Rate (5.0): The value-added rate measures the extent to which the adjusted score listed above exceeds the six-year grad rate for the university as a whole. **The university-wide rate is 50.0%.** Note: This measure generally favors programs within universities with relatively lower test scores for the student population as a whole.

Ratio of Staff to Honors Students (4.5): There is 1 staff member for every **92.9** students. (Mean ratio for all 50 programs is 1 staff member for every 135.6 students.)

Honors Residence Halls, Amenities (3.0): About 138 honors students live in Knowles Hall, which has traditional double rooms and hall baths. Freshmen and upperclassmen reside in Knowles. The residence is not air-conditioned, although the concern in Missoula is more about warmth than coolness. The nearest dining facility is the Food Zoo.

Honors Residence Halls, Availability (4.0): This rating compares the number of places in honors residence halls to the number of honors freshman and sophomore members in good standing, 325. The ratio for the honors program is **.42** rooms for each first- and second-year student. The average for all fifty programs is .63 places.

Prestigious Awards (4.5): UM students are among the national leaders in winning Udall scholarships, with 40 to date, the highest number of any program under review. The university is also a leader in Rhodes scholarships, with 27 in the history of the awards. Another 14 Goldwater scholarships have been won by UM students.

UNRATED FEATURES

Continuation Requirements: 3.00 GPA, to stay in the program and 3.00 overall and 3.40 in major to graduate.

Academic Strengths, National Rankings: This is based on national rankings of *graduate* programs in 15 disciplines, except engineering and business, where undergraduate rankings are used.

The UM has nationally ranked programs in earth sciences, biology, chemistry, education, and psychology.

"The Davidson Honors College is home to the University of Montana's award winning Climate Change Studies Program. Students have the opportunity to pursue a degree program in Climate Change Studies, or to take advantage of individual seminars in the program."

Undergraduate Research: "ALL (100%) of honors students who wish to graduate with University Scholar distinction complete a Senior Research Project," the Dean says, "and some first, second, and third-year students conduct formal undergraduate research before beginning work on their Senior Project. A conservative estimate is that 25-30% of our entire student body is conducting formal, mentored research at any point in time during the academic year."

"Every one of our graduating students works with a faculty mentor on a Senior Research/Creative Scholarship Project. It is a requirement for a student to graduate with University Scholar distinction."

"Additionally, the Davidson Honors College hosts the Annual University of Montana Conference on Undergraduate Research. UMCUR is now in its fifteenth year, and we have over 140 poster and oral presentations each year, along with a special Visual and Performing Arts Exhibition.

The Davidson Honors College has also driven UM's success in hosting (twice) the Annual National Conference on Undergraduate Research (NCUR)."

Honors Study Abroad: "We don't calculate our total number of students studying abroad, but I estimate it to be about 65-75 (approximately 10% of total honors student body) each year. The DHC supports approximately two-dozen students with study abroad scholarships totaling over $30,000 each year.

"Additionally, the Davidson Honors College runs an honors-only study abroad program to Ireland every other winter session. The trip is a rich, deep introduction to the history, literature, religion, politics, and other elements of Irish culture. Throughout Ireland, students visit ancient ruins, medieval monasteries and castles, beautiful sea cliffs, and sites of literary, political, and emigration history. In addition, they have the benefit of several extremely talented and knowledgeable professional tour guides.

"The Davidson Honors College also has extensive connections with annual study abroad trips to Vietnam, Guatemala, Tanzania, and Germany."

Financial Aid:

Presidential Leadership Scholarships

"Our flagship scholarship program is the Presidential Leadership Scholarship," the Dean tells us. "Presidential Scholars are chosen solely on academic merit with scholarships being renewable for a total of four years. Approximately 25 PLS awards are made each year to incoming freshman. Resident students receive a full tuition waiver. Non-resident students either have their tuition discounted through the WUE program or they receive a waiver equivalent to in-state tuition (currently $4,373). All PLS recipients also receive a stipend of $7,500 for the Gold Level or $5,000 for the Silver Level."

Western Undergraduate Exchange Scholarships

"Students awarded the WUE scholarship receive a discounted tuition rate equivalent to 150% of resident tuition. For the 2016-17 academic year this is equivalent to a scholarship of $15,267. To qualify for a WUE Scholarship, students need to have a 3.50 GPA or higher (with an ACT of 28 or higher and an SAT of 1860 or higher). Students with a 3.75 GPA or higher, an ACT score of 25 or higher or an SAT of 1700 or higher will suffice for a WUE."

Leadership and Service Scholarships

"For Autumn 2016, students from non-western states may qualify for the LAS scholarship, renewable for 4 years. Students with a 3.50 GPA and an ACT of 28 or higher will receive a scholarship of $5,000 per year."

Montana Academic Achievement Scholarships (MAA)

"Montana Academic Achievement Scholarships awards are tuition-designated scholarships or Montana resident students. They cannot exceed the cost of tuition when combined with other tuition designated awards such as tuition waivers. Students with a GPA between 3.50 and 3.75 and an ACT score of 28 or higher will receive $2,000, while students with a GPA of 3.75 or higher and an ACT score of 28 or higher will receive $3,000."

National Merit Scholarships

National Merit **Scholars attending the University of Montana receive a $2,500 National Merit Scholarship.**

Other Scholarships

"Every year, the Davidson Honors College offers our continuing students over $35,000 in additional scholarships for study abroad and undergraduate research."

Honors Fees: None.

Placement Experiences: "SAMPLE OF PLACEMENTS (of students currently enrolled or matriculating in graduate programs):

PhD Programs (sample, not exhaustive):
Union Theological Seminary, New York University (history PhD), University at Arizona School of Health Sciences, Washington University in St. Louis (PhD in economics), University of Chicago (English Literature).

Medical Schools (sample, not exhaustive):
University of Washington Medical School, University of Colorado Medical School, University of Virginia Medical School, Cornell Medical School.

Law Schools (sample, not exhaustive):
University of Oregon, University of Washington, University of Michigan, University of Southern California, UC Irvine, University of Texas, Notre Dame, University of Wisconsin, University of Denver.

Degree of Difference: This is based on the differences between (1) the average (2015, two-part) SAT scores for enrolled honors students (1265) and (2) the average test scores for all students in the university (1070) as a whole. The test scores may be an indication of how "elite" honors students may be perceived as compared to students in the university as a whole. The scores can also provide an indication of how well prepared the non-honors students in the university may be. **Please keep in mind that neither high nor low test scores determine the overall quality of a program.**

NAME: ALBERT DORMAN HONORS COLLEGE, NEW JERSEY INSTITUTE OF TECHNOLOGY.

Date Established: 1995.

Location: Newark, New Jersey.

University Full-time Undergraduate Enrollment: 5,923.

Honors Members in Good Standing: 716 (mean size of all 50 programs is 1,742).

Honors Average Admission Statistics: Old two-part SAT, 1380. Est. new SAT score, 1430.

Average High School GPA/Class Rank: 3.6 minimum; top 10% of class.

Basic Admission Requirements: ACT, 29. Old SAT, 1300; est. new SAT, 1360.

Application Deadline(s): *Please verify with each program, as some deadlines could change.*

February 1, 2017.

Honors Programs with old SAT scores from 1351—1396: Purdue, Oregon, Alabama, Massachusetts, Penn State, Indiana, CUNY Macaulay, Texas A&M, NJIT, Missouri, Oregon State, Delaware, LSU, Vermont, Temple.

Administrative Staff: 10 FTEs.

RATINGS AT A GLANCE: For all mortarboard ratings immediately below, a score of 5 is the maximum and represents a comparison with all 50 honors colleges and programs. More detailed explanations follow the "mortarboard" ratings.

PERCEPTION* OF UNIVERSITY AS A WHOLE, NOT OF HONORS: 🎓🎓🎓 $^{1/2}$

*Perception is based on the university's ranking among public universities in the 2016 U.S. News Best Colleges report. Please bear in mind that the better the U.S. News ranking, the more difficult it is for an honors college or program to have a rating that equals or improves on the magazine ranking.

OVERALL HONORS RATING: 🎓🎓🎓🎓🎓

Curriculum Requirements: 🎓🎓🎓🎓🎓

Number of Honors Classes Offered: 🎓🎓🎓🎓🎓

Number of Honors Classes in Key Disciplines: 🎓🎓🎓🎓🎓

Extent of Honors Enrollment: 🎓🎓🎓🎓

Honors-only Class Size: 🎓🎓🎓🎓

Overall Class Size (Honors-only plus mixed, contract): 🎓🎓🎓🎓

Honors Grad Rate: 🎓🎓🎓🎓

Value-Added Grad Rate: 🎓🎓🎓🎓🎓

Ratio of Staff to Students: 🎓🎓🎓🎓🎓

Priority Registration: Yes, honors students have priority registration for all courses, in the form of being able to register with the class ahead of them.

Honors Housing Amenities: 🎓🎓🎓🎓[1/2]

Honors Housing Availability: 🎓🎓🎓🎓🎓

Prestigious Awards: 🎓🎓🎓

RATING SCORES AND EXPLANATIONS:

Curriculum Requirements (5.0): The most important rating category, the curriculum completion requirement (classes required to complete honors) defines not only what honors students should learn but also the extent to which honors students and faculty are connected in the classroom. If there is a thesis or capstone requirement, it reinforces the individual contact and research skills so important to learning.

The average number of honors semester hours required for completion across all 50 programs is 29.0.

The *Course-Intensive* option at NJIT requires a minimum of **33 credits** for completion. Students must complete 24 credits in honors courses, with a maximum of 9 credits in contract sections. A **3-credit thesis** or capstone is included, as are **240 community service hours.**

The *Research Option* requires 24 total credit hours, including 16 colloquium hours. Contract courses are not counted as credit toward completion. At least 3 credits must be in departmental honors work, and a **6-credit research paper or product** (e.g., prototype, patent application) is required. The community service requirement is also 240 hours.

For completion of the *Professional Development* track, students must take a minimum of 24 total credits hours, including the same colloquium requirement, service requirement, and 3-credit requirement in a departmental class. Students must also complete a 3-credit capstone project.

The *Study Abroad Option* requirement is essentially the same as the Professional Development track above, except students must achieve course credit for at least one full semester of studying abroad.

"The Dorman Honors College offers both regular and *accelerated/combined programs in Medicine, Dentistry, Optometry, Physical Therapy (Doctor of Physical Therapy), and Law.* In accelerated programs, students complete all of their General University requirements and most of the major courses in three years at NJIT. The first year of professional school completes the Bachelors (BA/BS) degree requirements."

AP/IB credits are not counted as replacements for honors courses.

Number of Honors Classes Offered (5.0): This is a measure of the total **adjusted** honors main sections available in the term reported, not including labs and thesis. (Please read the section titled "All about Honors Classes".) An adjusted main section has 3 or more semester credits, or equivalent, and sections with fewer credits receive a lower prorated value.

The honors college offered an adjusted section for every **6.9** enrolled students. The average for all 50 programs is 14.2 students. The lower the number, the better.

In the term reported, **72.6%** of honors enrollment was **in honors-only sections; 16.6% in mixed honors sections (honors and non-honors students); and 10.8% reported in contract sections (regular sections in which honors students "contract" to do extra work).** The averages for all fifty programs are 81.3% in honors-only sections; 13.6 % in mixed honors sections; and 5.1% in contract sections.

Number of Honors Classes in Key Disciplines (5.0): The 15 "key" disciplines are biological sciences; business (all); chemistry; communications (especially public speaking); computer science; economics; engineering (all); English; history; math (all); philosophy; physics; political science; psychology; and sociology/anthropology/gender studies. Interdisciplinary sections, such as those often taken for General Education credit in the first two years, do receive a lesser, prorated discipline "credit" because they introduce students to multiple disciplines in an especially engaging way, often with in-depth discussion.

For this measure, mixed and contract sections are not counted as a section in a key discipline unless students taking the sections for honors credit make up at least 10% of the total section enrollment.

In the term reported, the program had a ratio of **8.2 honors students** per each main section in some or all "key disciplines." The mean for all 50 programs is 26.3. The lower the ratio, the better.

Out of **63 adjusted sections in key disciplines**, the program had **40 honors-only sections.** The most sections were in *engineering (12), an extremely high total;* biology (9), computer science (8), math (7), English and communications (5 each), history (4), business, chemistry, and physics (3 each). Economics, political science, and psychology were not listed.

The program also offered only 7 seminar sections, including at least three in "Writing, Reading, Thinking," along with "The Philosophy of Plato" and "History of the American Suburb."

The emphasis on courses in the disciplines, especially STEM disciplines, makes the program a strong **discipline-based program,** though one with some seminars.

Extent of Honors Enrollment (5.0:): Not all honors students take an honors class each term, especially after the first two years. Programs that have fewer honors classes for upper-division honors students will generally have fewer total members in good standing who are actually enrolled in a given term. (Please be aware, however, that honors students not enrolled in a class for a term are still connected to the honors community through residential and extracurricular activities.)

For example, if honors students in a program occupy 1,800 honors classroom seats in a given term, and there are 3,000 honors students in good standing, the extent of enrollment is .67. For programs that require a thesis, the ratio (score) reported below might in fact be somewhat higher, since we only count "regular" class enrollment for this measure, and not thesis enrollment. The college **has a ratio of 1.60**; the mean is 1.13 for all 50 programs. The higher the ratio, the better.

Average Class Size, Honors-only Sections (4.0): Offered mostly in the first two years, honors-only classes tend to be smaller and, as the name implies, have no or very few students other than those in the honors program. These class sections are almost always much smaller than mixed or contract sections, or regular non-honors class sections in the university.

The average honors-only class size in the honors program is **19.7 students**. The average for all 50 programs is 19.0 students.

Along with the honors-only average of 19.7 students, the mixed honors sections average **32.3 students,** and the contract sections with honors credit for individual honors students average **32.7 students.** Across all fifty programs, the average mixed honors section has 51.1 students, and the average contract section has 60.1 students.

Average Class Size, Overall (4.0): The overall class calculation is based on the *proportion* of honors students in each type of class (honors-only, mixed honors, and honors contract sections). Thus it is not a raw average. The overall honors-credit class size is **23.2 students**, versus the average for all 50 programs of 26.3 students.

These class size averages also do not correspond to the number of students per honors sections numbers above. The reason is that, in computing average class size metrics, we include enrollment in each 1-2-credit section, not just sections with 3 or more credits.

Honors Graduation Rate (4.0): The rating is based on the actual grad rate for students who entered the program six years earlier, whether or not the students remained in honors. The **actual rate of 86.0%** is also compared to the rates of other programs with the same test score entry requirement range, and then adjusted to the **score of 86.0%.** In some cases this measure favors programs within universities with relatively higher test scores for the student population as a whole. The average honors graduation rate for all programs with similar test scores required for admission is 86.2%.

Value-Added Grad Rate (5.0): The value-added rate measures the extent to which the adjusted score listed above exceeds the six-year grad rate for the university as a whole. **The university-wide rate is 59%.** Note: This measure generally favors programs within universities with relatively lower test scores for the student population as a whole.

Ratio of Staff to Honors Students (5.0): There is 1 staff member for every **71.6** students. (Mean ratio for all 50 programs is 1 staff member for every 135.6 students.)

Honors Residence Halls, Amenities (4.5): The honors college offers housing in five residence halls, but about 70% of honors students in honors housing live in one, the Honors Residence Hall. The co-ed dorm features suite-style rooms with shared baths; it is fully air-conditioned. Dining is very convenient at Campus Center. Like all of the honors residences at NJIT except Oak Hall, both freshmen and upperclassmen live in each hall. Oak is for upperclassmen only.

The rest of honors students in honors housing are in Laurel, Oak, Cypress, and Redwood Halls. All have suite-style rooms with air-conditioning. For all, the most convenient dining is also at the Campus Center.

Honors Residence Halls, Availability (5.0): This rating compares the number of places in honors residence halls to the number of honors freshman and sophomore members in good standing, about 358. The ratio for the honors program is **1.30** rooms for each first- and second-year student. The average for all fifty programs is .63 places.

Prestigious Awards (3.0): The awards that we track and include are listed in the section titled "Prestigious Scholarships." The awards are sometimes won by students who are not in an honors college or program, but increasingly many are enrolled in honors programs. It is also a trend that honors colleges and programs help to prepare their students for the awards competitions.

"NJIT has recently increased its efforts to successfully compete for prestigious national fellowships and scholarships," the Interim Dean told us. "In recent years our students have received Goldwater scholarships (5) (plus one Honorable Mention), NSF Graduate Research Fellowships (2), and a Truman Fellowship. We have also had students win a DOE Computational Sciences Graduate Fellowship, a National Defense Science and Engineering Graduate Fellowship and two Whitaker Fellowships. This year, we recommended four candidates for Fulbright Awards, and we have our first Fulbright Award winner. In addition, one of our Goldwater Scholarships, and our Honorable Mention, were won this year. All of the students mentioned above have been Honors Scholars.

"NJIT has also established a National Fellowships and Awards Committee to provide needed structure and support to our students as they enter these competitions. The committee has begun meeting in spring 2016 and is comprised of members of all our colleges, as well as the Provost's office. It is understood that the very large majority of students who apply for these fellowships will be Honors Scholars, and therefore the Honors College has a large presence on this committee. The committee is chaired by the Associate Dean of the Honors College, and contains two other members of the Honors College."

UNRATED FEATURES

Continuation Requirements: 3.20; 3.5 for accelerated programs (medicine, dentistry, physical therapy, optometry, and law).

Academic Strengths, National Rankings: This is based on national rankings of *graduate* programs in 15 disciplines, except engineering and business, where undergraduate rankings are used.

The *graduate* program in engineering is ranked 92nd in the nation, with specialty rankings as follow: environmental engineering (67); biomedical engineering (70); chemical engineering (74); civil engineering (81); electrical engineering (88); and mechanical engineering (89). Other national rankings include computer science (90); math (103); and physics (131).

Undergraduate Research: "Although we don't have a formal research requirement in the honors program, we do have a research track curriculum option."

Study Abroad: "The Honors College recently approved three new curricular tracks that provide students with new options for co-curricular experiences that will enrich their educational opportunities. One of these tracks is the Study Abroad track in which students will receive a two-course reduction in required honors courses if they study abroad for one semester. The university currently has several [memoranda of understanding] with international universities for student exchange with a primary focus on Business courses. As part of the commitment, the university will heavily promote these programs especially amongst the Honors College, where Business is the second most popular minor.

"Examples of existing programs --China (Fujian University of Technology, Shanghai Lixin University of Commerce); France (Esdes - Lyon, Kedge Business School, Skema Business School); South Korea (Hanyang University); Spain (Cesine Business School, Universitat Politecnica de Valencia); Sweden (Linkoping University)."

Financial Aid: "NJIT offers incoming students very generous merit-based faculty scholarships, as well as supplementary Honors Awards. *100% of the 175 incoming Honors Scholars in fall 2015 received significant awards. More than 80% received scholarships that covered at least full tuition.* Furthermore, 26 (15%) received full tuition, fees, room and board, and an additional 54 (31%) received full tuition, fees and room." [Emphasis added.]

Honors Fees: None.

Placement Experiences: "For the class of 2015, 46% of graduates reported they were attending graduate or professional school immediately upon graduation. Another 30% had already accepted offers of employment at the time of the survey (May 2015)."

Degree of Difference: This is based on the differences between (1) the average (2015, two-part) SAT scores for enrolled honors students (1380) and (2) the average test scores for all students in the university (1155) as a whole. The test scores may be an indication of how "elite" honors students may be perceived as compared to students in the university as a whole. The scores can also provide an indication of how well prepared the non-honors students in the university may be. **Please keep in mind that neither high nor low test scores determine the overall quality of a program.**

NAME: UNIVERSITY OF NEW MEXICO HONORS COLLEGE.

Date Established: 2013; formerly the University Honors Program, founded in 1957.

Location: Albuquerque, New Mexico.

University Full-time Undergraduate Enrollment: 16,384.

Honors Members in Good Standing: 1,582 (mean size of all 50 programs is 1,742).,

Honors Average Admission Statistics: ACT, 28.4. Most applicants have ACT scores; old SAT equivalent, approximately 1275; new SAT, 1335.

Average High School GPA/Class Rank: 3.6 minimum; top 10% of class.

Basic Admission Requirements: ACT, 28. Old SAT, 1260; est. new SAT, 1320. "[An] entering student who does not meet the minimum criteria stated above is encouraged to submit additional material in support of his or her application. Upon review, some of these students are admitted provisionally. If a provisionally-admitted student has achieved a 3.2 GPA at UNM in his or her first semester, that student becomes an Honors student in good standing. Of 2014 Freshmen who were provisionally admitted, more than 90% attained full status by earning a 3.2 or greater GPA."

Application Deadline(s): *Please verify with each program, as some deadlines could change.*

University final deadline is May 1, 2017.

Honors Programs with old SAT scores from 1240—1291: Arkansas, Oklahoma State, Texas Tech, Montana, Washington State, New Mexico, South Dakota, Colorado State, Arizona, Montana State, Arizona State.

Administrative Staff: 17.5 FTEs.

RATINGS AT A GLANCE: For all mortarboard ratings immediately below, a score of 5 is the maximum and represents a comparison with all 50 honors colleges and programs. More detailed explanations follow the "mortarboard" ratings.

PERCEPTION* OF UNIVERSITY AS A WHOLE, NOT OF HONORS:
*Perception is based on the university's ranking among public universities in the 2016 U.S. News Best Colleges report. Please bear in mind that the better the U.S. News ranking, the more difficult it is for an honors college or program to have a rating that equals or improves on the magazine ranking.

OVERALL HONORS RATING: 1/2

Curriculum Requirements:

Number of Honors Classes Offered:

Number of Honors Classes in Key Disciplines: 🎓🎓🎓 1/2

Extent of Honors Enrollment: 🎓🎓🎓

Honors-only Class Size: 🎓🎓🎓🎓🎓

Overall Class Size (Honors-only plus mixed, contract): 🎓🎓🎓🎓🎓

Honors Grad Rate: 🎓🎓🎓🎓🎓

Value-Added Grad Rate: 🎓🎓🎓🎓🎓

Ratio of Staff to Students: 🎓🎓🎓🎓 1/2

Priority Registration: Yes, honors students register for all courses, honors and otherwise, with the first group of students during each year they are in the program.

Honors Housing Amenities: 🎓🎓🎓 1/2

Honors Housing Availability: 🎓🎓🎓

Prestigious Awards: 🎓🎓🎓🎓

RATING SCORES AND EXPLANATIONS:

Curriculum Requirements (5.0): The most important rating category, the curriculum completion requirement (classes required to complete honors) defines not only what honors students should learn but also the extent to which honors students and faculty are connected in the classroom. If there is a thesis or capstone requirement, it reinforces the individual contact and research skills so important to learning. The average number of honors semester hours required for completion across all 50 programs is 29.0. The honors college is one of only a few that confer their own degrees.

For **B.A. in Interdisciplinary Liberal Arts conferred by the Honors College, 36 credit hours** of honors, distributed as at least 3 credit hours (freshman) level, at least 3 credit hours (sophomore) level, and additional upper division hours described below:

- Required 6-credit "integrative block" taken concurrently in a semester or across two consecutive semesters addressing a single theme from multiple lenses;
- Required 12 credit hours in a single non-English language (or equivalent proficiency);
- Honors thesis hrs.= 6 – 9 credit hours at the senior level;
- Honors capstone hrs.= the 6-credit thesis is one option for the capstone; the other two capstone options (service learning; teaching) also require 6-9 credit hours at the senior level;
- *We require a second major or minor in a discipline and additional upper division course work in yet another discipline. (So, the BA is earned in Honors, the other major/minor from a*

- different college, the additional course work in another discipline outside of Honors, but possibly the same college as the second major/minor).

The **Interdisciplinary Liberal Arts Minor** requires 24 credit hours, including 15 offered by the honors college. Up to 9 additional credits can be offered by another academic unit if the course meets honors criteria. At least half of the total credit hours must be upper division honors courses.

The **Honors College Transcripted Designation** requires15 credit hours, 9 must be honors courses and up to 6 credit hours in approved other-department courses. At least 6 credit hours must be at the upper-division level.

The Honors Distinction in International Studies does not require total credit hours that exceed one of the other options, but it does specify the manner in which an 18-credit minor must be earned. For the minor, 6 credit hours must be earned abroad (either through a faculty-led program or individual study abroad program), *plus* 12 credit hours in a Foreign Language *or* 12 credit hours in an international topics course (in Honors or in another UNM Department).

Finally, there is a *combined degree option:* **Bachelor of Arts in Interdisciplinary Liberal Arts from the Honors College *and* a Master of Business Administration.** Students seeking the combined BA/MBA are allowed to apply 18 credits of graduate work in business toward their BA in Honors total credit requirement of 36. The 6-credit thesis is still required.

AP/IB credits are not counted as replacements for honors courses.

Number of Honors Classes Offered (4.0): This is a measure of the total **adjusted** honors main sections available in the term reported, not including labs and thesis. (Please read the section titled "All about Honors Classes".) An adjusted main section has 3 or more semester credits, or equivalent, and sections with fewer credits receive a lower prorated value. The honors college offered an adjusted section for every 14.2 enrolled students. The average for all 50 programs is 14.2 students. The lower the number, the better.

In the term reported, **93.8%** of honors enrollment was **in honors-only sections; 2.5% in mixed honors sections (honors and non-honors students); and 4.7% reported in contract sections (regular sections in which honors students "contract" to do extra work).** The averages for all fifty programs are 81.3% in honors-only sections; 13.6 % in mixed honors sections; and 5.1% in contract sections.

Number of Honors Classes in Key Disciplines (3.5): The 15 "key" disciplines are biological sciences; business (all); chemistry; communications (especially public speaking); computer science; economics; engineering (all); English; history; math (all); philosophy; physics; political science; psychology; and sociology/anthropology/gender studies. Interdisciplinary sections, such as those often taken for General Education credit in the first two years, do receive a lesser, prorated discipline "credit" because they introduce students to multiple disciplines in an especially engaging way, often with in-depth discussion.

For this measure, mixed and contract sections are not counted as a section in a key discipline unless students taking the sections for honors credit make up at least 10% of the total section enrollment.

In the term reported, the program had a ratio of **30.9 honors students** per each main section in some or all "key disciplines." The mean for all 50 programs is 26.3. The lower the ratio, the better.

Out of **18 adjusted sections in key disciplines**, the program had **18 honors-only sections, most in interdisciplinary classes that had a predominant focus on one discipline.** The most sections were in English (4), history and philosophy (3), and sociology, anthropology, and genders studies combined (6). *The program is centered on interdisciplinary seminars, about 43 total, to an extent greater than almost all other programs under review. Unlike other programs that have a preponderance of these classes, UNM extends them to upper-division courses in addition to the more typical Gen Ed substitute courses for lower-division students.*

The seminars included "Soviet History through Underground Literature"; the Legacy series ("Legacy of Gods and Men," "Legacy of Dreams," "Legacy of Social Justice"; and, as well, "Individuals in Conflict with the Collective" and "Things that Make Us Smart."

The focus on interdisciplinary sources makes the program a complete **core** program, though it has more extension into junior and senior years than most core programs have.

Extent of Honors Enrollment (3.0:): Not all honors students take an honors class each term, especially after the first two years. Programs that have fewer honors classes for upper-division honors students will generally have fewer total members in good standing who are actually enrolled in a given term. (Please be aware, however, that honors students not enrolled in a class for a term are still connected to the honors community through residential and extracurricular activities.)

For example, if honors students in a program occupy 1,800 honors classroom seats in a given term, and there are 3,000 honors students in good standing, the extent of enrollment is .67. For programs that require a thesis, the ratio (score) reported below might in fact be somewhat higher, since we only count "regular" class enrollment for this measure, and not thesis enrollment. The college **has a ratio of .56**; the mean is 1.13 for all 50 programs. The higher the ratio, the better.

Average Class Size, Honors-only Sections (5.0): Offered mostly in the first two years, honors-only classes tend to be smaller and, as the name implies, have no or very few students other than those in the honors program. These class sections are almost always much smaller than mixed or contract sections, or regular non-honors class sections in the university.

The average honors-only class size in the honors program is **14.6 students**. The average for all 50 programs is 19.0 students.

Average Class Size, Overall (5.0): The overall class calculation is based on the *proportion* of honors students in each type of class (honors-only, mixed honors, and honors contract sections). Thus it is not a raw average. The overall honors-credit class size is **15.7 students**, versus the average for all 50 programs of 26.3 students.

These class size averages also do not correspond to the number of students per honors sections numbers above. The reason is that, in computing average class size metrics, we include enrollment in each 1-2-credit section, not just sections with 3 or more credits.

Along with the honors-only average of 15.7 students, the mixed honors sections average **18.0 students,** and the contract sections with honors credit for individual honors students average **32.4** students. Across all fifty programs, the average mixed honors section has 51.1 students, and the average contract section has 60.1 students.

Honors Graduation Rate (5.0): The rating is based on the actual grad rate for students who entered the program six years earlier, whether or not the students remained in honors. The **actual rate of 92.1%** is also compared to the rates of other programs with the same test score entry requirement range, and then adjusted to the **score of 92.8%.** In some cases this measure favors programs within universities with relatively higher test scores for the student population as a whole. The average honors graduation rate for all programs with similar test scores required for admission is 85.6%.

Value-Added Grad Rate (5.0): The value-added rate measures the extent to which the adjusted score above exceeds the six-year grad rate for the university as a whole. **The university-wide rate is 48%.** Note: This measure generally favors programs within universities with relatively lower test scores for the student population as a whole.

Ratio of Staff to Honors Students (4.5): There is 1 staff member for every **90.4** students. (Mean ratio for all 50 programs is 1 staff member for every 135.6 students.)

Honors Residence Halls, Amenities (3.5): Most honors students in honors housing live in Hokona Hall, which has a mix of traditional single and double rooms, mostly the latter, and hall baths. Hokona is air-conditioned and houses freshmen and upperclassmen. The nearest dining is at La Posada.

A few freshmen and most upperclassmen living in honors housing reside in the SRC Apartments. The apartments are air-conditioned, and each apartment has its own kitchen. The most convenient outside dining is at La Posada.

Honors Residence Halls, Availability (3.0): This rating compares the number of rooms in honors residence halls to the number of honors freshman and sophomore members in good standing, about 788. The ratio for the honors program is **.19** rooms for each first- and second-year student. The average for all fifty programs is .63 rooms.

Prestigious Awards (4.0): The awards that we track and include are listed in the section titled "Prestigious Scholarships." The awards are sometimes won by students who are not in an honors college or program, but increasingly many are enrolled in honors programs. It is also a trend that honors colleges and programs help to prepare their students for the awards competitions.

UNM students have won 10 Udall scholarships, 17 Goldwater scholarships, and 4 Boren scholarships. In addition, UNM has had 16 Rhodes scholars, 4 Marshall scholars, and 12 Truman scholars.

UNRATED FEATURES

Continuation Requirements: 3.20 to continue; 3.5 for BA.

Academic Strengths, National Rankings: This is based on national rankings of *graduate* programs in 15 disciplines, except engineering and business, where undergraduate rankings are used.

The average departmental ranking at UNM is between 90 and 100. The highest-ranked department is earth sciences (49). Next in line are political science (76), English (77), sociology (78), history (80), computer science (82), and physics (85). The anthropology department, though not tracked, is almost certainly among the top 40-50.

Undergraduate Research: "The Honors College offers multiple resources to support undergraduate research in addition to the required research thesis/capstone for our majors.

1.The Honors Research Institute funds research collaborations between faculty members and students. Recent HRI funded projects:

- Transcription, translation and restoration of archival material that included music, lyrics and journal entries of turn of the century composer Manuel Areu;
- Digging for fossil evidence in Uruguay;
- Archival work at historic sports venues in St. Louis, Missouri and Colorado Springs, Colorado;
- Field study of quinoa production in the US;
- Study of coral reef microbial symbionts on the Great Barrier Reef, Australia.

"Several of these projects have led to publications, or are the basis for currently developing journal articles for which students are authors, including one paper from the Australia study that has been accepted with another under review and one paper in process regarding the Areu history. This spring the New Mexico Philharmonic Orchestra will perform works that the students restored as part of its regular concert series.

"2. The Mellon Mays Undergraduate Fellowship program at UNM funds students over the course of their junior and senior years (including summers) who are conducting research with a faculty mentor. Students receive summer and academic year stipends, travel and research funding and access to Mellon-sponsored workshops, conferences and summer programs. Five students are selected each year during their sophomore year.

"3. The Lobo Scholars Program supports the scholarly work, including research, of our Division I athletes who are also Honors students. This spring the program will host a research symposium on issues affecting collegiate athletics."

Study Abroad: "*Conexiones* is the oldest faculty-led study abroad program at the University of New Mexico. The program is an intensive four-week summer language and culture study program offered each summer, with alternating locations in Spain and in Latin America. Sponsored by the Honors College in conjunction with the Department of Spanish & Portuguese, students earn 3 hours of Spanish language credit and 4 hours of Honors Humanities credit. This summer (2016) students will live with families in the Ecuadorian colonial city of Cuenca, study Spanish, and participate in field study.

"While *Conexiones* is the Honors College's marquee annual international program, three faculty-led course based trips have been offered in the past two years. "Drums and Dreams" included a Spring Break trip to Argentina (Spring 2014).

- "Shakespeare Abroad" students went to England at the end of the Spring 2014 semester.
- "Sounds of Havana" included a Spring Break trip to Cuba (Spring 2015).

"Honors students at UNM are better able to afford and fit into their packed schedules international study experiences that are offered during academic breaks."

Financial Aid: "UNM offers a number of merit-based scholarships, described below. In addition, beginning in their second semester at UNM, New Mexico students receive the Legislative Lottery scholarship, funded by the New Mexico Lottery. To qualify, students must have attended UNM in the first semester after high school and earned 15 credit hours in their first semester with a 2.5 GPA. This scholarship currently pays 90% of tuition for up to 7 semesters. The Honors College awards several small scholarships and monetary awards each year.

Regents Scholarship – Student qualifies for consideration with a 31 ACT (1380 SAT) and 3.9 unit GPA with a submitted application by December 1. Recipients receive an amount that represents tuition/fees, books/supplies and room/board ($17,803 for the 2016-2017 year). Regents Scholars must participate in the Honors College and live in Hokona Hall as freshmen.

National Scholars-- *Student qualifies for consideration as a National Merit* **Finalist.** *Recipients receive an amount that represents tuition/fees, books/supplies and room/board ($17,803 for the 2016-2017 year).*

National Hispanic Scholars--NM resident students qualify for consideration as a National Hispanic finalist admitted by February 1. Recipients will receive approximately $8,446 for the 2016-2017 year.

National American Indian Scholars--American Indian students from New Mexico, Colorado, Arizona, or Colorado with high academic achievements qualify for consideration if admitted by February 1. Recipients will receive approximately $8,446 for the 2016-2017 year.

Honors Fees: None. "New Mexico has the highest poverty rate of any state in the country. We are committed to providing the highest quality liberal arts education possible to motivated and able students regardless of socioeconomic background. Therefore we do not charge additional fees for participation in the Honors College or the Honors residence."

Placement Experiences: "In Academic Year 2014-15, approximately 80% of Honors graduates entered graduate or professional school immediately (82% of Fall 2014 grads; 79% of Spring 2015 grads)."

Degree of Difference: This is based on the differences between (1) the average (2015, two-part) SAT scores for enrolled honors students (1275) and (2) the average test scores for all students in the university (1050) as a whole. The test scores may be an indication of how "elite" honors students may be perceived as compared to students in the university as a whole. The scores can also provide an indication of how well prepared the non-honors students in the university may be. **Please keep in mind that neither high nor low test scores determine the overall quality of a program.**

NAME: HONORS CAROLINA.

Date Established: 1954.

Location: Chapel Hill, North Carolina.

University <u>Full-time Undergraduate</u> Enrollment: 17,570.

Honors Members in Good Standing: 1,957 (mean size of all 50 programs is 1,742).,

Honors <u>Average</u> Admission Statistics: ACT, 32.3; old two-part SAT, 1413. Est. new SAT score, 1465.

Average High School GPA/Class Rank: Top 3.5% of class.

<u>Basic</u> Admission Requirements: None listed.

Application Deadline(s): *Please verify with each program, as some deadlines could change.*

Must be accepted by university first, followed by honors invitation. University early action deadline is October 15, 2016, with decision by late January 2017. Regular deadline is January 15, 2017, with notification in late March. Final university deadline is February 15, 2017, with decision by mid-April.

Honors Programs with old SAT scores from 1402—1469: UCF, Connecticut, Kentucky, Washington, Maryland, North Carolina, UC Irvine, Kansas, Minnesota, Tennessee, South Carolina, Clemson, UT Austin, Georgia.

Administrative Staff: 11.

RATINGS AT A GLANCE: For all mortarboard ratings immediately below, a score of 5 is the maximum and represents a comparison with all 50 honors colleges and programs. More detailed explanations follow the "mortarboard" ratings.

PERCEPTION* OF UNIVERSITY AS A WHOLE, <u>NOT</u> OF HONORS: 🎓🎓🎓🎓🎓

*Perception is based on the university's ranking among public universities in the 2016 U.S. News Best Colleges report. Please bear in mind that the better the U.S. News ranking, the more difficult it is for an honors college or program to have a rating that equals or improves on the magazine ranking.

OVERALL HONORS RATING: 🎓🎓🎓🎓 1/2

Curriculum Requirements: 🎓🎓🎓🎓

Number of Honors Classes Offered: 🎓🎓🎓🎓 1/2

Number of Honors Classes in Key Disciplines: 🎓🎓🎓🎓

Extent of Honors Enrollment: ⚏⚏⚏^1/2

Honors-only Class Size: ⚏⚏⚏⚏^1/2

Overall Class Size (Honors-only plus mixed, contract): ⚏⚏⚏⚏⚏

Honors Grad Rate: ⚏⚏⚏⚏⚏

Value-Added Grad Rate: ⚏⚏⚏

Ratio of Staff to Students: ⚏⚏⚏^1/2

Priority Registration: "…members of Honors Carolina register for honors courses before other eligible students each semester. They also receive priority status for wait listing of honors courses."

Honors Housing Amenities: ⚏⚏⚏⚏

Honors Housing Availability: ⚏⚏⚏^1/2

Prestigious Awards: ⚏⚏⚏⚏⚏

RATING SCORES AND EXPLANATIONS:

Curriculum Requirements (4.0): The most important rating category, the curriculum completion requirement (classes required to complete honors) defines not only what honors students should learn but also the extent to which honors students and faculty are connected in the classroom. If there is a thesis or capstone requirement, it reinforces the individual contact and research skills so important to learning.

The average number of honors semester hours required for completion across all 50 programs is 29.0.

Graduation with Honors or Highest Honors requires a minimum of **30 credits** for first-year entrants: 24 course credit hours and a **6-credit thesis.**

To be an Honors Carolina Laureate, students admitted as first-semester freshmen must complete 24 credits; second-semester first-year students must earn 18 honors credits; and students admitted as first-semester second-year students must earn 15 credits.

AP/IB credits are not counted as replacements for honors courses.

Number of Honors Classes Offered (4.5): This is a measure of the total **adjusted** honors main sections available in the term reported, not including labs and thesis. (Please read the section titled "All about Honors Classes".) An adjusted main section has 3 or more semester credits, or equivalent, and sections with fewer credits receive a lower prorated value.

Honors Carolina offered an adjusted section for every **12.4** enrolled students. The average for all 50 programs is 14.2 students. The lower the number, the better.

In the term reported, **99.3%** of honors enrollment was **in honors-only or mostly honors sections; none in mixed honors sections (honors and non-honors students); and .7% reported in contract sections (regular sections in which honors students "contract" to do extra work).** It should be noted that Honors Carolina allows a few highly qualified students who are not in the program to enroll in honors classes. Since this percentage is quite small, the classes are counted as "honors-only." The averages for all fifty programs are 81.3% in honors-only sections; 13.6 % in mixed honors sections; and 5.1% in contract sections.

Number of Honors Classes in Key Disciplines (4.0): The 15 "key" disciplines are biological sciences; business (all); chemistry; communications (especially public speaking); computer science; economics; engineering (all); English; history; math (all); philosophy; physics; political science; psychology; and sociology/anthropology/gender studies. Interdisciplinary sections, such as those often taken for General Education credit in the first two years, do receive a lesser, prorated discipline "credit" because they introduce students to multiple disciplines in an especially engaging way, often with in-depth discussion.

For this measure, mixed and contract sections are not counted as a section in a key discipline unless students taking the sections for honors credit make up at least 10% of the total section enrollment.

In the term reported, the Honors Carolina had a ratio of **21.3 honors students** per each main section in some or all "key disciplines." The mean for all 50 programs is 26.3. The lower the ratio, the better.

Out of **60 adjusted sections in key disciplines**, Honors Carolina had about **50 honors-only sections.** The most sections were in English (10), history (8), political science (8), biology, computer science, and economics (6 each), chemistry and philosophy (4 each), business (3), and math (2). There were no sections in engineering or physics. UNC does not have an engineering school.

In all, there were more than 100 sections in key disciplines.

The emphasis on courses in the disciplines makes the program a very strong **discipline-based program.**

Extent of Honors Enrollment (3.5:): Not all honors students take an honors class each term, especially after the first two years. Programs that have fewer honors classes for upper-division honors students will generally have fewer total members in good standing who are actually enrolled in a given term. (Please be aware, however, that honors students not enrolled in a class for a term are still connected to the honors community through residential and extracurricular activities.)

For example, if honors students in a program occupy 1,800 honors classroom seats in a given term, and there are 3,000 honors students in good standing, the extent of enrollment is .67. For programs that require a thesis, the ratio (score) reported below might in fact be somewhat higher, since we only count "regular" class enrollment for this measure. Honors Carolina **had a ratio of .81**; the mean is 1.13 for all 50 programs. The higher the ratio, the better. It should be noted that the university has strong upper-division courses generally, and many Honors Carolina students also take graduate courses (not included in this measure) for honors credit.

Average Class Size, Honors-only Sections (4.5): Offered mostly in the first two years, honors-only classes tend to be smaller and, as the name implies, have no or very few students other than those in the honors program. These class sections are almost always much smaller than mixed or contract sections, or regular non-honors class sections in the university.

The average honors-only class size in the honors program is **17.9 students**. The average for all 50 programs is 19.0 students.

Average Class Size, Overall (5.0): The overall class calculation is based on the *proportion* of honors students in each type of class (honors-only, mixed honors, and honors contract sections). Thus it is not a raw average. The overall honors-credit class size is **18.0 students**, versus the average for all 50 programs of 26.3 students.

These class size averages also do not correspond to the number of students per honors sections numbers above. The reason is that, in computing average class size metrics, we include enrollment in each 1-2-credit section, not just sections with 3 or more credits.

Along with the honors-only average of 17.9 students, the mixed honors sections average **(NA) students,** and the contract sections with honors credit for individual honors students average **23.9** students. Across all fifty programs, the average mixed honors section has 51.1 students, and the average contract section has 60.1students.

Honors Graduation Rate (5.0): The rating is based on the actual grad rate for students who entered the program six years earlier, whether or not the students remained in honors. The **actual rate of 93.5%** is also compared to the rates of other programs with the same test score entry requirement range, and then adjusted to the **score of 93.6%.** In some cases this measure favors programs within universities with relatively higher test scores for the student population as a whole. The average honors graduation rate for all programs with similar test scores required for admission is 92.6%.

Value-Added Grad Rate (3.0): The value-added rate measures the extent to which the adjusted score listed above exceeds the six-year grad rate for the university as a whole. **The university-wide rate is 88%.** Note: This measure generally favors programs within universities with relatively lower test scores for the student population as a whole.

Ratio of Staff to Honors Students (3.5): There is 1 staff member for every **177.9** students. (Mean ratio for all 50 programs is 1 staff member for every 135.6 students.)

Honors Residence Halls, Amenities (4.0): Most first-year honors students reside in Khoury Hall, which features air-conditioned, suite-style rooms with shared baths. The nearest dining is at the Rams Head. Another 30% of honors students live in Ehringhaus Hall, with similar features and dining at Rams Head.

Honors Residence Halls, Availability (3.5): This rating compares the number of places in honors residence halls to the number of honors freshman and sophomore members in good standing, about 979. The ratio for the honors program is **.35** rooms for each first- and second-year student. The average for all fifty programs is .63 places. *Note: Honors Carolina offers honors housing to all freshmen, and the*

Associate Dean tells us that 55% of freshmen choose honors housing while the rest to do not. Honors Carolina does not offer honors housing to sophomores.

Prestigious Awards (5.0): The awards that we track and include are listed in the section titled "Prestigious Scholarships." The awards are sometimes won by students who are not in an honors college or program, but increasingly many are enrolled in honors programs. It is also a trend that honors colleges and programs help to prepare their students for the awards competitions.

UNC is one of the top two or three public universities in the achievement of prestigious awards at both the undergraduate and post-graduate level, and is likely the top public university when the following awards are combined: Rhodes (49), Gates Cambridge (5), Marshall (17), Churchill (16), and Truman (30).

UNC undergraduates have also won 44 Goldwater scholarships, and 15 Udall awards. Although we do not track Luce scholarships, for study in Asia, UNC students have won 37, "more than any other four-year institution, public or private."

UNRATED FEATURES

Continuation Requirements: 3.00 for continuation; 3.3 or higher overall, plus a range of higher requirements set by individual departments for coursework within students' major fields of study.

Academic Strengths, National Rankings: This is based on national rankings of *graduate* programs in 15 disciplines, except engineering and business, where undergraduate rankings are used.

The average departmental rank at UNC is 25th or better nationwide among all universities. Outstanding departments are sociology (6), business (7), history (11), psychology (12), political science (13), chemistry and English (15 each), computer science (25), biology (26), and math (28). Only one department is ranked lower than 40th in the nation. Again, please note that UNC does not have an engineering department.

Undergraduate Research: "Cutting-edge research is an integral part of the culture at Carolina. Honors Carolina students enjoy countless opportunities to work with faculty members conducting breakthrough research in almost any field. Honors Carolina students get involved in research projects, and many begin that work as early as their first year. Research may take the form of a senior honors thesis project, an advanced course in the major, a faculty-mentored research project, or participation in one of our competitive summer research fellowships.

"Burch Fellowships – Burch Fellows create their own unique educational experiences and travel the globe to pursue their passions. Designed for students with extraordinary ability, promise, and imagination, *Burch Fellowships provide up to $6,000 to support off-campus learning experiences like these: working with NASA astrobiologists to answer questions about the possibility of life on other planets; jamming with jazz musicians in Cuba; traveling to the Philippines to study how bamboo can mitigate the effects of climate change.*

"Carolina Blue Honors Fellowships in International Sports Entrepreneurship – The Carolina Blue Honors

Fellowship enables students to embark on *a self-designed project focused on international sports entrepreneurship. Fellows receive up to $5,000* to support experiences like these: working for an Australian Baseball league franchise; leading a social media campaign for a pro cricket franchise in the India Premier League; helping a soccer start-up get off the ground in Tanzania.

"Froelich Honors Fellowships – The Will Froelich Honors Fellowship allows incoming first year students to study abroad, pursue a project of civic engagement, finance an internship, or work with a faculty mentor on independent research. Fellows receive $7,500 to fund experiences throughout their undergraduate career.

"Robinson Honors Fellowships – Robinson Honors Fellows delve deeply into the history and culture of Europe and the Mediterranean, from the golden age of Greece to the upheaval of World War I. Fellows receive up to $6,000 to pursue projects that explore art, literature, history, music, philosophy, political thought, and religion.

"Taylor and Gold Summer Research Fellowships – Taylor and Gold Fellowships support students engaged in faculty-mentored research projects during the summer. Fellows receive up to $4,000 to continue work they have begun with a faculty member, to get a head start on a Senior Honors Thesis, or to travel to distant libraries, labs, or archives that might otherwise be beyond reach.

"Thesis Research Grants – Research grants are available to help offset the cost of conducting a Senior Honors Thesis. The grants, up to $500, can cover the cost of equipment, supplies, software, publications, transportation, and other expenses."

Study Abroad (and Off-Campus Study): Honors Carolina students have access to so many study-abroad and off-campus programs that not all of the information can be included here. Below are some of the opportunities:

"Honors Study Abroad programs are open to all UNC undergraduate students who are in good standing and have a 3.0 GPA. Financial aid can be applied to the program costs and Honors Carolina offers additional need- and merit-based scholarships. During the 2014- 2015 academic year, Honors Carolina awarded twenty-nine study abroad scholarships totaling, $55,000. In addition, three Weir Fellows received support totaling $65,440.

"Honors Semester in London (Fall and Spring)--*Students study at Honors Carolina's own Winston House on historic Bedford Square*, attend seminars within the shadow of the British Museum, conduct research at the British Library, and learn from professors who make London their home. Internships are available in fields ranging from global finance to healthcare and the arts.

"Weir Honors Fellowships in Asian Studies--(Spring and Summer) Weir Honors Fellows become fluent in Mandarin and gain practical, independent work experience in China, home to one of the world's oldest civilizations and the 21st century's fastest growing economy. Fellows spend the Spring semester in Beijing for intensive language study, then complete an eight-week summer internship in either Beijing or Shanghai exploring careers in fields such as banking, law, journalism, public health, and historic preservation.

"Honors Semester in Cape Town (Fall)--Students intern full-time and complete two academic courses on contemporary South Africa. Internships are available in public health, refugee resettlement, conflict resolution, medicine, urban planning, journalism, environmental conservation, the arts, and other areas.

"Honors Public Policy Seminar in Washington, D.C.: Domestic and Global Affairs Internship Program (Spring)--Students enjoy first-hand engagement with the actors and organizations that influence domestic and international affairs in Washington, D.C. The seminar exposes students to a range of public policies which influence U.S. economic prosperity, national security, and America's role in the broader global community.

"Entrepreneurship in Silicon Valley (beginning in spring 2017)--Students will work four days per week in internships and complete the requirements for an academic minor in entrepreneurship. Internships are available in young and maturing start-ups venture capital firms.

"Honors Carolina also offers a changing roster of field research seminars. These programs send faculty and students off campus to work on shared scholarly interests. Recent topics and locations include public health in Vietnam, energy and sustainable development in Germany and the Netherlands, Jewish life and the Holocaust in Poland, and security studies in Vienna, Bosnia, and Kosovo."

Financial Aid: "UNC's Office of Scholarships and Student Aid, along with the Morehead-Cain Foundation and the Robertson Scholars program, award merit- and need-based scholarships to members of Honors Carolina.

"Of the 594 incoming first-year members of Honors Carolina last fall (Fall 2015), 165 (28%) were awarded some form of merit scholarship."

Honors Fees: None.

Placement Experiences: None listed, but Carolina graduates attend the most prestigious institutions in America and abroad, and have excellent opportunities for employment as well.

Degree of Difference: This is a based on the differences between (1) the average (2015, two-part) SAT scores for enrolled honors students (1413) and (2) the average test scores for all students in the university (1305) as a whole. The test scores may be an indication of how "elite" honors students may be perceived as compared to students in the university as a whole. The scores can also provide an indication of how well prepared the non-honors students in the university may be. **Please keep in mind that neither high nor low test scores determine the overall quality of a program.**

NAME: JOE C, AND CAROLE KERR McCLENDON HONORS COLLEGE.

Date Established: 1996; preceded by Honors Program founded in 1964.

Location: Norman, Oklahoma.

University Full-time Undergraduate Enrollment: 18,764.

Honors Members in Good Standing: 2,300 (mean size of all 50 programs is 1,742).,

Honors Average Admission Statistics: ACT, 33.5. OU is one of the most selective programs under review.

Average High School GPA/Class Rank: Not listed.

Basic Admission Requirements: ACT, 30. High school GPA, 3.75; top 10% of class.

Application Deadline(s): *Please verify with each program, as some deadlines could change.*

"University scholarship deadline is December 15, 2016. Final deadline is February 1, 2017. No separate deadline for honors college."

Honors Programs with old SAT scores (or ACT equivalent) of 1500 or higher: Oklahoma, Illinois.

Administrative Staff: 9.

RATINGS AT A GLANCE: For all mortarboard ratings immediately below, a score of 5 is the maximum and represents a comparison with all 50 honors colleges and programs. More detailed explanations follow the "mortarboard" ratings.

PERCEPTION* OF UNIVERSITY AS A WHOLE, NOT OF HONORS: 🎓🎓🎓🎓

*Perception is based on the university's ranking among public universities in the 2016 U.S. News Best Colleges report. Please bear in mind that the better the U.S. News ranking, the more difficult it is for an honors college or program to have a rating that equals or improves on the magazine ranking.

OVERALL HONORS RATING: 🎓🎓🎓 1/2

Curriculum Requirements: 🎓🎓🎓 1/2

Number of Honors Classes Offered: 🎓🎓🎓🎓

Number of Honors Classes in Key Disciplines: 🎓🎓🎓🎓

Extent of Honors Enrollment: 🎓🎓🎓

Honors-only Class Size: 🎓🎓🎓🎓¹ᐟ²

Overall Class Size (Honors-only plus mixed, contract): 🎓🎓🎓¹ᐟ²

Honors Grad Rate: 🎓🎓🎓🎓🎓

Value-Added Grad Rate: 🎓🎓🎓🎓¹ᐟ²

Ratio of Staff to Students: 🎓🎓🎓

Priority Registration: For National Merit Scholars only.

Honors Housing Amenities: 🎓🎓🎓🎓

Honors Housing Availability: 🎓🎓🎓¹ᐟ²

Prestigious Awards: 🎓🎓🎓🎓¹ᐟ²

RATING SCORES AND EXPLANATIONS:

Curriculum Requirements (3.5): The most important rating category, the curriculum completion requirement (classes required to complete honors) defines not only what honors students should learn but also the extent to which honors students and faculty are connected in the classroom. If there is a thesis or capstone requirement, it reinforces the individual contact and research skills so important to learning.

The average number of honors semester hours required for completion across all 50 programs is 29.0.

Completion requires a minimum of 18 credits plus a 3-credit **thesis,** for a total of about **21** credits. Graduation at one of three levels depends on GPA.

The 18 credits include two 3-credit honors college courses taught by honors college faculty. Three more credits may be earned through an honors experience, often study abroad. A 3-credit colloquium (capstone) is also required, as is, separately, a 3-credit thesis. The remaining three credits (often more, by choice) are in departmental honors courses especially tailored for honors college students.

Honors students who complete the requirements with a 3.40-3.59 GPA are eligible to graduate *cum laude*; students with a GPA of 3.60-3.79 are eligible to graduate *magna cum laude*; and students with a GPA of 3.80 or higher are eligible to graduate *summa cum laude*.

Although not courses in the formal sense, the informal reading groups sponsored by the honors college each semester are an excellent addition. "The groups meet just one hour per week, with 10-15 students and one faculty member from the Honors College, to discuss about 50 pages of reading from specific books" the Dean tells us. "The books cover a very wide range of topics, and most have been recommended by Honors students. To participate, the only commitment is that each student makes a good-faith effort to do the reading and come to the group meeting as often as possible, with the understanding there may be one or two weeks when students need to do other things." In Spring 2014, the reading groups had more than 50 wonderful books to choose from, and about 500 honors students participated. And…they get to keep the books.

AP/IB credits are not counted as replacements for honors courses.

Number of Honors Classes Offered (4.0): This is a measure of the total **adjusted** honors main sections available in the term reported, not including labs and thesis. (Please read the section titled "All about Honors Classes".) An adjusted main section has 3 or more semester credits, or equivalent, and sections with fewer credits receive a lower prorated value.

The college offered a section for every **15.9** enrolled students. The average for all 50 programs is 14.2. The lower the number, the better.

In the term reported, **90.8%** of honors enrollment was **in honors-only sections; 6.6% in mixed honors sections (honors and non-honors students); and 2.6% in contract sections (regular sections in which honors students "contract" to do extra work).** The averages for all fifty programs are 81.3% in honors-only sections; 13.6 % in mixed honors sections; and 5.1% in contract sections.

Number of Honors Classes in Key Disciplines (4.0): The 15 "key" disciplines are biological sciences; business (all); chemistry; communications (especially public speaking); computer science; economics; engineering (all); English; history; math (all); philosophy; physics; political science; psychology; and sociology/anthropology/gender studies. Interdisciplinary sections, such as those often taken for General Education credit in the first two years, do receive a lesser, prorated discipline "credit" because they introduce students to multiple disciplines in an especially engaging way, often with in-depth discussion.

For this measure, mixed and contract sections are not counted as a section in a key discipline unless students taking the sections for honors credit make up at least 10% of the total section enrollment.

In the term reported, the program had a ratio of **26.3 honors students** per each main section in some or all "key disciplines." The mean for all 50 programs is 26.3. The lower the ratio, the better.

Out of **36 adjusted sections in key disciplines**, the Honors College had **27** that were **honors-only sections.** The most sections were in English, history, and math (5each), economics (4), physics and political science (3 each), and biology, chemistry, and communications (2 each).

The college also offered about 20 interdisciplinary sections and seminars, as well as several similar courses that had more of a disciplinary focus. Among the former were "American History through Biology"; "What Is Science?"; "Cultures of Modernity"; and "Death, Dying, and Religion."

The honors college, with an excellent mix of interdisciplinary classes and sections in the academic disciplines, is a **blended honors program.**

Extent of Honors Enrollment (3.0): Not all honors students take an honors class each term, especially after the first two years. Programs that have fewer honors classes for upper-division honors students will

generally have fewer total members in good standing who are actually enrolled in a given term. (Please be aware, however, that honors students not enrolled in a class for a term are still connected to the honors community through residential and extracurricular activities.)

For example, if honors students in a program occupy 1,800 honors classroom seats in a given term, and there are 3,000 honors students in good standing, the extent of enrollment is .67. For programs that require a thesis, the ratio (score) reported below might in fact be somewhat higher, since we only count "regular" class enrollment for this measure, and not thesis enrollment. The college **has a ratio of .52**; the mean is 1.13 for all 50 programs. The higher the ratio, the better.

Average Class Size, Honors-only Sections (4.5): Offered mostly in the first two years, honors-only classes tend to be smaller and, as the name implies, have no or very few students other than those in the honors program. These class sections are almost always much smaller than mixed or contract sections, or regular non-honors class sections in the university.

The average honors-only class size in the honors program is **16.4 students**. The average for all 50 programs is 19.0 students.

Average Class Size, Overall (3.5): The overall class calculation is based on the *proportion* of honors students in each type of class (honors-only, mixed honors, and honors contract sections). Thus it is not a raw average. The overall honors-credit class size is **33.2 students**, versus the average for all 50 programs of 26.3 students.

These class size averages also do not correspond to the number of students per honors sections numbers above. The reason is that, in computing average class size metrics, we include enrollment in each 1-2-credit section, not just sections with 3 or more credits.

Along with the honors-only average of 16.4 students, the few mixed honors sections average **261.5 students**, and the contract sections with honors credit for individual honors students average **44.2 students**. Across all fifty programs, the average mixed honors section has 51.1 students, and the average contract section has 60.1 students.

Honors Graduation Rate (5.0): The rating is based on the actual grad rate for students who entered the program six years earlier, whether or not the students remained in honors. The **actual rate of 95.0%** is also compared to the rates of other programs with the same test score entry requirement range, and then adjusted to the **score of 95.2%**. In some cases this measure favors programs within universities with relatively higher test scores for the student population as a whole. The average honors graduation rate for all programs with similar test scores required for admission is 95.0%.

Value-Added Grad Rate (4.5): The value-added rate measures the extent to which the adjusted score listed above exceeds the six-year grad rate for the university as a whole. **The university-wide rate is 67%.** Note: This measure generally favors programs within universities with relatively lower test scores for the student population as a whole.

Ratio of Staff to Honors Students (3.0): There is 1 staff member for every **255.2 students**. (Mean ratio for all 50 programs is 1 staff member for every 135.6 students.)

Honors Residence Halls, Amenities (4.0): Students in honors college housing are about evenly divided between Boren (Honors) Hall and Walker Tower, the latter for National Merit Scholars only. Boren Hall, with mostly freshmen residents, has traditional rooms with hall baths, and the rooms are not air-conditioned. Laundry service is not located within the residence. The most convenient dining is in Couch Cafeteria or Cate Food Court.

Walker Tower features air-conditioned, suite-style rooms with shared baths. All residents are freshmen. Dining is in Couch Cafeteria.

Honors Residence Halls, Availability (3.5): This rating compares the number of places in honors residence halls to the number of honors freshman and sophomore members in good standing, about 1,150. The ratio for the honors program is **.33** rooms for each first- and second-year student. The average for all fifty programs is .63 places.

Prestigious Awards (4.5): The awards that we track and include are listed in the section titled "Prestigious Scholarships." The awards are sometimes won by students who are not in an honors college or program, but increasingly many are enrolled in honors programs. It is also a trend that honors colleges and programs help to prepare their students for the awards competitions.

"This year [2015] we have had three Goldwater Scholars and a Truman Scholar, plus numerous Fulbright Scholars, a Boren Scholar, and two recent alumni who won the Paul and Daisy Soros New Americans fellowships. Over time, we have had 29 Rhodes Scholars."

OU students have also won 1 Gates Cambridge scholarship, 6 Marshall scholarships, and 16 Truman scholarships. The total number of Goldwater scholars is 47, along with 3 Udall scholarships, and 12 Boren scholarships.

UNRATED FEATURES

Continuation Requirements: 3.40.

Academic Strengths, National Rankings: This is based on national rankings of *graduate* programs in 15 disciplines, except engineering and business, where undergraduate rankings are used.

The average departmental ranking at OU is 80-85 nationally. Leading departments are earth sciences (60), business (61), history (64), and math (73).

Undergraduate Research: "We have five separate undergraduate research programs – the First-Year Research Experience (now with 75 freshmen mostly in science departments), Undergraduate Research Opportunities (funded research that the students propose and conduct), Honors Research Assistant Program (funded research assistance to faculty working on faculty research, an annual Honors Undergraduate Research Journal (now in its 15th year, both hard-copy and digital, run by a student editorial board, and an Honors Undergraduate Research Day. Several of our students are co-authors on published research in disciplinary scholarly journals."

Study Abroad: "We have our own Honors-at-Oxford program, which includes one month in Norman studying British history and British literature with Honors faculty, then one month in the UK where students are assigned their own individual Oxford tutor."

Financial Aid: "The University gives a very substantial package to National Merit Scholars. In August 2014 we enrolled 315 entering freshmen National Merit Scholars, the most of any university in the country, public or private, including all the Ivies and MIT. In August 2015 we enrolled close to 300 freshmen, although I don't know where that ranked nationally. Our President is a very strong supporter of this program and of the Honors College in general."

(OU currently does have more university-sponsored National Merit Scholars than any other school.)

The National Merit Scholar Package, Value: Tuition--$88,000; $22,000 to offset books, room, and board; cash stipend of $5,000; housing scholarship, $4,200; technology allowance, $2,000; travel stipend, $2,000. The tuition and books, room and board awards "can be used toward any graduate/professional program at OU if funds remain after completion of undergraduate degree (including medical school and law school)." Total value is $124,000. Any additional scholarships are not reduced. To receive the housing allowance portion ($4,200), students must live in the OU residence halls during freshman year.

Honors Fees: None.

Placement Experiences: "We actually don't collect placement information, although our best students are at Harvard Medical School, Johns Hopkins, Mayo, and we have had two students turn down Yale Law to go to Stanford Law, and several turn down Stanford law to go to Harvard Law."

Degree of Difference: This is based on the differences between (1) the average (2015, two-part) SAT scores for enrolled honors students (est. SAT equivalent to ACT, 1505) and (2) the average test scores for all students in the university (1100) as a whole. The test scores may be an indication of how "elite" honors students may be perceived as compared to students in the university as a whole. The scores can also provide an indication of how well prepared the non-honors students in the university may be. **Please keep in mind that neither high nor low test scores determine the overall quality of a program.**

NAME: OKLAHOMA STATE UNIVERSITY HONORS COLLEGE.

Date Established: "The first class of Honors graduates (three students) earned Bachelor's Degrees with Honors in the 1968-1969 academic year, and the Arts & Sciences Honors Program formed the basis for the university-wide Honors Program that was created in 1989."

Location: Stillwater, Oklahoma.

University <u>Full-time Undergraduate</u> Enrollment: 18,156.

Honors Members in Good Standing: 1,486 (mean size of all 50 programs is 1,742).,

Honors <u>Average</u> Admission Statistics: ACT, 28.4. Old SAT, 1237; est. new SAT, 1310.

Average High School GPA/Class Rank: 4.02 (3.89 unweighted).

<u>Basic</u> Admission Requirements: ACT, 27. Old SAT, 1220; est. new SAT, 1290. High school GPA, 3.75.

Application Deadline(s): *Please verify with each program, as some deadlines could change.*

February 1, 2017, with admission on a rolling basis until the deadline; after that on space-available basis.

Honors Programs with old SAT scores from 1240—1291: Arkansas, Oklahoma State, Texas Tech, Montana, Washington State, New Mexico, South Dakota, Colorado State, Arizona, Montana State, Arizona State.

Administrative Staff: 7.

RATINGS AT A GLANCE: For all mortarboard ratings immediately below, a score of 5 is the maximum and represents a comparison with all 50 honors colleges and programs. More detailed explanations follow the "mortarboard" ratings.

PERCEPTION* OF UNIVERSITY AS A WHOLE, <u>NOT</u> OF HONORS: 🎓🎓🎓 1/2

*Perception is based on the university's ranking among public universities in the 2016 U.S. News Best Colleges report. Please bear in mind that the better the U.S. News ranking, the more difficult it is for an honors college or program to have a rating that equals or improves on the magazine ranking.

OVERALL HONORS RATING: 🎓🎓🎓🎓 1/2

Curriculum Requirements: 🎓🎓🎓🎓 1/2

Number of Honors Classes Offered: 🎓🎓🎓🎓

Number of Honors Classes in Key Disciplines: 🎓🎓🎓🎓

Extent of Honors Enrollment: 🎓🎓🎓🎓🎓

Honors-only Class Size: 🎓🎓🎓🎓$^{1/2}$

Overall Class Size (Honors-only plus mixed, contract): 🎓🎓🎓🎓

Honors Grad Rate: 🎓🎓🎓🎓

Value-Added Grad Rate: 🎓🎓🎓🎓🎓

Ratio of Staff to Students: 🎓🎓🎓

Priority Registration: Yes, honors students register for all courses, honors and otherwise, with the first group of students during each year they are in the program.

Honors Housing Amenities: 🎓🎓🎓🎓

Honors Housing Availability: 🎓🎓🎓🎓

Prestigious Awards: 🎓🎓🎓$^{1/2}$

RATING SCORES AND EXPLANATIONS:

Curriculum Requirements (4.5): The most important rating category, the curriculum completion requirement (classes required to complete honors) defines not only what honors students should learn but also the extent to which honors students and faculty are connected in the classroom. If there is a thesis or capstone requirement, it reinforces the individual contact and research skills so important to learning.

The average number of honors semester hours required for completion across all 50 programs is 29.0.

The total for the honors college is 39 credits, but the college allows AP credits to offset as many as 6 credits; therefore, the rated curriculum total is **33** credits.

The Honors College Degree is earned by completion of both the General Honors Award and the College or Departmental Honors Award with a minimum of 39 honors credit hours, with grades of "A" or "B" and a cumulative graduation/retention GPA of 3.50 or higher at the time of graduation. Students earning the Honors College Degree are the only undergraduates who wear a baccalaureate hood at commencement ceremonies, they receive a special honors diploma, and the Honors College Degree is posted to their undergraduate transcripts. The degree requires 21 credits in honors courses in general honors, with a maximum of 6 credits in honors experiences (e.g., study abroad); 9 credits in honors departmental courses; 6 credits in honors courses or honors contract courses; and a 3-credit **thesis.**

"Students may also earn the Honors College Degree with International Study Emphasis by completing one of several specified academic minors and an approved study-abroad experience."

The General Honors Award requires 21 hours of honors courses, no more than 9 of which can be by honors contract.

The Departmental/Honors College Award requires 12 credit hours, with no limit on the number of contract hours, and "most hours are completed through contracts." Also required is a 3-hour thesis.

AP/IB credits can count for up to 6 honors credits. AP test score minimum is 4; IB minimum is 5.

Number of Honors Classes Offered (4.0): This is a measure of the total **adjusted** honors main sections available in the term reported, not including labs and thesis. (Please read the section titled "All about Honors Classes".) An adjusted main section has 3 or more semester credits, or equivalent, and sections with fewer credits receive a lower prorated value.

The college offered a section for every **15.1** enrolled students. The average for all 50 programs is 14.2. The lower the number, the better.

In the term reported, **93.6%** of honors enrollment was **in honors-only sections; .5% in mixed honors sections (honors and non-honors students); and 5.9% in contract sections (regular sections in which honors students "contract" to do extra work).** The averages for all fifty programs are 81.3% in honors-only sections; 13.6 % in mixed honors sections; and 5.1% in contract sections.

Number of Honors Classes in Key Disciplines (4.0): The 15 "key" disciplines are biological sciences; business (all); chemistry; communications (especially public speaking); computer science; economics; engineering (all); English; history; math (all); philosophy; physics; political science; psychology; and sociology/anthropology/gender studies. Interdisciplinary sections, such as those often taken for General Education credit in the first two years, do receive a lesser, prorated discipline "credit" because they introduce students to multiple disciplines in an especially engaging way, often with in-depth discussion.

For this measure, mixed and contract sections are not counted as a section in a key discipline unless students taking the sections for honors credit make up at least 10% of the total section enrollment.

In the term reported, the program had a ratio of **26.3 honors students** per each main section in some or all "key disciplines." The mean for all 50 programs is 26.3. The lower the ratio, the better.

Out of **60 adjusted sections in key disciplines**, the Honors College had **49** that were **honors-only sections.** The most sections were in English (11), business and math (7), biology, engineering, history, and political science (5 each), and philosophy and psychology (3 each). Sociology, anthropology, and gender studies had 3 sections combined.

The college also offered about 18 interdisciplinary sections and seminars, as well as others courses that had more of a disciplinary focus. Among the former were "First Amendment Freedoms"; "Medicine in the 21st Century"; and "U.S. Versus the World, Education Systems."

The honors college, with an excellent mix of interdisciplinary classes and sections in the academic disciplines, is a **blended honors program.**

Extent of Honors Enrollment (5.0): Not all honors students take an honors class each term, especially after the first two years. Programs that have fewer honors classes for upper-division honors students will generally have fewer total members in good standing who are actually enrolled in a given term. (Please be aware, however, that honors students not enrolled in a class for a term are still connected to the honors community through residential and extracurricular activities.)

For example, if honors students in a program occupy 1,800 honors classroom seats in a given term, and there are 3,000 honors students in good standing, the extent of enrollment is .67. For programs that require a thesis, the ratio (score) reported below might in fact be somewhat higher, since we only count "regular" class enrollment for this measure, and not thesis enrollment. The college **has a ratio of 1.39**; the mean is 1.13 for all 50 programs. The higher the ratio, the better.

Average Class Size, Honors-only Sections (4.5): Offered mostly in the first two years, honors-only classes tend to be smaller and, as the name implies, have no or very few students other than those in the honors program. These class sections are almost always much smaller than mixed or contract sections, or regular non-honors class sections in the university.

The average honors-only class size in the honors program is **16.5 students**. The average for all 50 programs is 19.0 students.

Average Class Size, Overall (4.0): The overall class calculation is based on the *proportion* of honors students in each type of class (honors-only, mixed honors, and honors contract sections). Thus it is not a raw average. The overall honors-credit class size is **24.2 students**, versus the average for all 50 programs of 26.3 students.

These class size averages also do not correspond to the number of students per honors sections numbers above. The reason is that, in computing average class size metrics, we include enrollment in each 1-2-credit section, not just sections with 3 or more credits.

Along with the honors-only average of 16.5 students, the mixed honors sections average **4.7 students**, and the contract sections with honors credit for individual honors students average **148.3 students**. Across all fifty programs, the average mixed honors section has 51.1 students, and the average contract section has 60.1 students.

Honors Graduation Rate (4.0): The rating is based on the actual grad rate for students who entered the program six years earlier, whether or not the students remained in honors. The **actual rate of 87.9%** is also compared to the rates of other programs with the same test score entry requirement range, and then adjusted to the **score of 88.2%**. In some cases this measure favors programs within universities with relatively higher test scores for the student population as a whole. The average honors graduation rate for all programs with similar test scores required for admission is 85.6%.

Value-Added Grad Rate (5.0): The value-added rate measures the extent to which the adjusted score listed above exceeds the six-year grad rate for the university as a whole. **The university-wide rate is 61%.**

Note: This measure generally favors programs within universities with relatively lower test scores for the student population as a whole.

Ratio of Staff to Honors Students (3.0): There is 1 staff member for every **212.3** students. (Mean ratio for all 50 programs is 1 staff member for every 135.6 students.)

Honors Residence Halls, Amenities (4.0): About 75% of honors students in honors housing reside in Stout Hall. Stout has traditional rooms with hall baths. It is air-conditioned and houses both freshmen and upperclassmen. The nearest dining hall is the Service Station.

The other honors students living in honors housing reside in West Bennett, which has air-conditioned suite-style rooms and shared baths. Dining is on site.

Honors Residence Halls, Availability (4.0): This rating compares the number of places in honors residence halls to the number of honors freshman and sophomore members in good standing, about 743. The ratio for the honors program is **.46** rooms for each first- and second-year student. The average for all fifty programs is .63 places.

Prestigious Awards (3.5): The awards that we track and include are listed in the section titled "Prestigious Scholarships." The awards are sometimes won by students who are not in an honors college or program, but increasingly many are enrolled in honors programs. It is also a trend that honors colleges and programs help to prepare their students for the awards competitions.

OSU students have won 1 Rhodes scholarship, 2 Gates Cambridge scholarships, 2 Marshall scholarships, and 17 Truman scholarships. In addition, as for Goldwater scholarships (most won by honors students) OSU students have won 19. The Udall total is 15 scholarships.

UNRATED FEATURES

Continuation Requirements: 3.50.

Academic Strengths, National Rankings: This is based on national rankings of *graduate* programs in 15 disciplines, except engineering and business, where undergraduate rankings are used.

The highest ranking departments at OSU are engineering and math (87 each) followed by business (93).

Undergraduate Research: Honors students, though only about 8% of the undergraduate student body, account for almost 60% of the students participating in these programs:

2015-16 The Niblack Research Scholars--Each year, the program awards an $8,000 scholarship to 12 students, who have the unique opportunity to conduct research in a university lab, assisted by a faculty sponsor and graduate student mentor.

2015-16 Wentz Scholars--Each year, $4,500 one-year Wentz Research Grants are given to undergraduates to conduct independent research with the guidance of a faculty mentor in any field of study (major).

2015-16 Freshman Research Scholars--Oklahoma State University's Freshman Research Scholars program provides students a $1,000 scholarship and the opportunity to go beyond the classroom and take part in research with experienced faculty.

2015-16 The Life Sciences Freshman Research (LSFRS) Program--This is part of an effort to involve students in authentic research during their introductory science experiences. Award is $1,000.

Study Abroad: "Cowboys in Cambridge is an OSU summer study-abroad opportunity with honors sections available. Honors students who participate in the program receive three honors hours after two weeks of study abroad at Magdalene College, University of Cambridge, and completion of a course project. Students must apply to the program and it is attended by top OSU students. All students admitted to the program receive significant financial support."

"Each year the two-week course explores a new topic. Recent topics include terrorism and insurgency in Britain, England during the time of Charles Dickens, and the Life and Work of Charles Darwin."

Financial Aid: OSU is now a major player in the National Merit Scholarship world. "Resident National Merit Finalists are eligible for a cash and tuition scholarship package valued at approximately $64,100," and out-of-state National Merit Finalists "are eligible for a cash and tuition scholarship package valued at approximately $130,100."

However, these might not be offered to a high number of students. The scholarship deadline is February 1, 2017.

The university has many other merit scholarships, including these based on test scores and high school GPA. Many honors students should be eligible.

Among these awards are Academic Excellence Scholarships of $2,000 per year, with a matrix requirement of test score and high school GPA (the higher the test score, the lower the GPA has to be). *All SAT scores below are based on the old tables.*

Example: 28-29 ACT or 1250-1320 SAT requires an unweighted high school GPA of 3.25; but with a 24 ACT or a 1090 SAT, a recipient would need a 3.80 unweighted high school GPA.

Non-residents can reap major benefits if they meet the matrix requirements. In this case, the dollar amount of the awards declines as the test scores and high school GPA's go down. At the high end, an out-of-state applicant with a 30 ACT or 1330 SAT and an unweighted high school GPA of 3.0 may receive an award of up to $12,500 a year.

On the low end, an out-of-state applicant with a 24 ACT or a 1090 ACT must have an unweighted high school GPA of 3.0 and may receive up to $8,000 per year.

Honors Fees: None.

Placement Experiences: "Of the 92 graduating students who completed our graduate questionnaire during the 2014-2015 and 2015-2016 academic years, 60 are attending graduate school, 21 have found a position and will begin working at their first job, and 11 were seeking employment at the time of graduation.

"We would also like to note that of the 187 students graduating in 2015-2016 with an Honors College award, 18% students are from under-represented groups. Over half of these students are Native American. Oklahoma State University as a whole is #1 in the nation among public land-grant colleges and universities for graduating Native American students five years in a row."

Degree of Difference: This is based on the differences between (1) the average (2015, two-part) SAT scores for enrolled honors students (1240) and (2) the average test scores for all students in the university (1150) as a whole. The test scores may be an indication of how "elite" honors students may be perceived as compared to students in the university as a whole. The scores can also provide an indication of how well prepared the non-honors students in the university may be. **Please keep in mind that neither high nor low test scores determine the overall quality of a program.**

NAME: ROBERT D. CLARK HONORS COLLEGE AT THE UNIVERSITY OF OREGON.

Date Established: 1960.

Location: Eugene, Oregon.

University Full-time Undergraduate Enrollment: 18,673.

Honors Members in Good Standing: 776 (mean size of all 50 programs is 1,742).

Honors Average Admission Statistics: Old SAT, 1358; est. new SAT, 1420.

Average High School GPA/Class Rank: 3.85; class rank is not considered.

Basic Admission Requirements: "While there is no minimum threshold, incoming students typically possess a mean GPA of 3.80 or higher and score in the 90+ percentile of test takers. Our holistic admissions review incorporates a self-introduction, essay, description of accomplishments, transcripts, test scores, and letters of recommendation from two teachers in differing disciplines. We seek bright, thoughtful, and academically motivated students to bring diversity to our community of scholars. All interested students who would enjoy the rigor and challenge of interdisciplinary critical thinking, reading, and writing are encouraged to apply."

Application Deadline(s): *Please verify with each program, as some deadlines could change.*

Early action deadline November 1, 2016, with all materials due November 7, 2016; notification December 15, 2017. Regular deadline January 15, 2017, with all materials due February 1, 2017; notification April 1, 2017.

Honors Programs with old SAT scores from 1351—1396: Purdue, Oregon, Alabama, Massachusetts, Penn State, Indiana, CUNY Macaulay, Texas A&M, NJIT, Missouri, Oregon State, Delaware, LSU, Vermont, Temple.

Administrative Staff: 14.

RATINGS AT A GLANCE: For all mortarboard ratings immediately below, a score of 5 is the maximum and represents a comparison with all 50 honors colleges and programs. More detailed explanations follow the "mortarboard" ratings.

PERCEPTION* OF UNIVERSITY AS A WHOLE, NOT OF HONORS:

*Perception is based on the university's ranking among public universities in the 2016 U.S. News Best Colleges report. Please bear in mind that the better the U.S. News ranking, the more difficult it is for an honors college or program to have a rating that equals or improves on the magazine ranking.

OVERALL HONORS RATING:

Curriculum Requirements: 🎓🎓🎓🎓

Number of Honors Classes Offered: 🎓🎓🎓🎓

Number of Honors Classes in Key Disciplines: 🎓🎓🎓🎓$^{1/2}$

Extent of Honors Enrollment: 🎓🎓🎓🎓🎓

Honors-only Class Size: 🎓🎓🎓🎓$^{1/2}$

Overall Class Size (Honors-only plus mixed, contract): 🎓🎓🎓🎓🎓

Honors Grad Rate: 🎓🎓🎓$^{1/2}$

Value-Added Grad Rate: 🎓🎓🎓🎓

Ratio of Staff to Students: 🎓🎓🎓🎓🎓

Priority Registration: Yes, honors students register for all courses, honors and otherwise, immediately after athletes and veterans (the first group), during each year they are in the program.

Honors Housing Amenities: 🎓🎓🎓🎓🎓

Honors Housing Availability: 🎓🎓🎓🎓

Prestigious Awards: 🎓🎓🎓🎓

RATING SCORES AND EXPLANATIONS:

Curriculum Requirements (4.0): The most important rating category, the curriculum completion requirement (classes required to complete honors) defines not only what honors students should learn but also the extent to which honors students and faculty are connected in the classroom. If there is a thesis or capstone requirement, it reinforces the individual contact and research skills so important to learning.

The average number of honors semester hours required for completion across all 50 programs is 29.0.

"The Clark Honors College's curriculum, most of which occurs in Clark Honors College-only classes, satisfies/replaces the "general education" required of all University of Oregon graduates. In addition the Clark Honors College requires a thesis, completed in the student's major. On average undergraduate students complete 45-50 courses for the completion of a bachelor's degree from the university, or 180 credits. Converted to semester hours, the minimum would be about **30 credits.**

AP/IB credits are not counted as replacements for honors courses.

Number of Honors Classes Offered (4.0): This is a measure of the total **adjusted** honors main sections available in the term reported, not including labs and thesis. (Please read the section titled "All about Honors Classes".) An adjusted main section has 3 or more semester credits, or equivalent, and sections with fewer credits receive a lower prorated value.

The college offered a section for every **13.1** enrolled students. The average for all 50 programs is 14.2. The lower the number, the better.

In the term reported, **100.0%** of honors enrollment was **in honors-only sections; none in mixed honors sections (honors and non-honors students); and none in contract sections (regular sections in which honors students "contract" to do extra work).** The averages for all fifty programs are 81.3% in honors-only sections; 13.6 % in mixed honors sections; and 5.1% in contract sections.

Number of Honors Classes in Key Disciplines (4.5): The 15 "key" disciplines are biological sciences; business (all); chemistry; communications (especially public speaking); computer science; economics; engineering (all); English; history; math (all); philosophy; physics; political science; psychology; and sociology/anthropology/gender studies. Interdisciplinary sections, such as those often taken for General Education credit in the first two years, do receive a lesser, prorated discipline "credit" because they introduce students to multiple disciplines in an especially engaging way, often with in-depth discussion.

For this measure, mixed and contract sections are not counted as a section in a key discipline unless students taking the sections for honors credit make up at least 10% of the total section enrollment.

In the term reported, the program had a ratio of **11.2 honors students** per each main section in some or all "key disciplines." The mean for all 50 programs is 26.3. The lower the ratio, the better.

Out of **35 sections in key disciplines offered in one quarter**, the program had **all honors-only sections.** The most sections (adjusted to semester based on 1.5 quarters) were in English (16), and history (14), with the remaining sections being in economics, math, and physics.

The college also offered about a dozen interdisciplinary sections, including "The Middle East and the USA"; "Atrocities and Genocide"; "War and Peace"; and "Human Rights Today."

The Honors College combines interdisciplinary classes with several departmental honors classes, but it is essentially a **core honors program, with disciplinary offerings as well.** This mix of core seminars and classes in a few major disciplines is similar to that in the UT Austin Plan II Honors Program.

Extent of Honors Enrollment (5.0): Not all honors students take an honors class each term, especially after the first two years. Programs that have fewer honors classes for upper-division honors students will generally have fewer total members in good standing who are actually enrolled in a given term. (Please be aware, however, that honors students not enrolled in a class for a term are still connected to the honors community through residential and extracurricular activities.)

For example, if honors students in a program occupy 1,800 honors classroom seats in a given term, and there are 3,000 honors students in good standing, the extent of enrollment is .67. For programs that require a thesis, the ratio (score) reported below might in fact be somewhat higher. The college **has a ratio of 1.90**; the mean is 1.14 for all 50 programs. The higher the ratio, the better.

Average Class Size, Honors-only Sections (4.5): Offered mostly in the first two years, honors-only classes tend to be smaller and, as the name implies, have no or very few students other than those in the honors program. These class sections are almost always much smaller than mixed or contract sections, or regular non-honors class sections in the university.

The average honors-only class size in the honors program is **17.0 students**. The average for all 50 programs is 19.0 students.

Average Class Size, Overall (5.0): The overall class calculation is based on the *proportion* of honors students in each type of class (honors-only, mixed honors, and honors contract sections). Thus it is not a raw average. The overall honors-credit class size is **17.0 students**, versus the average for all 50 programs of 26.3 students.

These class size averages also do not correspond to the number of students per honors sections numbers above. The reason is that, in computing average class size metrics, we include enrollment in each 1-2-credit section, not just sections with 3 or more credits.

Along with the honors-only average of 17.0 students, the mixed honors sections average **(NA)** students, and the contract sections with honors credit for individual honors students average **(NA)** students. Across all fifty programs, the average mixed honors section has 51.1 students, and the average contract section has 60.1 students.

Honors Graduation Rate (3.5): The rating is based on the actual grad rate for students who entered the program six years earlier, whether or not the students remained in honors. The **actual rate of 82%** is also compared to the rates of other programs with the same test score entry requirement range, and then adjusted to the **score of 81.6%.** In some cases this measure favors programs within universities with relatively higher test scores for the student population as a whole. The average honors graduation rate for all programs with similar test scores required for admission is 86.2%.

Value-Added Grad Rate (4.0): The value-added rate measures the extent to which the adjusted score listed above exceeds the six-year grad rate for the university as a whole. **The university-wide rate is 69%.** Note: This measure generally favors programs within universities with relatively lower test scores for the student population as a whole.

Ratio of Staff to Honors Students (5.0): There is 1 staff member for every **55.4** students. (Mean ratio for all 50 programs is 1 staff member for every 135.6 students.)

Honors Residence Halls, Amenities (5.0): The Global Scholars Residence Hall houses about 189 honors students, both freshmen and upperclassmen. The residence has a mix of singles, doubles, triples, and suite-style rooms, all of which are air-conditioned. A great feature is on-site dining at the Fresh Market Café.

Honors Residence Halls, Availability (4.0): This rating compares the number of places in honors residence halls to the number of honors freshman and sophomore members in good standing, about 388 . The ratio for the honors program is **.49** rooms for each first- and second-year student. The average for all fifty programs is .63 places.

Prestigious Awards (4.0): The awards that we track and include are listed in the section titled "Prestigious Scholarships." The awards are sometimes won by students who are not in an honors college or program, but increasingly many are enrolled in honors programs. It is also a trend that honors colleges and programs help to prepare their students for the awards competitions.

U of O students have won an impressive 19 Rhodes scholarships, along with 3 Gates Cambridge, 4 Marshall, and 8 Truman scholarships. Oregon students have also won 24 Goldwater and 4 Boren awards for undergraduates.

"Beginning in the 2015-2016 academic year, Clark Honors College hired Dr. Elizabeth Raisanen into the new position of Director of Undergraduate Advising. Dr. Raisanen is focused on increasing student awareness around distinguished scholarships through direct student outreach, workshops, and one-on-one mentoring. Dr. Raisanen also is a first-stop for students within the Clark Honors College, and can connect students to other resources throughout the university that the students may not have been aware of. This includes the Office of National and International Distinguished Scholarships at the University of Oregon.

"This office manages all aspects of students applying for distinguished scholarships, including applying, mock interviews, coaching and mentoring."

UNRATED FEATURES

Continuation Requirements: 3.00, and the same for graduation.

Academic Strengths, National Rankings: This is based on national rankings of *graduate* programs in 15 disciplines, except engineering and business, where undergraduate rankings are used.

The U of O has an excellent faculty, with departments averaging 50-55 in the nation. Among the most recognized departments are education (12), psychology (30), earth sciences (34), business (50), English (52), physics (54), biology (55), and economics, history, and math (all 56).

Undergraduate Research: "*Every* student who graduates from Clark Honors College must research, write and orally defend an undergraduate thesis. This process often takes more than a year, and the experience of defining a unique research question, conducting research, writing and defending the thesis in front of a committee of faculty members gives Clark Honors College students excellent preparation for graduate school. Many theses have become published articles in refereed journals.

"Additionally, the University of Oregon holds a campus-wide celebration of undergraduate research, creative and performance works--the Undergraduate Symposium--each May. While the Clark Honors College student body represents just under 4% of the UO's undergraduate population, each year Clark Honors College students represent 30% or more of the participants in the Undergraduate Symposium. Many of the posters and oral presentations result from the direct experience Clark Honors College students have conducting research in the mandatory lower division humanities or social science research course, class projects from research-intensive upper division honors colloquia, lab assistant or work study jobs in faculty research laboratories across campus, and from their independent thesis research."

Study Abroad: "The Clark Honors College offers honors specific study abroad programs, led by CHC faculty. These programs are designed to cater to students majoring in the sciences (36% of CHC students) by offering programs taught in English, which do not require proficiency in a second language, and through summer session courses which allow science students to complete the full academic-year science series they must take to fulfill their majors. These programs also cater to students pursuing more than one major (21% of CHC students) and who are therefore on a stricter course schedule in order to complete coursework for multiple majors in four years, by creating study abroad curriculum that qualifies for use towards mandatory upper division colloquia credits:

"Clark Honors College @ Oxford brings honors students to live in the center of the city of Oxford, England. The quarter-long program, in parallel with Oxford's Trinity term, provides students with an honors college colloquia, taught by Oregon and Oxford faculty, and two Oxford tutorials, taught by Oxford faculty at the oldest university in the English-speaking world. The tutorial program, where students meet one-on-one with a faculty advisor for each class once a week, is an extremely rigorous program, and excellent preparation for the independent study skills students will need during the completion of their honors thesis. The program and students are housed at the Centre for Medieval and Renaissance Studies, affiliated with Keble College, Oxford University, and located at the heart of the city and its ancient colleges.

"The Genius of Study Abroad is a course of active, activist global learning that considers the interactive, international, and interdisciplinary aspects of creativity in revolutionary imagination as seen in movements in architecture, landscape, arts, science and technology, and legislation on human rights and equality on both sides of the Channel. It takes students on tour of Dublin, London, Oxford and Paris, where students will retrace the literal and intellectual paths of historical figures who developed new ways to conceive of and express our world. Students earn the equivalent of two upper division colloquia (8 credits) and develop their own portfolio of writing and reflections. Activities include lectures, discussions, interactive performance, walking excursions and guest speakers.

"Research in Rapa Nui is a special study abroad program led by Clark Honors College Dean Terry Hunt. Hunt leads students to Rapa Nui (Easter Island) for a combined seminar-style intensive course and grand "field trip" to witness the island's most remarkable archaeology. Hunt is a leading Rapa Nui expert, whose work has been featured in a National Geographic cover story (July 2012), on Nova-National Geographic TV, and in his award-winning book with Carl Lipo, *The Statues that Walked* (2011). Students will complement assigned readings with daily field excursions around the island, with emphasis on seminar-style discussion and assigned readings. There is a preparatory part of the program to take place on the campus of the University of Oregon prior to departure."

Financial Aid: "The Clark Honors College incoming class of fall 2015, comprised of 236 students, received $1.87 million in scholarship awards. *92% of incoming students received merit and need-based awards, and 26% of incoming students received more than one award."* [Emphasis added.]
The college provided a long list of awards; below are the most generous:

Stamps Scholarship--$125,651 in awards across 5 students (2% of incoming class). The Stamps Scholarship—the University of Oregon's most prestigious and generous undergraduate scholarship—is awarded competitively to outstanding incoming freshmen from Oregon. Twenty students—five per year—will be awarded this merit-based scholarship by the Stamps Family Charitable Foundation in partnership with the University of Oregon.

"Stamps Scholars receive full UO tuition, room, and board for four years of undergraduate study. Recipients will also benefit from up to $12,000 in enrichment funds to be used over four years to help them pursue study abroad, unpaid internships, or other experiences. The total award is approximately $110,000 over four years. In addition to unprecedented levels of financial support, Stamps Scholars are automatically granted admission to the University of Oregon's Robert D. Clark Honors College.

"Presidential Scholarship--$270,000 in awards across 30 students (13% of incoming class). Presidential Scholarships are awarded competitively to outstanding incoming freshmen from Oregon. Approximately 50 freshmen receive this scholarship each year, and the awarding process is highly selective. Presidential Scholars receive up to $36,000 over four years of undergraduate study--$9,000 per year--which covers 64% of combined in-state university and honors differential tuition.

"Pathway Oregon--$61,378 in awards across 18 students (8% of incoming class). Oregon students who are Federal Pell Grant-eligible may attend the University of Oregon and Clark Honors College as part of the Pathway Oregon program. The program covers all UO tuition and fees for up to four years.

"Summit Scholarship--$1,233,000 in awards across 185 students (78% of incoming class). Summit Scholarships reward scholars for reaching the peak of high school achievement. The Summit Scholarship awards Oregon top scholars $24,000 over four years--$6,000 per year. Due to the difference in tuition, out-of-state top scholars will receive $36,000 over four years--$9,000 per year. This covers 42% of combined in-state university and honors differential tuition for Oregon students, and 25% for out-of-state students."

Honors Fees: "The Clark Honors College charges differential tuition, which allows us to maintain small class sizes, and ensures that all classes are taught by faculty and not graduate students.

"For both the 2015-2016 academic year and the 2016-2017 academic year *differential tuition is assessed at $3,834 annually*. This assumes a typical enrollment of 15 credits for each of 3 terms (45 credits per year)." [Emphasis added.]

Placement Experiences: None listed.

Degree of Difference: This is based on the differences between (1) the average (2015, two-part) SAT scores for enrolled honors students (1358) and (2) the average test scores for all students in the university (1130) as a whole. The test scores may be an indication of how "elite" honors students may be perceived as compared to students in the university as a whole. The scores can also provide an indication of how well prepared the non-honors students in the university may be. **Please keep in mind that neither high nor low test scores determine the overall quality of a program.**

NAME: OREGON STATE UNIVERSITY HONORS COLLEGE.

Date Established: 1995.

Location: Corvallis, Oregon.

University Full-time Undergraduate Enrollment: 18,477.

Honors Members in Good Standing: 1,143 (mean size of all 50 programs is 1,742).

Honors Average Admission Statistics: ACT, 30.26; Old SAT three-part, 2006; est. new SAT, 1430.

Average High School GPA/Class Rank: 3.93.

Basic Admission Requirements: ACT, 27. Old SAT three-part, 1820; est. new SAT, 1300.

Application Deadline(s): *Please verify with each program, as some deadlines could change.*

Early round deadline is November 1, with notification by December 31; primary round deadline is February 1, with notification by March 31.

Honors Programs with old SAT scores from 1351—1396: Purdue, Oregon, Alabama, Massachusetts, Penn State, Indiana, CUNY Macaulay, Texas A&M, NJIT, Missouri, Oregon State, Delaware, LSU, Vermont, Temple.

Administrative Staff: 13.

RATINGS AT A GLANCE: For all mortarboard ratings immediately below, a score of 5 is the maximum and represents a comparison with all 50 honors colleges and programs. More detailed explanations follow the "mortarboard" ratings.

PERCEPTION* OF UNIVERSITY AS A WHOLE, NOT OF HONORS: 🎓🎓🎓 1/2

*Perception is based on the university's ranking among public universities in the 2016 U.S. News Best Colleges report. Please bear in mind that the better the U.S. News ranking, the more difficult it is for an honors college or program to have a rating that equals or improves on the magazine ranking.

OVERALL HONORS RATING: 🎓🎓🎓 1/2

Curriculum Requirements: 🎓🎓🎓

Number of Honors Classes Offered: 🎓🎓🎓 1/2

Number of Honors Classes in Key Disciplines: 🎓🎓🎓🎓

Extent of Honors Enrollment: 🎓🎓🎓🎓

Honors-only Class Size: 🎓🎓🎓🎓🎓

Overall Class Size (Honors-only plus mixed, contract): 🎓🎓🎓🎓🎓

Honors Grad Rate: 🎓🎓🎓🎓

Value-Added Grad Rate: 🎓🎓🎓🎓^{1/2}

Ratio of Staff to Students: 🎓🎓🎓🎓^{1/2}

Priority Registration: "Students at Oregon State University register based on class standing, which is determined by credit hours earned (seniors first, juniors second, etc.). Honors students register for all courses in advance of the registration date established for all other students with the same class standing (but not in advance of classes of higher rank). This is the case in all terms except the fall term of students' first years: all students incoming to the university register at summer advising sessions."

Honors Housing Amenities: 🎓🎓🎓🎓^{1/2}

Honors Housing Availability: 🎓🎓🎓^{1/2}

Prestigious Awards: 🎓🎓🎓^{1/2}

RATING SCORES AND EXPLANATIONS:

Curriculum Requirements (3.0): The most important rating category, the curriculum completion requirement (classes required to complete honors) defines not only what honors students should learn but also the extent to which honors students and faculty are connected in the classroom. If there is a thesis or capstone requirement, it reinforces the individual contact and research skills so important to learning.

The average number of honors semester hours required for completion across all 50 programs is 29.0.

Graduation as an Honors Scholar requires 30 quarter hours, or about **20** semester hours.

Of the 30 **quarter** hours that are required, 6 credits must be in honors baccalaureate core classes; 6 credits in honors colloquia; 12 credits in honors electives; and 6 credits for the **honors thesis research project.**

There is a lesser requirement, called the Honors Associate track, which is for students who have already completed their baccalaureate core classes and who typically have only two years of coursework left before graduation. This track requires 15 quarter credits minimum, including 6 credits in honors colloquia, 6 credits in honors electives, and 3 credits for the honors thesis research project.

AP/IB credits are not counted as replacements for honors courses.

Number of Honors Classes Offered (3.5): This is a measure of the total **adjusted** honors main sections available in the term reported, not including labs and thesis. (Please read the section titled "All about Honors Classes".) An adjusted main section has 3 or more semester credits, or equivalent, and sections with fewer credits receive a lower prorated value.

The college offered a section for every **18.1** students. The average for all 50 programs is 14.2. The lower the number, the better.

In the term reported, **100.0%** of honors enrollment was **in honors-only sections; none in mixed sections (with honors discussion sections or labs); and none in contract sections (regular sections in which honors students "contract" to do extra work).** The averages for all fifty programs are 81.3% in honors-only sections; 13.6 % in mixed honors sections; and 5.1% in contract sections.

Number of Honors Classes in Key Disciplines (4.0): The 15 "key" disciplines are biological sciences; business (all); chemistry; communications (especially public speaking); computer science; economics; engineering (all); English; history; math (all); philosophy; physics; political science; psychology; and sociology/anthropology/gender studies. Interdisciplinary sections, such as those often taken for General Education credit in the first two years, do receive a lesser, prorated discipline "credit" because they introduce students to multiple disciplines in an especially engaging way, often with in-depth discussion.

For this measure, mixed and contract sections are not counted as a section in a key discipline unless students taking the sections for honors credit make up at least 10% of the total section enrollment.

In the term reported, the program had a ratio of **27.8 honors students** per each main section in some or all "key disciplines." The mean for all programs is 26.3. The lower the ratio, the better.

In one quarter, the college offered **32 adjusted sections in key disciplines**, the program had **all honors-only sections.** The most sections were in English and math (7 each), engineering (4), biology, chemistry, and history (3 each), and business and computer science (1 each). Sociology, anthropology, and genders studies combined has 3 sections.

The college offered about 15 one- and two-credit seminars. These included "God, Pain, and the Problem of Evil: An Introduction to C.S. Lewis"; "Energy IQ: Resources, Responsibility, and Renewability"; and "Connecting the Arts and Sciences: A Short Exploration."

The college combines interdisciplinary classes with honors classes in the disciplines, and is an example of a **blended program.**

Extent of Honors Enrollment (4.0): Not all honors students take an honors class each term, especially after the first two years. Programs that have fewer honors classes for upper-division honors students will generally have fewer total members in good standing who are actually enrolled in a given term. (Please be aware, however, that honors students not enrolled in a class for a term are still connected to the honors community through residential and extracurricular activities.)

For example, if honors students in a program occupy 1,800 honors classroom seats in a given term, and there are 3,000 honors students in good standing, the extent of enrollment is .67. For programs that require a thesis, the ratio (score) reported below might in fact be somewhat higher, since we only count

"regular" class enrollment for this measure, and not thesis enrollment. The college has a ratio of **.99**; the mean is 1.13 for all 50 programs. The higher the ratio, the better.

Average Class Size, Honors-only Sections (5.0): Offered mostly in the first two years, honors-only classes tend to be smaller and, as the name implies, have no or very few students other than those in the honors program. These class sections are almost always much smaller than mixed or contract sections, or regular non-honors class sections in the university.

The average honors-only class size in the honors program is **12.2 students**. The average for all 50 programs is 19.0 students.

Average Class Size, Overall (5.0): The overall class calculation is based on the *proportion* of honors students in each type of class (honors-only, mixed honors, and honors contract sections). Thus it is not a raw average. The overall honors-credit class size is **13.2 students**, versus the average for all 50 programs of 26.3 students. *This is the lowest overall class size among all programs reviewed.*

These class size averages also do not correspond to the number of students per honors sections numbers above. The reason is that, in computing average class size metrics, we include enrollment in each 1-2-credit section, not just sections with 3 or more credits.

Along with the honors-only average of 13.2 students, the mixed honors sections average **(NA)** students, and the contract sections with honors credit for individual honors students average **(NA)** students. Across all fifty programs, the average mixed honors section has 51.1students, and the average contract section has 60.1 students.

Honors Graduation Rate (4.0): The rating is based on the actual grad rate for students who entered the program six years earlier, whether or not the students remained in honors. The **actual rate of 87.6%** is also compared to the rates of other programs with the same test score entry requirement range, and then adjusted to the **score of 87.9%**. In some cases this measure favors programs within universities with relatively higher test scores for the student population as a whole. The average honors graduation rate for all programs with similar test scores required for admission is 86.2%.

Value-Added Grad Rate (4.5): The value-added rate measures the extent to which the adjusted score listed above exceeds the six-year grad rate for the university as a whole. **The university-wide rate is 63%.** Note: This measure generally favors programs within universities with relatively lower test scores for the student population as a whole.

Ratio of Staff to Honors Students (4.5): There is 1 staff member for every **89.8** students. (Mean ratio for all 50 programs is 1 staff member for every 135.6 students.)

Honors Residence Halls, Amenities (4.5): About 185 first-year students live in West Hall, which has suite-style, air-conditioned rooms and shared baths. The nearest dining is at Marketplace West.

Another 33 students, mostly in their first year, reside in Sackett Hall. "Sackett Hall offers double rooms, and rooms with separate sleeping porch and walk-in closets….Floors typically have 16 residents of a single gender sharing a single gender restroom. Floors alternate between male and female." The most convenient dining is also at Marketplace West.

"In addition to Honors College lounges in the official honors residential facilities in West and Sackett Hall, the college has a student lounge, computer lab, and study room in its administrative and teaching spaces.

"The Honors College also has an agreement with an apartment complex immediately adjacent to campus (but privately managed), the GEM, that provides Honors College students with application and room selection priority."

Honors Residence Halls, Availability (3.5): This rating compares the number of places in honors residence halls to the number of honors freshman and sophomore members in good standing, about 571. The ratio for the honors program is **.38** rooms for each first- and second-year student. The average for all fifty programs is .63 places.

Prestigious Awards (3.5): The awards that we track and include are listed in the section titled "Prestigious Scholarships." The awards are sometimes won by students who are not in an honors college or program, but increasingly many are enrolled in honors programs. It is also a trend that honors colleges and programs help to prepare their students for the awards competitions.

"Oregon State University has an advisor for prestigious scholarships. This is a new university-wide position, created in 2015, and is located in the Honors College and supervised by the Honors College dean. The advisor works closely with Honors College staff in the identification of candidates and is an accessible, visible resource for honors students."

OSU students have already won an impressive 10 Udall scholarships, 27 Goldwater scholarships, 2 Rhodes scholarships, and Marshall and Gates Cambridge awards (1 each).

UNRATED FEATURES

Continuation Requirements: 3.25, and the same for graduation.

Academic Strengths, National Rankings: This is based on national rankings of *graduate* programs in 15 disciplines, except engineering and business, where undergraduate rankings are used.

OSU has seven departments ranked within the top 100 in the nation, including earth sciences (34), computer science (67), engineering (70), math (73), biology (75), and physics (77).

Undergraduate Research: "Honors students must complete a thesis involving original research in a recognized scholarly field. This research can be conducted in any area the student chooses and is not necessarily in the student's major field(s) of study. Research is conducted under the mentorship of a tenure/tenure-track faculty member or senior instructor and is supported and assessed by this mentor and two other committee members, one of whom must also be a tenure/tenure-track faculty member or senior instructor at Oregon State University."

Study Abroad: "Honors College students can apply for scholarship support of up to $1,000 to assist in funding experiential opportunities, including study abroad, international and domestic service learning, research, and professional development. In the 2014-2015 academic year, the college provided over $100,000 to approximately 125 students in support of experiential learning.

"As mentioned above, the Honors College offers an international service learning course each year and, in the summer of 2016, will offer an honors study abroad opportunity in London, England with four Honors College courses."

Financial Aid: "The Honors College separately administers and awards approximately 155 scholarships each year. These are primarily $1,000, one-year awards. Recipients are determined through review of, for incoming students, Honors College application materials and special scholarship requirements and, for returning students, academic performance, progression through Honors College degree requirements, financial need, and special scholarship requirements. As mentioned previously, the college also makes a large number of experiential learning scholarships each year. Honors College students are eligible to receive university-wide scholarships and awards through their major degree programs as well."

Honors Fees: "Honors College students pay a differential tuition of approximately $451/term for fall, winter, and spring terms (fall term, 2016 rate). This primarily supports the Honors College curriculum offerings, but also funds student programming."

Placement Experiences: "We do not have this information. In a recent, non-comprehensive and voluntary survey of our alumni, 90% of respondents went to graduate school of some kind. The remaining 10% were primarily employed in professions such as engineering."

Degree of Difference: This is based on the differences between (1) the average (2015, two-part) SAT scores for enrolled honors students (1385) and (2) the average test scores for all students in the university (1105) as a whole. The test scores may be an indication of how "elite" honors students may be perceived as compared to students in the university as a whole. The scores can also provide an indication of how well prepared the non-honors students in the university may be. **Please keep in mind that neither high nor low test scores determine the overall quality of a program.**

NAME: SCHREYER HONORS COLLEGE AT THE PENNSYLVANIA STATE UNIVERSITY.

Date Established: Endowed as college in 1997, University Scholars Program established in 1980.

Location: University Park, Pennsylvania.

University Full-time Undergraduate Enrollment: 39,357.

Honors Members in Good Standing: 1,900 (mean size of all 50 programs is 1,742).

Honors Average Admission Statistics: Est. ACT, 31; est. old SAT, 1368; est. new SAT, 1420.

Average High School GPA/Class Rank: Est. 4.15.

Basic Admission Requirements: "The Schreyer Honors college does not set minimum academic requirements for grades or standardized tests. Candidates will be assessed based on the academic and extracurricular documents submitted with the application, as well as responses to essay questions and letters of recommendation. An interview is also an optional component of the application process."

Application Deadline(s): *Please verify with each program, as some deadlines could change.*

Priority deadline November 30, 2016, allows for interviews by end of January; final deadline January 16, 2017; notification by mid-March 2017.

Honors Programs with old SAT scores from 1351—1396: Purdue, Oregon, Alabama, Massachusetts, Penn State, Indiana, CUNY Macaulay, Texas A&M, NJIT, Missouri, Oregon State, Delaware, LSU, Vermont, Temple.

Administrative Staff: 24.

RATINGS AT A GLANCE: For all mortarboard ratings immediately below, a score of 5 is the maximum and represents a comparison with all 50 honors colleges and programs. More detailed explanations follow the "mortarboard" ratings.

PERCEPTION* OF UNIVERSITY AS A WHOLE, NOT OF HONORS: 🎓🎓🎓🎓🎓

*Perception is based on the university's ranking among public universities in the 2016 U.S. News Best Colleges report. Please bear in mind that the better the U.S. News ranking, the more difficult it is for an honors college or program to have a rating that equals or improves on the magazine ranking.

OVERALL HONORS RATING: 🎓🎓🎓🎓🎓

Curriculum Requirements: 🎓🎓🎓🎓🎓

Number of Honors Classes Offered: 🎓🎓🎓🎓🎓 1/2

Number of Honors Classes in Key Disciplines: 🎓🎓🎓🎓 1/2

Extent of Honors Enrollment: 🎓🎓🎓🎓 1/2

Honors-only Class Size: 🎓🎓🎓🎓 1/2

Overall Class Size (Honors-only plus mixed, contract): 🎓🎓🎓 1/2

Honors Grad Rate: 🎓🎓🎓🎓 1/2

Value-Added Grad Rate: 🎓🎓🎓

Ratio Staff to Students: 🎓🎓🎓🎓🎓

Priority Registration: Yes, honors students register for all courses, honors and otherwise, with the first group of students during each year they are in the program.

Honors Housing Amenities: 🎓🎓🎓 1/2

Honors Housing Availability: 🎓🎓🎓🎓🎓

Prestigious Awards: 🎓🎓🎓🎓🎓

RATING SCORES AND EXPLANATIONS:

Curriculum Requirements (5.0): The most important rating category, the curriculum completion requirement (classes required to complete honors) defines not only what honors students should learn but also the extent to which honors students and faculty are connected in the classroom. If there is a thesis or capstone requirement, it reinforces the individual contact and research skills so important to learning.

The average number of honors semester hours required for completion across all 50 programs is 29.0.

Schreyer Honors College has one set of completion requirements totaling about **35 credits.** Honors options (contract courses) can be used to meet some of the requirements. Specific yearly requirements are as follows:

To meet *first-year* requirements, students must earn 6 credits in Rhetoric and Civic Life, courses that emphasize speaking, writing, online communications, and visual presentations, during their first two semesters at Penn State.

The first-year academic plan is due one day prior to priority registration in the fall semester. The sophomore-year academic plan is due in the spring semester. In addition, it is recommended that first-year students earn an additional 6 honors credits.

Sophomore students must complete a four-semester total of 21 credits in honors courses. "While we do not mandate credit distribution between freshman and sophomore years, it is preferable to complete 12 honor credits in the first year and 9 honor credits during the second year at Penn State." Sophomores should also start planning for the honors thesis.

In the *junior year*, Schreyer students must complete the adviser-approved Academic Plan for all juniors for senior year, in the spring semester of the junior year. Juniors begin the completion of at least 14 honors credits required during the junior/senior block, and continue implementing the honors thesis plans. Students must submit a thesis proposal one year prior to intended semester of graduation. The thesis may be 6 credits, but it must be at least 3 credits.

Honors college *seniors* must complete a current, adviser-approved Academic Plan. They must file a new one, for a fifth year, if graduation is extended beyond eight semesters. The up-to-date thesis proposal must be on file and be approved by the thesis supervisor and the appropriate honors adviser.

Seniors must complete at a minimum the 14 honors credits required during the junior/senior block. Finally, seniors must submit the completed honors thesis, with original signatures of all readers, by the deadline.

AP/IB credits are not counted as replacements for honors courses.

Number of Honors Classes Offered (4.5): This is a measure of the total **adjusted** honors main sections available in the term reported, not including labs and thesis. (Please read the section titled "All about Honors Classes".) An adjusted main section has 3 or more semester credits, or equivalent, and sections with fewer credits receive a lower prorated value.

The program offered a section for every **9.9** students. The average for all 50 programs is 14.2. The lower the number, the better.

In the term reported, **19.6%** of honors class enrollment was **in honors-only sections; 45.2% in mixed honors sections (honors and non-honors students); and 35.2% in contract sections (regular sections in which honors students "contract" to do extra work).** The averages for all fifty programs are 81.3% in honors-only sections; 13.6 % in mixed honors sections; and 5.1% in contract sections.

Number of Honors Classes in Key Disciplines (4.5): The 15 "key" disciplines are biological sciences; business (all); chemistry; communications (especially public speaking); computer science; economics; engineering (all); English; history; math (all); philosophy; physics; political science; psychology; and sociology/anthropology/gender studies. Interdisciplinary sections, such as those often taken for General Education credit in the first two years, do receive a lesser, prorated discipline "credit" because they introduce students to multiple disciplines in an especially engaging way, often with in-depth discussion.

For this measure, mixed and contract sections are not counted as a section in a key discipline unless students taking the sections for honors credit make up at least 10% of the total section enrollment.

In the term reported, the program had a ratio of **17.8 honors students** per each main section in some or all "key disciplines." The mean for all programs is 26.3. The lower the ratio, the better.

In the term reported, the program offered **107 adjusted sections in key disciplines**, and **about 30 were honors-only sections; but in the high number of mixed sections, Schreyer students account for more than 40% of the enrollment, on average.** English had the most sections (21), followed by engineering (17-a high total), communications (13), biology and math (8 each), business (6), history, philosophy, and psychology (5 each), economics and political science (4 each), and chemistry (3). The only discipline not represented was computer science.

The college also offered about 25 sections in "Rhetoric and Civic Life," a required freshmen course.

Even though the Rhetoric classes are interdisciplinary (speaking and writing skills), the college is essentially an example of an excellent **discipline-based program.**

Extent of Honors Enrollment (4.5): Not all honors students take an honors class each term, especially after the first two years. Programs that have fewer honors classes for upper-division honors students will generally have fewer total members in good standing who are actually enrolled in a given term. (Please be aware, however, that honors students not enrolled in a class for a term are still connected to the honors community through residential and extracurricular activities.)

For example, if honors students in a program occupy 1,800 honors classroom seats in a given term, and there are 3,000 honors students in good standing, the extent of enrollment is .67. For programs that require a thesis, the ratio (score) reported below might in fact be somewhat higher, since we only count "regular" class enrollment for this measure, and not thesis enrollment. The program has a ratio of **1.36**; the mean is 1.13 for all 50 programs. The higher the ratio, the better.

Average Class Size, Honors-only Sections (4.5): Offered mostly in the first two years, honors-only classes tend to be smaller and, as the name implies, have no or very few students other than those in the honors program. These class sections are almost always much smaller than mixed or contract sections, or regular non-honors class sections in the university.

The average honors-only class size in the honors program is **16.3 students**. The average for all 50 programs is 19.0 students.

Average Class Size, Overall (3.5): The overall class calculation is based on the *proportion* of honors students in each type of class (honors-only, mixed honors, and honors contract sections). Thus it is not a raw average. The overall honors-credit class size is **33.0 students**, versus the average for all 50 programs of 26.3 students.

These class size averages also do not correspond to the number of students per honors sections numbers above. The reason is that, in computing average class size metrics, we include enrollment in each 1-2-credit section, not just sections with 3 or more credits.

Along with the honors-only average of 16.3 students, the mixed honors sections average **18.2 students,** and the contract sections with honors credit for individual honors students average **61.2 students.** Across all fifty programs, the average mixed honors section has 51.1 students, and the average contract section has 60.1 students.

Honors Graduation Rate (4.5): The rating is based on the actual grad rate for students who entered the program six years earlier, whether or not the students remained in honors. The **actual rate of 93%** is also compared to the rates of other programs with the same test score entry requirement range, and then adjusted to the **score of 93%.** In some cases this measure favors programs within universities with relatively higher test scores for the student population as a whole. The average honors graduation rate for all programs with similar test scores required for admission is 86.2%. *The college also had a four-year graduation rate of 88%.*

Value-Added Grad Rate (3.0): The value-added rate measures the extent to which the adjusted score listed above exceeds the six-year grad rate for the university as a whole. **The university-wide rate is 86%.** Note: This measure generally favors programs within universities with relatively lower test scores for the student population as a whole.

Ratio of Staff to Honors Students (5.0): There is 1 staff member for every **79.2** students. (Mean ratio for all 50 programs is 1 staff member for every 135.6 students.)

Honors Residence Halls, Amenities (3.5): Assignment of honors dorm space for freshmen and upperclassmen is about evenly divided between two long-time residences for honors students: Atherton and Simmons. About 95% of the rooms in both halls are traditional doubles with hall baths. Neither dorm is air-conditioned. The most convenient dining for both Atherton and Simmons is Redifer Commons. Both residences are coed.

Honors Residence Halls, Availability (5.0): This rating compares the number of places in honors residence halls to the number of honors freshman and sophomore members in good standing, about 950. The ratio for the honors program is **1.23** rooms for each first- and second-year student. The average for all fifty programs is .63 places.

Prestigious Awards (5.0): The awards that we track and include are listed in the section titled "Prestigious Scholarships." The awards are sometimes won by students who are not in an honors college or program, but increasingly many are enrolled in honors programs. It is also a trend that honors colleges and programs help to prepare their students for the awards competitions.

"Penn State University has an Office of Undergraduate Fellowships, where all Penn State students can explore options for prestigious scholarship/fellowship awards. The honors college works very closely with this office to promote these opportunities to Schreyer Scholars. Recent results have included Schreyer Scholars receiving a Churchill Scholarship, Marshall Scholarship, Gates-Cambridge Scholarship, recognition as Junior Fellow of the Carnegie Endowment for International Peace and numerous Fulbright Scholarship winners."

In all, PSU students have won 2 Rhodes scholarships, 9 Gates Cambridge awards, 7 Marshall scholarships, a Churchill scholarship, and 8 Truman awards. PSU undergraduates have an outstanding record of winning Udall scholarships (21) and Goldwater scholarships (61).

UNRATED FEATURES

Continuation Requirements: For continuation and for graduation, a 3.40 GPA is required.

Academic Strengths, National Rankings: This is based on national rankings of *graduate* programs in 15 disciplines, except engineering and business, where undergraduate rankings are used.

Penn State has one of the top faculties in the country, with the average departmental ranking being better than 30th in the nation. The most outstanding departments are earth sciences (6), sociology (17), engineering (18), chemistry (21), business (22), physics (23), English (26), economics (27), math and political science (both 28), computer science (29), and psychology (30).

Undergraduate Research: "All Schreyer Scholars are required to complete an undergraduate honors thesis. This work represents the culmination of a student's honors experience. Through the thesis, the student demonstrates a command of relevant scholastic work and a personal contribution to that scholarship.

"The thesis project can take many forms--from laboratory experiments all the way to artistic creations. The thesis document captures the relevant background, methods and techniques, as well as describing the details of the completion of the individual project.

"In addition to writing the thesis, most Scholars conduct other kinds of undergraduate research during their years at Schreyer Honors College.

"We feature in-person research presentations from our scholars each month during an undergraduate research forum, titled 'Scones and Scholarship' in the honors college.

"All Scholars are encouraged to record a 2-3 minute video highlighting the salient features of their research."

Study Abroad: "Penn State offers nearly 300 programs each year to many different countries spread across six continents. Schreyer Scholars take advantage of these programs to enhance their academic experience and are eligible to receive Schreyer Ambassador Travel Grants to help meet their travel expenses. Over $200,000 in travel grant funds are awarded each year to scholars studying overseas.

"Schreyer Honors College Programs Include:

"India: In the spring, students take a three-credit honors interdisciplinary course that introduces them to contemporary India. This course follows the specific disciplinary interests of the instructors, but includes a wide range of topics and issues to prepare students for the in-country experience.

"South America: We are applying the model of the (continuing) India program to South America, specifically to Brazil and Colombia. Brazil is, of course, the largest country in South America by a wide margin in both area and population, while Colombia is the largest Spanish-speaking country in South America by population.

"London Study Tour: For thirty-two years the SHC has offered a short-term theatre and cultural studies program in London over spring or winter break. Our goal is to provide Scholars who otherwise would not have an opportunity for arts and humanities study abroad with an honors-quality experience that will make a lasting impact on them, and we know from our alums that the LST has done that.

"Freiburg Honors Exchange: Within the overall Penn State-University of Freiburg exchange framework, the SHC and University College Freiburg (UCF) started an honors-to-honors exchange in 2014-15."

Financial Aid: "The Schreyer Honors College offers a $4,500 Academic Excellence Scholarship to all scholars entering the college their freshmen year. This award is renewable for each of the four years they are enrolled in the honors college.

"Additional need and merit based scholarships are available to Schreyer Scholars. Each academic year, the honors college awards over $1 million to scholars to support their academic studies, research and internship experiences.

"Our development team also conducts an annual campaign with the parents of our current scholars. They raise funds for our emergency scholarship program which supports scholars who find themselves in unanticipated financial crises. This campaign typically raises $35-40,000 each year, which supports between 15-20 scholars during the academic year."

Honors Fees: A $25/semester fee is assessed to all Schreyer scholars to support the programming efforts of the college. This fee also grants all scholars access to the residence hall facilities, regardless of where they might live on campus.

Placement Experiences: "Highlights for the 2015 graduating class include: 37% of our graduates went directly into graduate school; 52% reported going directly into the workforce; 11% chose other options, including service and research opportunities

"The Schreyer Honors College recently undertook a ground-breaking research project to determine the *success of our graduates five and ten years post-graduation.* By obtaining data through the National Student Clearinghouse, we have been able to determine a complete and accurate picture of the academic paths of our graduating scholars. [Emphasis added.]

"This research has resulted in our accurately being able to report the following data, also available on our web site: 29% of our graduates earned an advanced degree within 5 years of earning their bachelor's degree: 74% of our graduates earned an advanced degree within 10 years of earning their bachelor's degree; after 10 years, 58 of the 454 members of the 2005-06 graduating class had earned a doctoral degree."

Degree of Difference: This is based on the differences between (1) the average (2015, two-part) SAT scores for enrolled honors students (est. 1368) and (2) the average test scores for all students in the university (1190) as a whole. The test scores may be an indication of how "elite" honors students may be perceived as compared to students in the university as a whole. The scores can also provide an indication of how well prepared the non-honors students in the university may be. **Please keep in mind that neither high nor low test scores determine the overall quality of a program.**

NAME: PURDUE UNIVERSITY HONORS COLLEGE.

Date Established: The University Honors Program was established in 2005, and transitioned to the Purdue University Honors College in 2013.

Location: West Lafayette, Indiana.

University Full-time Undergraduate Enrollment: 27,881.

Honors Members in Good Standing: 1,888 (mean size of all 50 programs is 1,742).

Honors Average Admission Statistics: ACT, 31.68; old SAT, 1357; est. new SAT, 1420.

Average High School GPA/Class Rank: 3.95.

Basic Admission Requirements: "We use a holistic review process."

Application Deadline(s): *Please verify with each program, as some deadlines could change.*

Priority deadline using Common or Coalition App is November 1, 2016.

Honors Programs with old SAT scores from 1351—1396: Purdue, Oregon, Alabama, Massachusetts, Penn State, Indiana, CUNY Macaulay, Texas A&M, NJIT, Missouri, Oregon State, Delaware, LSU, Vermont, Temple.

Administrative Staff: 25.

RATINGS AT A GLANCE: For all mortarboard ratings immediately below, a score of 5 is the maximum and represents a comparison with all 50 honors colleges and programs. More detailed explanations follow the "mortarboard" ratings.

PERCEPTION* OF UNIVERSITY AS A WHOLE, NOT OF HONORS: 🎓🎓🎓🎓 1/2

*Perception is based on the university's ranking among public universities in the 2016 U.S. News Best Colleges report. Please bear in mind that the better the U.S. News ranking, the more difficult it is for an honors college or program to have a rating that equals or improves on the magazine ranking.

OVERALL HONORS RATING: 🎓🎓🎓🎓

Curriculum Requirements: 🎓🎓🎓 1/2

Number of Honors Classes Offered: 🎓🎓🎓🎓

Number of Honors Classes in Key Disciplines: 🎓🎓🎓🎓

Extent of Honors Enrollment: 🎓 🎓 🎓 🎓

Honors-only Class Size: 🎓 🎓 🎓 🎓 1/2

Overall Class Size (Honors-only plus mixed, contract): 🎓 🎓 🎓 🎓 1/2

Honors Grad Rate: 🎓 🎓 🎓 1/2

Value-Added Grad Rate: 🎓 🎓 🎓 1/2

Ratio of Staff to Students: 🎓 🎓 🎓 🎓 🎓

Priority Registration: Yes, honors students register for all courses, honors and otherwise, with the first group of students during each year they are in the program.

Honors Housing Amenities: 🎓 🎓 🎓 🎓 🎓

Honors Housing Availability: 🎓 🎓 🎓 🎓 🎓

Prestigious Awards: 🎓 🎓 🎓 🎓 1/2

RATING SCORES AND EXPLANATIONS:

Curriculum Requirements (3.5): The most important rating category, the curriculum completion requirement (classes required to complete honors) defines not only what honors students should learn but also the extent to which honors students and faculty are connected in the classroom. If there is a thesis or capstone requirement, it reinforces the individual contact and research skills so important to learning.

The average number of honors semester hours required for completion across all 50 programs is 29.0.

Graduation from the Honors College requires a minimum of **24** honors course credits, including a thesis or scholarly project.

Students must have 2 credits from the first-year honors seminar credits and an additional 3 credits from an HONR designated course. The other 19 honors course credits may be earned through higher level HONOR courses, honors contract courses, graduate courses, or research credits. Research credits must be part of the work toward a thesis.

Students may satisfy the thesis or scholarly project requirement by choosing ONE of the following options: a departmental or college honors thesis or honors capstone project; an interdisciplinary honors thesis/scholarly project; or a scholarly project approved by a faculty committee appointed by the Dean of the Honors College.

AP/IB credits are not counted as replacements for honors courses

Number of Honors Classes Offered (4.0): This is a measure of the total **adjusted** honors main sections available in the term reported, not including labs and thesis. (Please read the section titled "All about Honors Classes".) An adjusted main section has 3 or more semester credits, or equivalent, and sections with fewer credits receive a lower prorated value.

The program offered a section for every **15.0** students. The average for all 50 programs is 14.2. The lower the number, the better.

In the term reported, **93.8%** of honors class enrollment was **in honors-only sections; none in mixed honors sections (honors and non-honors students); and 6.2% reported in contract sections (regular sections in which honors students "contract" to do extra work).** The averages for all fifty programs are 81.3% in honors-only sections; 13.6 % in mixed honors sections; and 5.1% in contract sections.

Number of Honors Classes in Key Disciplines (4.0): The 15 "key" disciplines are biological sciences; business (all); chemistry; communications (especially public speaking); computer science; economics; engineering (all); English; history; math (all); philosophy; physics; political science; psychology; and sociology/anthropology/gender studies. Interdisciplinary sections, such as those often taken for General Education credit in the first two years, do receive a lesser, prorated discipline "credit" because they introduce students to multiple disciplines in an especially engaging way, often with in-depth discussion.

For this measure, mixed and contract sections are not counted as a section in a key discipline unless students taking the sections for honors credit make up at least 10% of the total section enrollment.

In the term reported, the program had a ratio of **29.0 honors students** per each main section in some or all "key disciplines." The mean for all programs is 26.3. The lower the ratio, the better.

The college offered **48 adjusted sections in key disciplines**, and **46 were honors-only sections.**

The honors college shows a commitment to developing communications skills, an important complement to the excellence in the STEM disciplines that the university offers. There are 7 honors sections on the Fundamentals of Speech, while 3 others focus on organizational communication, technical communication, and the interpretation of communications. With the 9th ranked engineering school offering the highest level of instruction in all engineering disciplines, the honors college nevertheless had 4 sections in engineering. Other key sections were in math and psychology (7 each) and philosophy and physics (3 each). The remaining sections were in chemistry, English, and history (2 each). Sociology, anthropology, and/or gender studies combined had 7 more sections.

The college also offered more than 40 seminar sections, including 22 in the 1-credit course titled "The Evolution of Ideas," in which students, over eight weeks, are introduced "to critical thinking, cultural critique, and the history of ideas. Each section of the course focuses on a single 'idea' that is significant for modern life." Another dozen or so 3-credit seminars included "Reading & Seeing Middle Ages"; "Paradigm Shifts Biology & Medicine"; and "Animals, Science, and Education."

The honors college, with interesting seminars and courses in the disciplines, is a strong example of a **blended honors program.**

Extent of Honors Enrollment (4.0): Not all honors students take an honors class each term, especially after the first two years. Programs that have fewer honors classes for upper-division honors students will generally have fewer total members in good standing who are actually enrolled in a given term. (Please be aware, however, that honors students not enrolled in a class for a term are still connected to the honors community through residential and extracurricular activities.)

For example, if honors students in a program occupy 1,800 honors classroom seats in a given term, and there are 3,000 honors students in good standing, the extent of enrollment is .67. For programs that require a thesis, the ratio (score) reported below might in fact be somewhat higher, since we only count "regular" class enrollment for this measure, and not thesis enrollment. The program **has a ratio of 1.15**; the mean is 1.13 for all 50 programs. The higher the ratio, the better.

Average Class Size, Honors-only Sections (4.5): Offered mostly in the first two years, honors-only classes tend to be smaller and, as the name implies, have no or very few students other than those in the honors program. These class sections are almost always much smaller than mixed or contract sections, or regular non-honors class sections in the university.

The average honors-only class size in the honors program is **16.5 students**. The average for all 50 programs is 19.0 students.

Average Class Size, Overall (4.5): The overall class calculation is based on the *proportion* of honors students in each type of class (honors-only, mixed honors, and honors contract sections). Thus it is not a raw average. The overall honors-credit class size is **20.5 students**, versus the average for all 50 programs of 26.3 students.

These class size averages also do not correspond to the number of students per honors sections numbers above. The reason is that, in computing average class size metrics, we include enrollment in each 1-2-credit section, not just sections with 3 or more credits.

Along with the honors-only average of 16.5 students, the mixed honors sections average **(not applicable)**, and the contract sections with honors credit for individual honors students averaged **81.6** students. Across all fifty programs, the average mixed honors section has 51.1 students, and the average contract section has 60.1 students.

Honors Graduation Rate (3.5): The rating is based on the actual grad rate for students who entered the program six years earlier, whether or not the students remained in honors. The **actual rate of 81.9%** is also compared to the rates of other programs with the same test score entry requirement range, and then adjusted to the **score of 81.5%.** In some cases this measure favors programs within universities with relatively higher test scores for the student population as a whole. The average honors graduation rate for all programs with similar test scores required for admission is 86.2%. Note: The Honors College rate is far lower than the rate reported in the 2014 edition, and it is our understanding that a brief change in selection procedures, now no longer in place, caused the drop in the graduation rate for students who began honors in 2009. The rate in the 2014 edition was 94%.

Value-Added Grad Rate (3.5): The value-added rate measures the extent to which the adjusted score listed above exceeds the six-year grad rate for the university as a whole. **The university-wide rate is 74%.**

Note: This measure generally favors programs within universities with relatively lower test scores for the student population as a whole.

Ratio of Staff to Honors Students (5.0): There is 1 staff member for every **75.5** students. (Mean ratio for all 50 programs is 1 staff member for every 135.6 students.)

Honors Residence Halls, Amenities (5.0): Important news on the housing front: "Beginning in August, 2016, we will transition all freshmen and several hundred upper-division students to our new 322,000 square-foot complex that includes the Honors College offices, study spaces, STEAM lab, music practice rooms, art and maker spaces, on-site restaurant, gardens, and the Innovation Forum to display research."

The new Honors College and Residences complex is home to almost 800 honors students. The facility combines ready access to college staff with air-conditioned, suite-style rooms and on-site dining. Formerly, freshman honors students lived in Shreve Hall. An additional 100 upper-division honors women reside in historic Duhme Hall, and 150 upper-division students live in the Third Street Suites, a coed facility. Both feature air-conditioned, suite-style rooms with shared baths. Dining for Duhme is at Windsor Dining Court; for Third Street Suites, it is Wiley Dining Court, also convenient to the Honors College and Residences.

Honors Residence Halls, Availability (5.0): This rating compares the number of places in honors residence halls to the number of honors freshman and sophomore members in good standing, about 944. The ratio for the honors program is **1.08** rooms for each first- and second-year student. The average for all fifty programs is .63 places.

Prestigious Awards (4.5): The awards that we track and include are listed in the section titled "Prestigious Scholarships." The awards are sometimes won by students who are not in an honors college or program, but increasingly many are enrolled in honors programs. It is also a trend that honors colleges and programs help to prepare their students for the awards competitions.

"The National and International Scholarships Office (NISO) is housed within the Honors College," the Dean reports. "The initial investments we have made are paying off with a 2015-2016 Churchill Scholar and Purdue's first Mitchell Scholar to Ireland. For reference, the Mitchell Scholarship is for Irish universities what the Marshall Scholarship is for British universities, and its Scholars have a similar profile. Renewed, strong faculty support for Fulbright U.S. Student Program applicants has led to large increases in participation for Fulbright across campus. Purdue kept up its tradition of STEM students receiving Goldwater Scholarships this year and is one of a handful of public universities with Astronaut Scholars."

As one would expect, Purdue students have a strong record of winning awards that are associated with excellence in the STEM disciplines, including 45 Goldwater scholarships and 12 Churchill scholarships, the latter total ranking third among all public universities. Purdue students have also won 2 Rhodes scholarships and 6 Marshall scholarships, along with a high number of NSF graduate research fellowships.

UNRATED FEATURES

Continuation Requirements: For continuation and for graduation, a 3.50 GPA is required.

Academic Strengths, National Rankings: This is based on national rankings of *graduate* programs in 15 disciplines, except engineering and business, where undergraduate rankings are used.

Academic departments at Purdue have an average national ranking of about 40-42. Along with the previously mentioned (and renowned) engineering department (9), outstanding departments include computer science (20), chemistry (21), business (22), math (28), and earth sciences, economics, and education (42 each).

Undergraduate Research: "The curriculum requires that students complete a 'thesis or scholarly project' that is either a research or creative project, depending on the student's field and interests. This independent thesis project pairs the student with a faculty mentor or mentors and takes place outside of traditional coursework. Students may undertake either a disciplinary thesis through their home department/college or an interdisciplinary thesis through the Honors College. In either the disciplinary or interdisciplinary case, students are required to present the findings of their project in a public forum (e.g. publication or poster session.)

"If students participate in the interdisciplinary thesis program, they are required to take two courses: HONR 399, Thesis Prep Workshop; and HONR 399, Thesis Writing Workshop. The first course offers instruction on research methodologies and practices, and it takes students through the definition of a research question and the writing of a research proposal. The second course instructs them on how to write up and present research findings. These two courses are supported by online research modules, developed in collaboration with Purdue Libraries, which are available to all Honors College students.

"In addition to the thesis/scholarly project program, all Honors College students may apply for research funding through the college to support their research work. They can use this money to travel to conferences, purchase equipment, or pay for housing during an unpaid research experience, for example."

Study Abroad: "The Purdue Honors College's major achievement in just its third year of existence was the establishment of an exchange program between the Purdue Honors College and the University of Padua's honors college, the Scuola Galileiana di Studi Superiori. The basis of the exchange is that one student from the Scuola Galileiana di Studi Superiori attends Purdue as a member of the Honors College during the fall semester, while the PHC sends two of its students to Padua's honors college during the spring semester. The program and the PHC students selected as 'Copernican Scholars' for the spring of 2016 in Padua served as his ambassadors. *The Purdue Honors College is very proud of this opportunity for our students to study abroad in an Italian honors college (for less money than they would owe to stay at Purdue), thanks to Honors College and Purdue University scholarships.*" [Emphasis added.]

"To help incentivize study abroad experiences for Purdue students, the University provides Purdue Moves scholarships for everyone who qualifies as a student in good standing. For example, our Copernican Scholars received $3,000 through Purdue's incentive for students who spend a semester or year abroad, and they also received a travel grant from the Purdue Honors College for their travel to and from Padua. Purdue also provides $2,000 scholarships to students spending at least six weeks studying abroad in the summer and earn at least six credits, and there are $1,000 scholarships for shorter term summer, winter, and spring programs.

"Also, starting with the summer of 2015, the Purdue Honors College has offered its own honors-only programs led by at least one Honors College core faculty member. The three initial programs offered (one during May and early June 2015 and two offered during spring break 2016 have enrolled 48 Purdue Honors Students. Offerings of such programs will increase in the future."

Financial Aid: A total of 510 first-year honors students received scholarships in 2015:

11 honors students won either a Stamps or Beering scholarship, each providing most or all costs of attendance;

83 received a Trustee scholarship, $10,000 a year for residents (29) and $16,000 a year for non-residents (54);

332 received a Presidential scholarship, ranging in value from $4,000 to $10,000 a year;

34 received Emerging Leader scholarships, valued at $10,000 a year for residents (23) and $15,000 a year for non-residents (11);

50 received National Merit scholarships valued at $1,000.

Honors Fees: None.

Placement Experiences: "Approximately 75% of honors completers continue their educational studies in graduate or professional programs. The remaining 25% pursue positions in industry."

Degree of Difference: This is based on the differences between (1) the average (2015, two-part) SAT scores for enrolled honors students (1357) and (2) the average test scores for all students in the university (1205) as a whole. The test scores may be an indication of how "elite" honors students may be perceived as compared to students in the university as a whole. The scores can also provide an indication of how well prepared the non-honors students in the university may be. **Please keep in mind that neither high nor low test scores determine the overall quality of a program.**

NAME: SOUTH CAROLINA HONORS COLLEGE, UNIVERSITY OF SOUTH CAROLINA.

Date Established: 1965 as a program, 1978 as a college.

Location: Columbia, South Carolina.

University <u>Full-time Undergraduate</u> Enrollment: 23,177.

Honors Members in Good Standing: 1,706 (mean size of all 50 programs is 1,742).

Honors <u>Average</u> Admission Statistics: ACT, 32.4; old SAT equivalent, 1431; est. new SAT, 1480.

Average High School GPA/Class Rank: 4.65; top 4%.

<u>Basic</u> Admission Requirements: None listed. "Students not accepted into the Honors College initially may apply to transfer into the Honors College after the freshman year. Transfer admission is competitive and is based on GPA, letters of recommendation, an essay, and availability of space."

Application Deadline(s): *Please verify with each program, as some deadlines could change.*

Deadline for scholarships and honors college admission is November 15, 2016, with notification of university admission in late December, 2016. Honors notification in late February, 2017.

Honors Programs with old SAT scores from 1402—1469: UCF, Connecticut, Kentucky, Washington, Maryland, North Carolina, UC Irvine, Kansas, Minnesota, Tennessee, South Carolina, Clemson, UT Austin, Georgia.

Administrative Staff: 28.5

RATINGS AT A GLANCE: For all mortarboard ratings immediately below, a score of 5 is the maximum and represents a comparison with all 50 honors colleges and programs. More detailed explanations follow the "mortarboard" ratings.

PERCEPTION* OF UNIVERSITY AS A WHOLE, <u>NOT</u> OF HONORS: 🎓🎓🎓🎓

*Perception is based on the university's ranking among public universities in the 2016 U.S. News Best Colleges report. Please bear in mind that the better the U.S. News ranking, the more difficult it is for an honors college or program to have a rating that equals or improves on the magazine ranking.

OVERALL HONORS RATING: 🎓🎓🎓🎓🎓

Curriculum Requirements: 🎓🎓🎓🎓🎓

Number of Honors Classes Offered: 🎓🎓🎓🎓🎓

Number of Honors Classes in Key Disciplines: 🎓🎓🎓🎓🎓

Extent of Honors Enrollment: 🎓🎓🎓🎓🎓

Honors-only Class Size: 🎓🎓🎓🎓^{1/2}

Overall Class Size (Honors-only plus mixed, contract): 🎓🎓🎓🎓^{1/2}

Honors Grad Rate: 🎓🎓🎓🎓🎓

Value-Added Grad Rate: 🎓🎓🎓🎓

Ratio of Staff to Students: 🎓🎓🎓🎓🎓

Priority Registration: Yes, honors students register for all courses, honors and otherwise, with the first group of students during each year they are in the program.

Honors Housing Amenities: 🎓🎓🎓🎓🎓

Honors Housing Availability: 🎓🎓🎓🎓🎓

Prestigious Awards: 🎓🎓🎓🎓^{1/2}

RATING SCORES AND EXPLANATIONS:

Curriculum Requirements (5.0): The most important rating category, the curriculum completion requirement (classes required to complete honors) defines not only what honors students should learn but also the extent to which honors students and faculty are connected in the classroom. If there is a thesis or capstone requirement, it reinforces the individual contact and research skills so important to learning.

The average number of honors semester hours required for completion across all 50 programs is 29.0.

The minimum requirement for Graduating with Honors from the South Carolina Honors College is **45 honors credits,** but the college has two other options that require **69 honors credits.**

The 45-credit requirement includes a minimum of 39 credits in honors courses, a 3-credit **thesis**, and 3 credits from "Beyond the Classroom" options, such as credits for research, internships, study abroad, or from service-learning credits. "Students on average complete about 54 honors credit hours," the Dean tells us.

A more research-intensive option is the **Baccalaureus Artium et Scientiae (BARSC)** degree. The degree requires **69 credits,** including a research/thesis component of 9-15 credits. Another 3 credits from "Beyond the Classroom" options are required.

The **BARSC/MD** program has requirements similar to the BARSC above, but it *"allows students in it to graduate with the degree and one year of medical school completed. Students completing this program are automatically admitted into the University of South Carolina School of Medicine, Columbia. The Honors College also has an early admission program with the University's other medical school, the School of Medicine, Greenville."*

AP/IB credits are not counted as replacements for honors courses.

Number of Honors Classes Offered (5.0): This is a measure of the total **adjusted** honors main sections available in the term reported, not including labs and thesis. (Please read the section titled "All about Honors Classes".) An adjusted main section has 3 or more semester credits, or equivalent, and sections with fewer credits receive a lower prorated value.

The program offered a section for every **8.3** students. The average for all 50 programs is 14.2. The lower the number, the better.

In the term reported, **88.8%** of honors class enrollment was **in honors-only sections; 11.2% in mixed honors sections (honors and non-honors students); and none in contract sections (regular sections in which honors students "contract" to do extra work).** The averages for all fifty programs are 81.3% in honors-only sections; 13.6 % in mixed honors sections; and 5.1% in contract sections.

Number of Honors Classes in Key Disciplines (5.0): The 15 "key" disciplines are biological sciences; business (all); chemistry; communications (especially public speaking); computer science; economics; engineering (all); English; history; math (all); philosophy; physics; political science; psychology; and sociology/anthropology/gender studies. Interdisciplinary sections, such as those often taken for General Education credit in the first two years, do receive a lesser, prorated discipline "credit" because they introduce students to multiple disciplines in an especially engaging way, often with in-depth discussion.

For this measure, mixed and contract sections are not counted as a section in a key discipline unless students taking the sections for honors credit make up at least 10% of the total section enrollment.

In the term reported, the program had a ratio of **12.8 honors students** per each main section in some or all "key disciplines." The mean for all programs is 26.3. The lower the ratio, the better.

The college offered **123 adjusted sections in key disciplines**, and **105 were honors-only sections.** English had the most sections (23), followed by business (17), math (13), chemistry (9), philosophy (8), engineering, history, and psychology (7 each), biology (6), physics (5), political science (4), communications and economics (3), and computer science (2). Sociology, anthropology, and/or gender studies combined had 10 more sections.

The college also offered about 30 seminar sections (in addition to others with a clear disciplinary emphasis that were included as "key disciplines" above). Among the seminar sections were "Pestilence, Plague, and Contagion in the Western Tradition"; "Connecting Life & Leadership"; "Authenticity: How to Live a Good Life and Be True To Yourself"; and "Brain and Evolution."

"The combination of interdisciplinary seminars with a very large number of honors classes in the disciplines is an outstanding example of a **blended honors program.**

Extent of Honors Enrollment (5.0): Not all honors students take an honors class each term, especially after the first two years. Programs that have fewer honors classes for upper-division honors students will generally have fewer total members in good standing who are actually enrolled in a given term. (Please be aware, however, that honors students not enrolled in a class for a term are still connected to the honors community through residential and extracurricular activities.)

For example, if honors students in a program occupy 1,800 honors classroom seats in a given term, and there are 3,000 honors students in good standing, the extent of enrollment is .67. For programs that require a thesis, the ratio (score) reported below might in fact be somewhat higher, since we only count "regular" class enrollment for this measure, and not thesis enrollment. The program has ratio of **1.82**; the mean is 1.13 for all 50 programs. The higher the ratio, the better.

Average Class Size, Honors-only Sections (4.5): Offered mostly in the first two years, honors-only classes tend to be smaller and, as the name implies, have no or very few students other than those in the honors program. These class sections are almost always much smaller than mixed or contract sections, or regular non-honors class sections in the university.

The average honors-only class size in the honors program is **17.8 students**. The average for all 50 programs is 19.0 students.

Average Class Size, Overall (4.5): The overall class calculation is based on the *proportion* of honors students in each type of class (honors-only, mixed honors, and honors contract sections). Thus it is not a raw average. The overall honors-credit class size is **20.5 students**, versus the average for all 50 programs of 26.3 students.

These class size averages also do not correspond to the number of students per honors sections numbers above. The reason is that, in computing average class size metrics, we include enrollment in each 1-2-credit section, not just sections with 3 or more credits.

Along with the honors-only average of 17.8 students, the mixed honors sections average **42.0 students,** and the contract sections with honors credit for individual honors students average **(NA)** students. Across all fifty programs, the average mixed honors section has 51.1 students, and the average contract section has 60.1 students.

Honors Graduation Rate (5.0): The rating is based on the actual grad rate for students who entered the program six years earlier, whether or not the students remained in honors. The **actual rate of 93%** is also compared to the rates of other programs with the same test score entry requirement range, and then adjusted to the **score of 93%.** In some cases this measure favors programs within universities with relatively higher test scores for the student population as a whole. *The college also had a four-year graduation rate of 88%.* The average honors graduation rate for all programs with similar test scores required for admission is 92.6%.

Value-Added Grad Rate (4.0): The value-added rate measures the extent to which the adjusted score listed above exceeds the six-year grad rate for the university as a whole. **The university-wide rate is 73%.** Note: This measure generally favors programs within universities with relatively lower test scores for the student population as a whole.

Ratio of Staff to Honors Students (5.0): There is 1 staff member for every **59.9** students. (Mean ratio for all 50 programs is 1 staff member for every 135.6 students.)

Honors Residence Halls, Amenities (5.0): The honors dorms are the Honors Residential Hall and the Historic Horseshoe. The Honors Residential Hall houses just over half of the honors students living on campus, with freshmen (70%) and upperclassmen (30%) sharing the hall. The residence has air-conditioned, suite-style rooms with shared baths, and its own dining hall, The Honeycomb Café. There are three living/learning themes: (Fine Arts, Sustainability, and Health and Wellness).

The residents of the Historic Horseshoe are about 88% upperclassmen. The residence has air-conditioned, apartment-style rooms, with kitchens, bathrooms, *and* washer/dryers in all apartments. Dining is at McCutcheon House located on the Horseshoe or at Russell House Student Union across the street. Historic Horseshoe has the same living/learning themes as the Honors Residential Hall.

650 Lincoln houses upperclassmen only. Residents live in apartments with features like those at the Historic Horseshoe. Dining is at the Community Table, on the first floor of the residence.

All of the residences are coed.

Honors Residence Halls, Availability (5.0): This rating compares the number of places in honors residence halls to the number of honors freshman and sophomore members in good standing, about 853. The ratio for the honors program is **1.16** rooms for each first- and second-year student. The average for all fifty programs is .63 places.

Prestigious Awards (4.5): The awards that we track and include are listed in the section titled "Prestigious Scholarships." The awards are sometimes won by students who are not in an honors college or program, but increasingly many are enrolled in honors programs. It is also a trend that honors colleges and programs help to prepare their students for the awards competitions.

"Established in 1994, the Office of Fellowships and Scholar Programs (six people) reports to the Dean of the South Carolina Honors College and is housed in the same building. In the 2014-2015 academic year, 237 applications were submitted by undergraduates, graduate students, and recent alumni in 55 competitions, with 57 winners earning awards totaling $2,280,000," the Dean reports.

"We have had national winners in every scholarship competition tracked (except Churchill which is invitation-only by institution), including: a Gates Cambridge Scholar in 2016, 24 consecutive years of Goldwater Scholars, two Marshall Scholars (the only institution in SC to have a Marshall Scholar), and eight Rhodes Scholars in the institution's history. In 2015 USC tied as a top producer of NOAA Hollings Scholars with nine, and another eight students were selected as Hollings Scholars in 2016. In the last three years, USC has had 94 applicants for the Gilman Scholarship and 32 winners.

"Goldwater, Udall, Hollings, Gilman and other undergraduate national fellowship winners that have yet to graduate serve as national fellowship interns and help with outreach and recruitment of future applicants. Approximately 65 faculty are appointed annually to serve as advisors and as members of nomination committees and practice interview teams." USC students have won an impressive 49 Goldwater scholarships and 14 Udall awards.

UNRATED FEATURES

Continuation Requirements: "There is a sliding GPA requirement. Students are required to maintain at least a 3.0 in their first two semesters (fall and spring), at least a 3.1 in their second two semesters, 3.2 in their third two major semesters, and 3.3 in their final semesters to remain in good standing and graduate 'with Honors'."

Academic Strengths, National Rankings: This is based on national rankings of *graduate* programs in 15 disciplines, except engineering and business, where undergraduate rankings are used.
The departments at South Carolina average between 90 and 100 in the nation. Especially strong departments are business (43—international business (1); political science (54), sociology (69), earth sciences and English (both 77), education (78), and chemistry and history (84).

Undergraduate Research: "In this current academic year, 426 honors students (24.9%) received research funding from the Honors College and/or completed a research project, including senior thesis research. An additional substantial number of students received research funding from the University, or worked for faculty on grant-funded projects, or volunteered as members of research teams. All students (100%) graduating 'with honors' complete a senior thesis, and the vast majority of these projects include 'research' in some sense. Overall, about 33% of honors students engage in research in addition to and apart from their senior thesis.

"The Honors College has a robust undergraduate research program. The Exploration Scholars Program is for Honors students in the arts, social sciences, humanities, journalism and other fields (qualitative research). The Science Undergraduate Research Fellowship is for students in natural sciences, technology, engineering, mathematics, and related fields. Out of an annual fund of $285,000, Honors students are eligible to receive up to $4,500 for research from the Honors College. They may also apply for an additional $4,500 in research funds from the University's Magellan Programs. Students may also apply for senior thesis grants and for travel grants to present their research findings.

"The Honors College Faculty Fellows, composed of 15 to 20 of the University's most illustrious faculty, serve two-year terms as mentors and advisors to honors students, and they often play an important role in helping students find research projects and directors. The Office of Undergraduate Research at USC also helps to connect students with faculty research mentors by means of a searchable data base of faculty mentors and research scholarships. There is an annual Discovery Day, a forum for students to present their research on campus, and 183 honors students participated in the most recent iteration of this event. Students also present their research findings at professional meetings and in professional journals."

Study Abroad: "About 50% of Honors graduates study abroad during their college career, including students in every major. They go all over, from Argentina to Zambia, but about 58% choose a country in Europe as their destination, followed by South America, Latin America and the Caribbean. Scholarship funds are available to all students, ranging up to $5,000, to help with study abroad expenses, with over $800,000 awarded in 2014-2015.

"Honors students are served by the University's Study Abroad Office, which offers over 1,500 different overseas programs in over 50 countries every year, and by the Honors College's own study-abroad program, which has sponsored trips to Brazil, Belize, Paris, Scotland, the Netherlands, Argentina,

Uruguay, Eastern Europe, and Japan during the period 2014-2016. The newest study-abroad relationship is with Oxford University (Lady Margaret Hall) and the International Business program."

Financial Aid: "All students accepted into the South Carolina Honors College receive a scholarship of some kind. These include University of South Carolina Scholarships and South Carolina Honors College Departmental Scholarships. The most valuable scholarships include the Belser Scholarship (full tuition) and the Top Scholars program, which includes Stamps Carolina, Carolina Scholars (88), McNair (80), Hamilton (12), and Horseshoe Scholars (7).

Some of these are extremely generous. The McNair Scholarship has a current four-year value of up to $138,000. The others listed above range from $7,000 to $11,000 per year.

For out-of-state students, the Horseshoe Scholarship has a four-year value of more than $114,800.

"Academic Profile for Top Scholars:

"Each group of Scholar Program applicants competes with itself. Therefore, there are no set minimum requirements. Below are some academic averages earned by past scholarship recipients.

"Last year, Carolina and Hamilton Scholars had an average SAT score of 1488 (ACT score of 33) and an average weighted GPA of 4.86.

"Last year, McNair and Horseshoe Scholars had an average SAT score of 1532 (ACT score of 34) and an average weighted high school GPA of 4.79."

Honors Fees: $475 per semester.

Placement Experiences: "Our survey of the 2015 Honors College graduates indicated that at the time of graduation, 30% had accepted enrollment in graduate school; 38% had accepted jobs; 11% had been accepted by and planned to attend medical school; 8% had been accepted by and planned to enroll in law school; 4% had been accepted by and planned to enroll in other professional schools, such as dentistry and physician assistant schools; 4% planned to take a gap year with deferred acceptances into professional or graduate schools; and 6% did not report their plans, were undecided, or were looking for employment."

Degree of Difference: This is based on the differences between (1) the average (2015, two-part) SAT scores for enrolled honors students (1431) and (2) the average test scores for all students in the university (1205) as a whole. The test scores may be an indication of how "elite" honors students may be perceived as compared to students in the university as a whole. The scores can also provide an indication of how well prepared the non-honors students in the university may be. **Please keep in mind that neither high nor low test scores determine the overall quality of a program.**

NAME: UNIVERSITY HONORS PROGRAM, UNIVERSITY OF SOUTH DAKOTA.

Date Established: 1967.

Location: Vermillion, South Dakota.

University Full-time Undergraduate Enrollment: 4,876.

Honors Members in Good Standing: 411 (mean size of all 50 programs is 1,742).

Honors Average Admission Statistics: ACT, 28.9; Old SAT, 1275; est. new SAT, 1335.

Average High School GPA/Class Rank: 3.92. Median class rank, top 7%.

Basic Admission Requirements: ACT, 27. Old SAT, 1267; est. new SAT, 1325. High school GPA, 3.75, top 10%.

Application Deadline(s): *Please verify with each program, as some deadlines could change.*

Applications are accepted on a rolling basis with no firm deadline, but it's recommended that you apply by January of your senior year in high school.

Honors Programs with old SAT scores from 1240—1291: Arkansas, Oklahoma State, Texas Tech, Montana, Washington State, New Mexico, South Dakota, Colorado State, Arizona, Montana State, Arizona State.

Administrative Staff: 4.

RATINGS AT A GLANCE: For all mortarboard ratings immediately below, a score of 5 is the maximum and represents a comparison with all 50 honors colleges and programs. More detailed explanations follow the "mortarboard" ratings.

PERCEPTION* OF UNIVERSITY AS A WHOLE, NOT OF HONORS: 🎓🎓🎓

*Perception is based on the university's ranking among public universities in the 2016 U.S. News Best Colleges report. Please bear in mind that the better the U.S. News ranking, the more difficult it is for an honors college or program to have a rating that equals or improves on the magazine ranking.

OVERALL HONORS RATING: 🎓🎓🎓 1/2

Curriculum Requirements: 🎓🎓🎓 1/2

Number of Honors Classes Offered: 🎓🎓🎓

Number of Honors Classes in Key Disciplines: 🎓🎓🎓🎓

Extent of Honors Enrollment: 🎓🎓🎓$^{1/2}$

Honors-only Class Size: 🎓🎓🎓🎓$^{1/2}$

Overall Class Size (Honors-only plus mixed, contract): 🎓🎓🎓🎓🎓

Honors Grad Rate: 🎓🎓🎓$^{1/2}$

Value-Added Grad Rate: 🎓🎓🎓🎓🎓

Ratio of Staff to Students: 🎓🎓🎓🎓$^{1/2}$

Priority Registration: Yes, honors students register for all courses, honors and otherwise, with the first group of students during each year they are in the program.

Honors Housing Amenities: 🎓🎓🎓🎓

Honors Housing Availability: 🎓🎓🎓🎓$^{1/2}$

Prestigious Awards: 🎓🎓🎓

RATING SCORES AND EXPLANATIONS:

Curriculum Requirements (3.5): The most important rating category, the curriculum completion requirement (classes required to complete honors) defines not only what honors students should learn but also the extent to which honors students and faculty are connected in the classroom. If there is a thesis or capstone requirement, it reinforces the individual contact and research skills so important to learning.

The average number of honors semester hours required for completion across all 50 programs is 29.0.

Graduation as a University Scholar requires about **22-23 credits** on average, including 3 credits each in honors speech, honors English, Ideas in History, Interdisciplinary Civilization, honors seminars (2), and an honors **thesis** of 3-6 credits. A 1-credit honors experience is optional.

Graduation as a Thesis Scholar requires two 3-credit honors seminars and an honors thesis of 3-6 credits.

AP/IB credits can in some cases count for up to three honors credits.

Number of Honors Classes Offered (3.0): This is a measure of the total **adjusted** honors main sections available in the term reported, not including labs and thesis. (Please read the section titled "All about Honors Classes".) An adjusted main section has 3 or more semester credits, or equivalent, and sections with fewer credits receive a lower prorated value.

The program offered a section for every **23.3** students. The average for all 50 programs is 14.2. The lower the number, the better.

In the term reported, **100%** of honors class enrollment was **in honors-only sections; none in mixed honors sections (honors and non-honors students); and none in contract sections (regular sections in which honors students "contract" to do extra work).** The averages for all fifty programs are 81.3% in honors-only sections; 13.6 % in mixed honors sections; and 5.1% in contract sections.

Number of Honors Classes in Key Disciplines (4.0): The 15 "key" disciplines are biological sciences; business (all); chemistry; communications (especially public speaking); computer science; economics; engineering (all); English; history; math (all); philosophy; physics; political science; psychology; and sociology/anthropology/gender studies. Interdisciplinary sections, such as those often taken for General Education credit in the first two years, do receive a lesser, prorated discipline "credit" because they introduce students to multiple disciplines in an especially engaging way, often with in-depth discussion.

For this measure, mixed and contract sections are not counted as a section in a key discipline unless students taking the sections for honors credit make up at least 10% of the total section enrollment.

In the term reported, the program had a ratio of **25.7 honors students** per each main section in some or all "key disciplines." The mean for all programs is 26.3. The lower the ratio, the better.

Out of **16 adjusted sections in key disciplines**, all were **honors-only sections.** The most sections were in English (6), communications (4), biology (2) and economics and philosophy (1 each). Sociology, anthropology, and gender studies combined had 2 sections.

The program also offered five seminars, but each had a disciplinary focus, including, for example, "Economic Approaches to Religion"; "Science Fiction: Exploring the Human"; and "Restoration Ecology."

The program combines seminar sections with several departmental honors classes, and is an example of a small **blended program.**

Extent of Honors Enrollment (3.5): Not all honors students take an honors class each term, especially after the first two years. Programs that have fewer honors classes for upper-division honors students will generally have fewer total members in good standing who are actually enrolled in a given term. (Please be aware, however, that honors students not enrolled in a class for a term are still connected to the honors community through residential and extracurricular activities.)

For example, if honors students in a program occupy 1,800 honors classroom seats in a given term, and there are 3,000 honors students in good standing, the extent of enrollment is .67. For programs that require a thesis, the ratio (score) reported below might in fact be somewhat higher, since we only count "regular" class enrollment for this measure, and not thesis enrollment. The program **has a ratio of .86**; the mean is 1.13 for all 50 programs. The higher the ratio, the better.

Average Class Size, Honors-only Sections (4.5): Offered mostly in the first two years, honors-only classes tend to be smaller and, as the name implies, have no or very few students other than those in the

honors program. These class sections are almost always much smaller than mixed or contract sections, or regular non-honors class sections in the university.

The average honors-only class size in the honors program is **17.7 students**. The average for all 50 programs is 19.0 students.

Average Class Size, Overall (5.0): The overall class calculation is based on the *proportion* of honors students in each type of class (honors-only, mixed honors, and honors contract sections). Thus it is not a raw average. The overall honors-credit class size is **17.7 students**, versus the average for all 50 programs of 26.3 students.

These class size averages also do not correspond to the number of students per honors sections numbers above. The reason is that, in computing average class size metrics, we include enrollment in each 1-2-credit section, not just sections with 3 or more credits.

Along with the honors-only average of 17.7 students, the mixed honors sections average **(NA)** students, and the contract sections with honors credit for individual honors students average **(NA)** students. Across all fifty programs, the average mixed honors section has 51.1 students, and the average contract section has 60.1students.

Honors Graduation Rate (3.5): The rating is based on the actual grad rate for students who entered the program six years earlier, whether or not the students remained in honors. The **actual rate of 82.5%** is also compared to the rates of other programs with the same test score entry requirement range, and then adjusted to the **score of 82.2%**. In some cases this measure favors programs within universities with relatively higher test scores for the student population as a whole. The average honors graduation rate for all programs with similar test scores required for admission is 85.6%.

Value-Added Grad Rate (5.0): The value-added rate measures the extent to which the adjusted score listed above exceeds the six-year grad rate for the university as a whole. **The university-wide rate is 57%.** Note: This measure generally favors programs within universities with relatively lower test scores for the student population as a whole.

Ratio of Staff to Honors Students (4.5): There is 1 staff member for every **102.8** students. (Mean ratio for all 50 programs is 1 staff member for every 135.6 students.)

Honors Residence Halls, Amenities (4.0): About 125 honors students live in Beede Hall, which has traditional double rooms and hall baths. Beede is air-conditioned. There is convenient dining at Student Dining Center (MUC) and Papa John's.

Honors Residence Halls, Availability (4.5): This rating compares the number of places in honors residence halls to the number of honors freshman and sophomore members in good standing, about 205. The ratio for the honors program is **.61** rooms for each first- and second-year student. The average for all fifty programs is .63 places.

Prestigious Awards (3.0): The awards that we track and include are listed in the section titled "Prestigious Scholarships." The awards are sometimes won by students who are not in an honors college or program, but increasingly many are enrolled in honors programs. It is also a trend that honors colleges and programs help to prepare their students for the awards competitions.

USD students have won 9 Rhodes scholarships and an impressive 16 Truman scholarships, along with 7 Udall scholarships and 13 Goldwater scholarships for undergraduates.

UNRATED FEATURES

Continuation Requirements: There is a sliding scale, all cumulative GPAs. At the end of the first year, 2.75; the end of the second year, 3.00; second year with intent to graduate in three years, 3.25; third year and after, 3.25.

Academic Strengths, National Rankings: This is based on national rankings of *graduate* programs in 15 disciplines, except engineering and business, where undergraduate rankings are used. USD has the highest participation in business, education, biology, psychology, and nursing.

Undergraduate Research: "All students are required to complete a thesis during their junior/senior years. The Honors thesis is meant to serve as the capstone of an Honors student's research experience at USD. It is an independent piece of sustained research conducted over the course of two semesters, guided by a Thesis Director and a Thesis Committee. As part of the process of writing this thesis, students submit a formal proposal and an abstract of the research to be performed to their committee. Ultimately, this research should result in a substantial academic work that will represent not only the apogee of the student's career at USD, but also be a contribution to the student's academic field. The thesis should be a major scholarly, creative, or investigative work consisting of some documentation that is publishable in a bound format for keeping of a permanent record in the library and the honors office."

Study Abroad: "USD Direct Programs are the most affordable study abroad option. USD has direct agreements with universities overseas which allow you to continue paying regular tuition and fees to USD, while not having to pay tuition to a foreign university. In exchange, we accept students from those universities here at USD for a semester or academic year. In most cases, you will fully enroll (matriculate) into the foreign university just like any other student and will have access to a broad range of courses, local student unions and organizations, public transportation and many other benefits enjoyed by the locals."

Examples of faculty-led programs include: Art and Art History in NYC; Ireland, History, Sport, and Culture; Isle of Greece: The Sporades Islands; The Republic of Empires: Rome, Florence, and Venice

In addition, there are direct exchange programs with universities in France, Germany, Japan, Spain, China, Australia, and various countries in South America.

Financial Aid: "The University of South Dakota has a centralized system for awarding the most valuable scholarships (most of which are awarded to Honors students), but there are no scholarships dedicated to the winners of national competitions."

Honors Fees: None.

Placement Experiences: For the graduating class of 2015, 33% entered employment, 57% went to graduate or professional school, and 10% unknown.

Degree of Difference: This is based on the differences between (1) the average (2015, two-part) SAT scores for enrolled honors students (1275=ACT equivalent) and (2) the average test scores for all students in the university (1050) as a whole. The test scores may be an indication of how "elite" honors students may be perceived as compared to students in the university as a whole. The scores can also provide an indication of how well prepared the non-honors students in the university may be. **Please keep in mind that neither high nor low test scores determine the overall quality of a program.**

NAME: TEMPLE UNIVERSITY HONORS PROGRAM.

Date Established: 1987.

Location: Philadelphia, Pennsylvania.

University Full-time Undergraduate Enrollment: 24,990.

Honors Members in Good Standing: 1,943 (mean size of all 50 programs is 1,742).

Honors Average Admission Statistics: ACT, 31. Old SAT, 1396; est. new SAT, 1450. (Late update: the average SAT for Fall 2016 was 1409 (old SAT); est. new SAT, 1460.

Average High School GPA/Class Rank: 3.91; top 9% of high school class.

Basic Admission Requirements: ACT, 30. Old SAT, 1340; est. new SAT, 1400; 3.70; top 10%. Temple Honors also participates in test-optional admissions.

Application Deadline(s): *Please verify with each program, as some deadlines could change.*

Early action deadline November 1, 2016; university deadline is February 1, 2017.

Honors Programs with old SAT scores from 1351—1396: Purdue, Oregon, Alabama, Massachusetts, Penn State, Indiana, CUNY Macaulay, Texas A&M, NJIT, Missouri, Oregon State, Delaware, LSU, Vermont, Temple.

Administrative Staff: 9 FTEs.

RATINGS AT A GLANCE: For all mortarboard ratings immediately below, a score of 5 is the maximum and represents a comparison with all 50 honors colleges and programs. More detailed explanations follow the "mortarboard" ratings.

PERCEPTION* OF UNIVERSITY AS A WHOLE, NOT OF HONORS: 🎓🎓🎓🎓

*Perception is based on the university's ranking among public universities in the 2016 U.S. News Best Colleges report. Please bear in mind that the better the U.S. News ranking, the more difficult it is for an honors college or program to have a rating that equals or improves on the magazine ranking.

OVERALL HONORS RATING: 🎓🎓🎓🎓1/2

Curriculum Requirements: 🎓🎓🎓🎓🎓

Number of Honors Classes Offered: 🎓🎓🎓🎓🎓

Number of Honors Classes in Key Disciplines: 🎓🎓🎓🎓1/2

Extent of Honors Enrollment: 🎓🎓🎓🎓🎓

Honors-only Class Size: 🎓🎓🎓 1/2

Overall Class Size (Honors-only plus mixed, contract): 🎓🎓🎓🎓 1/2

Honors Grad Rate: 🎓🎓🎓 1/2

Value-Added Grad Rate: 🎓🎓🎓🎓

Ratio of Staff to Students: 🎓🎓🎓

Priority Registration: Yes, honors students register for all courses, honors and otherwise, with athletes and veterans, during each year they are in the program.

Honors Housing Amenities: 🎓🎓🎓🎓 1/2

Honors Housing Availability: 🎓🎓🎓🎓 1/2

Prestigious Awards: 🎓🎓🎓

RATING SCORES AND EXPLANATIONS:

Curriculum Requirements (5.0): The most important rating category, the curriculum completion requirement (classes required to complete honors) defines not only what honors students should learn but also the extent to which honors students and faculty are connected in the classroom. If there is a thesis or capstone requirement, it reinforces the individual contact and research skills so important to learning.

The average number of honors semester hours required for completion across all 50 programs is 29.0.

Completion of the Temple curriculum requires at least 30 credits, including 10 honors courses. There is also a **thesis/capstone option.** The average completion is about **36-38 credits.** Honors contract courses can be used for up to 8 credits.

Students transferring in with 45-59 credits are required to take 8 honors courses rather than 10. Transfers with 60 or more credits must take 6 honors courses for completion.

AP/IB credits are not counted as replacements for honors courses.

Number of Honors Classes Offered (5.0): This is a measure of the total **adjusted** honors main sections available in the term reported, not including labs and thesis. (Please read the section titled "All about Honors Classes".) An adjusted main section has 3 or more semester credits, or equivalent, and sections with fewer credits receive a lower prorated value.

The program offered a section for every **7.4** enrolled students. The average for all 50 programs is 14.2 The lower the number, the better.

In the term reported, **89.3%** of honors enrollment was **in honors-only sections; 3.4% in mixed honors sections (honors and non-honors students); and 7.3% in contract sections (regular sections in which honors students "contract" to do extra work).** The averages for all fifty programs are 81.3% in honors-only sections; 13.6 % in mixed honors sections; and 5.1% in contract sections.

Number of Honors Classes in Key Disciplines (4.5): The 15 "key" disciplines are biological sciences; business (all); chemistry; communications (especially public speaking); computer science; economics; engineering (all); English; history; math (all); philosophy; physics; political science; psychology; and sociology/anthropology/gender studies. Interdisciplinary sections, such as those often taken for General Education credit in the first two years, do receive a lesser, prorated discipline "credit" because they introduce students to multiple disciplines in an especially engaging way, often with in-depth discussion.

For this measure, mixed and contract sections are not counted as a section in a key discipline unless students taking the sections for honors credit make up at least 10% of the total section enrollment.

In the term reported, the program had a ratio of **18.2 honors students** per each main section in some or all "key disciplines." The mean for all 50 programs is 26.3. The lower the ratio, the better.

Out of **66 adjusted sections in key disciplines**, the program had **59 honors-only sections.** The most sections were in business (14), English (10), math (7), engineering and political science (4 each), computer science, philosophy, and political science (3 each), and chemistry and history (2 each). Sociology, anthropology, and gender studies had 8 sections combined. There was at least one section in all 15 disciplines.

The program also offered only 25 three-credit interdisciplinary sections, titled "Intellectual Heritage." These count for Gen Ed credit. They "introduce students to foundational texts from cultural and intellectual traditions worldwide. Guiding themes such as 'journeys,' 'faith,' 'science,' and 'power' are the basis for reading, interrogating, and relating to texts that continue to shape self and society."

The Honors Program combines the Gen Ed interdisciplinary classes with extensive departmental honors classes, but it is essentially a **discipline-focused honors program.**

Extent of Honors Enrollment (5.0): Not all honors students take an honors class each term, especially after the first two years. Programs that have fewer honors classes and thesis options for upper-division honors students will generally have fewer total members in good standing who are actually enrolled in a given term. (Please be aware, however, that honors students not enrolled in a class for a term are still tied to the honors community through residential and extracurricular activities.)

For example, if a program has 1,800 individual students enrolled in a given term, and 3,000 students in good standing, the level of enrollment was .67, an indication that honors class enrollment is somewhat below average, especially in upper-division classes. The college **has a ratio of 1.43**; the mean is 1.13 for all 50 programs. The higher the ratio, the better.

Average Class Size, Honors-only Sections (3.5): Offered mostly in the first two years, honors-only classes tend to be smaller and, as the name implies, have no or very few students other than those in the honors program. These class sections are almost always much smaller than mixed or contract sections, or regular non-honors class sections in the university.

The average honors-only class size in the honors program is **21.6 students**. The average for all 50 programs is 19.0 students.

Average Class Size, Overall (4.5): The overall class calculation is based on the *proportion* of honors students in each type of class (honors-only, mixed honors, and honors contract sections). Thus it is not a raw average. The overall honors-credit class size is **22.0 students**, versus the average for all 50 programs of 26.3 students.

These class size averages also do not correspond to the number of students per honors sections numbers above. The reason is that, in computing average class size metrics, we include enrollment in each 1-2-credit section, not just sections with 3 or more credits.

Along with the honors-only average of 21.6 students, the mixed honors sections average **22.5 students,** and the contract sections with honors credit for individual honors students average **27.0 students.** Across all fifty programs, the average mixed honors section has 51.1 students, and the average contract section has 60.1 students.

Honors Graduation Rate (3.5): The rating is based on the actual grad rate for students who entered the program six years earlier, whether or not the students remained in honors. The **actual rate of 84%** is also compared to the rates of other programs with the same test score entry requirement range, and then adjusted to the **score of 83.9%.** In some cases this measure favors programs within universities with relatively higher test scores for the student population as a whole. The average honors graduation rate for all programs with similar test scores required for admission is 86.2%.

Value-Added Grad Rate (4.0): The value-added rate measures the extent to which the adjusted score listed above exceeds the six-year grad rate for the university as a whole. **The university-wide rate is 69%.** Note: This measure generally favors programs within universities with relatively lower test scores for the student population as a whole.

Ratio of Staff to Honors Students (3.0): There is 1 staff member for every **204.5** students. (Mean ratio for all 50 programs is 1 staff member for every 135.6 students.)

Honors Residence Halls, Amenities (4.5): The 1300 Residence Hall & Temple Towers house more than 700 honors students, including "about 35% of all Honors students and 80% of all honors freshmen. Of the Honors freshmen living on campus, 87% live in the Honors Living-Learning Community." The rooms are 70% suite-style with shared baths and about 30% apartment style (Temple Towers). They feature coed floors with single genders in each suite or apartment. The 2nd and 3rd floors of 1300 are for freshmen. Sophomores, juniors, and seniors reside in Temple Towers. All rooms are air-conditioned. There is a food court in Morgan Hall, next door.

Honors Residence Halls, Availability (4.5): This rating compares the number of places in honors residence halls to the number of honors freshman and sophomore members in good standing, about 972.

The ratio for the honors program is **.73** rooms for each first- and second-year student. The average for all fifty programs is .63 places.

Prestigious Awards (3.0): The awards that we track and include are listed in the section titled "Prestigious Scholarships." The awards are sometimes won by students who are not in an honors college or program, but increasingly many are enrolled in honors programs. It is also a trend that honors colleges and programs help to prepare their students for the awards competitions.

"In January 2013, Temple University created the Office of Development and Fellowships Advising. It is not officially affiliated with Honors, but it is proximate, works closely with Honors and is located within the same administrative portfolio." Temple undergraduates have won a large number of Udall scholarships, 13. Temple students have also won 4 Marshall scholarships and the same number of Truman scholarships.

UNRATED FEATURES

Continuation Requirements: 3.25.

Academic Strengths, National Rankings: This is based on national rankings of *graduate* programs in 15 disciplines, except engineering and business, where undergraduate rankings are used.

The average departmental ranking at Temple is in the 80-85 range. Leading departments include psychology (52), education (55), business (61), English (63), history and sociology (64 each), and political science (76).

Undergraduate Research: "While we do not know the percentage of Honors students that are participating in any form of research university wide, we do oversee our own thesis-level research track called the Honors Scholar Project. However, many of our students take advantage of the undergraduate research opportunities within their college and/or department (e.g., students in the College of Science and Technology can undertake research through the Undergraduate Research Program, the psychology department offers the Psychology Honors Research track, etc.). Last year we had 13 Honors Scholars, which made up 4% of our graduating seniors." These students have a special notation on their transcripts.

"Another research opportunity is for Honors students in the College of Science and Technology: The Science Scholars Program. This program supports exceptional incoming College of Science and Technology students from the Honors Program with paid summer research and academic and professional development."

Study Abroad: "Percentage of honors students who studied abroad for at least a full summer, quarter, or semester during the most recent academic year for which statistics are available:

2014-2015: 202 Honors students studied abroad, which is 24% of 843 undergrads who studied abroad that year;

2013-2014: 174 Honors students studied abroad, which is 20% of 886 undergrads who studied abroad that year.

"On average, about 30% of Honors students study abroad in contrast to about 15% of all undergraduate students at Temple who study abroad. In other words, Honors students study abroad about twice the rate of non-honors students.

"Honors is only 6% of the entire Temple University population and each year, we make up about 15-20% of the total students studying abroad.

"There are two foreign branch campuses, one in Rome, Italy and one in Tokyo, Japan. The Rome campus will be celebrating its 50th anniversary this year, and offers strong study abroad programs in the humanities, visual arts, architecture, and business to Temple students and students from many prominent institutions in the U.S. We are offering Honors courses at the Rome campus during the summer, with the intention to expand offerings abroad. The Tokyo campus has been in existence since 1982, and offers full undergraduate degrees in a variety of fields.

"In addition, Temple administers major study abroad programs in London, primarily for students in communications and related fields, and in Oviedo, Spain, which offers Spanish language courses at all levels.

"Temple has exchange agreements with a multitude of universities in Europe, Asia, and Latin America, faculty-led programs around the world (Brazil, Jamaica, Costa Rica, Ghana, India, and others), and also permits students to study at programs administered by other institutions and program providers.

"As evidence of Temple's support for study abroad, this year *Temple's Education Abroad Office is awarding $357,500 in study abroad scholarships to close to 245 students.* And in addition, Temple students successfully compete for regional and national scholarships, such as Fulbright, Boren and Gilman. [Emphasis added.]

Financial Aid: "Academic scholarships range from $3,000 to full tuition."

Honors Fees: None.

Placement Experiences: *Job Placement*: White House staff, Teach for America, GlaxoSmithKline, Boeing, Air Force, Peace Corps, Comcast, Showtime, MTV, PBS, Microsoft, Ebay, Google, Children's Hospital of Philadelphia, ESPN, and others. *Graduate/Professional School Placement*: Harvard, Columbia, Yale, Brown, Penn, Cornell, NYU, UC Berkeley, Maryland, UNC Chapel Hill, Virginia, and others.

Degree of Difference: This is based on the differences between (1) the average (2015, two-part) SAT scores for enrolled honors students (1396) and (2) the average test scores for all students in the university (1120) as a whole. This rating is an indication of how "elite" honors students may be perceived as compared to students in the university as a whole. The score also provides an indication of how well prepared the non-honors students in the university may be. **Please keep in mind that neither high nor low test scores determine the overall quality of a program.**

NAME: HONORS AND SCHOLARS PROGRAM, UNIVERSITY OF TENNESSEE.

Date Established: 1985.

Location: Knoxville, Tennessee.

University Full-time Undergraduate Enrollment: 20,337.

Honors Members in Good Standing: 1,500 (mean size of all 50 programs is 1,742).

Honors Average Admission Statistics: ACT, 32. Old SAT equivalent, 1410-1420; est. new SAT, 1470.

Average High School GPA/Class Rank: 4.41.

Basic Admission Requirements: ACT, 31. Old SAT, 1340; est. new SAT, 1400. 4.0 weighted GPA.

Application Deadline(s): *Please verify with each program, as some deadlines could change.*

November 1, 2016, in order to be eligible for major scholarships. Essay deadline is December 1, 2016.

Honors Programs with old SAT scores from 1402—1469: UCF, Connecticut, Kentucky, Washington, Maryland, North Carolina, UC Irvine, Kansas, Minnesota, Tennessee, South Carolina, Clemson, UT Austin, Georgia.

Administrative Staff: 9 FTEs.

RATINGS AT A GLANCE: For all mortarboard ratings immediately below, a score of 5 is the maximum and represents a comparison with all 50 honors colleges and programs. More detailed explanations follow the "mortarboard" ratings.

PERCEPTION* OF UNIVERSITY AS A WHOLE, NOT OF HONORS: 🎓🎓🎓🎓

*Perception is based on the university's ranking among public universities in the 2016 U.S. News Best Colleges report. Please bear in mind that the better the U.S. News ranking, the more difficult it is for an honors college or program to have a rating that equals or improves on the magazine ranking.

OVERALL HONORS RATING: 🎓🎓🎓🎓

Curriculum Requirements: 🎓🎓🎓🎓

Number of Honors Classes Offered: 🎓🎓🎓🎓^1/2

Number of Honors Classes in Key Disciplines: 🎓🎓🎓🎓🎓

Extent of Honors Enrollment: 🎓🎓🎓🎓^1/2

Honors-only Class Size: 🎓 🎓 🎓 🎓

Overall Class Size (Honors-only plus mixed, contract): 🎓 🎓 🎓 🎓

Honors Grad Rate: 🎓 🎓 🎓 🎓 1/2

Value-Added Grad Rate: 🎓 🎓 🎓 🎓

Ratio of Staff to Students: 🎓 🎓 🎓 1/2

Priority Registration: Yes, honors students register for all courses, honors and otherwise, with the first group of students during each year they are in the program.

Honors Housing Amenities: 🎓 🎓 🎓 🎓

Honors Housing Availability: 🎓 🎓 🎓 🎓

Prestigious Awards: 🎓 🎓 🎓 1/2

RATING SCORES AND EXPLANATIONS:

Curriculum Requirements (4.0): The most important rating category, the curriculum completion requirement (classes required to complete honors) defines not only what honors students should learn but also the extent to which honors students and faculty are connected in the classroom. If there is a thesis or capstone requirement, it reinforces the individual contact and research skills so important to learning.

The average number of honors semester hours required for completion across all 50 programs is 29.0.

The Honors and Scholars Program has two completion options, and they average about **28** credits.

The Chancellors Honors Program requires 21 honors credits and a **thesis,** 4-6 credits. Students may take one 3-credit contract class as part of the 21 credits.

The Haslam Scholars completion requirement is 24 credits, along with **a 6-credit thesis** and a 1-credit capstone/colloquium. Haslam Scholars all complete a 3-credit study-abroad requirement.

AP/IB credits are not counted as replacements for honors courses.

Number of Honors Classes Offered (4.5): This is a measure of the total **adjusted** honors main sections available in the term reported, not including labs and thesis. (Please read the section titled "All about Honors Classes".) An adjusted main section has 3 or more semester credits, or equivalent, and sections with fewer credits receive a lower prorated value.

The program offered a section for every **10.2** enrolled students. The average for all 50 programs is 14.2.

The lower the number, the better.

In the term reported, **82.2%** of honors enrollment was **in honors-only sections; 16.4% in mixed honors sections (honors and non-honors students); and 1.4% in contract sections (regular sections in which honors students "contract" to do extra work).** The averages for all fifty programs are 81.3% in honors-only sections; 13.6 % in mixed honors sections; and 5.1% in contract sections.

Number of Honors Classes in Key Disciplines (5.0): The 15 "key" disciplines are biological sciences; business (all); chemistry; communications (especially public speaking); computer science; economics; engineering (all); English; history; math (all); philosophy; physics; political science; psychology; and sociology/anthropology/gender studies. Interdisciplinary sections, such as those often taken for General Education credit in the first two years, do receive a lesser, prorated discipline "credit" because they introduce students to multiple disciplines in an especially engaging way, often with in-depth discussion.

For this measure, mixed and contract sections are not counted as a section in a key discipline unless students taking the sections for honors credit make up at least 10% of the total section enrollment.

In the term reported, the program had a ratio of **22.5 honors students** per each main section in some or all "key disciplines." The mean for all 50 programs is 26.3. The lower the ratio, the better.

Out of **87** adjusted sections in key disciplines, the program had **62** honors-only sections. A striking feature is that *there were 18 sections in engineering, an extraordinarily high number.* In other disciplines, English (11), math (8), philosophy (7), and business (5) followed. Next were psychology (5), history (4), and chemistry, communications, computer science, and political science (3 each). Sociology, anthropology, and gender studies had 13 sections combined, a very high total. All 15 key disciplines were represented.

Although there were 10 seminar sections, all had a disciplinary tilt. The program is almost a pure **discipline-based honors program.**

Extent of Honors Enrollment (4.5): Not all honors students take an honors class each term, especially after the first two years. Programs that have fewer honors classes and thesis options for upper-division honors students will generally have fewer total members in good standing who are actually enrolled in a given term. (Please be aware, however, that honors students not enrolled in a class for a term are still tied to the honors community through residential and extracurricular activities.)

For example, if a program has 1,800 individual students enrolled in a given term, and 3,000 students in good standing, the level of enrollment was .67, an indication that honors class enrollment is somewhat below average, especially in upper-division classes. The program **has a ratio of 1.16**; the mean is 1.13 for all 50 programs. The higher the ratio, the better. The higher the ratio, the better.

Average Class Size, Honors-only Sections (4.0): Offered mostly in the first two years, honors-only classes tend to be smaller and, as the name implies, have no or very few students other than those in the honors program. These class sections are almost always much smaller than mixed or contract sections, or regular non-honors class sections in the university.

The average honors-only class size in the honors program is **20.5 students**. The average for all 50 programs is 19.0 students.

Average Class Size, Overall (4.0): The overall class calculation is based on the *proportion* of honors students in each type of class (honors-only, mixed honors, and honors contract sections). Thus it is not a raw average. The overall honors-credit class size is **25.2 students**, versus the average for all 50 programs of 26.3 students.

These class size averages also do not correspond to the number of students per honors sections numbers above. The reason is that, in computing average class size metrics, we include enrollment in each 1-2-credit section, not just sections with 3 or more credits.

Along with the honors-only average of 20.5 students, the mixed honors sections average **45.2 students**, and the contract sections with honors credit for individual honors students average **69.2 students**. Across all fifty programs, the average mixed honors section has 51.1 students, and the average contract section has 60.1 students.

Honors Graduation Rate (4.5): The rating is based on the actual grad rate for students who entered the program six years earlier, whether or not the students remained in honors. The **actual rate of 90%** is also compared to the rates of other programs with the same test score entry requirement range, and then adjusted to the **score of 89.7%.** In some cases this measure favors programs within universities with relatively higher test scores for the student population as a whole. The average honors graduation rate for all programs with similar test scores required for admission is 92.6%.

Value-Added Grad Rate (4.0): The value-added rate measures the extent to which the adjusted score listed above exceeds the grad rate for the university as a whole. **The university-wide rate is 69%.** Note: This measure generally favors programs within universities with relatively lower test scores for the student population as a whole.

Ratio of Staff to Honors Students (3.5): There is 1 staff member for every **166.7** students. (Mean ratio for all 50 programs is 1 staff member for every 135.6 students.)

Honors Residence Halls, Amenities (4.0): Brown Hall is home to about 300 honors freshmen. The rooms are divided equally between traditional double rooms with hall baths and suite-style rooms with shared baths. The residence is fully air-conditioned and coed by pod. The nearest dining is in Presidential Court.

Honors Residence Halls, Availability (4.0): This rating compares the number of places in honors residence halls to the number of honors freshman and sophomore members in good standing, about 750. The ratio for the honors program is **.40** rooms for each first- and second-year student. The average for all fifty programs is .63 places.

Prestigious Awards (3.5): The awards that we track and include are listed in the section titled "Prestigious Scholarships." The awards are sometimes won by students who are not in an honors college or program, but increasingly many are enrolled in honors programs. It is also a trend that honors colleges and programs help to prepare their students for the awards competitions.

UT students have won 6 Udall scholarships and 30 Goldwater scholarships. In addition, students have won 7 Rhodes scholarships, 2 Marshall scholarships, and 4 Truman awards.

UNRATED FEATURES

Continuation Requirements: 3.50 cumulative; the same for graduation.

Academic Strengths, National Rankings: This is based on national rankings of *graduate* programs in 15 disciplines, except engineering and business, where undergraduate rankings are used.

UT departments average about 80th in the nation. Among the highest-rated are business (50), education (62), engineering (63), physics (65), computer science (70), and math (73).

Undergraduate Research: "While we do not have an exact number, 100% of our seniors are involved in research or creative production as part of their honors thesis work. We can estimate from advising notes that 17% of sophomores and 29% of juniors are engaged in undergraduate research activity.

"The office of research has an office of undergraduate research but it is not housed within honors. However, we do work closely with them and we have a staff member tasked specifically with supporting undergraduate research. We also sponsor research-related programming including a series each fall that discusses types of research (and how to get involved) by area (e.g., health, humanities, natural sciences, the arts, etc.)."

Study Abroad: "We have a 'ready for the world' requirement in the Chancellor's Honors Program that asks students to complete an international or intercultural learning experience. Most of them do study abroad or go on an international service trip of some kind.

"We offer 'ready for the world' grants to honors students for study abroad (more information below). The university also offers study abroad scholarships as do many of our academic colleges. These typically help to defray the costs of study abroad (not cover all expenses).

"We have two honors-exclusive study abroad programs: UT Honors at Cambridge, which has run for several years, awards credit for two honors courses, and carries the benefit of residence in Cambridge's Emmanuel College.

"UT Honors at oxford, begun in summer 2015, is a partnership program with two other universities which gives our students the opportunity to learn alongside students from different parts of the U.S. It awards credit for one honors course."

Financial Aid: "For most honors students, the financial aid/scholarships piece is kept separate. So while most of our students do enjoy some type of merit scholarship funding, we don't have a system that connects honors membership to scholarships, broadly speaking.

"The exception is a scholars program with a cohort of 15 students per year. The Haslam Scholars Program carries as a benefit one of the top merit scholarships at UTK (a chancellor's level scholarship—these are named awards) as well as other financial perks (research funding, all-inclusive group study abroad, etc.).

"We do support students on international experiences and undergraduate research through honors grants. These are awarded several times each year, based upon a competitive application process. In 2014, 2015, we awarded approximately $105k to students."

Honors Fees: None.

Placement Experiences: None listed.

Degree of Difference: This is based on the differences between (1) the average (2015, two-part) SAT scores for enrolled honors students (1420) and (2) the average test scores for all students in the university (1210) as a whole. The test scores may be an indication of how "elite" honors students may be perceived as compared to students in the university as a whole. The scores can also provide an indication of how well prepared the non-honors students in the university may be. **Please keep in mind that neither high nor low test scores determine the overall quality of a program.**

NAME: TEXAS A&M UNIVERSITY HONORS PROGRAM.

Date Established: 1968.

Location: College Station, Texas.

University Full-time Undergraduate Enrollment: 42,129.

Honors Members in Good Standing: 777 (mean size of all 50 programs is 1,742).

Honors Average Admission Statistics: ACT, 31. Old SAT, 1375; est. new SAT, 1430.

Average High School GPA/Class Rank: None reported.

Basic Admission Requirements: ACT, 27. Old SAT, 1220; est. new SAT, 1290.

Application Deadline(s): *Please verify with each program, as some deadlines could change.*

Application period begins August 1, 2016. No end date listed.

Honors Programs with old SAT scores from 1351—1396: Purdue, Oregon, Alabama, Massachusetts, Penn State, Indiana, CUNY Macaulay, Texas A&M, NJIT, Missouri, Oregon State, Delaware, LSU, Vermont, Temple.

Administrative Staff: 7.

RATINGS AT A GLANCE: For all mortarboard ratings immediately below, a score of 5 is the maximum and represents a comparison with all 50 honors colleges and programs. More detailed explanations follow the "mortarboard" ratings.

PERCEPTION* OF UNIVERSITY AS A WHOLE, NOT OF HONORS: 🎓🎓🎓🎓 1/2

*Perception is based on the university's ranking among public universities in the 2016 U.S. News Best Colleges report. Please bear in mind that the better the U.S. News ranking, the more difficult it is for an honors college or program to have a rating that equals or improves on the magazine ranking.

OVERALL HONORS RATING: 🎓🎓🎓🎓

Curriculum Requirements: 🎓🎓🎓🎓

Number of Honors Classes Offered: 🎓🎓🎓🎓

Number of Honors Classes in Key Disciplines: 🎓🎓🎓🎓

Extent of Honors Enrollment: 🎓🎓🎓🎓

Honors-only Class Size: 🎓🎓🎓

Overall Class Size (Honors-only plus mixed, contract): 🎓🎓🎓

Honors Grad Rate: 🎓🎓🎓🎓

Value-Added Grad Rate: 🎓🎓🎓¹ᐟ²

Ratio of Staff to Students: 🎓🎓🎓🎓¹ᐟ²

Priority Registration: Yes, honors students register for all courses, honors and otherwise, with the first group of students during each year they are in the program.

Honors Housing Amenities: 🎓🎓🎓🎓

Honors Housing Availability: 🎓🎓🎓🎓🎓

Prestigious Awards: 🎓🎓🎓🎓¹ᐟ²

RATING SCORES AND EXPLANATIONS:

Curriculum Requirements (4.0): The most important rating category, the curriculum completion requirement (classes required to complete honors) defines not only what honors students should learn but also the extent to which honors students and faculty are connected in the classroom. If there is a thesis or capstone requirement, it reinforces the individual contact and research skills so important to learning.

The average number of honors semester hours required for completion across all 50 programs is 29.0.

Graduation as an Honors Fellow requires **30 credits,** including 9 from core curriculum courses, 12 from upper-division courses, and 6 from a capstone/**thesis.**

Students can meet the honors requirement by taking any combination of departmental honors classes, graduate classes, honors contract classes, or independent-study classes. There is no limit on contract hours, but their principal function is to provide honors-level credit in a regular class section that the student wants or needs for enrichment or graduation.

AP/IB credits are not counted as replacements for honors courses.

Number of Honors Classes Offered (4.0): This is a measure of the total **adjusted** honors main sections available in the term reported, not including labs and thesis. (Please read the section titled "All about Honors Classes".) An adjusted main section has 3 or more semester credits, or equivalent, and sections with fewer credits receive a lower prorated value.

The college offered a section for every **15.1** enrolled students. The average for all 50 programs is 14.2. The lower the number, the better.

In the term reported, **63.0%** of honors enrollment was **in honors-only sections; 32.0% in mixed honors sections (honors and non-honors students); and 5.0% in contract sections (regular sections in which honors students "contract" to do extra work).** The averages for all fifty programs are 81.3% in honors-only sections; 13.6 % in mixed honors sections; and 5.1% in contract sections.

Number of Honors Classes in Key Disciplines (4.0): The 15 "key" disciplines are biological sciences; business (all); chemistry; communications (especially public speaking); computer science; economics; engineering (all); English; history; math (all); philosophy; physics; political science; psychology; and sociology/anthropology/gender studies. Interdisciplinary sections, such as those often taken for General Education credit in the first two years, do receive a lesser, prorated discipline "credit" because they introduce students to multiple disciplines in an especially engaging way, often with in-depth discussion.

For this measure, mixed and contract sections are not counted as a section in a key discipline unless students taking the sections for honors credit make up at least 10% of the total section enrollment.

In the term reported, the program had a ratio of **22.5 honors students** per each main section in some or all "key disciplines." The mean for all 50 programs is 26.3. The lower the ratio, the better.

The complexities of the TAMU data make it necessary to use percentages of sections instead of actual numbers of sections for this measure. Business, engineering, and math each accounted for a bit more than 20% of sections in key disciplines. Biology, English, and communications each accounted for about 6% of these sections. Philosophy and psychology each had about 5% of these sections. Chemistry and political science together made up about 5%. There were no sections in physics or economics.

The TAMU Honors Program is, as we have noted before, a straight from the shoulder program, all about classes in the disciplines. It is almost purely a **discipline-based honors program.**

Extent of Honors Enrollment (4.0): Not all honors students take an honors class each term, especially after the first two years. Programs that have fewer honors classes and thesis options for upper-division honors students will generally have fewer total members in good standing who are actually enrolled in a given term. (Please be aware, however, that honors students not enrolled in a class for a term are still tied to the honors community through residential and extracurricular activities.)

For example, if a program has 1,800 individual students enrolled in a given term, and 3,000 students in good standing, the level of enrollment was .67, an indication that honors class enrollment is somewhat below average, especially in upper-division classes. The college **has a ratio of 1.00**; the mean is 1.13 for all 50 programs. An honors thesis requirement can contribute to a higher ratio. The higher the ratio, the better.

Average Class Size, Honors-only Sections (3.0): Offered mostly in the first two years, honors-only classes tend to be smaller and, as the name implies, have no or very few students other than those in the honors program. These class sections are almost always much smaller than mixed or contract sections, or regular non-honors class sections in the university.

The average honors-only class size in the honors program is **26.3 students**. The average for all 50 programs is 19.0 students.

Average Class Size, Overall (3.0): The overall class calculation is based on the *proportion* of honors students in each type of class (honors-only, mixed honors, and honors contract sections). Thus it is not a raw average. The overall honors-credit class size is **47.6 students**, versus the average for all 50 programs of 26.3 students.

These class size averages also do not correspond to the number of students per honors sections numbers above. The reason is that, in computing average class size metrics, we include enrollment in each 1-2-credit section, not just sections with 3 or more credits.

Along with the honors-only average of 26.3 students, the mixed honors sections average **85.9 students**, and the contract sections with honors credit for individual honors students average **71.3 students**. Across all fifty programs, the average mixed honors section has 51.1 students, and the average contract section has 60.1 students.

Honors Graduation Rate (4.0): The rating is based on the actual grad rate for students who entered the program six years earlier, whether or not the students remained in honors. The **actual rate of 87%** is also compared to the rates of other programs with the same test score entry requirement range, and then adjusted to the **score of 87.1%.** In some cases this measure favors programs within universities with relatively higher test scores for the student population as a whole. The average honors graduation rate for all programs with similar test scores required for admission is 86.2%.

Value-Added Grad Rate (3.5): The value-added rate measures the extent to which the adjusted score listed above exceeds the six-year grad rate for the university as a whole. **The university-wide rate is 80%.** Note: This measure generally favors programs within universities with relatively lower test scores for the student population as a whole.

Ratio of Staff to Honors Students (4.5): There is 1 staff member for every **111.0** students. (Mean ratio for all 50 programs is 1 staff member for every 135.6 students.)

Honors Residence Halls, Amenities (4.0): The McFadden/Lechner honors residence halls can house about 400 freshmen students. The coed dorms have air-conditioned, suite-style rooms with shared baths. The nearest dining is at Sbisa.

Honors Residence Halls, Availability (5.0): This rating compares the number of places in honors residence halls to the number of honors freshman and sophomore members in good standing, about 389. The ratio for the honors program is **1.03** rooms for each first- and second-year student. The average for all fifty programs is .63 places.

Prestigious Awards (4.5): The awards that we track and include are listed in the section titled "Prestigious Scholarships." The awards are sometimes won by students who are not in an honors college or program, but increasingly many are enrolled in honors programs. It is also a trend that honors colleges and programs help to prepare their students for the awards competitions.

Aggies have won at least 5 Rhodes scholarships, 4 Marshall scholarships, and 4 Truman scholarships. Among the undergraduate awards won by Aggies, there have been at least 6 Udall scholars and 42 Goldwater scholars.

UNRATED FEATURES

Continuation Requirements: 3.50 cumulative. For honors graduation, 3.50 cumulative, with at least at 3.25 in honors courses.

Academic Strengths, National Rankings: This is based on national rankings of *graduate* programs in 15 disciplines, except engineering and business, where undergraduate rankings are used.

TAMU has an outstanding faculty, easily ranking among the top 50 in the nation. Among many strong departments are engineering (15), chemistry (19), political science (25), business (29), earth sciences (32), education (39), computer science (40), math (41), economics (42), physics (44), and sociology (46).

Undergraduate Research: "Undergraduate research opportunities for all students are run through our office. The thesis program is one of several options for Honors students to complete their capstone requirement."

Study Abroad: According to the Institute of International Education (2014 report), TAMU ranked third in the total number of students studying abroad among the top 40 doctorate institutions.

Financial Aid: Below please see the value of scholarship packages offered to National Merit Scholars:

"The scholarships listed below will be in addition to any other scholarships from our department, individual colleges or departments at Texas A&M, or from other outside donors.

"For out-of-state students, the value of the scholarship package could approach $100,000 due to the out-of-state tuition waiver, worth approximately $18,500 per year."

President's Endowed Scholarship--$12,000
NM Recognition Award--$26,000
Sponsorship (TAMU)--$2,000
Total over four years--$40,000 (in-state)

Study Abroad Stipend, $1,000
NMRA Supplemental for 5th year of study--$3,000
Total Potential Four Year Scholarship Award Package (stipend and 5th year) --$4,000

Honors Fees: None.

Placement Experiences: TAMU grads are viewed very positively by the business and engineering professions. Many honors grads go on to study at the nation's most prestigious universities.

Degree of Difference: This is based on the differences between (1) the average (2015, two-part) SAT scores for enrolled honors students (1375) and (2) the average test scores for all students in the university (1135) as a whole. The test scores may be an indication of how "elite" honors students may be perceived as compared to students in the university as a whole. The scores can also provide an indication of how well prepared the non-honors students in the university may be. **Please keep in mind that neither high nor low test scores determine the overall quality of a program.**

NAME: TEXAS TECH UNIVERSITY HONORS COLLEGE.

Date Established: 1999.

Location: Lubbock, Texas.

University Full-time Undergraduate Enrollment: 25,589.

Honors Members in Good Standing: 1,247 (mean size of all 50 programs is 1,742).,

Honors Average Admission Statistics: ACT, 28.1; old two-part SAT, 1242. Est. new SAT score, 1310.

Average High School GPA/Class Rank: None listed.

Basic Admission Requirements: Desired: ACT, 30. Old SAT, 1300. Est. new SAT, 1360.

Application Deadline(s): *Please verify with each program, as some deadlines could change.*

Application period begins August 1, 2016 and ends March 1, 2017.

Honors Programs with old SAT scores from 1240—1291: Arkansas, Oklahoma State, Texas Tech, Montana, Washington State, New Mexico, South Dakota, Colorado State, Arizona, Montana State, Arizona State.

Administrative Staff: 15.5 FTEs.

RATINGS AT A GLANCE: For all mortarboard ratings immediately below, a score of 5 is the maximum and represents a comparison with all 50 honors colleges and programs. More detailed explanations follow the "mortarboard" ratings.

PERCEPTION* OF UNIVERSITY AS A WHOLE, NOT OF HONORS: 🎓🎓🎓

*Perception is based on the university's ranking among public universities in the 2016 U.S. News Best Colleges report. Please bear in mind that the better the U.S. News ranking, the more difficult it is for an honors college or program to have a rating that equals or improves on the magazine ranking.

OVERALL HONORS RATING: 🎓🎓🎓🎓 1/2

Curriculum Requirements: 🎓🎓🎓🎓 1/2

Number of Honors Classes Offered: 🎓🎓🎓 1/2

Number of Honors Classes in Key Disciplines: 🎓🎓🎓🎓

Extent of Honors Enrollment: 🎓🎓🎓🎓

Honors-only Class Size: 🎓🎓🎓🎓

Overall Class Size (Honors-only plus mixed, contract): 🎓🎓🎓🎓^1/2

Honors Grad Rate: 🎓🎓🎓🎓

Value-Added Grad Rate: 🎓🎓🎓🎓^1/2

Ratio of Staff to Students: 🎓🎓🎓🎓🎓

Priority Registration: "Texas Tech University Honors College students receive priority registration as long as they are members of the Honors College. Honors College Seniors receive first day registration privileges and all other Honors students receive second day registration privileges."

Honors Housing Amenities: 🎓🎓🎓🎓🎓

Honors Housing Availability: 🎓🎓🎓🎓^1/2

Prestigious Awards: 🎓🎓🎓

RATING SCORES AND EXPLANATIONS:

Curriculum Requirements (4.5): The most important rating category, the curriculum completion requirement (classes required to complete honors) defines not only what honors students should learn but also the extent to which honors students and faculty are connected in the classroom. If there is a thesis or capstone requirement, it reinforces the individual contact and research skills so important to learning.

The average number of honors semester hours required for completion across all 50 programs is 29.0.

The honors college has two completion options (see below), but also has programs that lead to early acceptance to TTU medical and law schools:

Graduation with Honors--Students complete a total of 24 hours of honors credits, which must include at least 3 hours of upper-level honors seminar work and a 3-credit capstone requirement. A maximum of 6 credits of upper-level work in honors contract courses can be counted. All freshmen honors entrants must also complete an honors First Year Experience course, included in the total of 24 credits.

The Honors First-Year Experience (FYE) Program helps first-year students to transition into university life. Honors students take one of the core courses, each taught by an outstanding professor in a small group. First-year students have a built-in community through a designated Learning Community Group (LCG). These are taught by two upperclassmen "who function as Peer Mentors to guide freshmen though the adjustment phase and integrate them into the Honors and Tech communities."

Graduation with Highest Honors--Completion requires the same 24 honors credits along with an additional 6 credits of research, culminating in a senior honors **thesis**, for a total of 30 credits. A minimum grade of B- is required for honors credit in any honors college course or approved contract or graduate course.

The Honors College is a leader nationwide in crafting policies and requirements for honors contract classes. The College limits the number and level of honors contract courses that can count for honors credit and has well-defined procedures in place that are designed to ensure the highest levels of academic quality and integrity.

Early Acceptance to TTU Medical and Law Schools:

Medical School--"The joint TTU-TTUHSC Early Acceptance Program offers an exciting opportunity to select Honors College students by allowing them to waive the MCAT (Medical College Admissions Test) and to apply early to the TTUHSC's School of Medicine (SOM), typically in the junior year. Successful Early Acceptance applicants are notified of their acceptance to the School of Medicine in February and complete their baccalaureate degrees prior to admission.

"The primary goal of this special program is to encourage Honors students to broaden their educational experiences before they enroll in their professional studies. The waiver of the MCAT allows students to become actively involved in the Honors College and to include coursework or other experiences in areas such as languages, the humanities, mathematics, and business, enabling them to become more well-rounded professionals. This is not an accelerated program. Therefore, the School of Medicine reserves the right to deny acceptance through this program to students who may contemplate early graduation."

"A related opportunity is the **Health and Humanities track within the Honors Arts and Letters major,** designed to allow a flexible course of study for honors students that is firmly rooted in the Humanities in order to enable them to become more competitive applicants to medical schools and other professional healthcare programs which are increasingly seeking well-rounded applicants with a diverse and comprehensive undergraduate background. Students preparing for entrance to healthcare professional programs must complete all prerequisite courses for their desired program in addition to satisfying course requirements for the HAL major."

"Law School--"The Honors College and the Law School cooperate in an Early Decision Plan, which allows exceptional Law School applicants who are **Honors College students in good standing to receive notification of their acceptance to the Law School during their third year at Texas Tech**. Enrollment in the Law School would not occur until after the student receives a baccalaureate degree.

"To be eligible to apply for Law School Early Decision, applicants must have a minimum undergraduate GPA of at least 3.50; an LSAT score that places them in the top half nationwide (>152, approximately); an SAT of at least 1300 or an ACT of at least 29; and be enrolled in the Texas Tech University Honors College and making satisfactory progress toward a baccalaureate degree with a diploma designation in Honors studies.

"Students will apply during the fall semester of their third year (or during the fall semester of a year in which they are classified as juniors) and must have taken the LSAT by December of that year. Students who receive and accept an Early Decision must commit to enroll at the Texas Tech University School of Law and may not apply to other law schools."

AP/IB credits are not counted as replacements for honors courses.

Number of Honors Classes Offered (3.5): This is a measure of the total **adjusted** honors main sections available in the term reported, not including labs and thesis. (Please read the section titled "All about Honors Classes".) An adjusted main section has 3 or more semester credits, or equivalent, and sections with fewer credits receive a lower prorated value.

The honors college offered an adjusted section for every **16.3** enrolled students. The average for all 50 programs is 14.2 students. The lower the number, the better.

In the term reported, **97.8%** of honors enrollment was **in honors-only sections; none in mixed honors sections (honors and non-honors students); and 2.2% reported in contract sections (regular sections in which honors students "contract" to do extra work).** The averages for all fifty programs are 81.3% in honors-only sections; 13.6 % in mixed honors sections; and 5.1% in contract sections.

Number of Honors Classes in Key Disciplines (4.0): The 15 "key" disciplines are biological sciences; business (all); chemistry; communications (especially public speaking); computer science; economics; engineering (all); English; history; math (all); philosophy; physics; political science; psychology; and sociology/anthropology/gender studies. Interdisciplinary sections, such as those often taken for General Education credit in the first two years, do receive a lesser, prorated discipline "credit" because they introduce students to multiple disciplines in an especially engaging way, often with in-depth discussion.

For this measure, mixed and contract sections are not counted as a section in a key discipline unless students taking the sections for honors credit make up at least 10% of the total section enrollment.

In the term reported, the program had a ratio of **27.1 honors students** per each main section in some or all "key disciplines." The mean for all 50 programs is 26.3. The lower the ratio, the better.

Out of **41 adjusted sections in key disciplines**, the program had all were **honors-only sections.** The most sections were in math (7), business and physics (6 each), history (5), biology (4), and chemistry and engineering (3 each).

The college also offered more than 20 honors interdisciplinary seminars. Among them were "Booms, Busts, and Dust: Writings about Texans and their Land"; "History of Mathematics"; "Victorian Morals, Victorian Mayhem-Jack the Ripper & Microhistory."

The combination of interdisciplinary seminars and honors courses in the disciplines makes the program a strong **blended program.**

Extent of Honors Enrollment (4.0:): Not all honors students take an honors class each term, especially after the first two years. Programs that have fewer honors classes for upper-division honors students will generally have fewer total members in good standing who are actually enrolled in a given term. (Please be aware, however, that honors students not enrolled in a class for a term are still connected to the honors community through residential and extracurricular activities.)

For example, if honors students in a program occupy 1,800 honors classroom seats in a given term, and there are 3,000 honors students in good standing, the extent of enrollment is .67. For programs that require a thesis, the ratio (score) reported below might in fact be somewhat higher, since we only count "regular" class enrollment for this measure, and not thesis enrollment. The college **has a ratio of 1.14**; the mean is 1.13 for all 50 programs. The higher the ratio, the better.

Average Class Size, Honors-only Sections (4.0): Offered mostly in the first two years, honors-only classes tend to be smaller and, as the name implies, have no or very few students other than those in the honors program. These class sections are almost always much smaller than mixed or contract sections, or regular non-honors class sections in the university.

The average honors-only class size in the honors program is **19.0 students**. The average for all 50 programs is 19.0 students.

Average Class Size, Overall (4.5): The overall class calculation is based on the *proportion* of honors students in each type of class (honors-only, mixed honors, and honors contract sections). Thus it is not a raw average. The overall honors-credit class size is **19.7 students**, versus the average for all 50 programs of 26.3 students.

These class size averages also do not correspond to the number of students per honors sections numbers above. The reason is that, in computing average class size metrics, we include enrollment in each 1-2-credit section, not just sections with 3 or more credits.

Along with the honors-only average of 19.0 students, the mixed honors sections average **(NA)** students, and the contract sections with honors credit for individual honors students average **49.2** students. Across all fifty programs, the average mixed honors section has 51.1 students, and the average contract section has 60.1 students.

Honors Graduation Rate (4.0): The rating is based on the actual grad rate for students who entered the program six years earlier, whether or not the students remained in honors. The **actual rate of 85.0%** is also compared to the rates of other programs with the same test score entry requirement range, and then adjusted to the **score of 85.0%**. In some cases this measure favors programs within universities with relatively higher test scores for the student population as a whole. The average honors graduation rate for all programs with similar test scores required for admission is 85.6%.

Value-Added Grad Rate (4.5): The value-added rate measures the extent to which the adjusted score listed above exceeds the six-year grad rate for the university as a whole. **The university-wide rate is 59%.** Note: This measure generally favors programs within universities with relatively lower test scores for the student population as a whole.

Ratio of Staff to Honors Students (5.0): There is 1 staff member for every **80.5** students. (Mean ratio for all 50 programs is 1 staff member for every 135.6 students.)

Honors Residence Halls, Amenities (5.0): Tech honors students are fortunate to have two honors residence halls with suite-style rooms that are air-conditioned, with shared baths. The dorms are coed, with each shared suite all male or all female. Gordon Hall has dining on site at the Fresh Plate. Murray Hall students have the option of eating at Sam's Place, on site.

Honors Residence Halls, Availability (4.5): This rating compares the number of places in honors residence halls to the number of honors freshman and sophomore members in good standing, about 624. The ratio for the honors program is **.65** places for each first- and second-year student. The average for all fifty programs is .63 rooms.

Prestigious Awards (3.0): The awards that we track and include are listed in the section titled "Prestigious Scholarships." The awards are sometimes won by students who are not in an honors college or program, but increasingly many are enrolled in honors programs. It is also a trend that honors colleges and programs help to prepare their students for the awards competitions.

Tech students have won 1 Rhodes scholarship, 3 Gates Cambridge scholarships, and a Truman scholarship. They have also won 33 Goldwater scholarships and an above average share of Gilman scholarships.

UNRATED FEATURES

Continuation Requirements: 3.25 for continuation and graduation.

Academic Strengths, National Rankings: This is based on national rankings of *graduate* programs in 15 disciplines, except engineering and business, where undergraduate rankings are used.

The average national departmental ranking at Tech is about 120th in the nation, lead by engineering (87), earth sciences (89), and business (93).

Undergraduate Research: "The Honors [research] program is called Undergraduate Research Scholars (URS). URS is a year-long (or longer) program which culminates in the student's participation in the TTU Undergraduate Research Conference and/or thesis. Scholars receive a stipend through an endowment to participate in research with a faculty mentor. Scholars may participate in URS for two or more years."

Study Abroad: The honors college reported during the last review that it has "a $110,000 yearly scholarship fund to assist students wishing to study abroad. Awards vary depending on program length. Generally, a typical full semester award is $3,500." The university has exchange programs with 65 foreign universities, most of them in Europe, but there are programs in Australia, Brazil (several), Turkey, China, and Korea as well.

Perhaps the centerpiece of the university's study-abroad programs is the Texas Tech University Center in Sevilla, located on the Guadalquivir River in southern Spain, in the heart of the region known as Andalusia.

"A city of roughly 700,000 inhabitants, Sevilla offers all of the advantages of a big city while still maintaining a small-town feel. In Sevilla, students can still appreciate the splendor of Golden Age Spain as they meander through the nooks and crannies of the medieval city center, whose cathedral holds the tomb of Christopher Columbus, and at the same time take advantage of the modern cultural and leisure activities that this vibrant city has to offer.

"The Center allows students to take catalog TTU classes taught by Texas Tech faculty. The Center has a permanent staff as well as faculty that travel from Lubbock to Sevilla every semester (fall, spring and summer). The Center is located in a building that originally dates back to the 1890s, and today has all of the modern conveniences a university facility needs. It is conveniently situated in a bustling neighborhood, literally steps away from all sorts of eateries and shops."

Financial Aid: "The Honors College awarded $344,500 in scholarship funding in Academic Year 2015/2016. Scholarship decisions are based on exceptional performance as a TTU Honors College student. Scholarship considerations include: Honors experiences, overcoming adversity and challenges, work responsibilities, family circumstances, and volunteer experience. Most scholarship awards vary between $1,000 to $2,000 per year."

The National Merit Scholarship program was revitalized last year when Texas Tech University awarded full tuition and housing to seven National Merit Finalists.

Honors Fees: None.

Placement Experiences: None listed.

Degree of Difference: This is based on the differences between (1) the average (2015, two-part) SAT scores for enrolled honors students (1242) and (2) the average test scores for all students in the university (1100) as a whole. The test scores may be an indication of how "elite" honors students may be perceived as compared to students in the university as a whole. The scores can also provide an indication of how well prepared the non-honors students in the university may be. **Please keep in mind that neither high nor low test scores determine the overall quality of a program.**

NAME: UNIVERSITY OF CALIFORNIA, IRVINE, CAMPUSWIDE HONORS PROGRAM.

Date Established: 1988.

Location: Irvine, California.

University Full-time Undergraduate Enrollment: 24,139.

Honors Members in Good Standing: 750 (mean size of all 50 programs is 1,742).

Honors Average Admission Statistics: Old two-part SAT equivalent, 1419. (Used 3-part SAT, avg. 2120, SAT-R 706, SAT-M 713). Est. new SAT score, 1470.

Average High School GPA/Class Rank: 4.21.

Basic Admission Requirements: "All freshman applicants to UC Irvine are considered for admission to the Campuswide Honors Program. Applicants are invited to the program based on an application review by the faculty in each academic school. (There is no specific test score/HS GPA requirement.)"

Application Deadline(s): *Please verify with each program, as some deadlines could change.*

Application period for all UC campuses is August 1-November 30, 2016. Honors invitation after applicants confirm UC Irvine as choice on May 1, 2017.

Honors Programs with old SAT scores from 1402—1469: UCF, Connecticut, Kentucky, Washington, Maryland, North Carolina, UC Irvine, Kansas, Minnesota, Tennessee, South Carolina, Clemson, UT Austin, Georgia.

Administrative Staff: 7.

RATINGS AT A GLANCE: For all mortarboard ratings immediately below, a score of 5 is the maximum and represents a comparison with all 50 honors colleges and programs. More detailed explanations follow the "mortarboard" ratings.

PERCEPTION* OF UNIVERSITY AS A WHOLE, NOT OF HONORS: 🎓🎓🎓🎓🎓

*Perception is based on the university's ranking among public universities in the 2016 U.S. News Best Colleges report. Please bear in mind that the better the U.S. News ranking, the more difficult it is for an honors college or program to have a rating that equals or improves on the magazine ranking.

OVERALL HONORS RATING: 🎓🎓🎓🎓$^{1/2}$

Curriculum Requirements: 🎓🎓🎓🎓🎓

Number of Honors Classes Offered: 🎓🎓🎓$^{1/2}$

Number of Honors Classes in Key Disciplines: 🎓🎓🎓$^{1/2}$

Extent of Honors Enrollment: 🎓🎓🎓$^{1/2}$

Honors-only Class Size: 🎓🎓🎓🎓$^{1/2}$

Overall Class Size (Honors-only plus mixed, contract): 🎓🎓🎓🎓🎓

Honors Grad Rate: 🎓🎓🎓🎓🎓

Value-Added Grad Rate: 🎓🎓🎓$^{1/2}$

Ratio of Staff to Students: 🎓🎓🎓🎓$^{1/2}$

Priority Registration: Yes, honors students register for all courses, honors and otherwise, with the first group of students during each year they are in the program.

Honors Housing Amenities: 🎓🎓🎓$^{1/2}$

Honors Housing Availability: 🎓🎓🎓🎓$^{1/2}$

Prestigious Awards: 🎓🎓🎓🎓

RATING SCORES AND EXPLANATIONS:

Curriculum Requirements (5.0): The most important rating category, the curriculum completion requirement (classes required to complete honors) defines not only what honors students should learn but also the extent to which honors students and faculty are connected in the classroom. If there is a thesis or capstone requirement, it reinforces the individual contact and research skills so important to learning.

The average number of honors semester hours required for completion across all 50 programs is 29.0.

Completion of the program requires 54 *quarter* hours, which is the equivalent of **36** semester credits. A **thesis** is also required, included in the total above, and students must work on the thesis for at least two quarters.

First-year students must take the Honors Humanities Core sequence: 8 units for 3 quarters, or 24 units. Many sophomores take the Honors Social Science Core: 6 units for 3 quarters, or 18 units. Likewise, many juniors take the Honors Science Core Course: 4 units for 3 quarters, or 12 units.

"Students may switch the order in which they complete the Social Science and Science Cores, or take them simultaneously. Students who will not otherwise be taking any math or science courses as part of their curriculum in college may wish to take the Science Core during the sophomore year instead of the junior year, and postpone Social Science Core until junior year."

AP/IB credits are not counted as replacements for honors courses.

Number of Honors Classes Offered (3.5): This is a measure of the total **adjusted** honors main sections available in the term reported, not including labs and thesis. (Please read the section titled "All about Honors Classes".) An adjusted main section has 3 or more semester credits, or equivalent, and sections with fewer credits receive a lower prorated value.

The program offered an adjusted section for every **18.1** enrolled students. The average for all 50 programs is 14.2 students. The lower the number, the better.

In the term reported, **100%** of honors enrollment was **in honors-only sections.** The averages for all fifty programs are 81.3% in honors-only sections; 13.6 % in mixed honors sections; and 5.1% in contract sections.

Number of Honors Classes in Key Disciplines (3.5): The 15 "key" disciplines are biological sciences; business (all); chemistry; communications (especially public speaking); computer science; economics; engineering (all); English; history; math (all); philosophy; physics; political science; psychology; and sociology/anthropology/gender studies. Interdisciplinary sections, such as those often taken for General Education credit in the first two years, do receive a lesser, prorated discipline "credit" because they introduce students to multiple disciplines in an especially engaging way, often with in-depth discussion.

For this measure, mixed and contract sections are not counted as a section in a key discipline unless students taking the sections for honors credit make up at least 10% of the total section enrollment.

In the term reported, the program had a ratio of **48.5 honors students** per each main section in some or all "key disciplines." The mean for all 50 programs is 26.3. The lower the ratio, the better.

The "key discipline" score for the CHP derives entirely from the values assigned to interdisciplinary seminars for having at least some disciplinary content. The program does not offer courses strictly defined to one discipline (e.g., calculus I, or physics I). Examples of courses offered by the CHP in social sciences are "Jurisprudence and Constitutional Law"; "What is Space?"; and "Globalization and Human Security." Examples from the science core are "The Philosophy of Quantum Mechanics" and "The Impact of World War I on Physics, Chemistry, Astronomy and Other Sciences."

As fascinating as these sound, they remain interdisciplinary, as one can tell, especially by the titles of the science core courses. Those courses also help to explain why such courses definitely deserve some "points" for the key discipline metric.

The total emphasis on interdisciplinary seminars makes the program a pure **core honors program.**

Extent of Honors Enrollment (3.5:): Not all honors students take an honors class each term, especially after the first two years. Programs that have fewer honors classes for upper-division honors students will generally have fewer total members in good standing who are actually enrolled in a given term. (Please be

aware, however, that honors students not enrolled in a class for a term are still connected to the honors community through residential and extracurricular activities.)

For example, if honors students in a program occupy 1,800 honors classroom seats in a given term, and there are 3,000 honors students in good standing, the extent of enrollment is .67. For programs that require a thesis, the ratio (score) reported below might in fact be somewhat higher, since we only count "regular" class enrollment for this measure, and not thesis enrollment. The CHP **has a ratio of .94**; the mean is 1.13 for all 50 programs. The higher the ratio, the better.

Average Class Size, Honors-only Sections (4.5): Offered mostly in the first two years, honors-only classes tend to be smaller and, as the name implies, have no or very few students other than those in the honors program. These class sections are almost always much smaller than mixed or contract sections, or regular non-honors class sections in the university.

The average honors-only class size in the honors program is **16.4 students**. The average for all 50 programs is 19.0 students.

Average Class Size, Overall (5.0): The overall class calculation is based on the *proportion* of honors students in each type of class (honors-only, mixed honors, and honors contract sections). Thus it is not a raw average. The overall honors-credit class size is **16.4 students**, versus the average for all 50 programs of 26.3 students.

These class size averages also do not correspond to the number of students per honors sections numbers above. The reason is that, in computing average class size metrics, we include enrollment in each 1-2-credit section, not just sections with 3 or more credits.

Along with the honors-only average of 16.4 students, the mixed honors sections average **(NA)**students, and the contract sections with honors credit for individual honors students average **(NA)** students. Across all fifty programs, the average mixed honors section has 51.1 students, and the average contract section has 60.1 students.

Honors Graduation Rate (5.0): The rating is based on the actual grad rate for students who entered the program six years earlier, whether or not the students remained in honors. The **actual rate of 98.6%** is also compared to the rates of other programs with the same test score entry requirement range, and then adjusted to the **score of 99.2%.** In some cases this measure favors programs within universities with relatively higher test scores for the student population as a whole. The average honors graduation rate for all programs with similar test scores required for admission is 92.6%.

Value-Added Grad Rate (3.5): The value-added rate measures the extent to which the adjusted score listed above exceeds the six-year grad rate for the university as a whole. **The university-wide rate is a very high 87%.** Note: This measure generally favors programs within universities with relatively lower test scores for the student population as a whole.

Ratio of Staff to Honors Students (4.5): There is 1 staff member for every **107.1** students. (Mean ratio for all 50 programs is 1 staff member for every 135.6 students.)

Honors Residence Halls, Amenities (3.5): Freshmen living in honors housing are about evenly divided among three residences: The Shire, Loma, and Arroyo. While all of these have suite-style rooms and shared baths, they are not air-conditioned. However, the Irvine climate is generally mild, especially for the fall, winter, and spring quarters. The most convenient dining for Shire residents is Pippin; for the other freshman residences, it is the Anteatery.

Upperclassmen may choose to live in Arroyo Vista, with features similar to those in the freshmen dorms. Dining is conveniently located within the complex.

Honors Residence Halls, Availability (4.5): This rating compares the number of rooms in honors residence halls to the number of honors freshman and sophomore members in good standing, about 375.

The ratio for the honors program is **.71** places for each first- and second-year student. The average for all fifty programs is .63 places.

Prestigious Awards (4.0): The awards that we track and include are listed in the section titled "Prestigious Scholarships." The awards are sometimes won by students who are not in an honors college or program, but increasingly many are enrolled in honors programs. It is also a trend that honors colleges and programs help to prepare their students for the awards competitions.

Most UCI awards are won by CHP students. The total awards won by all UCI students are Rhodes scholarships (1), Gates Cambridge (2), Marshall (2), and Truman (7). UCI students do extremely well in winning Fulbright Student scholarships, and most of these are for research, and in winning NSF graduate fellowships. Students have also won 31 Goldwater scholarships.

UNRATED FEATURES

Continuation Requirements: Minimum GPAs are: Freshmen, 2.80; Sophomores, 3.00; Juniors and Seniors, 3.20; Graduation, 3.20.

Academic Strengths, National Rankings: This is based on national rankings of *graduate* programs in 15 disciplines, except engineering and business, where undergraduate rankings are used.

The average departmental rank at UCI is somewhere between 30th and 35th in the nation. Outstanding programs are in English (22), chemistry (24), education and sociology (25 each), computer science and physics (29 each), psychology (30), and biology, business, and earth sciences (all 34).

Undergraduate Research: "The Undergraduate Research Opportunities Program (UROP) encourages and facilitates research and creative activities by undergraduates from all schools and academic disciplines at UCI. The program offers assistance to students and faculty through all phases of the research process, whether it is with proposal writing, developing research plans through project management skills, awarding grants to fund research projects, scholarly journal writing through *The UCI Undergraduate Research Journal,* or presenting results of the research or creative project through the UCI Undergraduate Research Symposium."

Study Abroad: "Best time for CHP students to study abroad: fall of junior year, full year junior year, or fall of senior year. Take Honors Core courses early, before going abroad. Find a research advisor prior to studying abroad, even if you won't do research until you return. Discover or enhance your research topic while abroad. Enhance your resume--very helpful when applying for awards, scholarships, achievements, grad school, medical school, etc."

UCI does a good job of aligning study-abroad programs with academic majors. For example, students in biological sciences can easily find that they can study at the Bermuda Institute of Ocean Sciences or volunteer for an expedition with the Earthwatch Institute. Physics majors might choose Lund University in Sweden or the National University of Singapore.

"The Samueli School's Program in International Engineering (PIE) offers students a unique opportunity to train to be successful engineers in a truly global economy. The only such program offered in California, PIE provides *a course of study leading to both a B.S. degree in engineering and a B.A. degree in German.* A five-year program, PIE involves a study abroad component and an internship in a German-speaking country. Students will enter the workforce skilled in a field of engineering and with a deep understanding of a foreign language and culture."

Financial Aid: "The most prestigious merit award at UC campuses is the Regents' Scholarship, the amount of which varies each year. The amount can also vary according to the income level of the recipients. For engineering students, there is the Henry Samueli Endowed Scholarship. Each year, the UCI Alumni Association awards more than $85,000 in scholarships."

Placement Experiences: "UCI Campuswide Honors Program alumni attend some of the most prestigious graduate and professional schools in the nation, pursue careers in many different fields, and are active, engaged members of their communities."

Degree of Difference: This is based on the differences between (1) the average (2015, two-part) SAT scores for enrolled honors students (1419) and (2) the average test scores for all students in the university (1175) as a whole. The test scores may be an indication of how "elite" honors students may be perceived as compared to students in the university as a whole. The scores can also provide an indication of how well prepared the non-honors students in the university may be. **Please keep in mind that neither high nor low test scores determine the overall quality of a program.**

NAME: BURNETT HONORS COLLEGE, UNIVERSITY OF CENTRAL FLORIDA.

Date Established: 1998; preceded by Honors Program, 1982.

Location: Orlando, Florida.

University Full-time Undergraduate Enrollment: 36,428.

Honors Members in Good Standing: 1,948. (mean size of all 50 programs is 1,742).

Honors Average Admission Statistics: ACT, 31.6; old two-part SAT, 1402. Est. new SAT score, 1451.

Average High School GPA/Class Rank: 4.382; 80% ranked in the top 10th of their class.

Basic Admission Requirements: None listed.

Application Deadline(s): *Please verify with each program, as some deadlines could change.*

Deadline is March 31, 2017, but National Scholars are "guaranteed consideration" up to May 1, 2017.

Honors Programs with old SAT scores from 1402—1469: UCF, Connecticut, Kentucky, Washington, Maryland, North Carolina, UC Irvine, Kansas, Minnesota, Tennessee, South Carolina, Clemson, UT Austin, Georgia.

Administrative Staff: 26 FTEs.

RATINGS AT A GLANCE: For all mortarboard ratings immediately below, a score of 5 is the maximum and represents a comparison with all 50 honors colleges and programs. More detailed explanations follow the "mortarboard" ratings.

PERCEPTION* OF UNIVERSITY AS A WHOLE, NOT OF HONORS: 🎓🎓🎓

*Perception is based on the university's ranking among public universities in the 2016 U.S. News Best Colleges report. Please bear in mind that the better the U.S. News ranking, the more difficult it is for an honors college or program to have a rating that equals or improves on the magazine ranking.

OVERALL HONORS RATING: 🎓🎓🎓🎓[1/2]

Curriculum Requirements: 🎓🎓🎓🎓

Number of Honors Classes Offered: 🎓🎓🎓🎓🎓

Number of Honors Classes in Key Disciplines: 🎓🎓🎓🎓🎓

Extent of Honors Enrollment: 🎓🎓🎓🎓[1/2]

Honors-only Class Size: 🎓🎓🎓🎓

Overall Class Size (Honors-only plus mixed, contract): 🎓🎓🎓🎓 1/2

Honors Grad Rate: 🎓🎓🎓

Value-Added Grad Rate: 🎓🎓🎓🎓

Ratio of Staff to Students: 🎓🎓🎓🎓🎓

Priority Registration: Yes, honors students have priority registration for all courses, in the form of being able to register with the class ahead of them.

Honors Housing Amenities: 🎓🎓🎓🎓 1/2

Honors Housing Availability: 🎓🎓🎓🎓

Prestigious Awards: 🎓🎓🎓

RATING SCORES AND EXPLANATIONS:

Curriculum Requirements (4.0): The most important rating category, the curriculum completion requirement (classes required to complete honors) defines not only what honors students should learn but also the extent to which honors students and faculty are connected in the classroom. If there is a thesis or capstone requirement, it reinforces the individual contact and research skills so important to learning.

The average number of honors semester hours required for completion across all 50 programs is 29.0.

The average completion at the honors college requires at about **29** semester hours.

University Honors requires a 2-credit honors symposium; a 3-credit interdisciplinary seminar; and 18-24 departmental honors credits.

Honors in the Major requires a 3-credit honors directed reading course as well as a 3-credit **thesis.**

AP/IB credits are **not** counted as replacements for honors courses

Number of Honors Classes Offered (5.0): This is a measure of the total **adjusted** honors main sections available in the term reported, not including labs and thesis. (Please read the section titled "All about Honors Classes".) An adjusted main section has 3 or more semester credits, or equivalent, and sections with fewer credits receive a lower prorated value.

The honors program had a ratio of **9.6** enrolled students per each main section. The mean for all 50 programs is 14.2. The lower the ratio, the better.

In the term reported, **100.0%** of honors enrollment was **in honors-only sections.** The averages for all fifty programs are 81.3% in honors-only sections; 13.6 % in mixed honors sections; and 5.1% in contract sections.

Number of Honors Classes in Key Disciplines (5.0): The 15 "key" disciplines are biological sciences; business (all); chemistry; communications (especially public speaking); computer science; economics; engineering (all); English; history; math (all); philosophy; physics; political science; psychology; and sociology/anthropology/gender studies. Interdisciplinary sections, such as those often taken for General Education credit in the first two years, do receive a lesser, prorated discipline "credit" because they introduce students to multiple disciplines in an especially engaging way, often with in-depth discussion.

In the term reported, the program had ratio of **13.6 honors students** per each main section in some or all "key disciplines." The mean for all 50 programs is 26.3. The lower the ratio, the better.

Out of **82 adjusted sections in key disciplines**, all were **honors-only sections.** Math (15—a very high number), biology and communications (11 each), English (10), philosophy and physics (5 each), had the most sections, followed by history and psychology (4 each).

The program also offered about 30 honors symposium sections of 2 credits each, along with a dozen 3-credit interdisciplinary seminars, including "Terrorism from a Global Perspective"; "Analysis and Application of Ethics in Legal Context"; and "Religion and Medicine."

The combination of seminars and courses in the disciplines makes the program an example of a large **blended** program.

Extent of Honors Enrollment (4.5): Not all honors students take an honors class each term, especially after the first two years. Programs that have fewer honors classes for upper-division honors students will generally have fewer total members in good standing who are actually enrolled in a given term. (Please be aware, however, that honors students not enrolled in a class for a term are still connected to the honors community through residential and extracurricular activities.)

For example, if honors students in a program occupy 1,800 honors classroom seats in a given term, and there are 3,000 honors students in good standing, the extent of enrollment is .67. For programs that require a thesis, the ratio (score) reported below might in fact be somewhat higher, since we only count "regular" class enrollment for this measure, and not thesis enrollment. The college **has a ratio of 1.19**; the mean is 1.13 for all 50 programs. The higher the ratio, the better.

Average Class Size, Honors-only Sections (4.0): Offered mostly in the first two years, honors-only classes tend to be smaller and, as the name implies, have no or very few students other than those in the honors program. These class sections are almost always much smaller than mixed or contract sections, or regular non-honors class sections in the university.

The average honors-only class size in the honors program is **18.1 students**. The average for all 50 programs is 19.0 students.

Average Class Size, Overall (4.5): The overall class calculation is based on the *proportion* of honors students in each type of class (honors-only, mixed honors, and honors contract sections). Thus it is not a raw average. The overall honors-credit class size is **18.1 students**, versus the average for all 50 programs of 26.3 students.

These class size averages also do not correspond to the number of students per honors sections numbers above. The reason is that, in computing average class size metrics, we include enrollment in each 1-2-credit section, not just sections with 3 or more credits.

Along with the honors-only average of 18.1 students, the mixed honors sections average **(NA)** students, and the contract sections with honors credit for individual honors students average **(NA)** students. Across all fifty programs, the average mixed honors section has 51.1 students, and the average contract section has 60.1 students.

Honors Graduation Rate (3.0): The rating is the based on the actual grad rate for students who entered the program six years earlier, whether or not the students remained in honors. The **actual rate of 81.5%** is also compared to the rates of other programs with the same test score entry requirement range, and then adjusted to the **score of 80.4%.** In some cases this measure favors programs within universities with relatively higher test scores for the student population as a whole. The average honors graduation rate for all programs with similar test scores required for admission is 92.6%.

Value-Added Grad Rate (4.0): The value-added rate measures the extent to which the adjusted score listed above exceeds the grad rate for the university as a whole. **The university-wide rate is 70%.** Note: This measure generally favors programs within universities with relatively lower test scores for the student population as a whole.

Ratio of Staff to Honors Students (5.0): There is 1 staff member for every **111.2** students. (Mean ratio for all 50 programs is 1 staff member for every 135.6 students.)

Honors Residence Halls, Amenities (4.5): About 70% of honors students living in honors housing reside in Tower III, with the Towers at Knights Plaza. Tower III features air-conditioned *apartments* for both freshmen and upperclassmen. Dining is not on site, but it is within the Towers community.

The remaining 30% of students (all upperclassmen) who live in honors housing are divided about equally between the Lake Claire Apartments and the Neptune community. Both are air-conditioned, and Neptune features suite-style rooms with shared baths rather than apartments. The most convenient dining for Lake Claire is Knightros; for Neptune, 63 South.

Honors Residence Halls, Availability (4.0): This rating compares the number of places in honors residence halls to the number of honors freshman and sophomore members in good standing, just under 974. The ratio for the honors program is **.51** rooms for each first- and second-year student. The average for all fifty programs is .63 places.

Prestigious Awards (3.0): The awards that we track and include are listed in the section titled "Prestigious Scholarships." The awards are sometimes won by students who are not in an honors college or program, but increasingly many are enrolled in honors programs. It is also a trend that honors colleges and programs help to prepare their students for the awards competitions.

UCF graduates have won 1 Rhodes scholarship and 5 Goldwater awards. The best success has been in NSF grants for graduate study and Fulbright Student awards. The university is right at the mean for all programs under review for NSF grants and above the median for Fulbrights.

UNRATED FEATURES

Continuation Requirements: University Honors--3.20 overall GPA and 3.00 Honors GPA.

Honors in the Major--3.50 in the major GPA, and 3.20 upper division GPA. The same GPAs apply to graduating with honors.

Academic Strengths, National Rankings: This is based on national rankings of *graduate* programs in 15 disciplines, except engineering and business, where undergraduate rankings are used.

UCF has nationally ranked departments in criminology (26), engineering (82), physics (85), computer science (90), chemistry (117), and math (134).

Undergraduate Research: "The Burnett Honors College strongly nurtures and supports undergraduate research. Over $90,000 are awarded annually to Honors students who pursue research projects.

"Honors in the Major is the oldest and most prestigious undergraduate research program at the University of Central Florida. Honors in the Major provides students the opportunity to engage in independent and original research as principal investigators. Over the course of at least two semesters, students research, write, defend, and publish an original honors thesis that serves as the capstone project of their undergraduate career. Upon completion of the thesis, students earn Honors in the Major distinction on their diplomas and final transcripts.

"The Burnett Research Scholars program was also designed to align with the mission and vision of UCF and The Burnett Honors College. Burnett Research Scholars is designed to help students identify and work with a faculty mentor in a research area of shared interest, and to then assist these student-mentor teams with project funding. Students and mentors collaborate to write a formal grant proposal that includes the background of the project, budget, timeline, and overall contribution of the project to the discipline. Student-mentor teams are selected to receive funding based upon the scope, method, and impact of their grant proposals. The research grants are $1,000 for the student and $1,000 for the mentor."

Honors Study Abroad: "Because The Burnett Honors College values the transformative nature of international travel, several programs and scholarships are offered to students interested in a global experience," the Dean says. "During the summer, college offers short-term, international service-learning programs in countries such as South Africa and Nicaragua....Qualified students can apply for the President's Scholars Program which was created to support student travel in Honors study abroad programs. In addition, qualified Honors students are eligible for scholarships in support of semester and year-long study abroad programs that are administered by UCF's Study Abroad. Moreover, the college provides scholarships for qualified business majors interested in studying at the ICN Business School which has several campuses across Europe.

"Some Honors students pursue non-UCF sponsored international programs and internships such as the US Department of State Students Programs. Over *$65,000 is awarded annually to honors students* pursuing study abroad, both in scholarships and direct travel support."

Financial Aid: "The Burnett Honors College awards about 25 Honors Enhancement Scholarships for incoming freshmen for the first year. All other merit awards at UCF are administered by the Office of Undergraduate Admissions."

The UCF website states that "UCF is ranked among the *top 40 colleges* in the nation and second in Florida *for its number of enrolled National Merit Scholars.*"[Emphasis added.]

UCF scholarships: National Merit and National Hispanic Scholars, Provost Scholars (less than 10% of entering freshman class), Pegasus Award (less than 25% of entering freshman class). The Knights Achievement tuition waiver is for out-of-state outstanding applicants. National Achievement Scholarships were awarded only through 2015.

National Merit Finalists in state receive a package valued at $85,000, and for out-of-state finalists the package is valued at $144,000.

"Over 40% of the University Honors Freshman class consists of the top scholarship recipients (National Merit, National Hispanic and Provost Scholars.)

The Burnett Honors College also awards a multitude of grants and scholarships designed to support students' co-curricular pursuits."

Honors Fees: None.

Placement Experiences: The 2015 exit survey of honors grads that year lists medical school acceptances from Vanderbilt, UNC Chapel Hill, and Northwestern, among many others. Graduates were pursuing masters' or Ph.Ds. at Harvard, MIT, Cornell, Johns Hopkins, Michigan, Washington University St. Louis, Illinois, and UNC Chapel Hill.

Other grads are attending law school at Emory, Georgetown, Vanderbilt, USC, UCLA, College of William and Mary, Wake Forest, and UT Austin.

Still others report employment at American Express, Oracle, Harris Corporation, Institute for Simulation and Training, Deloitte Consulting, Digitec Interactive, Epic Software, Festivals at Sea Cruises, GOOGLE, Intergra Investments, KPMG, LLP, Lockheed Martin, Microsoft, Minneapolis Star Tribune, Novel Engineering, and many other corporations.

Degree of Difference: This is based on the differences between (1) the average (2015, two-part) SAT scores for enrolled honors students (1402) and (2) the average test scores for all students in the university (1185) as a whole. The test scores may be an indication of how "elite" honors students may be perceived as compared to students in the university as a whole. The scores can also provide an indication of how well prepared the non-honors students in the university may be. **Please keep in mind that neither high nor low test scores determine the overall quality of a program.**

NAME: PLAN II HONORS PROGRAM, UNIVERSITY OF TEXAS AT AUSTIN.

Date Established: 1935.

Location: Austin, Texas.

University Full-time Undergraduate Enrollment: 36,309.

Honors Members in Good Standing: 700 (mean size of all 50 programs is 1,742).

Honors Average Admission Statistics: ACT, 31-33; old two-part SAT, 1447. Est. new SAT score, 1488.

Average High School GPA/Class Rank: 70% in top 5% of class.

Basic Admission Requirements: None listed. Plan II definitely applies a "holistic" approach to admissions. The program requires **two** essays, a five-sentence personal statement, and an expanded resume, in addition to test scores, transcripts, recommendations, etc. Plan II seeks students with special experiences, talents, and insights, and these likely play a larger role in admissions than in other honors programs.

Application Deadline(s): *Please verify with each program, as some deadlines could change.*

May apply beginning August 1, 2016; recommended deadline is October 15, 2016, but final deadline is December 1, 2016.

Honors Programs with old SAT scores from 1402—1469: UCF, Connecticut, Kentucky, Washington, Maryland, North Carolina, UC Irvine, Kansas, Minnesota, Tennessee, South Carolina, Clemson, UT Austin, Georgia.

Administrative Staff: 8.

RATINGS AT A GLANCE: For all mortarboard ratings immediately below, a score of 5 is the maximum and represents a comparison with all 50 honors colleges and programs. More detailed explanations follow the "mortarboard" ratings.

PERCEPTION* OF UNIVERSITY AS A WHOLE, NOT OF HONORS: 🎓🎓🎓🎓🎓

*Perception is based on the university's ranking among public universities in the 2016 U.S. News Best Colleges report. Please bear in mind that the better the U.S. News ranking, the more difficult it is for an honors college or program to have a rating that equals or improves on the magazine ranking.

OVERALL HONORS RATING: 🎓🎓🎓🎓🎓

Curriculum Requirements: 🎓🎓🎓🎓🎓

Number of Honors Classes Offered: 🎓🎓🎓🎓

Number of Honors Classes in Key Disciplines: 🎓🎓🎓🎓

Extent of Honors Enrollment: 🎓🎓🎓🎓 1/2

Honors-only Class Size: 🎓🎓🎓 1/2

Overall Class Size (Honors-only plus mixed, contract): 🎓🎓🎓🎓 1/2

Honors Grad Rate: 🎓🎓🎓🎓 1/2

Value-Added Grad Rate: 🎓🎓🎓 1/2

Ratio of Staff to Students: 🎓🎓🎓🎓 1/2

Priority Registration: "Plan II students are guaranteed to get Plan II classes, with provisions. Although Plan II first-year students are not guaranteed to get in exactly the first-year World Literature class or exactly the first-year Signature course of their choosing, they are guaranteed to get one of each. "All second-year students are guaranteed to get into 1 of 3 sections of the year long Philosophy course.

"All students will take 2 Junior seminars, usually in their 3rd year; again, they may not all get their first choice seminar, but everyone will get two seminars.

"The Plan II Math, Biology, Physics and SS 301 are very similar. Everyone will get one if they need it (some will fulfill Math or Biology through pre-med or calculus if they are pursuing a major that requires those courses). These classes are restricted to only Plan II students."

Honors Housing Amenities: 🎓🎓🎓🎓

Honors Housing Availability: 🎓🎓🎓🎓

Prestigious Awards: 🎓🎓🎓🎓🎓

RATING SCORES AND EXPLANATIONS:

Curriculum Requirements (5.0): The most important rating category, the curriculum completion requirement (classes required to complete honors) defines not only what honors students should learn but also the extent to which honors students and faculty are connected in the classroom. If there is a thesis or capstone requirement, it reinforces the individual contact and research skills so important to learning.

The average number of honors semester hours required for completion across all 50 programs is 29.0.

The completion requirements for the Plan II degree is 51 credits counting the thesis, but because some of these credits may be offset by AP tests (Plan II biology, Plan II western civilization) or by taking a non-honors elective, the assessment is **42.5** credits.

Below is the official explanation of the curriculum requirements:

World Literature--This yearlong course is required of all Plan II first-year students and is of central importance in the curriculum. Students may not place out of this course. It is conducted as a seminar, with emphasis on discussion, and is a writing-intensive course= 6 credits.

First-Year Plan II--All freshmen take one Plan II Signature course in the fall or spring. The emphasis in these seminars is on discussion, critical thinking, and writing. Faculty from across the campus are specially selected to teach these courses. Recent seminar topics include "Philosophy and Emotions," "Right and Wrong in Politics," and "Shakespeare and Film"= 3 credits.

Social Science 301--This course is offered under several disciplines and is usually taken the second year, first or second semester. The content involves contemporary social issues, and students may select from economics, anthropology, government or psychology= 3 credits.

Second-Year Philosophy: Problems of Knowledge and Valuation --This yearlong course is also taken in the second year. Using ancient and modern texts, students usually consider problems in ethics, political theory, metaphysics, and epistemology= 6 credits.

Non-U.S. History --Two courses in the same geographical area are required: one from an older period of the area's history and the other from a more recent period. *Many elect to take a Western Civilization sequence which is designed for Plan II students, but students are free to take history sequences from other non-U.S. geographic areas (e.g., Africa, Asia, Europe, Latin America and the Middle East)= 6 credits.*

Math and Science --All students in Liberal Arts must take 18 hours of math and science. Twelve of these 18 hours are prescribed as follows for Plan II students:

- Plan II Logic (PHL 313Q) or Plan II Modes of Reasoning (TC 310)
- Mathematics for Plan II students (M 310P), or credit for an approved calculus sequence
- Physics for Plan II students (PHY 321)
- Biology for Plan II students (BIO 301E)

The above count for 12 credits.

Foreign Language Requirement --Proficiency through the fourth semester is required. Students may place out of some or all of the requirement.

Junior Seminars --Plan II students take two seminars in the junior year. Similar in format and approach to the first-year tutorials, the junior seminars often require term papers. Recent seminar topics include "Beauty and Politics," "Freedom of Expression," "Psychology and Religion," and "Lawyers, Ethics and Justice"= 6 credits.

Humanities/Fine Arts --One course in one of the following:

- Art History (any ARH course),
- Music History (see approved list),
- Theatre & Dance History (see approved list);

Honors Thesis—The thesis= 6 credits.

AP/IB credits are counted as replacements for honors courses, as follows: A score of 5 can count for the first biology class; a score of 4 or 5 can count for one course in western civilization or European history.

Number of Honors Classes Offered (4.0): This is a measure of the total **adjusted** honors main sections available in the term reported, not including labs and thesis. (Please read the section titled "All about Honors Classes".) An adjusted main section has 3 or more semester credits, or equivalent, and sections with fewer credits receive a lower prorated value.

The program offered a section for every **15.9** enrolled students. The average for all 50 programs is 14.2 students. The lower the number, the better.

In the term reported, **95.0%** of honors enrollment was **in honors-only sections, and about 5% was in mixed sections.** The averages for all fifty programs are 81.3% in honors-only sections; 13.6 % in mixed honors sections; and 5.1% in contract sections.

Number of Honors Classes in Key Disciplines (4.0): The 15 "key" disciplines are biological sciences; business (all); chemistry; communications (especially public speaking); computer science; economics; engineering (all); English; history; math (all); philosophy; physics; political science; psychology; and sociology/anthropology/gender studies. Interdisciplinary sections, such as those often taken for General Education credit in the first two years, do receive a lesser, prorated discipline "credit" because they introduce students to multiple disciplines in an especially engaging way, often with in-depth discussion.

In the term reported, the program had a ratio of **28.6 honors students** per each main section in some or all "key disciplines." The mean for all 50 programs is 26.3. The lower the ratio, the better.

Out of **18 adjusted sections in key disciplines**, the program had **18 honors-only sections.** English and philosophy led the way with 11 and 4 sections, respectively. There as 1 in biology, 1 in math, and 1 in physics. It should be noted that Plan II majors receive a degree in Plan II, but can also graduate with a Plan II degree in business honors and engineering. The UT Business Honors Program alone offers more than a dozen sections each term, and many Plan II majors also complete the BHP, as many as 55 or 60 in a given term. Neither the BHP courses nor any other courses are included in this metric. Finally, Plan II students can complete honors requirements in most of the university's other honors tracks, including Dean's Scholars, Health Science Scholars, Polymathic Scholars, Turing Scholars. A very high percentage of Plan II students pursue additional majors.

The program also offered more than 19 Plan II seminar sections, all with 3 credits. Among the many interesting course titles in the past are "The Veil: History, Culture, and Politics"; "What Is Power?"; "A History of the Self"; and "The Snow Bridge: Humanities & Neuroscience."

The combination of seminars and courses in the disciplines makes the program unusual. Mostly it is a core honors program, but its core contains more classes in the disciplines than other small core programs.

Extent of Honors Enrollment (4.5:): Not all honors students take an honors class each term, especially after the first two years. Programs that have fewer honors classes for upper-division honors students will generally have fewer total members in good standing who are actually enrolled in a given term. (Please be aware, however, that honors students not enrolled in a class for a term are still connected to the honors community through residential and extracurricular activities.)

For example, if honors students in a program occupy 1,800 honors classroom seats in a given term, and there are 3,000 honors students in good standing, the extent of enrollment is .67. For programs that require a thesis, the ratio (score) reported below might in fact be somewhat higher, since we only count "regular" class enrollment for this measure, and not thesis enrollment. The program **has a ratio of 1.37**; the mean is 1.13 for all 50 programs. The higher the ratio, the better.

Average Class Size, Honors-only Sections (3.5): Offered mostly in the first two years, honors-only classes tend to be smaller and, as the name implies, have no or very few students other than those in the honors program. These class sections are almost always much smaller than mixed or contract sections, or regular non-honors class sections in the university.

The average honors-only class size in the honors program is **21.8 students**. The average for all 50 programs is 19.0 students.

Average Class Size, Overall (4.5): The overall class calculation is based on the *proportion* of honors students in each type of class (honors-only, mixed honors, and honors contract sections). Thus it is not a raw average. The overall honors-credit class size is **21.8 students**, versus the average for all 50 programs of 26.3 students.

These class size averages also do not correspond to the number of students per honors sections numbers above. The reason is that, in computing average class size metrics, we include enrollment in each 1-2-credit section, not just sections with 3 or more credits.

There are no Plan II contract courses. The only sections that could be considered "mixed" are a few electives, the sections of which probably have a mix of Plan II and non-Plan II students.

Honors Graduation Rate (4.5): The rating is based on the actual grad rate for students who entered the program six years earlier, whether or not the students remained in honors. The **actual rate of 91.0%** is also compared to the rates of other programs with the same test score entry requirement range, and then adjusted to the **score of 90.8%.** In some cases this measure favors programs within universities with relatively higher test scores for the student population as a whole. The average honors graduation rate for all programs with similar test scores required for admission is 92.6%.

Plan II had an **85% graduation rate in four years.** Please note than Plan II is a difficult and demanding program on its own, and the fact that so many Plan II students seek second majors, or even another major in a different UT honors program, keeps the graduation rate a bit lower than it might otherwise be.

Value-Added Grad Rate (3.5): The value-added rate measures the extent to which the adjusted score listed above exceeds the six-year grad rate for the university as a whole. **The university-wide rate is 81%.** Note: This measure generally favors programs within universities with relatively lower test scores for the student population as a whole.

Ratio of Staff to Honors Students (4.5): There is 1 staff member for every **87.5** students. (Mean ratio for all 50 programs is 1 staff member for every 135.6 students.)

Honors Residence Halls, Amenities (4.0): The UT honors housing is in the Honors "Quad," and while the rooms are traditional with hall baths, the location is probably the best on campus. About 40% of Plan II freshmen live on campus, and a much lower percentage of upperclassmen. Freshmen and upperclassmen may live in Andrews, Blanton, Carothers and Littlefield. All rooms are air-conditioned. Dining is in nearby Kinsolving Hall.

Honors Residence Halls, Availability (4.0): This rating compares the number of places in honors residence halls to the number of honors freshman and sophomore members in good standing, about 350. The ratio for the honors program is **.51** rooms for each first- and second-year student. The average for all fifty programs is .63 places.

Prestigious Awards (5.0): The awards that we track and include are listed in the section titled "Prestigious Scholarships." The awards are sometimes won by students who are not in an honors college or program, but increasingly many are enrolled in honors programs. It is also a trend that honors colleges and programs help to prepare their students for the awards competitions.

UT Austin is among the top four or five public universities in the nation in this category. With an impressive 30 Rhodes scholarships, UT students have also earned 24 Marshall scholarships and 23 Truman awards. The university is also a national leader in NSF fellowship grants for graduate school and Fulbright student awards. Students have also won 38 Goldwater scholarships for undergraduate excellence in the STEM fields, and a very high number of Boren scholarships for study abroad.

Plan II students have won about two-thirds of the UT Truman Scholarships, and more than half of the UT Marshall Scholarships, despite the small size of the honors program.

UNRATED FEATURES

Continuation Requirements: 3.25 GPA.

Academic Strengths, National Rankings: This is based on national rankings of *graduate* programs in 15 disciplines, except engineering and business, where undergraduate rankings are used.

UT Austin has long been known for having one of the top faculties in the nation, with the *average* departmental ranking around 15th nationally among all universities public and private. Leading departments are business (7), earth sciences (8), computer science (9), education (10), engineering (11), chemistry (12), math, physics, psychology, and sociology (all 14), and English and history (both 17). The *lowest* ranked departments at UT are actually outstanding, including political science (21), economics (26), and biology (30).

The really good thing about such broad strength in the disciplines is that students, who often change their majors, can do so at UT and other leading public universities and still land in an outstanding department. Among public universities, UC Berkeley and Michigan have the highest rated departments, while UCLA and Wisconsin both have slightly higher overall departmental rankings than UT.

Undergraduate Research: None listed.

Financial Aid: "Plan II has a very small handful of scholarships that we can award incoming freshmen. These typically are around 10K for 4 years. We often receive out-of-state tuition waivers that we can award to two out of state students in each freshmen class, although these awards come from the college and are never a guarantee.

"Once students are here in Plan II, we have a healthy 'continuing student' scholarship fund, and every Plan II student is encouraged to apply and these awards can range from 3K-7K per year."

Honors Fees: None.

Placement Experiences: None listed, but Plan II graduates typically enroll in the most prestigious graduate and professional schools and do extremely well in finding employment.

Degree of Difference: This is based on the differences between (1) the average (2015, two-part) SAT scores for enrolled honors students (1447) and (2) the average test scores for all students in the university (1280) as a whole. The test scores may be an indication of how "elite" honors students may be perceived as compared to students in the university as a whole. The scores can also provide an indication of how well prepared the non-honors students in the university may be. **Please keep in mind that neither high nor low test scores determine the overall quality of a program.**

NAME: UNIVERSITY OF UTAH HONORS COLLEGE.

Date Established: 1962.

Location: Salt Lake City, Utah.

University <u>Full-time Undergraduate</u> Enrollment: 17,137.

Honors Members in Good Standing: 2,300 (mean size of all 50 programs is 1,742).

Honors <u>Average</u> Admission Statistics: The ACT for first-year entrants is 30; the old two-part SAT, 1361. Estimated new SAT score, 1390.

Average High School GPA/Class Rank: 3.90 GPA.

<u>Basic</u> Admission Requirements: None reported.

Application Deadline(s): *Please verify with each program, as some deadlines could change.*

Priority deadline November 1, 2016; final deadline March 1, 2017.

Honors Programs with old SAT scores from 1351—1396: Purdue, Oregon, Alabama, Massachusetts, Indiana, CUNY Macaulay, Texas A&M, NJIT, Missouri, Delaware, LSU, Vermont, Temple.

Administrative Staff: 14.

RATINGS AT A GLANCE: For all mortarboard ratings immediately below, a score of 5 is the maximum and represents a comparison with all 50 honors colleges and programs. More detailed explanations follow the "mortarboard" ratings.

PERCEPTION* OF UNIVERSITY AS A WHOLE, <u>NOT</u> OF HONORS: 🎓🎓🎓🎓

*Perception is based on the university's ranking among public universities in the 2016 U.S. News Best Colleges report. Please bear in mind that the better the U.S. News ranking, the more difficult it is for an honors college or program to have a rating that equals or improves on the magazine ranking.

OVERALL HONORS RATING: 🎓🎓🎓[1/2]

Curriculum Requirements: 🎓🎓🎓[1/2]

Number of Honors Classes Offered: 🎓🎓🎓[1/2]

Number of Honors Classes in Key Disciplines: 🎓🎓🎓🎓

Extent of Honors Enrollment: 🎓🎓🎓[1/2]

Honors-only Class Size: 🎓🎓🎓🎓

Overall Class Size (Honors-only plus mixed, contract): 🎓🎓🎓🎓^{1/2}

Honors Grad Rate: 🎓🎓🎓^{1/2}

Value-Added Grad Rate: 🎓🎓🎓🎓^{1/2}

Ratio of Staff to Students: 🎓🎓🎓^{1/2}

Priority Registration: Yes, honors students register for all courses, honors and otherwise, with the first group of students during each year they are in the program.

Honors Housing Amenities: 🎓🎓🎓🎓🎓

Honors Housing Availability: 🎓🎓🎓^{1/2}

Prestigious Awards: 🎓🎓🎓🎓^{1/2}

RATING SCORES AND EXPLANATIONS:

Curriculum Requirements (3.5): The most important rating category, the curriculum completion requirement (classes required to complete honors) defines not only what honors students should learn but also the extent to which honors students and faculty are connected in the classroom. If there is a thesis or capstone requirement, it reinforces the individual contact and research skills so important to learning.

The average number of honors semester hours required for completion across all 50 programs is 29.0.

"The College offers students the possibility of earning an Honors Bachelor's Degree. The degree requires a total of 24 credits, as follows:

- Four Honors core courses, which include two courses from the Honors Intellectual Traditions series, one Honors writing course and one Honors science course.

- Three Honors elective courses, which can be other Honors College courses such a "Praxis Lab", departmental honors classes, learning-abroad experiences or internships.

- One three-credit thesis course, and an honors thesis.

"Honors "Praxis Lab" courses take a pressing social topic and ask students to confront the issues and follow up with solutions or projects that are thoughtful, collaborative, and creative. Recent examples are listed below under the Range and Type of Honors Courses category.

AP/IB credits are not counted as replacements for honors courses.

Number of Honors Classes Offered (3.5): This is a measure of the total adjusted honors main sections available in the term reported, not including labs and thesis. (Please read the section titled "All about Honors Classes".) An adjusted main section has 3 or more semester credits, or equivalent, and sections with fewer credits receive a lower prorated value.

The honors college had a ratio of 18.04 enrolled students per each main section. The mean for all 50 programs is 14.2. The lower the ratio, the better.

In the term reported, In the term reported, 77.6% of honors enrollment was in honors-only sections; 22.4% in mixed honors sections (honors and non-honors students); and none reported in contract sections (regular sections in which honors students "contract" to do extra work). The averages for all fifty programs are 81.3% in honors-only sections; 13.6 % in mixed honors sections; and 5.1% in contract sections.

Number of Honors Classes in Key Disciplines (4.0): The 15 "key" disciplines are biological sciences; business (all); chemistry; communications (especially public speaking); computer science; economics; engineering (all); English; history; math (all); philosophy; physics; political science; psychology; and sociology/anthropology/gender studies. Interdisciplinary sections, such as those often taken for General Education credit in the first two years, do receive a lesser, prorated discipline "credit" because they introduce students to multiple disciplines in an especially engaging way, often with in-depth discussion.

In the term reported, the program had ratio of 27.9 honors students per each main section in some or all "key disciplines." The mean for all 50 programs is 26.3 The lower the ratio, the better.

Out of 55 adjusted sections in key disciplines, the college had 39 honors-only sections, with the remaining sections mostly filled with honors college students. Business (13 sections), history (12), and math (11) led the way, followed by English (8) and physics (4). There were no sections in communications, economics, engineering, or philosophy.

The college also offered about 50 interdisciplinary seminars, including several in the outstanding "Intellectual Traditions," series, ranging from "Antiquity and the Beginning of the Common Era," to the "Flowering of the Common Era & the Threshold of Modernity," and concluding with the "Rise of Modernity."

The combination of seminars and courses in the disciplines makes the honors college a **blended** program.

Extent of Honors Enrollment (3.5): Not all honors students take an honors class each term, especially after the first two years. Programs that have fewer honors classes for upper-division honors students will generally have fewer total members in good standing who are actually enrolled in a given term. (Please be aware, however, that honors students not enrolled in a class for a term are still connected to the honors community through residential and extracurricular activities.)

For example, if honors students in a program occupy 1,800 honors classroom seats in a given term, and there are 3,000 honors students in good standing, the extent of enrollment is .67. For programs that require a thesis, the ratio (score) reported below might in fact be somewhat higher, since we only count

"regular" class enrollment for this measure, and not thesis enrollment. The college has a ratio of **.86,** versus the mean of 1.13 for all 50 programs. The higher the ratio, the better.

Average Class Size, Honors-only Sections (4.0): Offered mostly in the first two years, honors-only classes tend to be smaller and, as the name implies, have no or very few students other than those in the honors program. These class sections always are much smaller than mixed or contract sections, or regular non-honors class sections in the university.

The average honors-only class size at the honors college is **19.2** students. The average for all 50 programs is 19.0 students.

Average Class Size, Overall (4.5): The overall class calculation is based on the *proportion* of honors students in each type of class (honors-only, mixed honors, and honors contract sections). Thus it is not a raw average. The overall honors-credit class size at the college is **20.2** students, versus the average for all 50 programs of 26.3 students.

These class size averages also do not correspond to the number of students per honors sections numbers above. The reason is that, in computing average class size metrics, we include enrollment in each 1-2-credit section, not just sections with 3 or more credits.

Along with the honors-only average of 19.2 students, the mixed honors sections average **23.9** students. No contract enrollment was reported. Across all fifty programs, the average mixed honors section has 51.1 students.

Honors Graduation Rate (3.5): The rating is the based on the actual grad rate for students who entered the program six years earlier, whether or not the students remained in honors. The actual rate of **82.0%** is also compared to the rates of other programs with the same test score entry requirement range, and then adjusted to the score of **81.7%.** In some cases this measure favors programs within universities with relatively higher test scores for the student population as a whole. The average honors graduation rate for all programs with similar test scores required for admission is 83.4%.

Value-Added Grad Rate (4.5): The value-added rate measures the extent to which the adjusted score listed above exceeds the six-year grad rate for the university as a whole. The **university-wide rate is 62%**. Note: This measure generally favors programs within universities with relatively lower test scores for the student population as a whole.

Ratio of Staff to Honors Students (3.5): There is 1 staff member for every **164.3** students. (Mean ratio for all 50 programs is 1 staff member for every 135.6 students.)

Honors Residence Halls, Amenities (5.0): "The Donna Garff Marriott Honors Residential Scholars Community (MHC) houses 309 honors students in apartment style living. The MHC offers both four-person and eight-person apartments with either single or double bedrooms. The MHC has 67 apartments in total and 75% of bedrooms are singles. The MHC is fully air-conditioned with multiple lounges, and on-site laundry. Each apartment suite has its own kitchen. The nearest dining hall is at the Peterson Heritage Center, a five-minute walk; however, the MHC has its own 24-hour convenience store and deli. Other amenities include cable TV with HBO package, a ski wax room, a music room, indoor bicycle storage, an honors library, and high-speed internet.

"The MHC includes three classrooms used exclusively for Honors classes. Freshmen and upperclassmen can choose from 11 living/learning themes communities in the MHC:

"First Year Experience; Outdoor Leadership and Education; Research in the Sciences; Health Fields; Eccles Scholars; Intellectual Traditions; Citizenship; Entrepreneurship; Business; Engineering; or the Thesis Mentoring Community.

"The Officers Circle Houses (OC) house 36 Honors students. Thirty-six Honors upperclassmen can live in the Honors Law House or one of the two Honors Thesis Mentoring Houses, small living/learning communities. Each house offers single and double room options. The Houses are co-ed, however, students of the same sex must share the doubles. Students enjoy the convenience of having on-site laundry, kitchens, and multiple lounge areas. The nearest dining for all four of these is at Peterson Heritage Center.

"The Sage Point Residence Hall Honors Floor. Twenty-four freshmen are also housed in Sage Point Hall, featuring suite-style singles and doubles. Students opting to leave in Sage Point share in the programming with the MHC Intellectual Living Learning Community. The nearest dining for all four of these is at Peterson Heritage Center."

Honors Residence Halls, Availability (3.5): This rating compares the number of places in honors residence halls to the number of honors freshman and sophomore members in good standing, just under 1,150. The ratio for the college is **.32 rooms** for each first- and second-year student. The average for all fifty programs is .63 places.

Prestigious Awards (4.5): The awards that we track and include are listed in the section titled "Prestigious Scholarships." The awards are sometimes won by students who are not in an honors college or program, but increasingly many are enrolled in honors programs. It is also a trend that honors colleges and programs help to prepare their students for the awards competitions.

In the case of Utah, students have won an impressive 22 Rhodes scholarships and 23 Truman awards, along with a very solid 33 Goldwater scholarships, awarded for undergraduate promise in the STEM disciplines. Students have also won a Gates Cambridge scholarship, a Marshall scholarship, and (the very rare) Churchill scholarship, as well as 3 Boren scholarships for postgraduate study abroad.

UNRATED FEATURES

Continuation Requirements: 3.50 GPA.

Academic Strengths, National Rankings: This is based on national rankings of *graduate* programs in all but engineering and business, where undergraduate rankings are used.

At the "U", the average department ranking nationwide is very high, better than 60th. Among the many outstanding departments are math (34), chemistry (35), and computer science (40). Close behind are earth sciences (42), business (50), and biology (55).

Undergraduate Research: "Honors students engage in a wide range of undergraduate research as part of their Honors Thesis Project," the college reports. "Designated faculty in each department help inform and direct Honors students to research opportunities in their major. The Honors College provides financial support for students to present their research at state and national conferences.

"In addition, through the University's Undergraduate Research Opportunities Program (UROP), Honors students also receive financial support for their research, present their research in a campus-wide Undergraduate Research Symposium and publish their research abstracts in the Undergraduate Research Abstracts Journal."

Honors Study Abroad: The 'U' offers 105 study-abroad programs, including Cuba: Community, Complexity, and Change during Fall break. Students go to Havana and Cien Fuegos for study. Also notable are the Freshman Business Scholars programs, one each in Paris and London. There are intensive language programs in Kiel, Germany; Grenoble, France; Siena, Italy; Osaka, Japan; Saratov, Russia; and Oviedo, Spain. We also like the summer program Underground London: Crime and Disorder, 1720-1890.

"The U offered $220,000 in study-abroad scholarships last year, and other scholarships are available within academic departments and the Honors College."

Financial Aid: The Associate Dean tells us that "for the incoming 2016 class, 95% of the students accepted into Honors received individual scholarships from the University of Utah. Additionally, Honors students have access to approximately $125,000 in achievement and completion-based scholarships through the Honors College."

The Honors College scholarships include the following:

George S. and Dolores Dore Eccles Scholarship--"This is the most prestigious award offered to incoming freshman at the U…recipients of the award receive a truly transformative educational experience through enrollment in the U's Honors College. Students receive tuition, fees, room, board and books and are mentored by extraordinary leaders and faculty on campus."

Beck Science Achievement Scholarship--"This award is given to students continuing or beginning their education at the University of Utah's Honors College. Qualified applicants must demonstrate tangible skill and interest in science-related areas of study, as well as commitment to attaining an Honors degree and completing their education with high academic standing."

C. Charles Hetzel III Scholarship--"This scholarship provides educational assistance to a deserving out-of-state Honors student who demonstrates high academic achievement. Up to $10,000 may be awarded. The award will be distributed over a period of two semesters toward tuition cost. Half of the scholarship funds will be deposited in the student's tuition account at the beginning of the first semester, and the other half will be deposited in the student's tuition account for use in the second semester."

Duane Harris Butcher Endowed Scholarship—"This scholarship is for students in the Honors College who are descendants of the Utah pioneers who emigrated from 1847-1897. Applicants will demonstrate appreciation for heritage and community through a one-page essay and demonstrate talent or aptitude in a chosen field." There are about 15 additional scholarships available to honors students at the "U" ranging from $1,000 to $5,000.

Honors Fees: $75 per semester, excluding summer.

Placement Experiences: "The Honors College recently surveyed its young alumni (those who completed the Honors Degree between 2010 to 2015). 71% of the respondents who pursued a graduate program immediately after completing their Honors Degree were admitted to their first-choice schools, including Stanford University, Duke University, Princeton, Massachusetts Institute of Technology, Brown University, University of Utah Medical School, and University of California Santa Barbara, to name a few. 71% of those who pursued employment after graduation found a career in their desired fields working.

Degree of Difference: This is based on the differences between (1) the average (2015, two-part) SAT scores for enrolled honors students (1331) and (2) the average test scores for all students in the university (1130) as a whole. The test scores may be an indication of how "elite" honors students may be perceived as compared to students in the university as a whole. The scores can also provide an indication of how well prepared the non-honors students in the university may be. Please keep in mind that neither high nor low test scores determine the overall quality of a program.

NAME: UNIVERSITY OF VERMONT HONORS COLLEGE.

Date Established: 2003.

Location: Burlington, Vermont.

University <u>Full-time Undergraduate</u> Enrollment (2015): 9,898.

Honors Members in Good Standing: 771; (mean size of all 50 programs is 1,742).

Honors <u>Average</u> Admission Test Score(s): ACT, 32; old SAT, 1392; est. new SAT, 1440.

Average High School GPA/Class Rank: Minimum 3.8; top 9%.

<u>Basic</u> Admission Requirements: ACT, 32. Old SAT, 1400; est. new SAT, 1450. (Yes, the basic requirement is somewhat higher than the average, but both are relatively high.)

Application Deadline(s): *Please verify with each program, as some deadlines could change.*

Early action November 1, 2016; regular deadline January 15, 2017.

Honors Programs with old SAT scores from 1351—1396: Purdue, Oregon, Alabama, Massachusetts, Penn State, Indiana, CUNY Macaulay, Texas A&M, NJIT, Missouri, Oregon State, Delaware, LSU, Vermont, Temple.

Administrative Staff: 7.

RATINGS AT A GLANCE: For all mortarboard ratings immediately below, a score of 5 is the maximum and represents a comparison with all 50 honors colleges and programs. More detailed explanations follow the "mortarboard" ratings.

PERCEPTION* OF UNIVERSITY AS A WHOLE, <u>NOT</u> OF HONORS: 🎓🎓🎓🎓

*Perception is based on the university's ranking among public universities in the 2016 U.S. News Best Colleges report. Please bear in mind that the better the U.S. News ranking, the more difficult it is for an honors college or program to have a rating that equals or improves on the magazine ranking.

OVERALL HONORS RATING: 🎓🎓🎓

Curriculum Requirements: 🎓🎓🎓

Number of Honors Classes Offered: 🎓🎓🎓

Number of Honors Classes in Key Disciplines: 🎓🎓🎓

Extent of Honors Enrollment: 🎓🎓🎓 1/2

Honors-only Class Size: 🎓🎓🎓🎓

Overall Class Size (Honors-only plus mixed, contract): 🎓🎓🎓🎓 1/2

Honors Grad Rate: 🎓🎓🎓

Value-Added Grad Rate: 🎓🎓🎓

Ratio of Staff to Students: 🎓🎓🎓🎓 1/2

Priority Registration: "All honors college students have at minimum in-class priority registration: they have the opportunity to register for all classes half an hour before the standard registration time for students in their class year (based on credits completed at the end of the previous semester). Students in highly structured majors, primarily in the professional programs and sciences, have overall priority registration status: they register the first day of registration week, before all other undergrads at the university, along with a small number of non-honors students who also have overall priority registration (some athletes, students with accommodations, etc.)."

Honors Housing Amenities: 🎓🎓🎓🎓🎓

Honors Housing Availability: 🎓🎓🎓🎓🎓

Prestigious Awards: 🎓🎓🎓 1/2

RATING SCORES AND EXPLANATIONS:

Curriculum Requirements (3.0): The most important rating category, the curriculum completion requirement (classes required to complete honors) defines not only what honors students should learn but also the extent to which honors students and faculty are connected in the classroom. If there is a thesis or capstone requirement, it reinforces the individual contact and research skills so important to learning.

The average number of honors semester hours required for completion across all 50 programs is 29.0

The honors college requires 20-22 credit hours for completion. The description from the honors director, used for the last edition, is still the best:

"The Honors College experience begins with a Fall semester course, *The Pursuit of Knowledge*, taught in the seminar format to classes of 21 students. In the Spring semester, first-year HCOL students take one section of HCOL 086, *Ways of Knowing*, a selection of special topics courses the majority of which fulfill one course of the University's two-course diversity requirement.

"Each of these courses applies some of the foundational knowledge learned in the first semester to particular sets of circumstances, often involving race and culture in the U.S. and beyond." The first-year requirement is 6 credits. Incoming students should be willing to participate very actively in the first-year seminars.

"Faculty teaching the first-year courses expect students not only to defend their opinions verbally but also in writing. The courses are designed to be writing-intensive, and to provide specialized writing instruction and support as students make the transition to college."

The work begins even before classes commence. Incoming first-year students receive a book to read at the June Orientation before classes begin. The students must then "complete a two-page essay that is due on the first day of class in the Fall."

On most Wednesday evenings during regular sessions, all honors students attend a plenary lecture series that is also open to the entire university community.

Each semester, sophomores take a three-credit honors seminar, "choosing from an extensive slate of offerings created for Honors College students by schools and colleges throughout the university. Topics vary from year to year."

During their junior year, students take a 3-credit honors course along with a 1-credit thesis preparation seminar. Also during their junior year students are required to take up undergraduate research and encouraged to study-abroad. In senior year, students complete a 6-credit **honors thesis**, typically in their major department.

AP/IB credits are **not** counted as replacements for honors courses.

Number of Honors Classes Offered (3.0): This is a measure of the total **adjusted** honors main sections available in the term reported, not including labs and thesis. An adjusted main section has 3 or more semester credits, or equivalent, and sections with fewer credits receive a lower prorated value.

UVM honors offered a section for every **24.2** enrolled students. The average for all 50 programs is 14.2 The lower the number, the better.

In the term reported, **87.2%** of honors enrollment was **in honors-only sections; none in mixed honors sections (honors and non-honors students), and 12.8% in contract sections were reported** The averages for all fifty programs are 81.3% in honors-only sections; 13.6 % in mixed honors sections; and 5.1% in contract sections.

Number of Honors Classes in Key Disciplines (3.0): The 15 "key" disciplines are biological sciences; business (all); chemistry; communications (especially public speaking); computer science; economics; engineering (all); English; history; math (all); philosophy; physics; political science; psychology; and sociology, anthropology, and gender studies. Interdisciplinary sections, such as those often taken for General Education credit in the first two years, do receive a lesser, prorated discipline "credit" because they introduce students to multiple disciplines in an especially engaging way, often with in-depth discussion.

For this measure, mixed and contract sections are not counted as a section in a key discipline unless students taking the sections for honors credit make up at least 10% of the total section enrollment.

In the term reported, the honors college only offered interdisciplinary seminar sections, each of which receives a reduced value when disciplines are rated. (This certainly does not mean that they are not "good" classes, but only reflects that they do not focus on a single discipline.) On the other hand, there are almost 30 of these classes.

In addition to the multiple sections of "Pursuit of Knowledge" and "Ways of Knowing," students could take "Political Economy for a Finite Planet," or "Crafting Democratic Institutions," as well as "Religion and Secularisms in the Modern World."

With the lack of classes in specific disciplines, the "credit" assigned to the college in this category is one section for every **62.0 honors students.** The average for all 50 programs is 26.3. The lower the number, the better.

The emphasis on interdisciplinary sections makes the honors college a **core honors program.**

Extent of Honors Enrollment (3.5): Not all honors students take an honors class each term, especially after the first two years. Programs that have fewer honors classes for upper-division honors students will generally have fewer total members in good standing who are actually enrolled in a given term. (Please be aware, however, that honors students not enrolled in a class for a term are still connected to the honors community through residential and extracurricular activities.)

For example, if honors students in a program occupy 1,800 honors classroom seats in a given term, and there are 3,000 honors students in good standing, the extent of enrollment is .67. For programs that require a thesis, the ratio (score) reported below might in fact be somewhat higher, since we only count "regular" class enrollment for this measure, and not thesis enrollment. **The college has a ratio of .80**; the average is 1.13 for all 50 programs. The higher the ratio, the better.

Average Class Size, Honors-only Sections (4.0): Offered mostly in the first two years, honors-only classes tend to be smaller and, as the name implies, have no or very few students other than those in the honors program. These class sections always are much smaller than mixed or contract sections, or regular non-honors class sections in the university.

The average honors-only class size at the honors college is **20.7 students**. The average for all 50 programs is 19.0 students.

Average Class Size, Overall (4.5): The overall class calculation is based on the *proportion* of honors students in each type of class (honors-only, mixed honors, and honors contract sections). Thus it is not a raw average. The overall honors-credit class size is **20.7 students**, versus the average for all 50 programs of 26.3 students.

Along with the honors-only average of 20.7students, the mixed honors sections average **(NA)** students, and the contract sections with honors credit for individual honors students average **19.8** students. Across all fifty programs, the average mixed honors section has 51.1 students, and the average contract section has 60.1 students.

These class size averages also do not correspond to the number of students per honors sections numbers above. The reason is that, in computing average class size metrics, we include enrollment in each 1-2-credit section, not just sections with 3 or more credits.

Honors Graduation Rate (3.0): The rating is the based on the actual grad rate for students who entered the program six years earlier, whether or not the students remained in honors. The **actual rate of 80.8%** is also compared to the rates of other programs with the same test score entry requirement range, and then adjusted to the **score of 80.3%.** The average honors graduation rate for all programs with similar test scores required for admission is 86.2%.

Value-Added Grad Rate (3.0): The value-added rate measures the extent to which the adjusted score above exceeds the six-year grad rate for the university as a whole. **The university-wide rate is 76.0%.**

Ratio of Staff to Honors Students (4.5): There is 1 staff member for every **96.4** students. (Mean ratio for all 50 programs is 1 staff member for every 135.6 students.)

Honors Residence Halls, Amenities (5.0): "University Heights North is the heart and home of the Honors College. The top three floors are the Honors residence hall, where the majority of the first-year and sophomore Honors College students live, as well as a handful of Honors juniors and seniors. The ground floor of the building houses the Honors College classrooms, where most first-year and sophomore seminar courses are taught. The Honors College administrative and advising offices, the Office of Fellowships Advising, and the Office of Undergraduate Research are also on the main floor of the building.

"University Heights North residence hall provides housing for Honors College students in a wide variety of spacious rooms in suite options, as well as single rooms. Faculty-in-residence play an important role in the HCOL community, leading book and film discussions and serving as advisors to groups of students. Because the HCOL classrooms and administrative offices are also located in UHN, students have easy access to advising and support from the staff and faculty."

About 400 honors first-year students and upperclassmen live in air-conditioned, suite-style rooms with shared baths between suites. Two laundry rooms are on site. Two dining options are nearby: Harris/Millis Dining Hall with fixed-price menus for every meal, and the University Marché, "a retail venue with multiple dining platforms including an open-concept Euro Kitchen offering plated lunch and dinner entrees, and a great selection of daily offerings from their deli case."

Honors Residence Halls, Availability (5.0): This rating compares the number of places in honors residence halls to the number of honors freshman and sophomore members in good standing, approximately 386. The ratio for the college is **1.03** rooms for each first- and second-year student. The average for all fifty programs is .63 places.

Prestigious Awards (3.5): UVM students have won 10 Rhodes scholarships, 10 Truman scholarships, five Udall awards, and nine Goldwater scholarships.

UNRATED FEATURES

Continuation Requirements: 3.20, but by the time of the thesis proposal, must be 3.40.

Academic Strengths, National Rankings: This is based on national rankings of *graduate* programs in all but engineering and business, where undergraduate rankings are used.

Nationally ranked disciplines at UVM include education (66) and psychology and statistics (78).

Undergraduate Research: "All HCOL seniors are required to do a senior thesis, the basis of which is undergraduate research. Many students are involved in research prior to embarking on thesis work.

"The Office of Undergraduate Research provides research grants, matches students with faculty conducting research, and co-sponsors an annual research symposium, Student Research Conference."

Honors Study Abroad: "The University of Vermont has study abroad options for the summer, a semester, or an academic year. The university offers exchange programs in Japan, Germany, Wales, Ireland, Australia, France, Finland, Mexico, New Zealand, Spain, England, Sweden, Austria, and Russia. In addition, the university enables students to pursue study abroad through many external study abroad programs. Finally, the Honors College has *summer research grants* that can be used to fund research projects abroad.

"The UVM Honors College has a special tie to Glasgow University in Scotland through the Principia Program. Students who participate in the program can complete a three-credit sophomore seminar requirement.

"Because of the nature of study abroad and the options students have for studying abroad through the university, an external program, a summer program, or through leave-of-absence, it is difficult to track the percentage of Honors College students who study abroad. That said, *31.2% of UVM students study abroad,* and we believe that that number is likely a good representation of Honors College students who study abroad."

Financial Aid: "Most students invited to the Honors College receive the top merit awards from the University of Vermont. This could include the **Presidential Scholarship**, the **Vermont Scholars Award**, the **Green Mountain Scholarship**, or others. Merit scholarships awarded at UVM can be for full tuition, room, and board (such as the **Green & Gold Scholarships**), or they can offer significant financial support to attend the university (many Honors College students receive the Presidential Scholarship, which can be for as much as $17,000 annually)."

For National Merit Scholars: UVM awards a Vermont Merit Scholarship to any Vermont student who has advanced to finalist status for the National Merit Scholarship. Recipients are awarded full in-state tuition for four years (a maximum of eight semesters). UVM also awards a Green Mountain Scholarship to any out-of-state student who has advanced to finalist status for the National Merit Scholarship. Green Mountain Scholarship recipients are awarded $10,000 annually for a maximum of four years (eight semesters).

For National Achievement Scholars: UVM awards a Vermont Merit Scholarship to any Vermont student who has advanced to semi-finalist status for the scholarship. Recipients are awarded full in-state tuition for four years (a maximum of eight semesters). UVM also awards a Green Mountain Scholarship to any out-of-state student who has advanced to semi-finalist status for the National Achievement Scholars program. Green Mountain Scholarship recipients are awarded $10,000 annually for a maximum of four years (eight semesters).

For National Hispanic Recognition Students: UVM offers the Vermont Merit Scholarship to any Vermont student who is selected as a National Hispanic Scholar. Recipients are awarded full in-state tuition for four years (a maximum of eight semesters). UVM also awards a Green Mountain Scholarship to any out-of-state student who has been selected as a National Hispanic Scholar. Green Mountain Scholarship recipients are awarded $10,000 annually for a maximum of four years (eight semesters). **Honors Fees:** None.

Placement Experiences: Recent UVM Honors College graduates are now pursuing:

- medical study at Harvard, Brown, and the UVM Medical School, among others;

- --graduate doctoral study at Cal Tech (chemistry), Vanderbilt (mathematics), Columbia (cell and molecular biology), Brown (pathobiology), and Harvard, UC-Berkeley, Johns Hopkins, Duke, the University of Warwick, among others;

- --vet school at Tufts, Cornell, and others;

- --law school at Duke, Penn, Georgetown, and Harvard, among others;

- --public health at Columbia University and Yale university, among others;

- --working at companies including Google, HBO, Global Foundries, Fuse Marketing, Flying Plow Farm, W. W. Norton & Company, NextCapital Group, the Burlington Free Press, and more;

- --founding their own companies or non-profit organizations, including ReWork, The Whole Human Upgrade, Books 4 Equality, and others;

- --employment in the public sector for the State Department, the Mayor of Burlington, Sen. Patrick J. Leahy, the State House of Vermont, Amnesty International, Vermont Public Interest Research Group (VPIRG), the U.S Army, and many others;

Degree of Difference: This is based on the differences between (1) the average (2015, two-part) SAT scores for enrolled honors students (1392) and (2) the average test scores for all students in the university (1185) as a whole. The test scores may be an indication of how "elite" honors students may be perceived as compared to students in the university as a whole. The scores can also provide an indication of how well prepared the non-honors students in the university may be. **Please keep in mind that neither high nor low test scores determine the overall quality of a program.**

NAME: VCU HONORS COLLEGE.

Date Established: 1983, as an honors program.

Location: Richmond, Virginia.

University Full-time Undergraduate Enrollment (2015): 20,294.

Honors Members in Good Standing: 996; (mean size of all 50 programs is 1,742).

Honors Average Admission Test Score(s): ACT, 31; old SAT, 1350; est. new SAT, 1410.

Average High School GPA/Class Rank: Minimum 3.50.

Basic Admission Requirements: ACT, 29. Old SAT, 1270; est. new SAT, 1330.

Application Deadline(s): *Please verify with each program, as some deadlines could change.*

September through April 30 of your senior year in high school. However, you are encouraged to apply by our **priority deadline of Feb. 1.** All prospective freshmen who apply to The Honors College by Feb. 1 will be notified of our admissions decision by April 1.

Honors Programs with old SAT scores from 1315—1350: Idaho, Georgia State, Virginia Tech, Utah, Iowa, Auburn, Houston, Mississippi, VCU.

Administrative Staff: 13.

RATINGS AT A GLANCE: For all mortarboard ratings immediately below, a score of 5 is the maximum and represents a comparison with all 50 honors colleges and programs. More detailed explanations follow the "mortarboard" ratings.

PERCEPTION* OF UNIVERSITY AS A WHOLE, NOT OF HONORS:

*Perception is based on the university's ranking among public universities in the 2016 U.S. News Best Colleges report. Please bear in mind that the better the U.S. News ranking, the more difficult it is for an honors college or program to have a rating that equals or improves on the magazine ranking.

OVERALL HONORS RATING:

Curriculum Requirements: 1/2

Number of Honors Classes Offered:

Number of Honors Classes in Key Disciplines: 1/2

Extent of Honors Enrollment: 🎓🎓🎓^{1/2}

Honors-only Class Size: 🎓🎓🎓🎓^{1/2}

Overall Class Size (Honors-only plus mixed, contract): 🎓🎓🎓🎓🎓

Honors Grad Rate: 🎓🎓🎓🎓^{1/2}

Value-Added Grad Rate: 🎓🎓🎓🎓🎓

Ratio of Staff to Students: 🎓🎓🎓🎓^{1/2}

Priority Registration: Yes, honors students register for all courses, honors and otherwise, with the first group of students during each year they are in the program.

Honors Housing Amenities: 🎓🎓🎓🎓^{1/2}

Honors Housing Availability: 🎓🎓🎓🎓

Prestigious Awards: 🎓🎓🎓

RATING SCORES AND EXPLANATIONS:

Curriculum Requirements (3.5): The most important rating category, the curriculum completion requirement (classes required to complete honors) defines not only what honors students should learn but also the extent to which honors students and faculty are connected in the classroom. If there is a thesis or capstone requirement, it reinforces the individual contact and research skills so important to learning.

The average number of honors semester hours required for completion across all 50 programs is 29.0

VCU honors requires a minimum of 24 credits. A thesis is not required.

Honors Writing Sequence--Students who enter the Honors College directly from high school are required to take an honors version of the university's writing sequence. Honors students take both Rhetoric and Expository Writing, effective Fall 2016. Successful completion of these two honors courses satisfies three university-required courses.

Honors Core--The Honors College require all students to complete 18 credits in the honors core. In addition to Rhetoric and Expository Writing, the core includes one designated honors course each in math, philosophy, physics, and political science.

Honors Electives--First-year members must take 6 credits in electives in order to meet the minimum honors credits. These electives can be satisfied through several options: honors contract courses, honors independent study, and honors seminars.

Departmental honors--Students may opt to pursue departmental honors in Arts or Business. This requires that students complete their University Honors requirements, and that 15 of their honors credits are earned in their discipline.

AP/IB credits are **not** counted as replacements for honors courses.

Number of Honors Classes Offered (4.0): This is a measure of the total **adjusted** honors main sections available in the term reported, not including labs and thesis. An adjusted main section has 3 or more semester credits, or equivalent, and sections with fewer credits receive a lower prorated value.

The honors college offered a section for every **17.8** enrolled students. The average for all 50 programs is 14.2. The lower the number, the better.

In the term reported, In the term reported, **90.5%** of honors enrollment was **in honors-only sections; and 8.0% in mixed honors sections (honors and non-honors students), and 1.5% in contract sections were reported** The averages for all fifty programs are 81.3% in honors-only sections; 13.6 % in mixed honors sections; and 5.1% in contract sections.

Number of Honors Classes in Key Disciplines (4.5): The 15 "key" disciplines are biological sciences; business (all); chemistry; communications (especially public speaking); computer science; economics; engineering (all); English; history; math (all); philosophy; physics; political science; psychology; and sociology, anthropology, and gender studies. Interdisciplinary sections, such as those often taken for General Education credit in the first two years, do receive a lesser, prorated discipline "credit" because they introduce students to multiple disciplines in an especially engaging way, often with in-depth discussion.

For this measure, mixed and contract sections are not counted as a section in a key discipline unless students taking the sections for honors credit make up at least 10% of the total section enrollment.

In the term reported, the honors college offered a very impressive 16 sections in English, along with 6 each in math, philosophy, and physics. There were 5 in political science, 3 in business, and 2 in biology. There were no sections that term in psychology or computer science. VCU offered a section in a key discipline for every **18.1 honors students.** The average for all 50 programs is 26.3. The lower the number, the better.

The college does offer seminars, 9 in the term reported, including "Political Documentary" and "The Molecular Basis for Human Disease."

Nevertheless, the college is essentially a **discipline-based program.**

Extent of Honors Enrollment (3.5): Not all honors students take an honors class each term, especially after the first two years. Programs that have fewer honors classes for upper-division honors students will generally have fewer total members in good standing who are actually enrolled in a given term. (Please be

aware, however, that honors students not enrolled in a class for a term are still connected to the honors community through residential and extracurricular activities.)

For example, if honors students in a program occupy 1,800 honors classroom seats in a given term, and there are 3,000 honors students in good standing, the extent of enrollment is .67. For programs that require a thesis, the ratio (score) reported below might in fact be somewhat higher, since we only count "regular" class enrollment for this measure, and not thesis enrollment. **VCU honors has a ratio of .87**; the average is 1.13 for all 50 programs. The higher the ratio, the better.

Average Class Size, Honors-only Sections (4.5): Offered mostly in the first two years, honors-only classes tend to be smaller and, as the name implies, have no or very few students other than those in the honors program. These class sections always are much smaller than mixed or contract sections, or regular non-honors class sections in the university.

The average honors-only class size at the honors college is **16.4 students**. The average for all 50 programs is 19.0 students.

Average Class Size, Overall (5.0): The overall class calculation is based on the *proportion* of honors students in each type of class (honors-only, mixed honors, and honors contract sections). Thus it is not a raw average. The overall honors-credit class size is **17.8 students**, versus the average for all 50 programs of 26.3 students.

These class size averages also do not correspond to the number of students per honors sections numbers above. The reason is that, in computing average class size metrics, we include enrollment in each 1-2-credit section, not just sections with 3 or more credits.

Along with the honors-only average of 16.4 students, the mixed honors sections average **26.7 students,** and the contract sections with honors credit for individual honors students average about **59.8 students.** Across all fifty programs, the average mixed honors section has 51.1 students, and the average contract section has 60.1 students.

Honors Graduation Rate (4.5): The rating is based on the actual grad rate for students who entered the program six years earlier, whether or not the students remained in honors. The **actual rate of 88.6%** is also compared to the rates of other programs with the same test score entry requirement range, and then adjusted to the **score of 88.9.%.** The average honors graduation rate for all programs with similar test scores required for admission is 83.4%.

Value-Added Grad Rate (5.0): The value-added rate measures the extent to which the adjusted score above exceeds the six-year grad rate for the university as a whole. **The university-wide rate is 59.0%.**

Ratio of Staff to Honors Students (4.5): There is 1 staff member for every **90.5** students. (Mean ratio for all 50 programs is 1 staff member for every 135.6 students.)

Honors Residence Halls, Amenities (4.5): About 87% of honors students living in honors housing reside in the Honors Residence, *featuring single apartments and private baths*. Both freshmen and upperclassmen may live in the residence, which is air-conditioned throughout. The remainder of honors residence space is in Brandt Hall (freshmen only) and West Grace Hall (upperclassmen only), both air-conditioned with suite-style rooms and shared baths. The Shafer Court Dining Center is the most convenient dining location. The only reason the rating is not 5.0 is that the Honors Residence does not include onsite dining. Otherwise, it is clear that the residence is outstanding.

Honors Residence Halls, Availability (4.0): This rating compares the number of places in honors residence halls to the number of honors freshman and sophomore members in good standing, approximately 498. The ratio for the college is **.40** rooms for each first- and second-year student. The average for all fifty programs is .63 places.

Prestigious Awards (3.0): "Since 2005, all ten Goldwater Scholars from VCU have been Honors College students. As of February 2016, 15 of 34 Fulbright Scholarship recipients were honors students or honors alumni (three declined). Most of the rest of the Fulbright Scholars were graduate students who did their undergraduate work elsewhere. At least three of VCU's recent NSF GRF recipients were honors alumni. Virtually all of our Rhodes, Marshall, and Truman nominees have been honors students or recent alums."

UNRATED FEATURES

Continuation Requirements: 3.50.

Academic Strengths, National Rankings: This is based on national rankings of *graduate* programs in all but engineering and business, where undergraduate rankings are used.

Nationally ranked disciplines at VCU include education (33), psychology and statistics (both 78), chemistry (106), engineering 133.

Undergraduate Research: "The Freshman Research Institute is designed to introduce 20-25 incoming freshmen to the nuances of undergraduate research at VCU. For instance, students interact with faculty across disciplines to learn about their research and the qualities that they are seeking in research assistants. Beyond learning about undergraduate research, this free program is designed to aid in transitioning to college and building community among honors students.

"The Honors Summer Undergraduate Research Program is a nine-week program designed to engage 20-25 students in faculty mentored research projects. Students are selected through a competitive process and receive on-campus housing, a stipend, professional development opportunities and one honors course credit.

"In addition, preparing for scholarly research is incorporated into our curriculum. All students enrolled in Rhetoric (which is required for freshmen and optional for those who enter as continuing or transfer students), are expected to submit a proposal to the National Conference on Undergraduate Research (NCUR). This April, the Honors College chartered a bus and the Director of Writing accompanied 37 (out of 60 accepted) students to the NCUR in Asheville, NC. For the past several years, the honors students have made Virginia Commonwealth University one of the best-represented schools at the conference."

Honors Study Abroad: "For honors study abroad trips, however, the Honors College also provides funding. For example, a $2,500 honors scholarship was available to each student accepted to the honors study abroad programs to Italy and Bolivia (Summer 2016) to assist with covering the costs of the program and/or travel."

Financial Aid: "The Honors College gives over $50,000 in scholarships each year to Honors College students. Scholarships awarded are by academic year, students may reapply each year. Scholarships range from $1,000-$3,000.

"Beginning in fall 2016, the *VCU Office of Admissions provides National Merit Scholars a scholarship valued at full in-state level, room, board, tuition and fees.* [Emphasis added.]

"In addition, all honors students are eligible for the university's merit-based scholarships, which include the Presidential, the Provost's, and the Dean's Scholarships. Honors students are highly competitive for these scholarships.

"The Honors College, in collaboration with the Office of Admissions, is able to provide many Honors College students with a $2,000 renewable scholarship. However, if students receive a higher level merit based scholarship from the University, they would forfeit the $2,000 renewable scholarship in order to accept the higher amount."

Honors Fees: $50.00 per semester.

Placement Experiences: For the 2016 graduating class, an extremely impressive 43% entered post-graduate professional school; 31% began their work careers; 18% went on to graduate school; 3% chose to travel; and the remainder were either not employed or not reporting their plans.

Degree of Difference: This is based on the differences between (1) the average (2015, two-part) SAT scores for enrolled honors students (1350) and (2) the average test scores for all students in the university (1105) as a whole. The test scores may be an indication of how "elite" honors students may be perceived as compared to students in the university as a whole. The scores can also provide an indication of how well prepared the non-honors students in the university may be. **Please keep in mind that neither high nor low test scores determine the overall quality of a program.**

NAME: UNIVERSITY HONORS AT VIRGINIA TECH (now called the Honors College).

Date Established: 1968.

Location: Blacksburg, Virginia.

University <u>Full-time Undergraduate</u> Enrollment (2015): 23,685.

Honors Members in Good Standing: 1,450; (mean size of all 50 programs is 1,742).

Honors <u>Average</u> Admission Test Score(s): ACT, 30.4; old SAT, 1327; est. new SAT, 1385.

Average High School GPA/Class Rank: 4.24.

<u>Basic</u> Admission Requirements: None listed.

Application Deadline(s): *Please verify with each program, as some deadlines could change.*

University early decision deadline November 1, 2016, with notification December 15; regular deadline is January 15, 2016, and notification by April 1, 2017.

Honors Programs with old SAT scores from 1315—1350: Idaho, Georgia State, Virginia Tech, Utah, Iowa, Auburn, Houston, Mississippi, VCU.

Administrative Staff: 13.

RATINGS AT A GLANCE: For all mortarboard ratings immediately below, a score of 5 is the maximum and represents a comparison with all 50 honors colleges and programs. More detailed explanations follow the "mortarboard" ratings.

PERCEPTION* OF UNIVERSITY AS A WHOLE, <u>NOT</u> OF HONORS: 🎓🎓🎓🎓$^{1/2}$

*Perception is based on the university's ranking among public universities in the 2016 U.S. News Best Colleges report. Please bear in mind that the better the U.S. News ranking, the more difficult it is for an honors college or program to have a rating that equals or improves on the magazine ranking.

OVERALL HONORS RATING: 🎓🎓🎓🎓

Curriculum Requirements: 🎓🎓🎓$^{1/2}$

Number of Honors Classes Offered: 🎓🎓🎓🎓$^{1/2}$

Number of Honors Classes in Key Disciplines: 🎓🎓🎓🎓$^{1/2}$

Extent of Honors Enrollment: 🎓🎓🎓

Honors-only Class Size: 🎓 🎓 🎓 🎓 🎓

Overall Class Size (Honors-only plus mixed, contract): 🎓 🎓 🎓 🎓

Honors Grad Rate: 🎓 🎓 🎓 🎓 $^{1/2}$

Value-Added Grad Rate: 🎓 🎓 🎓

Ratio of Staff to Students: 🎓 🎓 🎓 🎓

Priority Registration: Yes, students register first in their class year, except that first-year students do not register early in the Fall semester.

Honors Housing Amenities: 🎓 🎓 🎓

Honors Housing Availability: 🎓 🎓 🎓 🎓

Prestigious Awards: 🎓 🎓 🎓 $^{1/2}$

RATING SCORES AND EXPLANATIONS:

Curriculum Requirements (3.5): The most important rating category, the curriculum completion requirement (classes required to complete honors) defines not only what honors students should learn but also the extent to which honors students and faculty are connected in the classroom. If there is a thesis or capstone requirement, it reinforces the individual contact and research skills so important to learning.

The average number of honors semester hours required for completion across all 50 programs is 29.0.

The average number of honors credits required at Virginia Tech is approximately 27 credits. It should be noted, however, that the program offers many options and **the university has Bachelor/Master accelerated degree programs in many disciplines,** including biological sciences, most engineering disciplines, computer science, physics, math, and several disciplines in the social sciences and humanities.

"University Honors at Virginia Tech encourages students to earn honors credits through a multitude of ways." There are at least four ways: coursework, individualized learning, non-classroom experiences, and community learning.

Currently, there are six options:

The Honors Scholar option requires the completion of 18 honors credits.

The "in Honors" option requires the completion of 21 honors credits including 6 credits of undergraduate research—**and a thesis.**

The Honors Baccalaureate degree requires the completion of 24 honors credits including 6 credits of undergraduate research and 6 credits of tutorials. Students must have a minimum of two majors or one major and two minors. Students must create a thesis advisory committee with at least two faculty members. Students working toward a double major must include at least one faculty member from each major, and then complete an honors **thesis.**

The Scholar in Health Studies option requires 12 honors credits and the completion of the **minor in Medicine & Society.** "The MSOC minor engages students in a field called medical humanities, which focuses on the meanings and experiences of disease, medicine, and health. Our classes investigate pressing bioethical questions, explore the humanistic aspects of medical practice and research, and seek to understand medicine, illness and health across time periods, cultures, and contexts. The medical humanities provides an *essential education* about the nature and power of medicine in past eras and contemporary culture."

Commonwealth Scholars "are eligible for this diploma only if they transfer from another post-secondary institution; choose the accelerated undergraduate/graduate degree program; or, upon entering University Honors, have five or fewer semesters until graduation."

Honors Global Scholars must complete 12 honors credits including study abroad, which should last for one full semester or 9 credits. Global scholars must also complete six credits of language study, not counting high school AP/IP credits. Additional requirements include six credits in "global context" courses and 60 hours of unpaid global engagement service.

AP/IB credits are **not** counted as replacements for honors courses.

Number of Honors Classes Offered (4.5): This is a measure of the total **adjusted** honors main sections available in the term reported, not including labs and thesis. An adjusted main section has 3 or more semester credits, or equivalent, and sections with fewer credits receive a lower prorated value.

The program offered a section for every **10.6** enrolled students. The average for all 50 programs is 14.2. The lower the number, the better.

In the term reported, **70.5%** of honors enrollment was **in honors-only sections; and 29.4% in mixed honors sections (honors and non-honors students), and .1% in contract sections were reported** The averages for all fifty programs are 81.3% in honors-only sections; 13.6 % in mixed honors sections; and 5.1% in contract sections.

Number of Honors Classes in Key Disciplines (4.5): The 15 "key" disciplines are biological sciences; business (all); chemistry; communications (especially public speaking); computer science; economics; engineering (all); English; history; math (all); philosophy; physics; political science; psychology; and sociology, anthropology, and gender studies. Interdisciplinary sections, such as those often taken for General Education credit in the first two years, do receive a lesser, prorated discipline "credit" because they introduce students to multiple disciplines in an especially engaging way, often with in-depth discussion.

For this measure, mixed and contract sections are not counted as a section in a key discipline unless honors students taking the sections for honors credit make up at least 10% of the total section enrollment.

In the term reported, the program offered the most sections in English (22), followed by math (4), biology, economics, history, and political science (2 each), and business and chemistry (1 each). Counting the points allocated for interdisciplinary sections, there was a section in a key discipline for every **19.1 honors students.** The average for all 50 programs is 26.3. The lower the number, the better.

The program does offer seminars, about nine or 10, including "The Cultural Impacts of Taxation" and "Charles Darwin, Myths and Realities." Overall, this is a **blended** honors program.

Extent of Honors Enrollment (3.0): Not all honors students take an honors class each term, especially after the first two years. Programs that have fewer honors classes for upper-division honors students will generally have fewer total members in good standing who are actually enrolled in a given term. (Please be aware, however, that honors students not enrolled in a class for a term are still connected to the honors community through residential and extracurricular activities.)

For example, if honors students in a program occupy 1,800 honors classroom seats in a given term, and there are 3,000 honors students in good standing, the extent of enrollment is .67. For programs that require a thesis, the ratio (score) reported below might in fact be somewhat higher, since we only count "regular" class enrollment for this measure, and not thesis enrollment. **Virginia Tech honors has a ratio of .63**; the average is 1.13 for all 50 programs. The higher the ratio, the better.

Average Class Size, Honors-only Sections (5.0): Offered mostly in the first two years, honors-only classes tend to be smaller and, as the name implies, have no or very few students other than those in the honors program. These class sections always are much smaller than mixed or contract sections, or regular non-honors class sections in the university.

The average honors-only class size at the honors college is an extremely impressive **9.2 students**. The average for all 50 programs is 19.0 students.

Average Class Size, Overall (4.0): The overall class calculation is based on the *proportion* of honors students in each type of class (honors-only, mixed honors, and honors contract sections). Thus it is not a raw average. The overall honors-credit class size is **23.7 students**, versus the average for all 50 programs of 26.3 students.

These class size averages also do not correspond to the number of students per honors sections numbers above. The reason is that, in computing average class size metrics, we include enrollment in each 1-2-credit section, not just sections with 3 or more credits.

Along with the honors-only average of 35.1 students, the mixed honors sections average **42.9 students,** and the contract sections with honors credit for individual honors students average about **60 students.** Across all fifty programs, the average mixed honors section has 51.1 students, and the average contract section has 60.1 students.

Honors Graduation Rate (4.5): The rating is the based on the actual grad rate for students who entered the program six years earlier, whether or not the students remained in honors. The **actual rate of 89.6%** is also compared to the rates of other programs with the same test score entry requirement range, and then adjusted to the **score of 90.1.%.** The average honors graduation rate for all programs with similar test scores required for admission is 83.4%.

Value-Added Grad Rate (3.0): The value-added rate measures the extent to which the adjusted score listed above exceeds the six-year grad rate for the university as a whole. **The university-wide rate is relative high, at 83.0%.**

Ratio of Staff to Honors Students (4.0): There is 1 staff member for every **111.5** students. (Mean ratio for all 50 programs is 1 staff member for every 135.6 students.)

Honors Residence Halls, Amenities (3.0): About 75% of honors students living in honors housing reside in the Honors Residential Community. More than two-thirds of the rooms in this facility are traditional doubles with hall baths; the remaining rooms are suite or apartment-type rooms. All are air-conditioned.

"The Honors Residential Community (HRC) was founded in 2011…and comprised of more than 300 Junior Fellows (undergraduate students), several Graduate Fellows (graduate students), and more than 30 Senior Fellows…While the HRC is student-governed, it also receives consistent leadership from a Faculty Principal (live-in tenure-track faculty member) and Student Life Coordinator (live-in Housing and Residence Life staff member). They focus on fostering a supportive, yet challenging community that creates the conditions for students to pursue meaningful encounters with the wider world."

The remainder of honors students in honors dorms live in the Hillcrest Residential Community. All rooms there are suite-style—but not air-conditioned.

Honors Residence Halls, Availability (4.0): This rating compares the number of places in honors residence halls to the number of honors freshman and sophomore members in good standing, approximately 725. The ratio for the college is **.58** rooms for each first- and second-year student. The average for all fifty programs is .63 places.

Prestigious Awards (3.5): The awards that we track and include are listed in the section titled "Prestigious Scholarships." The awards are sometimes won by students who are not in an honors college or program, but increasingly many are enrolled in honors programs. It is also a trend that honors colleges and programs help to prepare their students for the awards competitions.

As might be expected from a university with such a strong focus on STEM disciplines, Tech students have won an impressive 43 Goldwater scholarships, awarded for undergraduate promise in research.

UNRATED FEATURES

Continuation Requirements: 3.50.

Academic Strengths, National Rankings: This is based on national rankings of *graduate* programs in all but engineering and business, where undergraduate rankings are used.

It is Virginia Tech—so the nationally-renowned engineering department leads the way, ranked number 15 nationwide. The overall ranking across 15 departments is better than 60 nationwide. Other leading departments are earth sciences (30), computer science (40), and business (43), and economics (58).

Undergraduate Research: "For the 2015-2016 academic year, a total of 208 honors students participated in undergraduate research. There were 111 students who worked on undergraduate research in fall 2015, and 97 who are working on undergraduate research in the spring of 2016. We do not have a formal undergraduate research program in honors, but there are two specific honors diplomas that recognize students who have written a thesis and participated in at least 6 credit hours of undergraduate research."

Honors Study Abroad: "An exceptionally special study abroad program within University Honors is the Presidential Global Scholars program. It is sponsored by University Honors, the Office of the President, and Office of Outreach and International Affairs. PGS, as it is often called, is designed as a collaborative living-learning community in which ambitious honors students and award-winning professors work in tandem with the resources and opportunities at Virginia Tech's Steger Center for International Scholarship in Riva San Vitale, Switzerland, and beyond to create an environment that allows the students to better understand the world and what they might accomplish in it.

"The Presidential Global Scholars experience is currently worth 16 honors credits and 19 university credits, and completes most of the requirements for the 'Honors Global Scholar' diploma. **However, the program is currently being revised and will soon be able to cover approximately half of the university's new general education requirements for participants.** The coursework is comprised of one-to-two week intensive courses taught by University Distinguished Professors (UDP's) and some of the universities most engaging faculty.

"Since the creation of the Presidential Global Scholars program back in the Spring of 2012, University Honors has awarded more than $275,000 in scholarships to the small cohorts that participate in the program every year.

"University Honors also works directly with students to help them obtain other needed scholarships and financial aid for any study abroad experience students wish to participate in, University Honors related or not. University Honors does this by using endowed study aboard scholarship funds that any honors student can apply for and by connecting students with other Virginia Tech related resources and outside the university funding options."

Financial Aid:

Freshman Recruitment Scholarships include the following:

Prospective freshmen applying to Virginia Tech and to University Honors will have the opportunity to apply for a variety of recruitment scholarships.

Stamps Scholarships--Merit scholarship available to incoming University Honors students who exemplify leadership, perseverance, scholarship, service and innovation. *This scholarship covers estimated cost of attendance for four years filling in after any other scholarships won.*

Calhoun Diversity Scholarships--Merit scholarships available to incoming University Honors students who are first generation or from underrepresented groups. Variable award from $1,000 - to full tuition, fees, room and board annually.

Calhoun Liberal Arts Scholarships--Merit scholarships available to incoming University Honors students who are majoring in the humanities and liberal arts. Variable award from $1,000 - to full tuition, fees, room and board annually.

McNamara Scholarships --Merit scholarships are available to incoming University Honors students from middle income families. Variable award from $1,000 - to full tuition, fees, room and board annually.

Alumni Presidential Scholarships--Merit scholarships available to incoming University Honors students. Variable award from $1,000 - $15,000 annually.

Honors Fees: None.

Placement Experiences: For the 2016 graduating class, 43% entered employment; 32% went to graduate school; 14% went to professional school; 9% took a gap year; and 2% entered military service.

Degree of Difference: This is based on the differences between (1) the average (2015, two-part) SAT scores for enrolled honors students (1327) and (2) the average test scores for all students in the university (1215) as a whole. The test scores may be an indication of how "elite" honors students may be perceived as compared to students in the university as a whole. The scores can also provide an indication of how well prepared the non-honors students in the university may be. **Please keep in mind that neither high nor low test scores determine the overall quality of a program.**

NAME: UNIVERSITY HONORS PROGRAM.

Date Established: 1961.

Location: Seattle, Washington.

University <u>Full-time Undergraduate</u> Enrollment (2015): 27,764.

Honors Members in Good Standing: 1,500; (mean size of all 50 programs is 1,742).

Honors <u>Average</u> Admission Test Score(s): ACT, 33; old SAT, est. 1410; est. new SAT, 1460.

Average High School GPA/Class Rank: Minimum 3.85-4.00.

<u>Basic</u> Admission Requirements: None listed.

Application Deadline(s): *Please verify with each program, as some deadlines could change.*

December 1, 2016; honors recommendations due January 16, 2017. Notification of honors admission March 23–April 15, 2017.

Honors Programs with old SAT scores from 1402—1469: UCF, Connecticut, Kentucky, Washington, Maryland, North Carolina, UC Irvine, Kansas, Minnesota, Tennessee, South Carolina, Clemson, UT Austin, Georgia.

Administrative Staff: 9.

RATINGS AT A GLANCE: For all mortarboard ratings immediately below, a score of 5 is the maximum and represents a comparison with all 50 honors colleges and programs. More detailed explanations follow the "mortarboard" ratings.

PERCEPTION* OF UNIVERSITY AS A WHOLE, <u>NOT</u> OF HONORS: 🎓🎓🎓🎓🎓

*Perception is based on the university's ranking among public universities in the 2016 U.S. News Best Colleges report. Please bear in mind that the better the U.S. News ranking, the more difficult it is for an honors college or program to have a rating that equals or improves on the magazine ranking.

OVERALL HONORS RATING: 🎓🎓🎓🎓

Curriculum Requirements: 🎓🎓🎓🎓🎓

Number of Honors Classes Offered: 🎓🎓🎓🎓^{1/2}

Number of Honors Classes in Key Disciplines: 🎓🎓🎓^{1/2}

Extent of Honors Enrollment: 🎓🎓🎓

Honors-only Class Size: 🎓🎓🎓

Overall Class Size (Honors-only plus mixed, contract): 🎓🎓🎓🎓

Honors Grad Rate: 🎓🎓🎓🎓🎓

Value-Added Grad Rate: 🎓🎓🎓$^{1/2}$

Ratio of Staff to Students: 🎓🎓🎓$^{1/2}$

Priority Registration: No.

Honors Housing Amenities: 🎓🎓🎓🎓

Honors Housing Availability: 🎓🎓🎓

Prestigious Awards: 🎓🎓🎓🎓🎓

RATING SCORES AND EXPLANATIONS:

Curriculum Requirements (5.0): The most important rating category, the curriculum completion requirement (classes required to complete honors) defines not only what honors students should learn but also the extent to which honors students and faculty are connected in the classroom. If there is a thesis or capstone requirement, it reinforces the individual contact and research skills so important to learning.

The average number of honors semester hours required for completion across all 50 programs is 29.0.

The University of Washington Honors program requires about 60 quarter hours for the highest level of completion, **equivalent to about 40 semester** credit hours. Below are three completion options.

Completion of **Interdisciplinary Honors** requires nine 5-unit honors core courses **(quarter system)** plus two 1-unit seminars. (To convert quarter units to semester hours, multiply the quarter units by two-thirds. In this case, 47 quarter units=31.3 semester hours.) In addition, completion requires students to participate in two experiential learning activities and maintain a continuing portfolio of their work and their reflections on cross-disciplinary learning what they have learned and the inter-connections of their learning in the classroom and out of the classroom. Experiential activities "should involve activities in the areas of leadership, research, service or international engagement."

"**Departmental Honors** allows students to explore their majors in greater depth by completing upper-level electives, research, or an extended thesis. Departmental Honors also exposes students to a close working relationship with faculty mentors. **Admission to Interdisciplinary Honors does not guarantee admission to Departmental Honors.** Admission procedures are specific to each department; students should consult with an academic adviser within their department for more information.

Departmental Honors completion requirements vary, "but usually constitute an additional 10-15 credits of upper-level coursework [6-10 semester hours], **additional research and/or an extended thesis.**

College Honors, the completion of **both Interdisciplinary Honors and Departmental Honors,** allows students to experience both Honors general education and the deeper understanding of their chosen disciplinary focus. College Honors completion is one of the most rigorous in the nation, requiring 57-62 honors quarter units (equivalent to 38-42 semester hours).

AP/IB credits are **not** counted as replacements for honors courses.

Number of Honors Classes Offered (4.5): This is a measure of the total **adjusted** honors main sections available in the term reported, not including labs and thesis. An adjusted main section has 3 or more semester credits, or equivalent, and sections with fewer credits receive a lower prorated value.

UW honors offered a section for every **8.5** enrolled students. The average for all 50 programs is 14.2. The lower the number, the better.

In the term reported, In the term reported, **58.6%** of honors enrollment was **in honors-only sections; 34.1% in mixed honors sections (honors and non-honors students); and 7.3% in contract sections were reported.** The averages for all fifty programs are 81.3% in honors-only sections; 13.6 % in mixed honors sections; and 5.1% in contract sections.

Number of. Honors Classes in Key Disciplines (3.5): The 15 "key" disciplines are biological sciences; business (all); chemistry; communications (especially public speaking); computer science; economics; engineering (all); English; history; math (all); philosophy; physics; political science; psychology; and sociology, anthropology, and gender studies. Interdisciplinary sections, such as those often taken for General Education credit in the first two years, do receive a lesser, prorated discipline "credit" because they introduce students to multiple disciplines in an especially engaging way, often with in-depth discussion.

For this measure, mixed and contract sections are not counted as a section in a key discipline unless students taking the sections for honors credit make up at least 10% of the total section enrollment.

In the *quarter* reported, the honors program offered two sections in English, along with one each in chemistry and math, and one each in physics and political science. The program offered a section in a key discipline for every **34.1 honors students.** The average for all 50 programs is 26.3. The lower the number, the better.

The program is strongly focused on interdisciplinary seminars, each of which receives a reduced value when disciplines are rated. (This only means that they do not focus on a *single* discipline.) In the quarter reported, there were 9 seminars, including "Philosophy of Gender in Western Thought"; and "Raid the Archives: Understanding Visual Literacy." There was also an excellent interdisciplinary series encompassing the humanities, fine arts, social sciences, and natural sciences.

Extent of Honors Enrollment (3.0): Not all honors students take an honors class each term, especially after the first two years. Programs that have fewer honors classes for upper-division honors students will generally have fewer total members in good standing who are actually enrolled in a given term. (Please be aware, however, that honors students not enrolled in a class for a term are still connected to the honors community through residential and extracurricular activities.)

For example, if honors students in a program occupy 1,800 honors classroom seats in a given term, and there are 3,000 honors students in good standing, the extent of enrollment is .67. For programs that require a thesis, the ratio (score) reported below might in fact be somewhat higher, since we only count "regular" class enrollment for this measure, and not thesis enrollment. **UW honors has a ratio of .76**; the average is 1.13 for all 50 programs. The higher the ratio, the better.

Average Class Size, Honors-only Sections (3.0): Offered mostly in the first two years, honors-only classes tend to be smaller and, as the name implies, have no or very few students other than those in the honors program. These class sections always are much smaller than mixed or contract sections, or regular non-honors class sections in the university.

The average honors-only class size in the UW Honors Program is **29.2 students**. The average for all 50 programs is 19.0 students.

Average Class Size, Overall (4.0): The overall class calculation is based on the *proportion* of honors students in each type of class (honors-only, mixed honors, and honors contract sections). Thus it is not a raw average.

The overall honors-credit class size is **27.4 students**, versus the average for all 50 programs of 26.3 students.

Note: These class size averages do not correspond to the number of students per sections ratios above. The reason is that, in computing average class size metric, we include enrollment in each 1-2-credit section, not just sections with 3 or more credits.

Along with the honors-only average of 29.2 students, at UW Honors the mixed honors sections average a very low **22.1 students,** and the relatively few contract sections with honors credit for individual honors students average **37.4 students.** Across all fifty programs, the average mixed honors section has 51.1 students, and the average contract section has 60.1 students.

Honors Graduation Rate (5.0): The rating is the based on the actual grad rate for students who entered the program six years earlier, whether or not the students remained in honors. The **actual rate of 93.3%** is also compared to the rates of other programs with the same test score entry requirement range, and then adjusted to the **score of 93.4%.** The average honors graduation rate for all programs with similar test scores required for admission is 92.6%.

Value-Added Grad Rate (3.5): The value-added rate measures the extent to which the adjusted score above exceeds the six-year grad rate for the university as a whole. **The university-wide rate is 84.0%.**

Ratio of Staff to Honors Students (3.5): There is 1 staff member for every **166.7** students. (Mean ratio for all 50 programs is 1 staff member for every 135.6 students.)

Honors Residence Halls, Amenities (4.0): Terry Hall is the home of about 190 honors students, freshmen and upperclassmen. Located in West Campus, Terry has double rooms, triples, and studios, all with ensuite bathrooms. Recently remodeled, the residence also has a rooftop deck with views of the Olympics and Portage Bay, a community kitchen, a great room, and floor lounges. Terry does not have room air-conditioning, although that is not the problem it would be in other parts of the country. The residence is extremely close to dining options at the District Market, Cultivate, and Local Point. The nearest dining is in Lander Hall.

Honors Residence Halls, Availability (3.0): This rating compares the number of places in honors residence halls to the number of honors freshman and sophomore members in good standing, approximately 750. The ratio for the college is **.26** rooms for each first- and second-year student. The average for all fifty programs is .63 places.

Prestigious Awards (5.0): UW is one of the six or seven leading public universities when it comes to its students' winning prestigious awards. UW students have won 37 Rhodes scholarships, 13 Truman scholarships, Marshall and Gates Cambridge awards, 5 each, 55 Goldwater scholarships, and 14 Udall awards. In addition, UW is a leader in National Science Foundation post-graduate grants and Fulbright scholarships.

UNRATED FEATURES

Continuation Requirements: 3.30.

Academic Strengths, National Rankings: This is based on national rankings of *graduate* programs in all but engineering and business, where undergraduate rankings are used.

The UW faculty and departments are very likely in the top 20 nationally among both private and public universities. The average departmental ranking across all major disciplines is about 22. The many outstanding departments include computer science (6), education (8), earth sciences (11), psychology (14), biology (19), business and physics (22), chemistry (24), and math (25). All of the 15 departments we track are ranked 40th in the nation or better.

Undergraduate Research: "Honors collaborates with the University Research Program in Undergraduate Academic Affairs which hosts a clearing house to put students in touch with research opportunities all across campus.

"All students in the Interdisciplinary and College Honors programs are required to complete two of four experiential learning requirements, one of which is research. Students in Departmental and College must complete a research project. Each year the UW offers an Undergraduate Research Symposium at which around 1,000 undergraduates present their research. The percentage listed above reflects those students who have used research as one of their experiential learning requirements. The percentage who actually participate in research is certainly much higher, but we don't have precise information – many students complete several research projects or positions during their undergraduate years."

Honors Study Abroad: 2016 Summer Programs included:

Rome, Italy - Art, Identity, and Structures of Exchange;
South Africa - Bantu Base Afrika: Linguistics and Health;
Peru - From Andes to Amazon: Biodiversity, Conservation and Sustainability in Peru;
Tanzania - Critical Perspectives on Ecotourism in Tanzania;
Romania and Georgia - Conflicting Currents: Romania and Georgia in a Turbulent Black Sea.

"In addition to our regular study abroad programs, the Honors Program also has Direct Exchange agreements with the following universities:

Tokyo, Japan - Waseda University Global Leadership Program (year-long);
Argentina - Universidad de San Andrés;
Netherlands - University of Utrecht Honors College.

Interdisciplinary Honors Field Studies. The UW Honors Program offers an average of three courses in its Interdisciplinary Field Studies Program. Courses demonstrate "field studies" in its broadest and most inclusive sense offering place and community based learning across a broad range of disciplines.

Global Challenges—Interdisciplinary Answers is an annual event held every year during autumn quarter bringing together an interdisciplinary panel to explore big questions that are posed by students' feedback.

Honors Diversity Courses. 25% of UW Honors courses are listed as "DIV" courses (Diversity). The UW requires a "DIV" graduation requirement.

Financial Aid: First year scholarships:

- Mary Gates Endowment Scholarship (2 year tuition for in-state students);
- Honors Undergraduate Scholar Award (4 year tuition waiver for in-state students);
- Honors Achievement Award (one-time partial tuition waiver for out-of-state students);
- Campbell Scholarship (one-time award of $3,000 for first generation student);
- Eberharter Scholarship (four-year $3,000 award for student interested in international studies, with support for study abroad);
- Clack Scholarship (one-time award of $3,500 for in-state resident from Spokane County with financial need);
- Lovsted Family Scholarship (4 year award $2,000/year).

Honors also has a number of one-time awards for continuing students:

- Bonderman Fellowship ($20,000 for each of 7 undergraduate awardees – not exclusive to Honors; students but the majority of recipients have been honors students, and the fellowship is housed in the University Honors Program);
- Bordeaux Scholarship (rising juniors in Interdisciplinary/College Honors; $1,500);
- Dilman Scholarship (rising seniors in Interdisciplinary/College Honors; $1,500);
- Friedman-Hechter Scholarship (Any year in Interdisciplinary/College Honors; $500);
- Honors Program Scholarship (Any year in Interdisciplinary/College Honors; $500);

- Greene Scholarship (Any year in Interdisciplinary/College Honors; one year of in-state tuition);
- Hennes Scholarship (Any year in Interdisciplinary, Departmental, or College Honors; $5,000);
- Mary Gates Achievement Scholarship (rising sophomores in Interdisciplinary/College Honors; one year of in-state tuition);
- Gerberding Scholarship (rising seniors and above in Interdisciplinary, Departmental, or College Honors; $1,500);
- Wang Scholarship (Any year in in Interdisciplinary, Departmental, or College Honors; $2,000;
- Mary Gates Achievement Scholarship (rising sophomores in Interdisciplinary Honors, WA resident);
- Distinguished Alumni Scholarship (rising senior in Interdisciplinary Honors $500).

Scholarship amounts may vary from year to year.

Honors Fees: None.

Placement Experiences: None available at this time.

Degree of Difference: This is based on the differences between (1) the average (2015, two-part) SAT scores for enrolled honors students (1410) and (2) the average test scores for all students in the university (1230) as a whole. The test scores may be an indication of how "elite" honors students may be perceived as compared to students in the university as a whole. The scores can also provide an indication of how well prepared the non-honors students in the university may be. **Please keep in mind that neither high nor low test scores determine the overall quality of a program.**

NAME: THE HONORS COLLEGE, WASHINGTON STATE UNIVERSITY.

Date Established: 1998.

Location: Pullman, Washington.

University <u>Full-time Undergraduate</u> Enrollment (2015): 20,843.

Honors Members in Good Standing: 703; (mean size of all 50 programs is 1,742).

Honors <u>Average</u> Admission Test Score(s): ACT, 28.1; old SAT, 1250; est. new SAT, 1310.

Average High School GPA/Class Rank: 3.86.

<u>Basic</u> Admission Requirements: None listed.

Application Deadline(s): *Please verify with each program, as some deadlines could change.*

January 31, 2017.

Honors Programs with old SAT scores from 1240—1291: Arkansas, Oklahoma State, Texas Tech, Montana, Washington State, New Mexico, South Dakota, Colorado State, Arizona, Montana State, Arizona State.

Administrative Staff: 10.

RATINGS AT A GLANCE: For all mortarboard ratings immediately below, a score of 5 is the maximum and represents a comparison with all 50 honors colleges and programs. More detailed explanations follow the "mortarboard" ratings.

PERCEPTION* OF UNIVERSITY AS A WHOLE, <u>NOT</u> OF HONORS: 🎓🎓🎓 1/2

*Perception is based on the university's ranking among public universities in the 2016 U.S. News Best Colleges report. Please bear in mind that the better the U.S. News ranking, the more difficult it is for an honors college or program to have a rating that equals or improves on the magazine ranking.

OVERALL HONORS RATING: 🎓🎓🎓 1/2

Curriculum Requirements: 🎓🎓🎓 1/2

Number of Honors Classes Offered: 🎓🎓🎓

Number of Honors Classes in Key Disciplines: 🎓🎓🎓 1/2

Extent of Honors Enrollment: 🎓🎓🎓🎓

Honors-only Class Size: 🎓🎓🎓🎓

Overall Class Size (Honors-only plus mixed, contract): 🎓🎓🎓🎓¹ᐟ²

Honors Grad Rate: 🎓🎓🎓🎓

Value-Added Grad Rate: 🎓🎓🎓🎓

Ratio of Staff to Students: 🎓🎓🎓🎓🎓

Priority Registration: Yes students register for all courses, honors and otherwise, with the first group of students during each year they are in the program

Honors Housing Amenities: 🎓🎓🎓🎓¹ᐟ²

Honors Housing Availability: 🎓🎓🎓¹ᐟ²

Prestigious Awards: 🎓🎓🎓

RATING SCORES AND EXPLANATIONS:

Curriculum Requirements (3.5): The most important rating category, the curriculum completion requirement (classes required to complete honors) defines not only what honors students should learn but also the extent to which honors students and faculty are connected in the classroom. If there is a thesis or capstone requirement, it reinforces the individual contact and research skills so important to learning.

The average number of honors semester hours required for completion across all 50 programs is 29.0.

The completion requirement at the honors college is **25** credits. These must include 21 credits in honors, one credit in an honors experience, and a 4-credit **thesis**.

The college strongly emphasizes educating its students for the increasing presence of a global economy. The honors site says that in a "recent article in the *Financial Times of London* it was reported that '[companies] hire more multilingual employees, because these employees can communicate better, have better intercultural sensitivity, are better at cooperating, negotiating, compromising. But they can also think more efficiently.'"

The foreign language requirement may be satisfied in one of the following ways:

- Satisfactory completion of the STAMP test;

- Satisfactory completion of a foreign language 204 level course;

- Completion of a minor in a foreign language;

- Earning the Honors College **Certificate of Global Competencies;**

- Students whose native language is not English and came to the United States after 8th grade will be exempt of this requirement upon discussion with an Honors adviser.

The Certificate of Global Competencies is a separate option that requires 15 credits and a thesis. It essentially requires study-abroad credits and courses in international studies, in addition to the foreign language requirement.

AP/IB credits are **not** counted as replacements for honors courses.

Number of Honors Classes Offered (3.0): This is a measure of the total **adjusted** honors main sections available in the term reported, not including labs and thesis. An adjusted main section has 3 or more semester credits, or equivalent, and sections with fewer credits receive a lower prorated value.

The college offered a section for every **22.4** enrolled students. The average for all 50 programs is 14.2. The lower the number, the better.

In the term reported, the percentage of honors enrollment was **88.8 % in honors-only sections; and 11.2% in mixed honors sections (honors and non-honors students). No contract sections were reported** The averages for all fifty programs are 81.3% in honors-only sections; 13.6 % in mixed honors sections; and 5.1% in contract sections.

Number of Honors Classes in Key Disciplines (3.5): The 15 "key" disciplines are biological sciences; business (all); chemistry; communications (especially public speaking); computer science; economics; engineering (all); English; history; math (all); philosophy; physics; political science; psychology; and sociology, anthropology, and gender studies. Interdisciplinary sections, such as those often taken for General Education credit in the first two years, do receive a lesser, prorated discipline "credit" because they introduce students to multiple disciplines in an especially engaging way, often with in-depth discussion.

For this measure, mixed and contract sections are not counted as a section in a key discipline unless students taking the sections for honors credit make up at least 10% of the total section enrollment.

In the term reported, the honors college offered nine sections in English, two in economics, and one in math and physics each. (Bear in mind that the college is a small program.) Counting the reduced points allocated for interdisciplinary sections, a section in a key discipline for every **46.1 honors students.** The average for all 50 programs is 26.3. The lower the number, the better.

The college does offer classes, about 21, including "Contextual Understanding in the Arts and Humanities"; "Science as a Way of Knowing"; and multiple sections on "Global Issues" in science, social sciences, and the arts and humanities.

The honors college is a **core** program, most interdisciplinary and strongly focused on internationalism.

Extent of Honors Enrollment (4.0): Not all honors students take an honors class each term, especially after the first two years. Programs that have fewer honors classes for upper-division honors students will generally have fewer total members in good standing who are actually enrolled in a given term. (Please be aware, however, that honors students not enrolled in a class for a term are still connected to the honors community through residential and extracurricular activities.)

For example, if honors students in a program occupy 1,800 honors classroom seats in a given term, and there are 3,000 honors students in good standing, the extent of enrollment is .67. For programs that require a thesis, the ratio (score) reported below might in fact be somewhat higher, since we only count "regular" class enrollment for this measure, and not thesis enrollment. **The college has a ratio of 1.00**; the average of 1.13 for all 50 programs. The higher the ratio, the better.

Average Class Size, Honors-only Sections (4.0): Offered mostly in the first two years, honors-only classes tend to be smaller and, as the name implies, have no or very few students other than those in the honors program. These class sections always are much smaller than mixed or contract sections, or regular non-honors class sections in the university.

The average honors-only class size at the honors college is **19.5 students**. The average for all 50 programs is 19.0 students.

Average Class Size, Overall (4.5): The overall class calculation is based on the *proportion* of honors students in each type of class (honors-only, mixed honors, and honors contract sections). Thus it is not a raw average. The overall honors-credit class size is **18.2 students**, versus the average for all 50 programs of 26.3 students.

Note: These class size averages do not correspond to the number of students per sections ratios above. The reason is that, in computing average class size metric, we include enrollment in each 1-2-credit section, not just sections with 3 or more credits.

Along with the honors-only average of 18.2 students, the mixed honors sections average **33.0 students,** Across all fifty programs, the average mixed honors section has 51.1 students.

Honors Graduation Rate (4.0): The rating is based on the actual grad rate for students who entered the program six years earlier, whether or not the students remained in honors. The **actual rate of 86.8%** is also compared to the rates of other programs with the same test score entry requirement range, and then adjusted to the **adjusted score of 87.0%.** The average honors graduation rate for all programs with similar test scores required for admission is 85.3%.

Value-Added Grad Rate (4.0): The value-added rate measures the extent to which the adjusted score above exceeds the six-year grad rate for the university as a whole. **The university-wide rate is 67%.**

Ratio of Staff to Honors Students (5.0): There is 1 staff member for every **70.3** students. (Mean ratio for all 50 programs is 1 staff member for every 135.6 students.)

Honors Residence Halls, Amenities (4.5): Honors students can live in Honors Hall, a very attractive building with suite-style rooms and shared baths. The main floor is air-conditioned.

Honors Residence Halls, Availability (3.5): This rating compares the number of places in honors residence halls to the number of honors freshman and sophomore members in good standing, approximately 352. The ratio for the college is **.36** rooms for each first- and second-year student. The average for all fifty programs is .63 places.

Prestigious Awards (3.0): The awards that we track and include are listed in the section titled "Prestigious Scholarships." The awards are sometimes won by students who are not in an honors college or program, but increasingly many are enrolled in honors programs. It is also a trend that honors colleges and programs help to prepare their students for the awards competitions.

WSU students have won 10 Rhodes scholarships, as well as 23 Goldwater scholarships through 2016.

UNRATED FEATURES

Continuation Requirements: 3.20.

Academic Strengths, National Rankings: This is based on national rankings of *graduate* programs in all but engineering and business, where undergraduate rankings are used.

WSU has an average national departmental ranking across 15 departments that is better than 90th. Leading departments are sociology (45), earth sciences (69), computer science and engineering (both at 70), physics (77), and chemistry (80).

Undergraduate Research: All Honors College students, except those majoring in engineering, are required to complete an Honors thesis that involves research directly under the supervision of a faculty mentor. The students have to complete a written thesis and defend it orally in front of a faculty committee that includes at least one external examiner (i.e., not from the Honors College) and one faculty member from the Honors College. For students majoring in engineering (about 20% of our students) their capstone project (part of the ABET requirement) is counted in lieu of the Honors thesis. However, many of the engineering students in Honors also do undergraduate research. Undergraduate research is encouraged for all students in Honors.

Honors Study Abroad: The Honors College has three Honors Exchanges:

Two Universities in Wales: Aberystwyth and Swansea, and Southeast University in Nanjing, China.

"We offer 2-3 faculty led trips every summer, offered by Honors faculty. Honors has led the university in providing this type of experience since 1996," according to the Dean.

"Scholarships are available specifically for study-abroad programs. These are provided by Honors, the Office of International Programs, and through the academic degree-granting colleges."

Financial Aid: "The Honors College at Washington State University is very proud to have many alumni, friends, and programs dedicated to helping our students meet the financial demands as they earn their education in Honors and at WSU. Honors scholarships and awards for Honors College students are awarded based on or to support incoming freshmen, merit for outstanding grades and achievements, financial need as determined by FAFSA, diversity, study-and research-abroad experiences including foreign language immersion programs, undergraduate research, and pursuit of a specific major. Most scholarships go into student accounts and are used for tuition and/or fees. Each of our scholarship awards requires that applicants be current Honors students and have a WSU cumulative grade point average of at least 3.20."

Honors Fees: None.

Placement Experiences: No information provided.

Degree of Difference: This is based on the differences between (1) the average (2015, two-part) SAT scores for enrolled honors students (1270) and (2) the average test scores for all students in the university (1020) as a whole. The test scores may be an indication of how "elite" honors students may be perceived as compared to students in the university as a whole. The scores can also provide an indication of how well prepared the non-honors students in the university may be. **Please keep in mind that neither high nor low test scores determine the overall quality of a program.**

Please see following pages for Summary Reviews (unrated reviews) of ten more public university honors programs.

SUMMARY REVIEWS

The following reviews summarize the admissions information, curriculum requirements, class sizes, graduation rates, honors housing and other perks, along with each university's record of winning prestigious scholarships.

The honors colleges and programs in this section are not rated because (1) they simply did not have all the data that we requested for this edition; (2) they did not provide the data; (3) they had special features that we could not measure, especially open curriculum requirements; or (4) they were in the midst of major program changes or transitioning to an honors college from an honors program.

We hope it is clear that the placement of an honors college or program in this section does not mean that the program or college is somehow unworthy of a full, rated review, as evidenced by the inclusion of honors programs at the University of Michigan, University of Virginia, and the University of Wisconsin, all of which are institutions ranked among the top 50 national universities in the nation, public or private.

NAME: UNIVERSITY HONORS PROGRAM, UNIVERSITY OF CINCINNATI.

Editor's Note: The University Honors Program has not been reviewed in previous editions, but we are very pleased to include this summary review in the current edition. Along with the Pitt Honors College and the Echols Scholars Program at the University of Virginia, the UHP emphasizes maximum flexibility and choice for students. Although this can be a wonderful, enriching experience for students, it does not fit our methodology. But the UHP differs from Pitt and UVA, and from any other program we review, *in its emphasis on experiential learning in the curriculum.*

Date Established: "The honors program at the University of Cincinnati began in the late 1960's as the McMicken Honors Program, housed within the McMicken College of Arts and Sciences. In 1991, the program was expanded university-wide and became known as the Honors Scholars Program. In 2007, the program was completely revised with a focus on experiential learning and reflection to promote student self-growth and discovery alongside of academic rigor, and the name was changed to the University Honors Program (UHP). The UHP continues today to serve students from every undergraduate college on campus."

Location: Cincinnati, Ohio.

University Full-time Undergraduate Enrollment: 20,788.

Honors Members in Good Standing: 1,353. (Mean size of all 50 programs is 1,742).

Honors Average Admission Statistics: ACT median , 32.9; old SAT equivalent, 1450-1460; est. new SAT equivalent, 1490. High school GPA at least 3.85 unweighted.

Average High School GPA/Class Rank: 90% in top 10% of high school class.

Basic Admission Requirements: ACT, 29. Old SAT equivalent, 1290; est. new SAT equivalent, 1350.

Application Deadline(s): *Please verify with each program, as some deadlines could change.*

December 1, 2016.

Honors Programs with old SAT scores from 1402—1469: UCF, Connecticut, Kentucky, Washington, Maryland, North Carolina, UC Irvine, Kansas, Minnesota, Tennessee, South Carolina, Clemson, UT Austin, Georgia.

Administrative Staff: 11.

Priority Registration: "Yes, students can register 4 days in advance of all other students (including graduate students) for all courses every year."

Curriculum Requirements: "The University Honors Program (UHP) is built around an innovative pedagogical approach to honors education. It is focused on experiential, interdisciplinary, reflective and integrative learning as well as the following thematic areas:

- Research

- Global studies

- Leadership

- Community engagement

- Creativity

"UHP students own their honors experience – each student creates a pathway unique to their goals and aspirations. ***There is only one required class,*** a one-credit hour *Gateway to University Honors* (HNRS1010) course that all students take during their first year. Other than that, each student's pathway through the program is entirely their own.

"[A]ll students are required to complete five "Honors Experiences" during their time in our program and they must maintain their honors learning portfolio. These experiences must be grounded in one or more of our five thematic areas (see above and the attached Learning Outcomes).

"There are different types of honors experiences. The students have the freedom to choose any combination of honors experiences, as long as they complete at least five. Each experience is set up so that time on task (at least 75 hours) and learning is equivalent to a three credit hour course. Honors experiences fall within the following three categories:

"**Honor Seminar Courses**--These are special honors-only courses, usually about 30-40 per year, which are chosen from proposals submitted by faculty across the university in a competitive process.

"**Pre-Approved Experiences**--These are best practice experiential learning courses or existing programs offered at the university that our office has vetted as being appropriate for our students.… In most…cases, students must complete a full year of an activity or program in order for it to qualify as a pre-approved experience (at least 75 hours). The time-on-task and learning involved in a pre-approved experience is equivalent to that of a three-credit-hour course.

"**Self-Designed Experiences**--This option allows advanced students the freedom to create their own honors experience. Students must submit a proposal describing the course of study and then have that approved by our office. Examples of this type of experience often fall within the category of research (i.e., an honors student may work on the medical campus for 6-12 months with a faculty member on a specific project, resulting in a paper or poster presentation).

"In addition to fulfilling five honors experiences, students must also maintain an online learning portfolio to capture their growth and development across their entire college career. Learning portfolios provide UHP students with a place to reflect on and integrate their learning across experiences. This includes personal, academic and professional learning as well as curricular and co-curricular experiences. While students are required to include their honors experiences in portfolios, we encourage them to include any meaningful experience they engage in, honors-related or not."

AP/IB credits are not counted as replacements for honors courses.

Average Class Size: "All courses are small, ranging in enrollment from 4-28 students (average enrollment in 2014-15 was 17 students); the only classes with enrollment over 25 are sections of *Gateway to University Honors*, a required first-year course for students entering the UHP.

- 26 disciplines were represented in 2014-15, and
- 70 honors classes were offered in 2014-15; of these:
- 44 are seminar style = 2000- or 3000-level honors seminar courses ;
- 11 are small departmental honors classes (Physics, English Composition, Calculus, Chem labs;
- 15 are the one-credit hour Gateway to University Honors course that all first-year students take.

Honors Graduation Rate: The six-year graduation rate of first-year entrants who graduated from the university, whether or not the students completed the honors program, is 90.6%. The average honors graduation rate for all programs with similar test scores required for admission is 92.6%.

Value-Added Graduation Rate: The six-year honors graduation rate of 92% compares to the university-wide six-year rate of 65%.

Ratio of Staff to Honors Students: Since there is currently an overlap of staffing with the SAS Honors Program, we can only estimate the staff ratio for the new honors college: about 1 staff member for every **123** students. (Mean ratio for all 50 programs is 1 staff member for every 135.6 students.)

Honors Residence Halls: "Starting in Fall 2016, Honors housing will be consolidated into three buildings – Scioto Hall, Turner Hall and Daniels Hall. Honors housing in Scioto Hall includes the top three levels of UC's newest residence hall, Scioto Hall, a LEED-Silver certified building which offers apartment-style living. The other two remaining buildings for Honors housing are Daniels and Turner.

"This consolidation was made to take advantage of the opportunity to gain honors housing space in the new residence hall. The number of honors housing spaces on campus will not change, even though we have one less building. The new honors housing space in Scioto will accommodate the same number of students that were previously in both the Morgens and Stratford Heights buildings (see below).

"Prior to fall 2016, the UHP has had dedicated honors housing in four on-campus residence halls-- Stratford Heights, Turner Hall, Daniels Hall, and Morgens Hall.

- 533 honors students lived on campus during fall semester 2015 (39.4% of our students live on campus);

- 365 of these 533 students live in honors housing (27% of our students live in honors housing)."

Prestigious Awards: "Most recently, first-year UHP student Aswin Bikkani won the prestigious 2015 Tylenol Future Care Scholarship. This award is presented to 20 outstanding health-related undergraduate or graduate students from across the nation based on academic performance (other recipients were from Stanford, Harvard, and Washington University). Aswin Bikkani was also selected by the National Society of High School Scholars to be one of 25 participants worldwide (only 5 were invited from the United States) to attend the Stockholm University Nobel Week in Stockholm, Sweden this past December. During this event, the Nobel Prize Ceremonies took place, as well as the Nobel Lectures and other Nobel festivities.

"UHP students are also often at found at the highest levels of student leadership at the university (e.g., incoming Student Body President Mitchell Phelps and current Student Body Vice President Andrew Griggs). In addition, UHP students often earn the Presidential Leadership Medal of Excellence, UC's highest honor for an undergraduate student. For example, 5 of the 6 recipients of the 2016 Presidential Leadership Medal of Excellence were UHP students."

University of Cincinnati students have also won 4 Rhodes scholarships and 5 Goldwater scholarships.

Continuation Requirements: 3.20 GPA.

Academic Strengths, National Rankings: This is based on national rankings of *graduate* programs in 15 disciplines, except engineering and business, where undergraduate rankings are used.

UC is well-known for its undergraduate and graduate programs in music, and the graduate criminology program is ranked 3rd in the nation. Among the departments we track, engineering (83), earth sciences (88), biology and education (both 93), sociology (94), and chemistry (94) all rank in the top 100 nationally.

Undergraduate Research: "Research is strongly encouraged in our program as it is one of our five major thematic areas (in addition to leadership, community engagement, creative arts and global studies). Consequently, we strongly encourage our students engage in research and we have developed two programs through the UHP to allow them to do so. The two programs that are run through the UHP are:

"UHP Biomedical Research and Mentoring Program (RaMP) - developed by the UHP in collaboration with the UC College of Medicine and Cincinnati Children's Hospital Medical Center; and

"UHP+DISCOVER – a new UHP program for summer 2016 that pairs students and faculty for research projects in the humanities, social sciences, business, music, graphic design, and education and other non-STEM disciplines.

"UHP students can also participate in at least 16 different research opportunities that automatically qualify as one (or more) pre-approved honors experiences. These opportunities include:

"Women In Science and Engineering (WISE) – for female students who are paired with STEM faculty over 12 weeks during the summer;

"SURF – Summer Undergraduate Research Fellowship; offered through the UC College of Medicine;

"Protégé Undergraduate Research Program – for students in the College of Engineering and Applied Sciences; and

"TAFT Undergraduate Research Fellowship through the McMicken College of Arts and Sciences.

"In addition, UHP students are encouraged to develop their own research project with a faculty mentor within any area, and they can receive honors credit for doing so as part of the self-designed experience option (see above). Research activities requiring 75-249 hours per semester qualify the student to receive one honors experience, while research over 250 hours counts as two honors experiences. Several of our honors students also co-author peer-reviewed, scientific papers and/or present their research at professional meetings with their faculty mentors."

Study Abroad: "The Study Abroad experience is strongly emphasized in our program as we view this as critical in encouraging our students to become global citizens. During the 2014-15 academic year, our UHP students studied in 45 countries for 828 weeks. Our goal over the next 5 years is for 75% of our students to have a Study Abroad experience during their time at UC.

"To financially assist students, the UHP typically provides individual grants to students, in addition to separate funding provided by the Study Abroad office. UHP grants for international travel typically consist of up to $1200 for short-term study abroad (7 weeks or less) and up to $1500 for long-term study abroad (7-15 weeks); smaller grants of approximately $500 are also available for less expensive study abroad opportunities. The UHP has a close relationship with UC International (which oversees the Study Abroad program), as our Director, Dr. Raj Mehta, is also Vice-Provost for International Affairs."

Financial Aid: The main forms of scholarships for our honors students are as follows:

"**Cincinnatus Scholarship Program** – awarded to incoming freshmen; "The brightest and most promising prospective freshmen in all academic disciplines are selected to receive renewable awards totaling more than $22 million in University of Cincinnati four-year scholarships." These include: "10 Presidential awards – full tuition, fees, room, board and book allowance;

"Cincinnatus awards with varying amounts between $1500-6000 per year;

"**Cincinnatus Excellence Scholarship for National Merit and National Hispanic Scholar Finalists** – est. $17,500 per year, covers in-state tuition, fees, on-campus room, and a one-time $1,500 to support computer purchase, study abroad experience, or undergraduate research;

"**National Outreach Award** – a renewable $6000 award; 'The UC National Outreach Award is a scholarship program recognizing the academic merit of students coming to the University of Cincinnati from select, targeted geographic areas.'"

Degree of Difference: This is based on the differences between (1) the average (2015, two-part) SAT scores for enrolled honors students (1450-1460, ACT equivalent) and (2) the average test scores for all students in the university (1190-1200, ACT equivalent) as a whole. The test scores may be an indication of how "elite" honors students may be perceived as compared to students in the university as a whole. The scores can also provide an indication of how well prepared the non-honors students in the university may be. **Please keep in mind that neither high nor low test scores determine the overall quality of a program.**

NAME: FLORIDA STATE UNIVERSITY HONORS PROGRAM

Date Established: The university established multiple honors programs in 1932.

Location: Tallahassee, Florida.

University Full-time Undergraduate Enrollment: 29,211.

Honors Students in Good Standing: Estimated 2,500 (mean size of all 50 programs under review is 1,742).

Honors Average Admission Statistics: ACT, 32. Old SAT three-part, 2080; est. new SAT, 1440-1450. High school GPA (weighted), 4.20.

Minimum Admission Requirements: None listed.

Honors Programs with old SAT scores from 1351—1396: Purdue, Oregon, Alabama, Massachusetts, Penn State, Indiana, CUNY Macaulay, Texas A&M, NJIT, Missouri, Oregon State, Delaware, LSU, Vermont, Temple.

Administrative Staff: 4.

Priority Registration: Yes, honors students have "the privilege of being able to register at the same time as seniors" in the university.

Curriculum Requirements: The basic honors completion requirement at FSU is 18 credit hours in honors courses or an equivalent amount of credits including honors departmental research and thesis.

Of special interest to many prospective students are the programs for Honors Legal Scholars and Honors Medical Scholars, both designed for highly qualified honors students who want to earn **automatic admission to the FSU Law or an opportunity for a 7-year BS/MD degree sequence.**

"Honors Legal Scholars gain experience and knowledge through volunteer and educational activities as well as social gatherings. They are given pre-professional advising, meet with professors, observe classes, and shadow current students in the College of Law." Successful honors completion earns automatic law school admission at FSU.

Honors completion does not bring automatic admission into the College of Medicine, but "FSU Honors Medical Scholars who successfully complete the program and pre-medical requirements will be eligible to apply to the FSU College of Medicine through the early decision process. **The program allows eligible students to pursue a Bachelor of Science degree of their choice. In some cases it may be possible to finish the undergraduate and M.D. degrees in seven years depending on college credits earned before enrollment at FSU.**"

Here are the two basic options for honors completion:

Honors Finisher: "Students must earn eighteen honors points, which are usually honors credits earned through coursework. These eighteen honors points must include a minimum of nine semester hours of honors course work (honors sections of regular courses, honors seminars, the honors colloquium, honors-augmented courses). The remainder of the eighteen honors points can be earned through any combination of further honors coursework including honors Directed Individual Study (DIS), graduate classes, or Honors in the Major work (also known as honors thesis).

Honors in the Major: Students "are required to complete a minimum of 2 semesters and 6 credit hours in order to earn Honors in the Major. These semesters should be consecutive, with the exception of the summer semester if you will not be on campus. You can take up to 9 credit hours of Honors thesis work over 3 semesters if necessary. All requirements must be met and your thesis must be successfully defended before graduation from FSU with your bachelor's degree."

Honors in the Major (9-12 hours course work + 6-9 hours of thesis) is given special recognition at the awards ceremony and has both distinctions described here noted on their transcripts."

Average Class Size: No information available from the program. In 2014, we estimated the honors-only class size to be 20-25 students.

Graduation Rate: The six-year graduation rate of first-year entrants who graduated from the university, whether or not the students completed the honors program, was *estimated in 2014 to be* a **89.3%** The average honors graduation rate for all programs with similar test scores required for admission is 86.2%.

Value-Added Graduation Rate: The honors graduation rate is 89.3% compared to the university-wide six-year rate of 79%.

Ratio of Staff to Honors Students: Our estimate is that there is 1 staff member for every **250** students. (Mean ratio for all 50 rated programs is 1 staff member for every 135.6 students.)

Honors Residence Halls: "All Honors Freshman are strongly encouraged to live in Landis Hall or a Living-Learning Community. Living in Landis Hall allows for both a stronger connection with other honors students and close proximity to the Honors, Scholars, and Fellows House that has resources available for you to succeed."

Landis Hall has suite-style double rooms with a connecting bath. The halls are coed but gender-separated by suite. The residence is air-conditioned. Laundry is on site. Landis has a capacity of 403 residents, but we do not know how many Honors Program freshmen are residents. It is possible that Landis could accommodate all honors freshmen.

An important new addition is the Honors, Scholars and Fellows House. A large, multi-story facility, it has study facilities, lounges, classrooms, and meeting rooms. It is home to the University Honors Program, the Office of Undergraduate Research, the Office of Graduate Fellowships and Awards, the Florida State University Fellows Society, and the Program for Instructional Excellence. The space will also be used by the Undergraduate Research Opportunity Program.

Prestigious Awards: FSU has been recognized as a leading producer of Fulbright Student Scholars, a highly-competitive award to outstanding students selected to study or teach abroad. By our count, FSU students have won 25 Fulbright Scholarships during the most recent three years. FSU undergraduates have also won 20 Goldwater Scholarships, and university graduates have won 5 Rhodes Scholarships and 6 Truman Scholarships.

Continuation Requirements: 3.20 cumulative GPA.

Academic Strengths: FSU has a highly respected faculty, with four departments ranking in the top 50 among all universities public or private. These include education (37), sociology (39), political science (40), physics (44), and chemistry (49).

Undergraduate Research: The *Undergraduate Research Opportunity Program* (UROP) offers an opportunity for students to partner with excellent faculty as research assistants. Students in UROP work closely with faculty and peers, receive mentorship and training in the UROP Colloquium class, and present their contributions in the Spring Research Symposium. UROP aims to enhance the academic culture of our student body, helping them to achieve their academic, personal, and career goals, and better contribute to the world."

Study Abroad: FSU ranks among the leaders in the number of students who study abroad. The university offers Global Scholars Travel Award stipends on a need basis, assisting students in participating in FSU's Global Scholars program "who may not otherwise be able to take part due to financial obstacles."

Recipients will receive a stipend of up to $2,000 (up to $3,250 in some cases) to cover expenses associated with participating in FSU's Global Scholars Program. "Funds may be used for general program costs, living expenses, and/or travel."

Financial Aid:

National Merit Finalist Scholarship

"This scholarship is available to non-Florida residents listing FSU as their first choice with the National Merit Scholarship Corporation. The award includes a waiver of the out-of-state portion of tuition cost, the $9,600 University Freshman Scholarship, and any National Merit Scholarship. The total value of this scholarship is over $69,000 over four years and guarantees admission into FSU's University Honors Program."

Presidential Scholars Program

"Accepted freshmen that have received the University Freshman Scholarship are also eligible to apply for the Presidential Scholars Program. The Program application deadline is January 25, 2017. Students selected to be Presidential Scholars will receive the $2,400 per year University Freshman Scholarship plus a separate $2,400 Presidential Scholarship for a total of $4,800 per year ($19,200 over four years). An additional $12,000 will be granted for educational enrichment opportunities. The total value of this scholarship is $31,200 over four years. Out-of-state applicants will also receive a full out-of-state tuition waiver."

Benacquisto Scholarship (formerly Florida Incentive Scholarship Program)

"This prestigious scholarship is available to National Merit Finalists that are Florida residents graduating with a standard high school diploma or the equivalent in Florida. This award equals the institutional cost of attendance (minus the sum of Bright Futures and the National Merit scholarship). The total value of this scholarship is over $80,000 over four years and guarantees admission into FSU's University Honors Program."

Degree of Difference: This is based on the differences between (1) the average (2015, two-part) SAT scores for enrolled honors students (SAT two-part equivalent of 1394) and (2) the average test scores for all students in the university (1230 SAT equivalent) as a whole. The test scores may be an indication of how "elite" honors students may be perceived as compared to students in the university as a whole. The scores can also provide an indication of how well prepared the non-honors students in the university may be. **Please keep in mind that neither high nor low test scores determine the overall quality of a program.**

NAME: LSA HONORS PROGRAM, THE UNIVERSITY OF MICHIGAN.

Editor's Note: Reviewed previously in the 2012 and 2014 editions of *A Review of Fifty Public University Honors Programs,* the LSA Honors Program was either ranked or rated among the top public honors programs in the nation. For the present volume we could not obtain all of the data required for the new, more exacting methodology. That we do not have the necessary data does not mean that the LSA Program, housed within one of the leading research universities in the world, is not an outstanding option. As is the case with the Echols Scholars Program at the University of Virginia, LSA could be a decisive part of a student's decision to attend a public university rather than an elite private institution, but probably not to the extent that other honors programs might be. Given the overall prominence of both Michigan and UVA and the extremely high qualifications of their entire student populations, either institution is extremely appealing even without honors.

Date Established: 1957.

Location: Ann Arbor, Michigan.

University Full-time Undergraduate Enrollment: 27,395.

Honors Students in Good Standing: Est. 1,600-1,800 (mean size of all 50 programs under review is 1,742)

Honors <u>Average</u> Admission Statistics: *Estimated* old SAT score for enrolled LSA students is 1460-1470; est. new SAT, 1500. *Estimated* ACT average is 32-34.

Honors Programs with old SAT scores from 1402—1469: UCF, Connecticut, Kentucky, Washington, Maryland, North Carolina, UC Irvine, Kansas, Minnesota, Tennessee, South Carolina, Clemson, UT Austin, Georgia.

Administrative Staff: 9-10.

Priority Registration: No.

Curriculum Requirements: Honors completion in the LSA Program requires an average of **33-36 credits.** The average completion requirement for all 50 rated programs is 29.0 credits.

The basic four requirements for a lower-division Honors student are:

- an average of two Honors courses per term for the first four full terms of Honors,
- a course load of 14-18 credit hours,
- an overall grade point average (GPA) of 3.4 or better,
- three courses in the Honors Core curriculum, one in each division (Humanities, Natural Sciences, Social Sciences).

After the first two years, students pursue one of three options: the Honors in the Major Program; Honors Individualized Major Program; or Honors in Liberal Arts. The most typical route is the **Honors in the**

Major, in which the requirements depend on the department, but average about 9-12 credits, including departmental honors research and an honors **thesis.**

The **Honors Individualized Major Program (IMP)** requires students to "develop your ideas into a coherent intellectual statement of what you plan to study and a justification for why your study cannot be conducted in any single LSA department. With Dr. Wessel Walker, you will draw up a list of courses, both prerequisites and at least 30 upper-level credits that will constitute your major. At least two faculty will need to provide their support, not just at the beginning of your project, but supervising your work and guiding your study all along the way. One of them will serve as your thesis advisor and the other will serve as a second reader. Your proposal will include a description of the direction you expect your thesis to take. While you may pick and choose among courses as you go, and develop your thesis idea as you learn, you should have a fairly good idea of what you're doing when you submit your IMP proposal to the Honors Academic Board."

"A fairly new alternative to Honors in a major, **Honors in the Liberal Arts (HLA)** is interdisciplinary in nature, individually designed, and course-based rather than thesis based.

"If there is a topic or question that intrigues you but can be best studied from a variety of disciplinary perspectives, you can construct an HLA in which you can study that question through course work.

"With your Honors academic advisor, at the end of your second year or the beginning of the third, develop a plan of courses that you might take to look at the issue." Students must take at least five courses on their HLA list, keeping the work in those courses in a portfolio. In the spring of senior year, students write "a short reflection paper in which you discuss your topic, describe what you learned about it in the courses you took, and how those courses combine to provide you with an integrated look at the topic of your HLA." Students must then submit the essay and portfolio to the Honors Academic Board by April 1st of the senior year. Members of the Honors Faculty Advisory Board will read and evaluate your work, and decide whether to grant you Honors in the Liberal Arts.

Average Class Size: LSA allows contract (conversion) courses for honors credit, with appropriate approval, and we have no data on those sections. It appears that some core courses have somewhat large main sections of 125-140 students, and multiple discussion sections, each of which averages 7-17 students. The Ideas in Honors 1-credit mini-courses average 12 students each.

Graduation Rate: The six-year graduation rate of first-year entrants who graduated from the university, whether or not the students completed the honors program, was *estimated* in 2014 to be **95.6%** The average honors graduation rate for all programs with similar test scores required for admission is 92.6%.

Value-Added Graduation Rate: The honors graduation rate is 95.6%, compared to the university-wide six-year rate of 91%.

Ratio of Staff to Honors Students: Our estimate is that there is 1 staff member for every **175** students. (Mean ratio for all 50 rated programs is 1 staff member for every 135.6 students.)

Honors Residence Halls: Honors Housing is in the **newly renovated South Quad.** Honors has reserved spaces in the following South Quad Houses: Frederick, Taylor, Hunt, and Bush. "Single-gender and substance-free housing options are available in Frederick House. We plan to make Bush House (5th and

6th floors) our reserved space for returning Honors students (i.e. sophomores, juniors, and seniors), although we have also made selected singles in other houses available to returners."

South Quad, like the former honors housing in West Quad, has traditional corridor dorms with hall baths. The dorm rooms are not air-conditioned. But renovations have brought new features, including

- a central campus dining center in South Quad with a capacity for 950 diners;
- improved student bathrooms with new plumbing, fixtures and shower privacy stalls;
- **community lounges, with air conditioning;**
- better access from West Quadrangle and the Michigan Union;
- improved group study rooms, music practice rooms and two central laundry rooms.

"Honors students serve as Resident Advisors (HRAs) in Honors halls; they are responsible both to Housing and to Honors for their work with students, and for programming events. For their Honors events, HRAs seek to provide higher levels of intellectual and cultural engagement, and to probe issues more deeply than in other student programming."

Prestigious Awards: Michigan is the leader among all public universities in this category when it comes to its students winning the national awards that we track. These awards include 26 Rhodes scholarships, 7 Gates Cambridge, 18 Marshall, 13 Churchill, 25 Truman, and at least 57 Goldwater scholarships. Perhaps the most impressive achievement is in winning Fulbright Student Scholarships (first among public universities in the last three years) and NSF Graduate Fellowships (fourth among public universities in the last two years).

Continuation Requirements: At least at 3.40 GPA.

Academic Strengths: Next to UC Berkeley, Michigan has the most highly regarded faculty among public universities, and UM departments rank among the top 10 even when private elite universities are included. All 15 departments at Michigan that we track are ranked 19th or better nationally, averaging about 9th overall. Examples are business, political science, psychology, and sociology (all number 4), engineering (6), history (7), earth sciences (8), math (9), physics (11), education (12), computer science, economics and English (13), chemistry (15), and biology (19).

Undergraduate Research: The Undergraduate Research Opportunity Program (UROP) creates research partnerships between undergraduate students and University of Michigan researchers. All schools and colleges are active participants in UROP, which provides a wealth of interesting research topics for program participants. UROP started with 14 student/faculty partnerships in 1988, and has expanded to include more than 1300 students and 800 faculty researchers.

"UROP is now recognized as a model program for engaging undergraduate students in research. In 2002 U.S. News and World Report ranked UROP Number 1 in the category, Undergraduate Research/Creative Projects. UROP has consistently ranked at the top of this category in the ensuing years." Note: If students are accepted to a work-study gig in UROP, they receive $8.15-$15.00 per hour.

Study Abroad: The university ranks 5th among all universities in the number of students studying abroad. The university's Center for Global and Intercultural Study administers most of the programs. Students must attend a Ready, Set, Go Global (RSGG) session before making application. The application process requires a meeting with a UROP adviser, followed by an electronic application; it must include letters of recommendation from UM faculty who have taught and graded the student. UM has 60 programs for international study, not including foreign language study. Third and fourth year language study programs are available in China, France, Italy, Argentina, Spain, and Costa Rica.

Financial Aid: It is difficult to find many details about merit aid for Michigan students. LSA Honors has some donor funds "to provide grants for research expenses and travel, travel to present papers and posters at conferences, and to support study abroad travel. We have no scholarships or financial aid of our own for tuition or fees. We do participate in the College merit scholarship committee but that program is very small (fewer than 20 awards in a year) and not restricted to Honors students."

Michigan, like UC Berkeley, Virginia, Wisconsin, UCLA, UT Austin, and, more recently, UNC Chapel Hill and Ohio State, have sharply reduced or ceased university sponsorship of National Merit Scholars. This does not mean, however, that NMS awardees at these schools are not eligible for corporate-sponsored National Merit Scholarships.

Degree of Difference: This is based on the differences between (1) the average (2015, two-part) SAT scores for enrolled honors students (old SAT two-part equivalent of 1460-1470) and (2) the average test scores for all students in the university (old SAT two-part equivalent of 1360) as a whole. The test scores may be an indication of how "elite" honors students may be perceived as compared to students in the university as a whole. The scores can also provide an indication of how well prepared the non-honors students in the university may be. **Please keep in mind that neither high nor low test scores determine the overall quality of a program.**

NAME: UNIVERSITY HONORS PROGRAM, UNIVERSITY OF NEW HAMPSHIRE.

Editor's Note: This is the first appearance of UNH Honors in our review. With excellent curriculum requirements in place, the program is in the process of expanding and developing additional features.

Date Established: 1984.

Location: Durham, New Hampshire.

University Full-time Undergraduate Enrollment: 12,377.

Honors Students in Good Standing: 988. (mean size of all 50 programs under review is 1,742)

Honors Average Admission Statistics: ACT, 30. Old SAT three-part, 1985; est. new SAT, 1390. High school GPA (weighted), 4.13.

Minimum Admission Requirements: ACT, 29; Old SAT three-part, 1970; est. new SAT, 1380. Top 10% of high school class.

Honors Programs with old SAT scores from 1315—1350: Idaho, Georgia State, Virginia Tech, Utah, Iowa, Auburn, Houston, Mississippi, VCU.

Administrative Staff: 3.

Priority Registration: "We hold 'preregistration' for honors courses, which allows Honors students to reserve seats in advance of their official registration."

Curriculum Requirements: The average number of honors semester hours required for completion across all 50 rated programs is 29.0.

"Completion of the University Honors Program requires at least 32 credits of Honors work, which is typically begun in the Freshman year."

University Honors students must complete 16 credits in Honors Discovery courses, including at least 4 credits in an Honors Symposium.

They must also complete either Honors in the Major (as specified by the major department) OR Interdisciplinary Honors "Students who complete only Discovery Honors [16 credits] will not receive special recognition upon graduation."

Complete the requirements for Honors in the Major, as specified by the major OR complete the requirements for Interdisciplinary Honors. Honors in the Major requires at least 12 more credits in honors courses and a 4-8 credit **thesis**. Interdisciplinary Honors requires at least 12 credits in honors experiences in addition to the 16 credits in honors courses, and a 4-8 credit thesis. Examples of Honors experiences include studying abroad, internships, research experience, research presentation, co-authorship with publication in a peer-reviewed journal, and completion the application process for a major national scholarship.

"Students with a qualifying GPA may complete Honors in Major by itself, without participating in the University Honors Program or completing Discovery Honors requirements. Members of the University Honors Program who do not fulfill Discovery Honors requirements remain eligible to graduate with Honors in Major, but not University Honors."

"The Honors requirements can usually be completed by taking one Honors course each semester, though there is no requirement to do so. Many students follow a plan like the one below.

- **Freshman year:** One Honors Inquiry Seminar and one Honors Discovery course
- **Sophomore year:** Two Honors Discovery courses
- **Junior year:** Two Honors-in-Major courses
- **Senior year:** One or two Honors-in-Major course(s); one or two semester(s) of Honors Thesis

Average Class Size: The average honors-only class size is 16.4 students. For all rated programs, the average honors-only class size was 19.0 students.

Graduation Rate: The six-year graduation rate of first-year entrants who graduated from the university, whether or not the students completed the honors program, was **91.9%** The average honors graduation rate for all programs with similar test scores required for admission is 83.4%.

Value-Added Graduation Rate: The honors graduation rate is 91.9% compared to the university-wide six-year rate of 77%.

Ratio of Staff to Honors Students: Our estimate is that there is 1 staff member for every **329.3** students. (Mean ratio for all 50 rated programs is 1 staff member for every 135.6 students.)

Honors Residence Halls: The Honors residence is Hubbard Hall, which houses about 80 students. Hubbard is not air-conditioned, but that is not a major factor in New Hampshire. The rooms are traditional doubles with hall baths. The living/learning theme is "Making the Grade."

The ratio of room places in Hubbard is about .16 places per first- and second-year student. The average for all 50 rated programs is .63 places.

Prestigious Awards: "We have a fairly new Office of National Fellowships (a full-time director was hired in 2011) that coordinates closely with the Honors Program. In the past 2-3 years we have seen a great improvement in the number of students receiving prestigious awards, including Fulbrights, Goldwaters, NSF Graduate Fellowships, etc."

Continuation Requirements: 3.0 for freshmen, 3.40 thereafter; an increase to 3.20 for freshmen and 3.50 thereafter is pending. Graduation for University Honors in Major and University Interdisciplinary Honors require a 3.40 (a change to 3.50 is pending).

Academic Strengths: The highest nationally-rated department at UNH is earth sciences (77), followed by history and sociology (both 84).

Undergraduate Research: "We encourage students to participate in programs administered by the Hamel Center for Undergraduate Research. The Research Experience Apprenticeship Program, which students complete between the freshmen and sophomore years, is exclusive to Honors students, and a large proportion of students who receive other research awards (which fund summer and school year research) are within the Honors Program. In 2014-15, 46% of research awards went to Honors students, who comprised only 7% of the undergraduate body. Many more students complete in UNH's Undergraduate Research Conference, which is the largest in the country."

As of 2016, undergraduate research can count toward completion of the Honors Program in our Interdisciplinary Honors track.

Study Abroad: "We offer an Honors Exchange with University College Utrecht (the Honors College of Utrecht University). As of 2016, study abroad experiences may be used toward completion of Honors requirements via the Interdisciplinary Honors track.

"Many Honors students also take advantage of international research funding provided by the Hamel Center for Undergraduate Research (International Research Opportunity Program and Summer Undergraduate Research Fellowship)."

Financial Aid: "All entering Honors students receive a merit scholarship based on their qualifications (Presidential or Dean's Scholarship). Some major scholarships are restricted to Honors Program students (Governor's Success Scholarship, Hamel Scholarship). The Honors Program also administers several funds endowed to give scholarships to continuing students."

Presidential Scholarship: "New Hampshire Residents, $5,000; non-residents, $10,000. Rank in top 10% of graduating class (or equivalent level for unranked schools as determined by GPA and/or information on the school profile). Strong college preparatory curriculum and consistent achievement. Standardized test scores of 1390+ New SAT / 29+ ACT composite."

Dean's Scholarship: "New Hampshire Residents, $1,500; non-residents, $6,000. Rank in top 15% of graduating class (or equivalent level for unranked schools as determined by GPA and/or information on the school profile). Strong college preparatory curriculum and consistent achievement. Standardized test scores of 1260+ New SAT / 26+ ACT composite."

Degree of Difference: This is based on the differences between (1) the average (2015, two-part) SAT scores for enrolled honors students (old SAT two-part equivalent of 1330) and (2) the average test scores for all students in the university (old 1100 SAT equivalent) as a whole. The test scores may be an indication of how "elite" honors students may be perceived as compared to students in the university as a whole. The scores can also provide an indication of how well prepared the non-honors students in the university may be. **Please keep in mind that neither high nor low test scores determine the overall quality of a program.**

NAME: OHIO UNIVERSITY HONORS TUTORIAL COLLEGE.

Editor's Note: The Ohio University HTC is unique and, unfortunately, difficult to rate because with so many tutorial courses it is almost impossible to define class sizes and courses in each discipline. The HTC was rated in the 2014 edition, but only because some of the scores then were estimated; HTC received the lowest class size estimate in that edition. In the current edition, we did not believe we could incorporate the HTC into the new rating system, given that the class size and course section data from all other programs were so detailed. It is no fault of the HTC that its structure does not fit with our methodology. Its structure is what makes it not only unique but outstanding. *If* we could rate the HTC in this edition, it would certainly receive a very high rating, *at least* a 4.5, and it should be considered as equivalent in quality to any programs with that rating, or even the highest rating.

Date Established: 1972.

Location: Athens, Ohio.

University Full-time Undergraduate Enrollment: 17,019.

Honors Students in Good Standing: 280 (mean size of all 50 programs under review is 1,742)

Honors Average Admission Statistics: ACT, 31.6. Old SAT, 1350; est. new SAT, 1410. High school GPA, 3.92; top 8.4% of class.

Minimum Admission Requirements: SAT 1300, ACT, 30. Old SAT, 1300; est. new SAT, 1360. Top 10% of high school class.

Honors Programs with old SAT scores from 1315—1350: Idaho, Georgia State, Virginia Tech, Utah, Iowa, Auburn, Houston, Mississippi, VCU.

Administrative Staff: 9.

Priority Registration: "HTC students register before all other incoming freshman for their first semester but not before upperclassmen. In subsequent semesters, our students register before any other Ohio University students, including doctoral students. HTCers get first crack at all classes—undergraduate and graduate."

Curriculum Requirements: The average number of honors semester hours required for completion across all 50 rated programs is 29.0.

"Students in our 36 programs of study (majors) earn their degrees from the Ohio University Honors Tutorial College. Each program of study has a distinct curriculum that, in most cases, varies quite a bit from the traditional Ohio University degree in the same field. *Within their required curriculum, our students are able to substitute higher-level courses whenever appropriate. Those courses may include upper-level undergraduate courses or graduate courses, which our students are eligible to take at any time.* Course prerequisites are waived for our students, so they may register for the level that best fits their aptitude. It is possible for students in many of our degree programs to avoid large lecture and intro courses entirely.

"Our students do not have to fulfill the university's general education requirements, except for freshman and junior composition. We offer our own junior composition course that emphasizes academic writing and prepares students to write their senior theses. Most of our students earn a variety of minors and interdisciplinary certificates, along with their HTC degree.

"In each of our 36 programs of study, students take at least one one-on-one or small group tutorial with a faculty member every semester. Each tutorial ranges in credit hours from 2 to 15, depending on its content and goals. During students' final year in our program, they must complete a thesis or professional project that makes an original contribution to their discipline. The two senior thesis tutorials often are taken for 10 to 15 credits each.

"Double majors in our college take at least two tutorials per semester. Single majors may take up to two tutorials per term if they elect to do so.

"Tutorials may be taught by faculty in any field. Faculty members from the Heritage College of Osteopathic Medicine, for example, teach biomedical tutorials every term for students in our biological sciences, neuroscience, chemistry, and translational health programs. Applied research faculty from the Edison Biotechnology Institute also serve as regular tutors, as do faculty members from the Voinovich School of Leadership and Public Affairs graduate programs in public administration and environmental studies.

"Tutorials do not have to match the content of existing Ohio University courses, so they are highly flexible and customizable. Faculty members spend a minimum of 50 minutes per week meeting with students in tutorials, which are spirited conversations not lectures. In the natural sciences and mathematics, a student is often given a problem to solve at the board. The professor asks questions about each step of the solution. Upper-level tutorials may also take place in labs or in the field if the professor deems it most conducive to the learning process.

"Each semester, we offer one to four interdisciplinary special topics seminars that our students may choose to take. They are capped at either 10 or 20 students. The Dean teaches a mandatory 3-hour freshman seminar that introduces students to academic inquiry across disciplines and explores knowledge and its creation. We offer a 3-hour academic and research-writing seminar to juniors who want extra help in preparing their senior thesis prospectus.

"We offer more than 250 tutorials each term, plus two to six HTC seminars. **Our total number of sections multiplied by the total credits is a very high number, but it offers no basis for comparison with other programs because our curriculum is so different.** Also this number is very difficult for us to gather because the majority of tutorial sections are housed in individual academic units across campus. We are the degree-granting unit and have ultimate authority for the curriculum; however, the home departments schedule the sections and earn the credit for teaching them as part of our central budgeting process." [Emphases added.]

Average Class Size: Although HTC students will certainly have some large non-honors sections, the extremely small class size that goes along with the tutorial approach to teaching would yield the lowest average class size of any program under review.

Graduation Rate: The six-year graduation rate of first-year HTC entrants who graduated from the university, whether or not the students completed the honors program, was a very high **(95%)** The average honors graduation rate for all programs with similar test scores required for admission is 83.4%.

Value-Added Graduation Rate: The honors graduation rate is 95% compared to the university-wide six-year rate of 67%.

Ratio of Staff to Honors Students: Our estimate is that there is 1 staff member for every **31.1s** students, one of the distinct advantages of a small program. (Mean ratio for all 50 rated programs is 1 staff member for every 135.6 students.)

Honors Residence Halls: The honors residence hall is the Reed-Johnson Scholars Complex, a coed facility that features traditional double rooms and hall baths—and sinks in each room. It is available to *all* HTC freshmen and sophomores. The complex is air-conditioned and has on-site laundry facilities. The closest dining halls are Shively or Nelson Commons. The ratio of rooms to first- and second-year students is 1.0. The average ratio for rated programs is .63.

The complex is in East "Green," Ohio University's most convenient green for business, math, communication, and humanities majors due to its convenient location near Morton and College Green.

Prestigious Awards (3.5): The HTC has its own office of prestigious fellowships, which includes a full-time director and a host of campus partners. The university is developing a solid record of achievement in winning undergraduate awards, especially Udall and Goldwater Scholarships. "We have had 4 Marshall winners, including one in 2012-2013; 3 Truman winners; more than 120 Fulbright winners, at least 15 Goldwater winners, and 4 Udall winners."

Continuation Requirements: "We have set floors that students must meet in order to realistically reach our 3.5 GPA graduation requirement. Students must earn a 3.1 or higher at the end of their first year, a 3.3 or higher at the end of their second year, and a 3.4 or higher at the end of their third year. Students whose GPAs fall below a 3.4 in any year must meet with their faculty advisor and the associate dean to put an improvement plan in place." Graduation with honors requires a 3.5 cumulative GPA.

Academic Strengths: Journalism and communications are both very strong at Ohio University. English, physics, business, environmental studies and engineering are other solid programs at the university, as are many of the fine arts disciplines.

Undergraduate Research: "All of our students conduct original research or creative activity as part of their tutorial curriculum. Many attend academic conferences, and several publish in peer-reviewed journals each year.

"A senior thesis or professional project that makes an original contribution to the student's academic discipline is a graduation requirement for our students.

"We offer paid research apprenticeships during the summer. At least 30 students are paid to conduct research or creative activity with a faculty mentor for a minimum of 300 hours (usually 25 hours a week for 12 weeks)."

Study Abroad: "We invest more than $50,000 in student research and travel expenses. Often, we pay for students' study abroad travel costs. Students may participate in official Ohio University study abroad programs or those sponsored by other institutions. Many of students conduct thesis research abroad. We have special programs at Leipzig University and Chubu University [Japan].

"If our students study abroad during the fall or spring terms at an OU-affiliated program, their tuition scholarship may be applied to their host institution's tuition."

Financial Aid: "All students admitted to the Honors Tutorial College as incoming freshman receive a four-year renewable scholarship valued at full, in-state tuition. Out-of-state students receive an additional four-year renewable $6,000 scholarship to help offset the out-of-state differential. Several HTC students receive full tuition and room/board scholarships through the Templeton and Cutler Scholars Programs at Ohio University."

Degree of Difference: This is based on the differences between (1) the average (2015, two-part) SAT scores for enrolled honors students (SAT 1350) and (2) the average test scores for all students in the university (1100) as a whole. The test scores may be an indication of how "elite" honors students may be perceived as compared to students in the university as a whole. The scores can also provide an indication of how well prepared the non-honors students in the university may be. **Please keep in mind that neither high nor low test scores determine the overall quality of a program.**

NAME: UNIVERSITY HONORS COLLEGE, UNIVERSITY OF PITTSBURGH.

Editor's Note: The University Honors College was reviewed in the 2012 edition, but not in much depth. We are very pleased to include this summary review of the college in the current edition. Along with the University Honors Program at the University of Cincinnati and the Echols Scholars Program at the University of Virginia, the UHC emphasizes maximum flexibility and choice for students. Although this can be an exceptional experience for students, the open curricular requirements do not fit our methodology. But the UHC differs from the UHP at Cincinnati, and from all but a few programs we review, in offering its own degrees. And it is unique (that word again, applied also to the Honors Tutorial College at Ohio University, for different reasons) in opening itself to all students at Pitt "who choose to challenge themselves beyond the normal academic requirements" at the university.

Date Established: "The University of Pittsburgh began an Honors Program in 1978 and formally converted this program to the University Honors College in 1987."

Location: Pittsburgh, Pennsylvania.

University Full-time Undergraduate Enrollment: 17,694.

Honors Members in Good Standing: Varies. (Mean size of all 50 programs is 1,742).

Honors Average Admission Statistics: "Automatic eligibility to enroll in honors courses requires a minimum 3.25 cumulative GPA (or, if a first-year student, who has not yet established a GPA at Pitt, either 1400 combined SAT math and critical reading scores or a 32 ACT math and English subscores average). The new SAT score would be about 1450. High school class rank estimate, top 5%.

Average High School GPA/Class Rank: Varies.

Basic Admission Requirements: See above.

Application Deadline(s): *Please verify with each program, as some deadlines could change.*

No separate application from university application. University scholarship deadline is December 15.

Honors Programs with old SAT scores from 1402—1469: UCF, Connecticut, Kentucky, Washington, Maryland, North Carolina, UC Irvine, Kansas, Minnesota, Tennessee, South Carolina, Clemson, UT Austin, Georgia.

Administrative Staff: 16.

Priority Registration: No.

Curriculum Requirements: "Since its inception in 1987, the University Honors College (UHC) has been granted the authority to award the **Bachelor of Philosophy (BPhil) degree**. The BPhil is a unique undergraduate degree jointly awarded by UHC and any undergraduate school/college at Pitt, which is the "home school" of the recipient, signifying the highest level of scholarship attainable by an undergraduate student. The BPhil is the degree title and not related to the academic discipline of philosophy; one pursue the BPhil degree in any undergraduate discipline at the University of Pittsburgh.

"The BPhil degree replaces the standard bachelor's degree a student would receive; students do not receive a BPhil degree in addition to another undergraduate degree, such as a Bachelor of Arts (BA) or a Bachelor of Science (BS). Please note that in some professional schools the degree awarded will be a jointly-conferred BS or BA, not a BPhil; some professional schools may also give students the option of choosing between a BPhil degree or a jointly-conferred BS or BA degree.

Requirements: "In order to receive the BPhil degree, you must fulfill the degree requirements (major, general education, and/or other curricular requirements) of your 'home school'…and maintain a 3.50 cumulative GPA. The honors college, then, adds two additional requirements: a demanding program of study proposed by you and approved by the honors college, and independent research culminating in the production of an undergraduate **thesis.**

"Your program of study should have breadth, depth, and focus. Often, this is achieved through a double degree between schools or through double or triple majors in a single school. But even if you have only one major, you can meet the spirit of this requirement if your course work and related academic accomplishments are particularly noteworthy through their rigor. In sum, the program of study component is an indicator that you are willing to challenge yourself academically. To complete the thesis component, you identify and work closely with a faculty member to design and implement a research project related to your academic discipline (i.e., one of your majors) and write a thesis related to that research. You then defend your thesis before a faculty examination committee that includes a visiting external examiner from another college or university within the United States. *Students should strive to have the same research experience -- and produce the same caliber of thesis -- as that of a graduate student at the master's level within your academic discipline.*"[Emphasis added.]

The UHC also offers another, very rigorous degree. "The **politics and philosophy major,** a major in the Kenneth P. Dietrich School of Arts and Sciences, advised through the University Honors College, provides students with interdisciplinary training in the conceptual, empirical, and normative foundations of various fields of public policy. It enhances students' understanding of the moral and political complexities of public life and it offers preparation in both theory and practice to students interested in pursuing careers in social and public affairs.

"By combining course work from different disciplines -- political science, philosophy, and economics -- the program's scope is broad, yet the structure of the curriculum also requires depth. The thematic nature of the major allows for flexibility in course selection. In collaboration with the major advisor, students design a cohesive program of study tailored to meet their individual post-graduate/career interests and needs."

Requirements: Students must complete 7 courses in political science, at least 4 of which must be upper division; 7 courses in philosophy, at least 4 of which must be upper division; 3 courses in economics, including micro- and macro-economics; and a capstone. The capstone may be completion of the Bachelor of Philosophy thesis through the University Honors College; participation in a graduate level seminar (with permission from the instructor); or completion of a Directed Research Project, an Independent Study, or an Internship.

Average Class Size: The UHC offers about 80-100 honors courses each year. The average enrollment in honors humanities and social science courses is 18 students, but, as is the case with almost every honors program, there are some large sections, especially in science courses. The average honors-only class size for the 50 programs being rated is 19.0.

Honors Graduation Rate: Since there is no formal honors "membership" in the UHC, we do not have a graduation rate to report. The average honors graduation rate for all programs with similar test scores required for admission is 92.6%.

Value-Added Graduation Rate: The university-wide six-year rate of 82%.

Ratio of Staff to Honors Students: Again, because there is no definite number of honors students in the UHC, we do not have an actual ratio to report. (Mean ratio for all 50 programs is 1 staff member for every 135.6 students.) If this ratio is applied to the UHC, the number of students being served would be about 2,170.

Honors Residence Halls: First-year honors students live in Sutherland Hall, which houses 737 first-year men and women. "The complex is composed of Sutherland West and East, adjoined by a common building. The common area includes the Perch at Sutherland made-to-order restaurant facility, a Quick Zone convenience store, a computer center, the Hill O'Beans coffee cart, and a mail center. The air-conditioned rooms in Sutherland Hall are mostly doubles with semi-private baths. Laundry facilities and fitness rooms are on the ground floors of both Sutherland East and West."

Honors upperclassmen can choose to live in The Forbes Craig Apartments, located across from the Carnegie Museum of Art and Natural History, or Pennsylvania Hall, located near the Petersen Events Center on the upper campus.

The 39 apartment units in Forbes-Craig accommodate 102 students in single and double bedrooms. Pennsylvania Hall houses 420 students in four-person suites and doubles with private baths. Each floor includes a lounge and laundry facility. There is a fitness center on the ground floor. Pennsylvania Hall is home to two living learning communities: upper-class honors and health sciences.

Prestigious Awards: Pitt students, many of them graduates of the UHC, have an excellent record of winning prestigious awards. A total of 369 prestigious national and international awards have been won by students mentored through the UHC's national scholarship office since 2008.

In all, Pitt students have won 7 Rhodes scholarships and 47 Goldwater scholarships. In the last 20 years alone, Pitt students have also won 6 Marshall scholarships 5 Truman scholarships, 7 Udall scholarships, and a Churchill and Gates Cambridge scholarship, along with at least 23 Boren scholarships. Pitt graduates have won more than 40 Fulbright Student scholarships in the last three years, along with 25 NSF Graduate Research fellowships.

Continuation Requirements: 3.50 GPA.

Academic Strengths, National Rankings: This is based on national rankings of *graduate* programs in 15 disciplines, except engineering and business, where undergraduate rankings are used.

The faculty at Pitt is extremely well regarded, and the academic departments we track easily average among the top 50 in the nation. Outstanding departments include education and psychology (both 30), chemistry (35), economics and history (both 36), business and English (39), and political science (40).

Undergraduate Research: The **Beckman Scholars Program** provides "scientific training, professional development, and financial support for a cohort of outstanding undergraduate students to perform cutting-edge research during a 15-month time frame under the mentorship of renowned university faculty. The University of Pittsburgh was one of only 12 institutions nationwide that were selected for this prestigious award from the Arnold and Mabel Beckman Foundation.

"The Beckman research project must be performed in the laboratory of an approved faculty mentor (see below), who will provide training in the scientific development of the Scholar. Sessions on professional development will also be offered across the biomedical, engineering, and physical science disciplines. Scholars are expected to work in the laboratory full time (40 hours per week) for two summers and 10 hours per week during the Fall and Spring semesters in the intervening academic year. A total of six Scholars will be selected in 2015-2017, and the capstone of the Scholars' experience will be attendance and professional presentations at scientific meetings, including the annual Beckman Scholars Summer Symposium in California. It is expected that each Scholar also will contribute to the publication of at least one scientific manuscript. *The stipend for this position is: $13,600 for the first and second summer periods, and $4,600 for the intervening academic year (for a total of $18,200).* A travel and supply fund of $2,800 also is provided, as well as $5,000 in support of the Faculty Mentor's laboratory." [Emphasis added.]

Study Abroad: In 2014, the University of Pittsburgh announced a new opportunity for students interested in the Pitt in London program. Pitt in London Honors offers students the opportunity to study at one of the most prestigious English departments in the world, University College, London. "With courses ranging from Chaucer to the Modern period, courses have been specially selected to fit with Pitt's English Literature majors and minors. Studying alongside British peers [so to speak], students on the program will engage in the British tutorial system, offering unprecedented access to the foremost scholars in the field." Although it does not involve studying abroad, the UHC "provides a one-of-a-kind intellectual adventure for 20 students each summer in magnificent Yellowstone National Park and its stunning surroundings. Geological, ecological, and cultural dimensions of Yellowstone and its environs make this 30-day course an incomparable educational experience."

Another opportunity is the Wyoming Field Studies Program, "a unique introduction to the fundamental practices of paleontology, ecology, and archaeology, with a strong emphasis on field techniques. Students are given the opportunity to unlock a natural time capsule, one teeming with remnants of life that date back 150 million years. Thanks to the generous donation of land to the University of Pittsburgh by rancher Allen Cook, the University of Pittsburgh Honors College maintains stewardship of the Spring Creek Preserve, a bountiful 6000-acre tract that embraces pristine dinosaur-bone-bearing beds, Native American archaeology spanning 9,000 years, indigenous prairie ecology, and a section of the original grade of the 1869 trans-continental railroad. Located near Rock River, Wyoming, the Spring Creek Preserve includes prominent outcroppings of the Jurassic Morrison Formation…"

Financial Aid:. Among the most generous scholarships are the Stamps Leadership Scholarship, the Nordenberg Leadership Scholars Program, and the Chancellor's Scholarship.

In recent years, scholarship eligible students possessed <u>ALL</u> of the following:

- minimum SAT score of 1490 (math and critical reading scores only) or 33 ACT composite; overall 'A' average; top 5% class rank (if applicable) while participating in challenging high school curriculums consisting of AP/IB/Honors courses;
- record of excellence in various academic and nonacademic activities outside of the classroom.

"University of Pittsburgh academic scholarships may range in value from $2,000 per year to full tuition and room and board and are generally available for eight full time undergraduate terms, provided the recipient maintains a 3.0 GPA and meets all of the other terms and conditions of the specific award."

Degree of Difference: This is based on the differences between (1) the average (2015, two-part) SAT scores for enrolled honors students (1400) and (2) the average test scores for all students in the university (1270) as a whole. The test scores may be an indication of how "elite" honors students may be perceived as compared to students in the university as a whole. The scores can also provide an indication of how well prepared the non-honors students in the university may be. **Please keep in mind that neither high nor low test scores determine the overall quality of a program.**

NAME: HONORS COLLEGE, RUTGERS UNIVERSITY-NEW BRUNSWICK.

Editor's Note: In previous editions, we reviewed the School of Arts and Sciences Program (SAS Honors). The new Honors College, sure to have a significant impact on honors education, is still involved with the SAS program in some areas, so it could not receive a full, rated review in this book. The honors graduation rate (below) is for the SAS Program, not the Honors College. They have similar admissions requirements.

Date Established: 2015.

Location: New Brunswick, New Jersey.

University Full-time Undergraduate Enrollment: 32,411.

Honors Members in Good Standing: 530. "To be increased by 500 each year, for a total of approximately 2,000." (Mean size of all 50 programs is 1,742).

Honors Average Admission Statistics: ACT, 31.68; old SAT, 1440; est. new SAT, 1480.

Average High School GPA/Class Rank: 90% in top 10% of high school class.

Basic Admission Requirements: "No minimum requirements, per se. We use both GPA and board scores along with a holistic review process."

Application Deadline(s): *Please verify with each program, as some deadlines could change.*

December 1, 2016.

Honors Programs with old SAT scores from 1402—1469: UCF, Connecticut, Kentucky, Washington, Maryland, North Carolina, UC Irvine, Kansas, Minnesota, Tennessee, South Carolina, Clemson, UT Austin, Georgia.

Administrative Staff: 19 (but includes some staff from SAS Honors Program).

Priority Registration: Honors students register with the first group, but only for honors courses.

Curriculum Requirements: The average number of honors semester hours required for completion across all 50 programs is 29.0.

Graduation from the Honors College requires a minimum of 24 honors course credits and a 6-credit **thesis,** for a total of **30 credits.**

Students must have 2 credits from the first-year honors seminar credits and an additional 3 credits from an HONR designated course. The other 19 honors course credits maybe earned through higher level

HONOR courses, honors contract courses, graduate courses, or research credits. Research credits must be part of the work toward a thesis.

Students may satisfy the 6-credit thesis requirement by choosing ONE of the following options: a departmental or college honors thesis or honors capstone project; an interdisciplinary honors thesis/scholarly project; or a scholarly project approved by a faculty committee appointed by the Dean of the Honors College.

AP/IB credits are not counted as replacements for honors courses.

Average Class Size: The average honors-only class size in the honors college is about 19.5 students. The average for all 50 rated programs is 19.0 students.

Honors Graduation Rate: The six-year graduation rate of first-year entrants who graduated from the university, whether or not the students completed the honors program, is 92%. The average honors graduation rate for all programs with similar test scores required for admission is 92.6%.

Value-Added Graduation Rate: The honors graduation rate **(SAS Honors Program)** is 92%, compared to the university-wide six-year rate of 80%.

Ratio of Staff to Honors Students: Since there is currently an overlap of staffing with the SAS Honors Program, we can only estimate the staff ratio for the new honors college: about 1 staff member for every **112** students. (Mean ratio for all 50 programs is 1 staff member for every 135.6 students.)

Honors Residence Halls: "In their first-year, all Honors College students live in the Honors College facility. In their second and subsequent years, they have the option of a variety of honors-only communities (usually floors of residence halls) located across Rutgers. Honors College students participate in an early, exclusive lottery process. These communities provide students with the opportunity to live with students from across all honors programs on the Rutgers campus. Honors communities are strategically located across the five New Brunswick campuses to provide honors living opportunities for students who may want to live on a particular campus due to the location of courses in their major."

"The Honors College building houses all first-year Honors College students as well as being the home to three faculty fellows (including the Academic Dean of the Honors College), the Honors College administrative and advising offices, and six seminar rooms, one of which includes a mini Maker Space/ Innovation Lab."

The new facility, just opened in Fall 2016, can house 520 honors students. The rooms are almost all traditional doubles with air conditioning and hall baths. The most convenient dining is at Brower Hall.

Other honors residences are The Yard on College Avenue (apartments); Campbell Hall; BEST North; Thomas Suites; McCormick Suites; Quad III; New Gibbons; and Newell Apartments.

Prestigious Awards: The awards that we track and include are listed in the section titled "Prestigious Scholarships." The awards are sometimes won by students who are not in an honors college or program, but increasingly many are enrolled in honors programs. It is also a trend that honors colleges and programs help to prepare their students for the awards competitions. Since the Office of Distinguished Fellowships was established in the fall of 2007, the number of Rutgers students who have applied for nationally-competitive honors and awards has increased dramatically and with this almost exponential rise has come a higher yield of recipients than ever before in the University's history.

"For example, in the first 18 years of the competition for the Goldwater Scholarship (1989-2007), 16 Rutgers students were selected; in the 9 years since the Office of Distinguished Fellowships began to administer this award, 20 Rutgers students have been recognized as Goldwater Scholars, and we are especially proud that 8 of them have been women.

"Rutgers has also enjoyed a remarkable increase in the number of its students chosen for Fulbright's US Student program, and for the past 8 years consecutively has been ranked in the Top-Producing research institutions, including in 2013-14 when Rutgers was third in the country with 26 Fulbright Students, behind only Harvard and Michigan. Finally, in 2014-15, Rutgers was the only school in the nation who had its nominees honored with the Mitchell, Luce, Soros and Churchill Scholarships."

Rutgers students have also won 8 Rhodes scholarships, 8 Gates Cambridge scholarships, and 11 Truman scholarships.

Continuation Requirements: "It depends on the school of enrollment and ranges from 3.2 to 3.5."

Academic Strengths, National Rankings: This is based on national rankings of *graduate* programs in 15 disciplines, except engineering and business, where undergraduate rankings are used.

Academic departments at Rutgers have an average national ranking in the top 50. Outstanding departments include English (17), history (20), math (23), sociology (28), physics (29), computer science (34), economics (48), earth sciences (49), and engineering (51).

Undergraduate Research: "We are working closely with the Aresty Undergraduate Research Center, which serves all of Rutgers-New Brunswick, in providing our students with these opportunities. This summer, approximately 30 of our students will be participating in the Aresty Summer Research Program for rising sophomores. A far larger number have already begun working in research."

Study Abroad: "We do have dedicated scholarships for supporting Honors College students to study abroad (usually $1,000 to $2,000). We also feature a number of interdisciplinary honors seminars each year that have a 1-credit add-on element, in which students travel to the country studied for one-week over winter or spring break or immediately following the end of spring semester. This past year, these courses traveled, among other places, to Brazil, Spain, Ireland, Poland, and Holland."

Financial Aid: "All Honors College students receive a merit-based award, usually ranging from $10,000 to $26,200 (comparable to in-state tuition, fees, room, and board). Other merit and need-based awards are also available."

Degree of Difference: This is based on the differences between (1) the average (2015, two-part) SAT scores for enrolled honors students (1440) and (2) the average test scores for all students in the university (1205) as a whole. The test scores may be an indication of how "elite" honors students may be perceived as compared to students in the university as a whole. The scores can also provide an indication of how well prepared the non-honors students in the university may be. **Please keep in mind that neither high nor low test scores determine the overall quality of a program.**

NAME: ECHOLS SCHOLARS PROGRAM, UNIVERSITY OF VIRGINIA.

Editor's Note: The Echols Scholars Program has been reviewed in both previous editions and has received a "five mortarboard" rating, but the program cannot be broken down into the components necessary for the detailed quantitative methodology used for the 50 rated programs in this edition. Along with the Pitt Honors College, Echols emphasizes maximum flexibility and choice for its students. It is an excellent opportunity for extremely talented students who want or need an alternative to an Ivy or other elite college experience.

Date Established: 1960.

Location: Charlottesville, Virginia.

University Full-time Undergraduate Enrollment: 15,622.

Honors Members in Good Standing: Estimated at 925-975. (Mean size of all 50 programs is 1,742).

Honors Average Admission Statistics: Estimated ACT, 34. Estimated old SAT, 1500; est. new SAT, 1530-1540.

Average High School GPA/Class Rank: Estimated top 1-3%.

Basic Admission Requirements: All applicants to the College of Arts & Sciences' first-year class are automatically reviewed for selection to the Echols Scholars Program. About 6.5% of the incoming A&S class are invited, or approximately 225-250 students.

Application Deadline(s): *Please verify with each program, as some deadlines could change.*

Early Action deadline November 1, 2016; regular deadline January 1, 2017.

Honors Programs with old SAT scores of 1500 or more: Illinois, Oklahoma.

Administrative Staff: For purposes of computing the staff metric for our rating system, **we assigned a full-time equivalent staff of 7 to the Echols Program.** Three administrative staff members are the Echols Director, an Associate Dean/Assistant Director, and another Assistant Director, but one of their functions is to assign each Echols Scholar to a faculty advisor, who is often a tenured professor. Twenty faculty advisors from about a dozen departments work with incoming and continuing Echols Scholars.

Priority Registration: Echols Scholars register before other UVA students in the same class year.

Curriculum Requirements: "Echols Scholars are free from all area and competency requirements within the College of Arts & Sciences, including foreign language, natural science, non-western perspectives, historical and social science, and English composition requirements. The reason for this exemption is two-fold:

1. Most Echols Scholars have already met many of these requirements through AP or dual-enrollment college credits before enrolling at the University.

2. Echols Scholars are encouraged to take specialized higher-level classes from the outset of their matriculation. When the Echols Program was created in the 1960s, the Faculty Senate strongly believed that Scholars should be given the freedom to pursue their academic interests without first having to satisfy certain preliminaries.

"While a general exemption exists, Echols Scholars must still meet any Departmental requirements prior to declaring a major or a minor, since Echols status does not exempt them from these major or minor requirements."

"All students within the College [of Arts & Sciences], including Echols Scholars, are required to declare a major by the start of the fifth semester. Since the Echols Scholars Program is founded upon the principle of academic motivation and intellectual creativity, students in the program have the opportunity to define a course of study that will permit attainment of academic and career goals that fall outside existing majors or interdisciplinary programs within the college."

However…"The principle underlying the **Echols Interdisciplinary Major** is that no existing major, or combination of majors, fully satisfies a student's broader interests. *Students declaring the Echols Interdisciplinary Major do so with the provision that it will be their sole major.*"

Echols Scholars are encouraged to write a senior thesis, but they are not required to do so.

Another reason that Echols is not rated as an "honors program" in this edition is that, in some important ways, Echols is *not* like honors programs. The best way to describe Echols, in fact, is by saying what it is *not,* as in this excerpt from the 2014 edition:

"One thing is certain, the Echols administrators are unfazed about any second-guessing of their program, and if we find it difficult to say exactly what it *is***, they are eager to say exactly what it** *is not.* Echols, they assert emphatically, is "*not* a 'college within a college'. The Echols Program does *not* offer a special curriculum with certain 'core' courses or special sections of courses. It does *not* require a thesis or 'capstone' project. We do *not* wish to segregate Echols Scholars from other students in the College or to fit all Echols Scholars into the same academic mold. Rather than placing Scholars into a common introductory course (the 'college within a college' model) we wish to accelerate their progress into upper-level courses and individual areas of interest. The Echols first-year seminar is voluntary rather than mandatory, and is intended to facilitate academic debate rather than achieve a curricular goal."

AP/IB credits are counted at UVA and allow Echols Scholars to even more latitude in their choice of courses.

Average Class Size: In the 2014 edition, we estimated the average class size to be about 23 students.

Honors Graduation Rate: We do not know the six-year Echols graduation rate, but a conservative estimate would be 95%-97% The average honors graduation rate for rated programs with similar test scores required for admission is 95.0%.

Value-Added Graduation Rate: The six-year estimated honors graduation rate of 95-97%% compares to the university-wide six-year rate of 94%.

Ratio of Staff to Honors Students: Since there is currently an overlap of staffing with the SAS Honors Program, we can only estimate the staff ratio for the new honors college: about 1 staff member for every **135.7** students. (Mean ratio for all 50 programs is 1 staff member for every 135.6 students.)

Honors Residence Halls: "Echols Scholars are currently housed in the Balz-Dobie and Tuttle-Dunnington residence halls on Alderman Road during their first year. Echols Scholars are housed with Rodman Scholars, the Honors students in the School of Engineering and Applied Sciences, and College Science Scholars, creating a unique residential experience."

Tuttle-Dunnington is located across a green from Balz-Dobie and beyond a stand of trees. We do not know why the Echols Program chose a hall farther away from Balz-Dobie than the adjacent Watson-Webb (formerly used as one of the Echols dorms), but at least the renovation of Tuttle-Dunnington is more recent. All dorms are air-conditioned. They are not as convenient to most classroom buildings on "grounds" as the old residences in the heart of the campus, but they are not all that far away, either. There is a dining commons between Balz-Dobie and Watson-Webb.

Both Scholars' residence halls feature double rooms with shared hall baths. The laundry in Balz-Dobie has a remote sensor that can tell a student when a washer is available *and* let the student know when the clothes are done.

Prestigious Awards: UVA leads all public universities in the number of Rhodes Scholars, 51, and is second among public universities in Truman Scholars with 31. UVA students have also won 3 Gates Cambridge scholarships, 8 Marshall scholarships, and 4 Churchill scholarships. UVA undergraduates have won at least 57 Goldwater scholarships, a very high total.

Continuation Requirements: 3.00 GPA.

Academic Strengths, National Rankings: This is based on national rankings of *graduate* programs in 15 disciplines, except engineering and business, where undergraduate rankings are used.

UVA, while undoubtedly an elite university, does not have a research faculty with an overall ranking as high as, for example, the faculties at UC Berkeley, Michigan, UCLA, UW-Madison, or UT Austin. In this it is similar to some elite private universities, such as Brown in the Ivy League. But with an average national departmental ranking of 35 or so, UVA is still among the elite in this category. Outstanding departments include business (6), English (10), history (20), education (21), psychology (26), computer science (29), economics (30), and engineering (31).

Undergraduate Research: "The University of Virginia's Harrison Undergraduate Research Awards program funds outstanding undergraduate research projects to be carried out in the summer following application for the award and the subsequent academic year. Approximately forty awards of up to $3,000 each will be granted on a competitive basis to current first-, second-, and third-year undergraduate students. Applicants must be fulltime undergraduates at U.Va. and must remain enrolled at the University through the completion of their project."

One feature that contributes to the success of this program: "Harrison Award faculty advisors receive research support in the amount of $1,000."

Study Abroad: Along with scores of other study-abroad opportunities, UVA students can study at Mansfield College, Oxford, a small and collegial part of the world-famous university. "Each Visiting Student will study two tutorial courses per term. The Primary course shall be for eight tutorial meetings and the Secondary course shall be for four tutorial meetings. This course load shall enable the Visiting Students to earn the equivalent of twelve credits each term. Visiting Students will be expected to complete three full terms at Oxford, a period which corresponds to a full academic year at Virginia. In addition to tutorials, Visiting Students are encouraged to attend lectures, seminars and relevant classes.

"Visiting Students will normally be permitted to study tutorial subjects in the following areas: Economics, English, Geography, History, Human Sciences (Anthropology, Biology, Sociology, etc.), Oriental Studies (Middle Eastern Languages & Cultures), Philosophy, Politics, and Theology. All Virginia students will be encouraged to apply especially those in the academic areas of English, History and Politics as well as students in the International Residential College."

Financial Aid: Echols Scholars can also be named Jefferson Scholars, one of the most prestigious undergraduate scholarships in the nation. "Intended to cover the entire cost of attendance for four years at the University of Virginia plus coverage of the supplemental enrichment experiences," the scholarships are more than generous:

"Total value of the scholarship exceeds:

- **$240,000** for non-Virginian students;

- **$125,000** for Virginian students;

"The Jefferson Scholar Stipend in 2016-2017 will exceed:

- **$61,000** for non-Virginian students;

- **$31,000** for Virginian students."

Degree of Difference: This is based on the differences between (1) the average (2015, two-part) SAT scores for enrolled honors students (1500+) and (2) the average test scores for all students in the university (1370) as a whole. The test scores may be an indication of how "elite" honors students may be perceived as compared to students in the university as a whole. The scores can also provide an indication of how well prepared the non-honors students in the university may be. **Please keep in mind that neither high nor low test scores determine the overall quality of a program.**

NAME: LEE HONORS COLLEGE, WESTERN MICHIGAN UNIVERSITY.

Editor's Note: This is the first appearance of WMU and its Lee Honors College in our publication. As an already large but still developing honors program, Lee Honors College will play an increasingly important role in regional honors education.

Date Established: 1962 as an honors program.

Location: Kalamazoo, Michigan.

University Full-time Undergraduate Enrollment: 15,713.

Honors Students in Good Standing: 1,785 (mean size of all 50 programs under review is 1,742)

Honors <u>Average</u> Admission Statistics: None listed.

Basic Admission Requirements: ACT, 26. Old SAT, 1170; new SAT, 1240. High school GPA, 3.60.

Application Deadline(s): *Please verify with each program, as some deadlines could change.*

April 1, 2017.

Administrative Staff: 7.75 FTEs.

Priority Registration: Yes, honors students register for all courses, honors and otherwise, with the first group of students during each year they are in the program.

Curriculum Requirements: To graduate with honors from Lee Honors college requires at least **18 credits.** The average completion requirement for all 50 rated programs is 29.0 credits.

The specific requirements at the LHC are listed below:

- Complete 18 honors credits plus 3 credits of HNRS 4990: Honors Thesis by the time you graduate from WMU.
- Attend four honors college sponsored events during your freshman year and two honors college sponsored events during your sophomore year.
- Complete 20 hours of community service each year.
- Complete and defend an honors thesis or senior capstone project.
- Maintain a cumulative GPA of 3.5 or greater.
- Attend mandatory freshman advising.
- Complete both the graduation audit survey and graduation ceremony RSVP during the semester before your graduation from WMU. Links to these surveys will be emailed to all seniors each semester.

"Up to half of these credits may be earned in our 'experiential' category. We grant honors credit for study abroad, internships, field experiences, varsity sports, some music/dance ensembles, some foreign language study, with honors advisor/dean approval. At least half of credits must be completed by honors-only courses, such as those listed above."

AP/IB credits do **not** count as replacement credits for honors courses.

Average Class Size: LHC offered about a dozen honors seminars, with an average enrollment of about 14 students. An additional 30 or so sections in departmental honors courses had an average enrollment of about 17 students. Most of the major disciplines were represented, with the most sections in business, math, English, history, and philosophy.

Graduation Rate: The six-year graduation rate of first-year entrants who graduated from the university, whether or not the students completed the honors program, was **80.1%.** The average honors graduation rate for programs with somewhat higher test scores required for admission is 85.3%.

Value-Added Graduation Rate: The honors graduation rate is 81.0%, compared to the university-wide six-year rate of **54.0%.**

Ratio of Staff to Honors Students: Our estimate is that there is 1 staff member for every **231.8** students. (Mean ratio for all 50 rated programs is 1 staff member for every 135.6 students.)

Honors Residence Halls: The honors residence is Ackley/Shilling Hall, which houses 158 students. The rooms are suite-style with shared baths, but they are not air-conditioned. The nearest dining is at Valley I Dining Hall.

There are four honors floors in Ackley. Part of one floor, with 33 students, is for honors STEM students.

Prestigious Awards: "…in 2015 we formalized a prestigious [scholarship] advisor staff position. An honors college faculty specialist spends 0.5 FTE advising for prestigious scholarships with the remaining 0.5 FTE devoted to teaching honors sections. In 2014, we formed a university-wide committee to increase our applicant pool for prestigious scholarships. In our first year, one student won a Goldwater honorable mention (we focused on STEM, initially), and a pair of students won the MIT-Lemelson 'Cure It' innovation prize."

Continuation Requirements: At least at 3.50 GPA.

Academic Strengths: At WMU, the business school is one of the largest in the nation. The departments of English, earth sciences, history, and psychology are all ranked in the top 150 in the nation.

Undergraduate Research: "We strongly encourage our honors students to become engaged in undergraduate research and have plans to develop a more formalized student-faculty mentor pairing network so that it is easier for students to find faculty members earlier. We are a doctoral-granting, high research activity university and encourage honors students to take advantage of research facilities, work closely with faculty engaged in research and complete accelerated graduate degrees."

Study Abroad: "We offer competitive study abroad scholarships only available to honors students. In addition, we have a very active study abroad office, with over 100 programs available to our students and many scholarship opportunities (for all students, not just honors students).

"This year [2016] we piloted our new Global Discovery Experience. This is a pre-freshmen study abroad course offered only to honors students. 12 students traveled to Ireland in August with a faculty member from Global and International Studies."

Financial Aid: WMU conducts some of Michigan's biggest four-year scholarship competitions for talented incoming freshmen, annually awarding more than 30 Medallion and Foundation scholarships worth $50,000 each and 50 Multicultural Leader Scholarships worth $16,000 each.

"All first-year students with a GPA of at least 3.7 and ACT of at least 26 are invited to compete in our Medallion Scholarship competition. All competitors receive a 1-year $3,000 scholarship and automatic admission to the honors college. Semi-finalists receive $6,000 over 2 years and approximately 20 finalists receive $60,000 over 4 years. Finalists who complete an undergraduate degree in less than four years may use remaining funds for graduate study.

"We also offer honors scholarships for study abroad (up to $3,000) and to pursue research and creative activities (up to $3,000). These are awarded through a competitive application process. "

Degree of Difference: This is based on the differences between (1) the average (2015, two-part) SAT scores for enrolled honors students (1170) and (2) the average test scores for all students in the university (1030-1050) as a whole. The test scores may be an indication of how "elite" honors students may be perceived as compared to students in the university as a whole. The scores can also provide an indication of how well prepared the non-honors students in the university may be. **Please keep in mind that neither high nor low test scores determine the overall quality of a program.**

NAME: UNIVERSITY OF WISCONSIN-MADISON LETTERS AND SCIENCE HONORS PROGRAM.

Editor's Note: Reviewed previously in the 2012 and 2014 editions of *A Review of Fifty Public University Honors Programs,* the L&S Honors Program is not rated in this edition because, like another Big Ten honors program, the Ohio State Honors and Scholars Program, it is decentralized and based to a large extent in the academic departments. For the present volume we could not obtain all of the data required for the new, more exacting methodology, especially precise enrollment figures in departmental honors classes and in honors contract courses. The lack of the necessary data for a full rating does not mean that the L&S Honors Program, housed within one of the leading research universities in the nation and world, is not an excellent value for highly talented students.

Date Established: 1958.

Location: Madison, Wisconsin.

University Full-time Undergraduate Enrollment: 28,324.

Honors Students in Good Standing: 1,100 (mean size of all 50 programs under review is 1,742)

Honors <u>Average</u> Admission Statistics: ACT, 30.3. Old SAT, 1344; est. new SAT, 1400-1410. High school GPA, 3.70-3.90, top 8-9%.

Basic Admission Requirements: None reported.

Application Deadline(s): *Please verify with each program, as some deadlines could change.*

First Fall deadline is November 1, 2016, with notification by January 31, 2017; Second Fall deadline is February 1, 2017, with notification by March 31, 2017. Honors applicants have 30 days to apply for honors after they login.

Honors Programs with old SAT scores from 1315—1350: Idaho, Georgia State, Virginia Tech, Utah, Iowa, Auburn, Houston, Mississippi, VCU.
Administrative Staff: 4.

Priority Registration: "There are some courses that only students in an Honors Program can register for, but I think that would qualify as limited-enrollment courses rather than priority enrollment...."

Curriculum Requirements: Completion of Comprehensive Honors in the L&S Program requires at least **30 credits.** The average completion requirement for all 50 rated programs is 29.0 credits.

For Comprehensive Honors (a combination of Honors in the Liberal Arts and Honors in the Major) students must complete 24 honors credits and a 6-credit **thesis.** Students "must take 6 Honors credits in each breadth category: Science, Social Science, and Humanities (and another six in an area of their choice)."

Honors in the Liberal Arts requires only the 24 credits in honors courses, as described above.

Honors in the Major requires the thesis, as above, and any additional requirements the department may have for its honors majors.

AP/IB credits do **not** count as replacement credits for honors courses.

Average Class Size: L&S is certainly a **discipline-based** program, as there are no honors courses offered directly by honors with a separate honors departmental code. The departmental honors courses come in several forms—seminars, option courses (contracts, add-ons), and mixed sections that have honors and non-honors students. Although some of the seminars have 12-20 students, the overall honors class size is probably about 35 students.

There is an excellent range of disciplines available, including 4 biology sections and 7 chemistry sections, although we did not see honors math sections listed. Many more sections were in the humanities and social sciences, especially in psychology, philosophy, and political science.

Graduation Rate: The six-year graduation rate of first-year entrants who graduated from the university, whether or not the students completed the honors program, was **91.0%.** The average honors graduation rate for all programs with similar test scores required for admission is 83.4%.

Value-Added Graduation Rate: The honors graduation rate is 91.0%, compares to the university-wide six-year rate of 85.0%.

Ratio of Staff to Honors Students: Our estimate is that there is 1 staff member for every **275** students. (Mean ratio for all 50 rated programs is 1 staff member for every 135.6 students.)

Honors Residence Halls: "There is no 'Honors' housing on campus, but many of our students choose to live in Residential Learning Communities (RLC), which are the theme-based living opportunities at UW-Madison. About 20% of students living in housing live in one of these RLCs, and this model actually allows maximum flexibility for Honors students to select a housing option that corresponds to their academic and personal interests, rather than being limited to only one Honors housing option."

Prestigious Awards: UW-Madison is among the top four or five public universities in winning major national scholarships, including a (very high) 17 Udall scholarships, 59 Goldwater scholarships, and 14 Boren scholarships. In addition, UW-Madison graduates have won 32 Rhodes scholarships, 2 Gates Cambridge awards, 19 Marshall scholarships, 6 Churchill awards, and 22 Truman scholarships. The university has also produced a very high number of Fulbright Student scholars and NSF Graduate Research fellows.

Continuation Requirements: At least at 3.33 GPA; some departments have a higher requirement.

Academic Strengths: Following UC Berkeley, Michigan, and UCLA (barely), UW-Madison has the fourth highest ranked faculty among public universities, and UW-Madison departments rank among the top 12 or 13 even when private elite universities are included. *All 15 departments at Madison that we track are ranked 18th or better nationally.* Examples are sociology (1), education (4), chemistry (9), computer science (11), earth sciences and economics (13 each), engineering, history, and math (all 14), business and political science (15 each), English (17), and biology and physics (both 18).

Undergraduate Research: "We don't have complete numbers for how many L&S Honors students participate in research each year for the simple reason that there are so many ways in which students can participate in research that do not fall under the L&S Honors Program. Within the Honors Program itself, there are several avenues to getting involved in research, including a Sophomore Research Apprenticeship, as well as Senior Thesis Research Grants."

Study Abroad: "There are Honors-specific study abroad opportunities in Utrecht, Netherlands and Quito, Ecuador, but students can receive credit towards their Honors in the Liberal Arts degree while studying in any program through a petition process (obviously they also receive credit toward their UW-Madison degree). The university in general and the L&S Honors Program in particular have grants available to help offset the cost of studying abroad."

Financial Aid: The L&S Honors Program does not grant financial aid; that is handled through the university-wide office or the College of Letters & Science more generally.

UW-Madison, like UC Berkeley, Virginia, UCLA, and UT Austin, has sharply reduced or ceased university sponsorship of National Merit Scholars, but Madison, as one of the most egalitarian public universities in the nation, is gradually coming to terms with the need to provide more merit aid in order to keep the most talented students in state. Although the change has been written about, the university does not appear ready to identify or publicize the ways it is, or will be, increasing merit aid.

One scholarship that we found is the Carolyn B. Knapp and Charles H. Bernhard Scholarship, with a $7,000 renewable award—to one student.

Degree of Difference: This is based on the differences between (1) the average (2015, two-part) SAT scores for enrolled honors students (1344) and (2) the average test scores for all students in the university (1230) as a whole. The test scores may be an indication of how "elite" honors students may be perceived as compared to students in the university as a whole. The scores can also provide an indication of how well prepared the non-honors students in the university may be. **Please keep in mind that neither high nor low test scores determine the overall quality of a program.**

Curriculum—the formal course of study required for honors program completion and, often, for graduation with honors.

Honors Individuals—the unduplicated count of individual honors students enrolled in a given term, as opposed to honors "seats" or honors "members in good standing."

Honors Seats—the number of classroom spaces occupied by honors students in a given term, this is a number larger than the number of honors individuals because each individual honors student frequently takes more than one honors class per term, thereby occupying two or more classroom spaces, or seats, in that term. If 25 honors individuals within a group of 200 total honors individuals take two honors courses instead of one, and the other honors students take only one course each, then the number of honors seats would be 225, not 200.

Honors Members in Good Standing—represents yet another way to enumerate the number of honors students; the number of members in good standing includes all honors individuals enrolled in a given term *and* honors students who are still planning to complete the honors requirements but who are not taking an honors course in the term.

Discipline—a term that is synonymous with an academic subject, such as math, chemistry, or philosophy.

Academic Department—the administrative unit that organizes courses, almost always in a single discipline, and assigns faculty to courses and sections in the discipline.

Departmental Honors Program—easily confused with a department-*based* honors program, departmental honors programs are offered by the academic department, often with little or no coordination with a university-wide honors college or program. For example, the history department selects a small number of excellent, highly motivated students to pursue departmental honors by taking a special research course and then completing an honors thesis for six credits, under the supervision of a history faculty member.

Discipline or Department-Based Honors Program—an honors program or college that offers few or no sections of its own but instead coordinates with academic departments to arrange honors course sections. A program of this type is not likely to feature seminars or interdisciplinary sections. An honors thesis is a frequent requirement.

Core Honors Program—an honors program or college that offers many of its own courses, often including seminars and interdisciplinary courses. Some core program have set offerings in the academic disciplines as well, while others are entirely interdisciplinary in focus. Many core programs offer most of their courses in the first two years as honors versions of university General Education requirements, although this approach to meeting Gen Ed requirements is widely used by all types of honors programs. It is not unusual for most of the upper-division work for honors students in a core program to be centered on the honors thesis and associated research.

Blended Honors Program—an honors program or college using the most typical model of blending seminars, interdisciplinary courses, and discipline-specific courses. In many cases, these programs and those that are discipline-based (department-based) offer honors classes across all four years.

Honors Seminar—a small class section, usually with fewer than 25 students and often with 10-15 students, where class discussion and participation are the norm. Seminars might be interdisciplinary or they might focus on only one academic subject, or discipline.

Honors Colloquium—a seminar course that features different instructors and differing perspectives at each or several class meetings.

Honors-Only Section—as the name suggests, this is almost always a class with honors students only or, in a few honors programs, a class in which 80%-90% of the students are in a university honors program and the other students have high GPAs and like the challenge and stimulation of an occasional honors class. For our purposes, both types are considered honors-only classes.

Mixed Honors Section—is a course section that has honors and non-honors students enrolled in the same main section. Honors students in these main sections frequently meet in additional all-honors labs or discussion sections. Mixed sections are generally about twice the size of honors-only sections.

Honors Contract Section—also referred to as an honors option, conversion, or enhancement, these are regular courses in which one or a few honors program students "contract" with the instructor to extra work in order to earn honors credit. Contract courses are often taken for upper-division credit in order to meet major or minor requirements. They are generally more than twice the size of honors-only sections and somewhat larger than mixed honors sections.

Departmental Honors Course--is a course for honors credit that concerns only the academic discipline offered by the department. Sometimes these are a formal part of completing a university-wide honors program and sometimes these are taken only to complete the departmental honors requirements for the discipline.

Honors Experiences—are activities outside the university's classroom for which honors credit may be awarded. These often include internships, public service, study abroad, research projects, teaching assistantships, and leadership education.

Honors Thesis—is required by most honors programs for completion and graduation with some type of honors designation. The credit for an honors thesis can vary, with some having only 3 credits, many with 6 credits, and a few with 9-12 credits. Although some students with demanding majors, such as engineering, might avoid honors programs with a thesis requirement, the honors thesis is regarded as a very important component in the programs that require it. Often students are required to "defend" the thesis before faculty and other students or to make a thesis presentation. An honors thesis is excellent preparation for graduate or professional school and can be useful in gaining entrance to prestigious graduate programs.

Honors Capstone—is sometimes offered as an alternative or replacement for an honors thesis. A capstone is usually a project undertaken by the student to demonstrate mastery of a subject area or procedure. Engineering students, for example, often complete involved and demanding projects pursuant to completing a capstone requirement. Other students in STEM fields can fulfill the requirement with experimental projects.

Public University Press, in Portland, Oregon, has published two editions of *A Review of Fifty Public University Honors Programs* and the current edition, retitled *INSIDE HONORS: Ratings and Reviews of Sixty Public University Honors Programs.*

The editor is John Willingham, also the founder of the website PublicUniversityHonors.com. John began researching and writing about public university honors colleges and programs in 2011, a time when many states had already made several annual cuts in funding for higher education. Some political leaders had become so focused on applying business models of "productivity" and "efficiency" to state universities that they lost sight of the critical need to offer the highest levels of quality in those institutions.

As a way of exemplifying the excellence that can and should be sustained in public universities, the editor compiled a rudimentary ranking of the honors programs in major state universities in 2012, hoping that readers would not only gain some comparative knowledge about the programs but also develop a greater awareness of the value that they all offer to highly talented students. Good intentions aside, the 2012 edition was a broad-brush attempt at describing the variety and complexity of honors programs. The next edition, in 2014, was an improvement but still lacked the extensive data necessary for a truly comprehensive study of honors colleges and programs.

Inside Honors is the best attempt, thanks to the outstanding cooperation of more than 100 honors Deans, Directors, and professionals in honors colleges and programs across the nation. Most of them have endured our repeated entreaties with patience, and, while thanking those who offered encouragement, we are also grateful to the several who voiced criticisms or concerns. Because of them, we have made many changes to the methodology and presentation of honors data.

The reason that the term "editor" applies to John more than "author" is that so much of the information in the book has come from the honors community. Assisting him with copy editing and proofing is the assistant editor and marketing coordinator, Wendy Frizzell Willingham. Wendy is a graduate of the University of Wisconsin-Madison, where she was an honors student in foreign languages and education.

A Ph.D. scientist and professional statistician advises and assists the John in the development of a master data sheet, based on about 900 documents and spreadsheets. The master data sheet is a compilation of data received from honors professionals. John analyzes and categorizes all of the data from the programs and determines the impact of each category. The statistician standardizes and sums the raw data to produce both category and overall ratings. E-Book Adaptations in Akron, Ohio, has formatted all of our copy so that it can be uploaded for electronic and paperback publication.

John's background includes years of work in journalism and public administration, mostly in Texas. For three years, he was a regular contributor to the History News Network (HNN.us), writing several articles that covered the controversy in Texas over the adoption of social studies and science textbooks and curricula. His education includes a BA, with university honors, from the University of Texas at Austin, and an MA in history from UT Austin, including graduate minors in education and journalism. He is the author of an historical novel about the 1836 Texas Revolution, and his fiction and non-fiction have appeared in the *Southwest Review* literary quarterly, published by Southern Methodist University Press.